£4

To Stewart McGregor,

with the author's compliments.

Dugald Gardner

July 2013

My Path to Pathology

By Rivers, Lakes and Seas

An autobiography

Dugald Gardner

The ROYAL
SOCIETY *of*
MEDICINE
PRESS *Limited*

© 2012 Royal Society of Medicine Press Limited

Published by the Royal Society of Medicine Press Ltd
1 Wimpole Street, London W1G 0AE, UK
Tel: +44 (0)20 7290 2921
Fax: +44 (0)20 7290 2929
E-mail: publishing@rsm.ac.uk
Website: www.rsmpress.co.uk

British Library Cataloguing in Publication Data
A catalogue record for this book is available from the British Library

ISBN 978-1-85315-972-5

Distribution in Europe and Rest of World:
Marston Book Services Ltd
PO Box 269
Abingdon
Oxon OX14 4YN, UK
Tel:+44 (0)1235 465500
Fax: +44 (0)1235 465555
Email: direct.order@marston.com

Distribution in the USA and Canada:
Royal Society of Medicine Press Ltd
c/o BookMasters, Inc
30 Amberwood Parkway
Ashland, Ohio 44805, USA
Tel: +1 800 247 6553 / +1 800 266 5564
Email: order@bookmasters.com

Typeset by Phoenix Photosetting, Chatham, Kent, UK
Printed and bound by Replika Press Pvt. Ltd, India

Contents

Dedication   v
Foreword   vi
Preface   viii
Acknowledgements   x

I.   **From the English Channel to the Firth
        of Forth**
        1   **Inheritance**   1
            From the Clyde and the Thames
        2   **Early days**   9
            Near the Ouse
        3   **An English schoolboy**   25
            On the South Downs
        4   **A Scottish schoolboy**   33
            On the banks of the Esk

II.   **To East Anglia, the Water Of Leith and
        Lincolnshire**
        5   **An English student**   49
            Beside the Cam
        6   **A Scottish student**   61
            Near Dunsepie Loch
        7   **The National Health**   75
            In sight of Arthur's Seat
        8   **Marriage, then medicine**   87
            By the Spaarn and the Witham

III.   **From The Elbe to Lake Erie**
        9   **With the army**   97
            Beside the Elbe
        10 **Microscopes and men**   111
            A return to the Cam

11 **Rheumatism research**   121
By the Water of Leith

12 **To the United States and Canada**   137
On the banks of Lake Erie

13 **A Scottish university hospital**   155
A return to the Firth of Forth

IV. **From the Thames and the Lagan to the oceans of the World**

14 **A London first**   169
By the banks of the Thames

15 **Across the water**   185
To the Lagan

16 **Japan and a view of China**   203
Tokyo Bay and the Yellow Sea

17 **A sight of Brazil**   219
Towards the Amazon

V. **The rivers of Europe, Australia and the Middle East**

18 **Back to Britain**   235
Beside the Mersey

19 **A European scene**   253
From the Tagus to the canals of Mons

20 **Down under**   273
The Gulf of St Vincent and the Murray River

21 **Iraq and Israel**   291
From the Tigris to the Sea of Galilee

VI. **Home again**

22 **The fixed period**   307
In sight of Queensferry

23 **Jewel in a Crown**   321
A surgical museum

24 **Looking back – the end of my path**   337
The colour of life

Endnotes   353

References   385

Index   403

Dedication

Dedicated to the memory of
Philip Lindsay Gardner LL.B., 1957–1979

Foreword

This is a remarkable book for many reasons. The period Professor Gardner describes, from the inter-war years through to the present time, has been, and continues to be, one of the fastest-changing periods in British society, and this book recalls how these changes were felt.. The book also reflects the dramatic impact on health care of new understanding of disease and new pharmaceuticals, including the sulphonamides and penicillin, and the advent and embedding in everyday life of the National Health Service. Professor Gardner details the process of fashioning a career at the same time as building and enjoying a rich and stable family life. He records how the process of education flourishes when modern technology is matched with the innate human skills of instructing, communicating and inspiring. In particular he draws a vivid picture of the conflicting priorities in academic medicine – the allocation of time between diagnostic work, teaching and research.

All of this is chronicled faithfully and carefully by the author as he saw the world.. The face of the pre-war schoolboy at Loretto is the same as that of the house officer dutifully accompanying his consultant to the hospital car park, and the same again as the international medical scientist devoted to unravelling the process of rheumatic joint disease although the latter never overlays the junior self with the gloss of hindsight. The readers of this book will find themselves glimpsing Prof Gardner's family as they grew up, the towns he lived in, the little cars he drove, and his first impressions of USA, Japan, Russia, China, Eastern Europe, the Middle East, Australia and Brazil. In a day whose pain remains, he recounts with dignity the tragic loss of his son, to whose memory this book is dedicated.

In Prof Gardner's world "of rivers, lakes and seas", the reader will not only come across several "sailors" whose names are now famous, but many others, commended for their skills or admired for their character. There are few lasting enemies. Even the two senior men who, on separate occasions, told the ambitious young staff member "You'll have to go" are asked politely "Where to?" and are discovered later in a more favourable light. A recurrent philosophical theme runs through the book, that success owes much to serendipity. Yet Prof Gardner's own career will remind the thoughtful reader of the adage that "Chance favours the skilled observer."

I had the privilege of working in the same Department as Dugald when he returned to Edinburgh as a Senior Research Fellow and Conservator of the College of Surgeons of Edinburgh. By that time he had been Director of the Kennedy Institute for Rheumatic Diseases in London, and Head of University Departments of Pathology in Belfast and Manchester. He was justly famous for his pioneering work on the pathology and pathogenesis of the rheumatic diseases. Almost more impressive was the enthusiasm which he still exhibited in studying this complex, common and devastating family of diseases, using the technology and insights of modern microscopy immunology. If the reader wonders how Professor Gardner managed to be an expert diagnostic pathologist, a research leader, an innovative teacher, the designer of a brilliant museum, and a warm family man, I can only reply that I share that wonder, but indeed it is so.

Andrew H Wyllie FRS, FRSE, FRCPath
February 2012

Preface

Life on Earth pursues mutually exclusive conditions, Normality and Abnormality. The study of the former is Biology, the pursuit of the latter, Pathology, 'the knowledge and understanding of disease'. I have written this book to explain how chance led me to Pathology.

Pathology knows no boundaries and embraces all living creatures and every human race. All are prone to disease so that veterinarians who dissect the bodies of polar bears found dead in the Arctic are as much pathologists as laboratory workers who cultivate human cancer cells. With the growth of television drama, many think of pathologists as benign, white-coated men or women guiding police in their attempts to resolve the causes of crime. But these specialists are forensic pathologists. The majority investigating human disease are hospital workers, concerned with the identification of conditions affecting tissues removed by surgeons and in finding the causes of death in patients dying in hospital. Many others labour in research institutes and in the pharmaceutical and related industries.

In all our lives, chance plays an important part. This book tells how the failure of an examination introduced me to a nurse who became my wife. Graduating on the day on which the British National Health Service began, I became a physician but good fortune led me to laboratory medicine, to research and to a lifetime's university teaching and hospital diagnosis. Many years later, the fortuitous retirement of a surgical colleague allowed me to become Conservator of one of the world's finest medical museums.

The practice of Pathology is worldwide so that it is not surprising that, in the exchange of information, societies[1] and conferences took us to many parts of this and other countries. Our travels ranged from Lisbon and Hamburg in the West, to Okayama and Hong Kong in the East, as well as to North and South America and Australia. To emphasize the range of our journeys, I have arranged my chapters on a basis, associating our visits with the waterways we came to know so that my book bears the subtitle 'By Rivers, Lakes and Seas'.

During my lifetime, western societies have benefited from revolutionary advances in scientific technology. In my early hospital days, chemical measurements were centred on glass test tubes and burettes. Radiologists had begun to use plastic films but electrocar-

diograms were still recorded on glass plates. Antibiotics and intravenous anaesthetics were becoming realities but the autoanalyser,
computerised axial tomography, 'keyhole' surgery and organ transplantation remained distant dreams However, during my years,
advances such as the invention of the artificial kidney in 1943
began to offer new hope for the future just as the concept of the
double helix of DNA in 1953 suddenly presented the revolutionary
prospect of understanding the molecular basis of inheritance.

The serious pursuit of hospital pathology, in which patients' lives
and welfare depend on the precise identification of diseases of all
kinds, is demanding of time. When to this insistent pressure are
added the need to teach undergraduate and postgraduate students;
to administer a department; to prosecute competitive research; and
to travel frequently in this and other countries, then only the constant support of a devoted family can make life possible.

Looking back can be seen as a form of self indulgence and autobiography is beset with challenges[2]. Hans Krebs[3], quoted Goethe[4]
who wrote:

> 'If a person wishes to write about himself his motives are
> irrelevant. It is not at all necessary that he is a virtuous
> person and that his deeds are distinguished and virtuous.
> All that matters is that something is done which may be
> of use and give pleasure to others'.

None of us is spared loss and suffering but I shall remain ever grateful for the privileges, the immense satisfaction and the countless
opportunities I have been granted both in my family life and in my
profession.

Dugald Lindsay Gardner
Edinburgh 2012

Acknowledgements

Throughout the preparation of this book I have benefited from the advice and comments of friends and colleagues in the University of Edinburgh and in the Royal College of Surgeons of Edinburgh. I have been especially grateful to Donald Salter of the University School of Molecular and Clinical Medicine, to Iain MacLaren FRCSEd, emeritus member of the College Court of Regents, and to Sheena Jones, a former member of the College staff.

The Librarian of the Royal College of Surgeons of Edinburgh, Marianne Smith, gave generously of her time and skills, assisted enthusiastically by Steven Kerr and by Andrew Morgan and my work would not have been possible without their unremitting help. I express my thanks to Ian Milne, Librarian of the Royal College of Physicians of Edinburgh, and to his colleague Estela Dukan for their continual guidance and expert advice.

Sally Pagan of the University of Edinburgh Library assisted in the search for older photographs and the London School of Hygiene and Tropical Medicine provided information on the time spent at the School by Dr. Aldo Castellani and Dr. John Gordon Thomson. The Library of the Wellcome Centre for the History of Medicine and the Library of the Royal Society of Medicine provided invaluable assistance and I thank the Royal Commission on the Ancient and Historic Monuments of Scotland, the Central Library of the City of Edinburgh and the Newington Library, Edinburgh, for their patience in answering my enquiries. My special thanks are due to the Education Centre and Library of Lindsay House, Bathgate and in particular to Mrs Cavanagh, Blackburn.

Max McKenzie, formerly photographer to the Royal College of Surgeons of Edinburgh brought to my work the expert and willing help characteristic of his many years in the service of the College. In the same way, Kenny Ryan, Information Technology Manager, and his colleagues were continually helpful and I received valuable advice from Mark Baillie, Marketing and Communications Officer.

The Department of Pathology of the University of Cambridge enabled me to trace records of some of my former colleagues and the office of the Principal of the University of Edinburgh, Sir Timothy O'Shea, drew my attention to the period in office of the former Vice Chancellor, Sir Edward Appleton.

Dr Frank Anderson, Chairman of the Croydon Airport Society provided me with a photograph of this famous rendezvous. The assistance of other organisations in finding illustrations is acknowledged in the text.

Alison Campbell and Mark Sanderson of the Publications Department of the Royal Society of Medicine have been unfailingly supportive in assisting me in taking my manuscript to Press.

I am deeply grateful to members of my family for their support. Iain was an enthusiastic advisor, Rosalind gave me photographs of her children and David passed me some of his images of Brighton. Perry Gardner, my nephew, provided valuable guidance as did Denise, my sister-in-law and Gordon, my brother-in-law. John Welchman's studies of my mother's inheritance proved invaluable.

Words alone cannot sufficiently express my gratitude to my wife Helen without whose tolerant support the completion of this work would not have been possible. Her comments and contributions, often taken from her own diaries, have proved invaluable.

Dugald Lindsay Gardner

I.

From the English Channel to the Firth of Forth

CHAPTER 1

Inheritance

From the Clyde and the Thames

You must consider this too, that we are born, each of
us, not for ourselves alone but partly for our country,
partly for our parents and partly for our friends

Plato[1]

Choose your parents with care, I was told! But my inheritance was determined not by choice but by a virus. Influenza, the 'Spanish' flu, spread across the world between 1918 and 1920, killing five in every hundred of the world's population. Among them was my father's first wife.

Chapter summary
- **War, then influenza**
- **Marjorie Welchman**
- **Marriage again**

My story can be said to begin with my great-grandfather, Thomas Gardner, born in the Gorbals, Glasgow, on 8th April 1815, within days of the Battle of Waterloo. On 19th October 1838, he married Jean Livingstone. The eldest of their six children[A] was also named Thomas, the youngest – who was to be my grandfather – was Dugald.

After his wife's death on 24th June 1855, my great-grandfather left for New Zealand and died at Coromandel, near Auckland, on 5th July 1880. Dugald married Jean Muir. They had one son, again called Thomas (Tom). He was born in Govan, Lanarkshire on 8th August 1880 and became my father. He had one sister, Annie.

My grandfather left Scotland for South Africa at the time of the 1880s gold rush, leaving his impoverished family at Gardnerswell, Bathgate, West Lothian, where my grandmother, Jean, cared for Tom and for his much loved cousin Madge Garroway, the daughter of Jean's sister Catherine.[B] Dugald died in Dar es Salaam, Portuguese East Africa. The *Evening News* gave the date of his death as 9th April 1900, the cause 'fever'.

My father's early years were fraught with difficulty. He attended Bathgate Academy but left school when he was no more than 12 years old. To support his mother, he had no choice but to seek work as a builder's boy. Housing was proliferating, industrial developments springing up as the country prospered. Shale oil as well as coal

Figure 1.1 *The silver quaich given to me on my first birthday by the Reverend John Lindsay, my godfather.*

was in demand and the land was bespattered with 'bings', great hills of earth, rocks and soil brought from underground workings.

With the friendship and support of the Reverend John Lindsay,[C] minister to St John's United Free Church, Bathgate,[D] Tom gained admission to the University of Edinburgh to read medicine, the class fees ranging from one to four guineas. John Lindsay continued to help during the succeeding years of struggle and became my godfather. On my first birthday, he gave me an inscribed silver *quaich* (Figure 1.1), a treasured possession.

Imbued with determination, reserved but innately proud, thrifty but instinctively generous, my father had the good fortune to become a student of Thomas Annandale, Joseph Lister's successor in the Chair of Clinical Surgery, and of Henry Littlejohn, who had revolutionized the health of the citizens of Edinburgh before becoming Professor of Forensic Medicine. Tom graduated MB, ChB (Bachelor of Medicine and Bachelor of Surgery) in 1908, aged 28. Lacking the professional and social contacts that were keys to securing an appointment in the teaching hospital, the Royal Infirmary of Edinburgh, he obtained a position as House Surgeon to the Bridgwater General Hospital, Somerset, at a generous salary of £10 a month. It was the first step on a path that led to a lifelong devotion to the West Country. That the hospital had recently paid £50 for the revolutionary new X- (Röntgen) ray apparatus[2] speaks of the values of the time.

Seeking promotion, my father moved to London. Determined to succeed, in 1910 he was awarded the degree of MD for a University of Edinburgh thesis on pneumonia.[3] He worked first as an Assistant Medical Officer at the Chelsea Hospital for Women, then as Resident Surgical Officer to the Bethnal Green Infirmary (Figure 1.2). It was here that he met the nurse who was to become his first wife, Muriel Rose Milne, the daughter of Oswald Ivan Milne and Rose Welchman, the family with which he was intimately associated for the remainder of his life. Perhaps to enhance his income, he joined a 'panel' medical practice in Lillie Road, Fulham of the kind established after Lloyd George's 1911 National Insurance Act. He married Muriel on 17th April 1916, some months before his 36th birthday. She was 10 years younger.

War, then influenza

The outbreak of hostilities in 1914 changed the life of every family in the land. By 1916, the war had stretched the country's resources to their limits. Conscription was brought in, but there was a particular shortage of medical officers. Barely six months after his marriage, on 19th October 1916, Tom was called to the Royal Army Medical

Figure 1.2 *Dr Thomas Gardner (second from the right, middle row) at Bethnal Green Infirmary in 1912. One of the nurses, Muriel Welchman, was to become his first wife.*

Corps, gazetted Temporary Lieutenant and taken with the army, via Durban, to German East Africa (Figure 1.3). From the moment his ship left in convoy from Chatham, he kept a handwritten diary.[E] During the following two years in Africa, he joined the Ross Malaria Commission, his contribution recorded in their Report of 1919.[4,F] In the following year, he was promoted to Captain. However, towards the end of 1917, he contracted dysentery and was sent home. Returning to England, the dreadful impact of the influenza pandemic became only too clear when Muriel was taken ill and died. In the face of this tragedy, my grandmother Jean and Tom's cousin Madge came from Scotland to offer support.

Marjorie Welchman

Not many months later, my father was introduced to his late wife's first cousin, Marjorie Welchman.[5] The circumstance in which Tom and Marjorie met was their shared love for the West Country of England (Figure 1.4). My father had a deep affec-

Figure 1.3 *Lieutenant Thomas Gardner, RAMC, 1916.*

Figure 1.4. *Tar Steps, a Stone Age crossing, in Somerset.*

Figure 1.5. *Grace Beatrice (Bici) Rickard, Marjorie Gardner's mother, a daguerreotype of 1888.*

tion for north Somerset, a region he had come to know well during his time in Bridgwater, while Marjorie had fallen in love with Exmoor when on holiday with her grandparents in Lynton and Lynmouth. A tiny volume of *Lorna Doone*,[6] inscribed in my father's minuscule handwriting 'Marjorie Welchman, Minehead, 28th April 1920', may have been an engagement present.

Lorna Doone, set in the seventeenth century, tells of the vicious, isolated Doone family and their attacks on the farming communities of Somerset. The long tale leads towards the Monmouth rebellion of 1685 and the union of the hero, John Ridd, with his beloved Lorna, who, it transpires, is the daughter of Lord and Lady Dugal. One excerpt exemplifies Blackmore's romantic style – 'By the side of the stream, she was coming towards me, even among the primroses, as if she loved them all; and every flower looked brighter, as her eyes were on them' – and explains my parents' life-long fondness for primroses, which they used to send, like Easter cards but in little boxes, to all their friends.

Born on 21st November 1889, Marjorie would be my mother. She came from an Oxfordshire family and was the daughter of Herbert Guy Welchman (1860–1940) and Gladys Beatrice (Bici) Rickard (Figure 1.5).

Herbert Guy could trace his origins back to a John Welchman who died in 1591. He was one of the four sons of Thomas Guy (Figure 1.6) and Emma Welchman (neé Skeet) and was a businessman who sold bicycles in Biggleswade. In 1888, he married Bici, the youngest of the four daughters of Richard White Rickard and Margaret Elizabeth Davey, Cornishwoman. Richard Rickard's engineering work took him to many parts of the world and Bici was born in Leghorn, Italy. For the whole of her life, Marjorie retained a deep affection for Bici's sister Caroline, 'Auntie Car', whose husband, A. H. (Harry) Young,[G] had been Professor of Anatomy at Owens College, Manchester. Like Thomas and Marjorie, Herbert and Bici are thought to have met in the West Country, where Thomas Guy and Emma Welchman took their four sons – Herbert, Frank, Arthur and George – and five daughters on holiday. Marjorie, an only child, was soon orphaned when Bici died in 1890 following an infection said to have been contracted during a coach journey. Tuberculosis was rife and may have underlain Bici's premature death. My mother was brought up by her grandparents at 16 Carlton Road, Putney. Her grandfather died in 1909, her grandmother in 1915.

Figure 1.6. *Thomas Guy Welchman at Bluecoats School (Christ's Hospital, Horsham) in the early years of the nineteenth century.*

Some years after his wife's death, Marjorie's father, Herbert Guy, took up fruit farming[H] and moved to Westfield House, Terrington St Clement, Norfolk. On 1st May 1900, he married Mary Cicely Newnum, daughter of the vicar of Tilney All Saints, a parish adjoining Terrington. Cicely did not choose to care for Marjorie, and she remained with her grandparents. Together, Herbert and Cecily had three sons and three daughters.[I] Herbert was financially successful and retired at the age of 60 (Figure 1.7). With his large family, he settled at Grove House, St Cross, Winchester, a large mansion that we visited each year as we made our annual pilgrimage to Minehead, Somerset (p. 18).

Figure 1.7. *Herbert Guy Welchman, Marjorie Gardner's father.*

In later years, Marjorie spoke little of her early life and of the cloistered existence she had led before her marriage, within a strictly disciplined but affluent Victorian home where two of her uncles, Frank and Arthur, were living. George had died at an early age. Marjorie came to act as a young house-companion to her two surviving uncles, caring for their domestic needs. Frank was quiet, reserved and highly intelligent. He became a medical student at Guy's Hospital, qualifying in 1902 in the same year as Gowland Hopkins (p.55). He acted as a locum for Dr Dobson in Windermere (see below) and, from time to time, for my father when my parents went on holiday. There is little evidence that Frank ever accepted regular employment – he and Arthur had been left considerable sums of money by their father. Frank enjoyed Alpine holidays with his brother and their cousin Phyllis Milne. Later in life, I was impressed by how, at the age of 70, he went for walks of 15 or more miles each afternoon after completing the *Times* crossword puzzle every morning. Arthur qualified as a chartered accountant, worked in the City and, latterly, lived in Cromwell Road. His lifestyle was flamboyant and Marjorie had the responsibility of unlocking her grandfather's front door when, late on Saturday nights, Arthur returned from the Hammersmith Palais. In notes written in her 80th year, she recalled:

> Uncle Arthur's arrival home each evening brought a breath of fresh air to the house, even though it meant a lot of teasing for me. At weekends he was off to dances. I would often be awakened by the peeling of the front door bell in the early hours of the morning and had to go down and let him in – he'd forgotten his latch key or, as sometimes happened, couldn't get it in to the keyhole!

Blessed with self-confidence, assiduity and honesty, Marjorie made many friends. They included Norah Falshaw and Emily Swinhoe, who settled in Eastbourne with her numerous cats, her sister and her wealthy brother. Two of Marjorie's closest friends, Vera Devereux and Thersie Jackman, lived in Minehead. The fact that Vera's Roman Catholicism was not shared did not diminish the love of her associates for her exuberant personality.

> Another close friend was Alice (Alcie) Dobson, the daughter of Dr Dobson, who had been a general medical practitioner in Windermere, Westmoreland. Alcie's brother, GMB Dobson FRS, was a distinguished scientist who became Reader in Geology at the University of Oxford.[7] Marjorie's friendship with Alcie came from the association of her (Marjorie's) uncle Frank with Dr Dobson. Alcie, the local Commissioner for Girl Guides, was aided in this work by devotion to her car, but she was an uncertain driver – the fact that she did not have more accidents was almost certainly due to the low volume of motor traffic in the 1920s and 1930s. There were few traffic signals – the first was erected in Piccadilly in 1926 – and Alcie rarely looked to right or left at road junctions! She built her own home, 'High Biggin', close to her father's old mansion, both overlooking Lake Windermere. Behind the mansions, steeply rising areas of wooded and rocky land extended to the magnificent hills, which we visited on occasional holidays (p.18).

Marjorie's notes recorded that the road in front of her grandparents' house in Putney was of rough stones, not yet surfaced with tarmac. She described five postal deliveries daily, all on time. Her love of music was evident from an early age,[J] and during her long years in London she immersed herself in musical entertainment and theatre, not only as forms of escape from the tedium of her grandmother's eagle eye but as passions that she enjoyed for the whole of her long life. During the First World War, Marjorie and her London friends were confronted with food shortages as they glimpsed the defence balloons that floated over London, offering scant protection from the zeppelins, the German airships. Aware of the Battle of the Somme,[8,9] Marjorie, a very practical person, recalled few contemporary comments, perhaps because they were so dreadful. Her many friends drew her into a social scene in which charitable work with the Waifs and Strays (later the Church of England Children's Society) and the Red Cross played important parts. However, as she freely admitted, she learnt little during her adolescence of the harsh realities of life.

Meanwhile, Thomas Gardner's sister, Annie Gardner (Figure 1.8), had been promoted to be Deputy Matron of the Edinburgh District Mental Hospital, Bangour. She had trained as a theatre nurse under the direction of Sir William Macewen in Glasgow before moving to West Lothian to become Matron of Bangour in 1931.

Figure 1.8. *Thomas Gardner's sister, Annie Gardner, Matron of Edinburgh District Mental Hospital, Bangour 1931.*

Marriage again

My parents were married on 8th September 1920 and for three years lived in Fulham. After his remarriage, my father was pre-occupied with financial security, although he retained his contacts with the London School for Tropical Medicine as it changed to become the London School of Hygiene and Tropical Medicine (Figure 1.9). He realized that, for professional advancement, he needed additional qualifications and entered for the examinations for the Fellowship of the Royal College of Surgeons of Edinburgh, the FRCSEd. At his first attempt, in 1923, he failed. The reason: he had misread a question on the surgical operation of ovariectomy and, in error, had written about a different operation, ovariotomy. When I became a medical student (p.49), he used this mistake to remind me of the importance of reading examination papers with proper care! At his second attempt at the FRCSEd examinations, early in 1924, he not only passed but narrowly missed being awarded a medal: as 'runner-

up', he was given a steel case of scalpels and other instruments inscribed with his name and the date. The case is now in the keeping of my son, Iain Dugald Gardner, FRCSEng.

The sudden approach of marriage in 1920 was a turning point that severely tested Marjorie's character and that of my father, who had lost Muriel, the love of his life, only a few months previously. I was never privileged to know the inmost thoughts of my parents, but my brother Colin and I were well aware that, over the years, Marjorie rarely referred to her husband as 'Tom' or 'Thomas' but as 'The Doctor', recalling how Mrs Proudie in Barchester[10] often addressed her husband as 'Bishop'.

Figure 1.9. *Dr Thomas Gardner with Dr Aldo (later Sir Aldo) Castellani, at that time a lecturer at the London School of Hygiene and Tropical Medicine.*

CHAPTER 2

Early days

Near the Ouse

'Begin at the beginning,' the King said, gravely,
'and go on till you come to the end; then stop.'

Lewis Carroll[1]

From the islands of Jersey and Guernsey, the rolling waves of the English Channel sweep north-westwards, separating England and France, a barrier in war, a shared pathway in times of peace. A dreaded obstacle to early settlers, to Napoleon and then to Adolf Hitler, the Channel shores were peopled over thousands of years by fishermen and farmers and proved a refuge for city dwellers seeking escape from the towns of the Industrial Revolution.

Chapter summary
- Life in a medical practice
- A family at home
- Holidays
- A glance at Hitler's Germany
- The end of the beginning

Memory is like quicksilver. One moment a flash of recollection, the next moment nothing!

I was born at 12 Upper Park Fields, Putney on 30th May 1924. My father was Dr Thomas Gardner, my mother, Marjorie, his second wife (Figure 2.1). The circumstances of his first wife's death are described in Chapter 1. Soon after my birth, my parents moved to the south coast. My father wished to practise outside the National Health Insurance Act of 1911 and had few friends in the capital.[A] He selected Brighton and chose wisely – not only were the town and its neighbour Hove known for their health and wealth, but the countryside was renowned for its compelling beauty.

Figure 2.1 *My mother, Marjorie, cradles me in her arms in 1924.*

The little fishing village of Brighthelmstone that became Brighton evolved in the thirteenth and four-teenth centuries. In 1514, the village survived destruction by the French. In the eighteenth century, Brighthelmstone came to the attention of the Prince Regent, later to be King George IV. As Rowlandson recorded in his cartoons, the aristocracy disported themselves in the nearby sea, bathing with modesty and discretion, concealed from prying eyes by timber huts on wheels that were dragged to the water's edge. The Prince Regent visited Brighton in 1783 and in 1786 took a 21-year lease on a farmhouse in the seaside area called the Steine. Henry Holland was engaged to enlarge the house and to construct a French interior for what became a Royal Pavilion. During 1815–23, John Nash designed an Indian-style exterior for the Pavilion (Figure 2.2) in the resplendent style of an Indian Maharajah's palace with a Chinese interior. Queen Victoria did not share King George's tastes and sold the Royal Pavilion to the municipal authority. During the First World War, the Pavilion provided accommodation for wounded Indian troops.

Figure 2.2 *The Royal Pavilion, Brighton.*

My father bought a share of the medical practice of a Dr George Morgan[B] and found a nearby house, 2 Old Steine, Brighton. Old Steine (Figure 2.3), within easy walking distance of the Brighton Pavilion, was part of a corner block of Regency terraced buildings of an attractive pale yellow–ochre colour, although Number 2 retained its original brick façade. On 3rd July 1926, my brother Colin Guy

Figure 2.3 *Corner of Pavilion Parade, Brighton (left) and Old Steine (right).*

Muir[C] was born there, cared for by a much loved Nurse Pemberton. Old Steine was near the shopping centres of West Street, North Street and East Street and continued into Pavilion Parade. North Street led up to the Clock Tower and from there to the Brighton railway station. Our home faced south, welcoming the summer sun. The pavement took passers-by to the War Memorial and to Pool Valley, which had become a bus station. Not far away were the 'Lanes', a maze of narrow pedestrian walkways lined by the antiquarian booksellers, jewellers and philatelists so beloved by some members of the Royal family and in particular by Queen Mary.

Those parts of Brighton and Hove near the sea were known as 'The Front'. As many as a quarter of a million people could be found on sunny weekends, lazing on the shingle beaches and watching a little cruise vessel, the *Skylark*. The terraced houses of Marine Parade, favoured by the actors and actresses of the time, were separated from the sea by Madeira Drive, while a 'Middle Walk', a raised and covered esplanade in which green-painted cast-iron Victorian decorative pillars created a sheltered terrace, was preferred by the old and the young. In Victorian times, a West Pier (1863–66), an Aquarium (1872) and the Palace Pier (1899) were among many other attractions. From a little station built above the sea, Volk's Electric Railway was a never-ending joy. In places, the railway passed over the water, supported on huge timber beams. Below the cliffs, a concrete wall defended the coast against an insistent sea. In modern times, the defensive wall had become an immense bulwark of concrete. On its upper part, a broad pathway was laid. Along this protected route, pedestrians, perambulators and itinerants walked to Rottingdean and Seahaven, interrupted only when huge waves threw great showers of water across them. Further east, modern roads carried travellers towards Folkestone, Eastbourne and, ultimately, Dover. The war of 1939–45 made dramatic but temporary changes to the Brighton Front. The sea wall (p.46) was identified as a potential landing ground for an invading German army and, covered with barbed wire, became a defensive platform on which anti-aircraft guns were sited, while mines were laid on the innocent, shingled beaches.

Life in a medical practice

Our early years were spent in a busy medical household. In 1926, my father bought the remainder of Dr Morgan's practice and his house and we moved round the corner to 6 Pavilion Parade. It was the year of the General Strike and I recall the crowds in the streets. Number 6 was part of an imposing array of Victorian villas, each of six floors, the stonework grey–black in the face of the ravages of the English Channel weather. There was a main door reached between iron railings, and a gate opened on to a flight of stone steps and a gloomy basement. The front rooms faced the Pavilion, while a rear door led through the kitchen to a glass-paned conservatory and small garden. My father and mother were fond of dogs and a black terrier ran freely around the house. On the wall of the dimly lit dining room hung a Scottish scene inscribed with the Selkirk Grace:

> *Some hae meat and canna eat,*
> *And some wad eat that want it:*
> *But we hae meat and we can eat*
> *And sae the Lord be thankit.*

My father worked alone, visiting patients by day and occasionally by night. He employed neither nurse nor secretary, so my mother acted as receptionist, nurse, secretary and bookkeeper. The 'surgery' occupied much of the ground floor. My mother's Victorian upbringing ensured she was 'house-proud', and each Wednesday morning she rose at seven o'clock, donned an overall and cleaned the dining room. As children, we had no understanding of the demands on her time and it was only after my father's death that we understood what she meant when she spoke of 'my widow's freedom'. She was loving if old-fashioned, and spent much time taking us to Hannington's drapery and clothing store. At children's 'fancy dress' parties, boys and girls rivalled each other in their elegance and, aged 9, to my instant dislike, she dressed me in a satin blouse and velvet trousers, the style of Little Lord Fauntleroy.[D]

Our (children's) bedroom was on the fifth floor, our nursery on the sixth. It was a mansion demanding much maintenance, but the nursery maid and housekeeper found time to take us for walks towards the 'Front'. Motorized traffic was slight. The delivery of coal for the fire and the kitchen boiler was made by horse-drawn wagon; the milkman conducted his daily rounds by means of a horse and cart; and ice cream came from Wall's peddle tricycles labelled 'Stop Me and Buy One', ridden by uniformed salesmen. The 'best buys' were long one-penny water ices, triangular in cross-section. Two-penny cream ices, held between wafers, were prohibitively expensive for children whose pocket money was sixpence (2.5 pence in modern decimal currency) per week, a figure from which the occasional three pence for a haircut was deducted.

By 1933, increased financial security enabled my father to move house again to be closer to the centre of his practice – many patients lived in the inland part of Brighton. Guided by an agent, Mr Bradshaw, my father bought a new home, 24 Windlesham Road (Figure 2.4), near the Seven Dials, an important junction less than half a mile from Dyke Road, which carried traffic from beyond the South Downs towards the town centre. The purchase included land between Windlesham Road and Montefiore Road, and this uncultivated ground became a fruit garden and a lawn. The house was a late Edwardian three-storey red-brick mansion. Within the outer, oak front door was a stained-glass inner door. One day, a grateful but eccentric patient offered my father a substantial bequest provided that my father would agree to place at the front door *in perpetuity* a life-size statue of St Roc, the patron saint of dogs. It was an offer that had to be politely refused!

Facing west was a grand 'consulting room', above it a drawing room of equal size and above it again the 'nursery' – a room that kept its childhood name long after Colin and I had left home. On the ground floor, a dining room with elegant, glass-fronted bookcases gave entry to the garden. An open coal fire welcomed guests, while an oval 'leaved' mahogany table catered for family birthdays and for Christmas. On the left of the door to the garden lay a small back yard and a splendid new greenhouse; beyond them, the bricked surface of a runway sloped down to a long garage.

My father was well liked both socially and professionally. However, he maintained an instinctive silence concerning personal matters to the extent that even Colin and I learnt little of the struggles that he had endured during and after the First World War (p.2). At mealtimes, he spoke relatively little, generally about problems

Figure 2.4 *24 Windlesham Road, Brighton.*

encountered in his practice but occasionally using a few words of Swahili, the language he had mastered during the campaigns of 1916–18 (p.3).

As signs of war approached in 1939, discussion of a possible National Health Service (the NHS) became widespread, but it was to be nine years before the NHS changed the face of British medicine. The Beveridge Report[2] evoked great interest but my father disliked the idea of becoming a 'paid employee of the State'. His practice was 'private', so that each patient might be asked to pay either for a consultation at 24 Windlesham Road or for a visit to their own home. The poorest paid nothing, but others could be charged 5 shillings (25 pence in decimal currency), a wealthy country patient as much as £5. The practice accounts were prepared by my mother, but I have no recollection of any financial advisor. The practice papers were held in the Victorian bureau given to her by the Waifs and Strays at the time of her marriage in 1920 and bequeathed to my wife Helen in 1987. In the consulting room, French's *Index of Differential*

Diagnosis was prominent. Beside the oaken bookcase stood a filing cabinet, while to one side of a splendid coal-burning stove was an instrument cupboard with drawers containing bandages, scissors, a scalpel and forceps. The test tubes and spirit lamp needed to test urine for sugar and albumin were kept on a glass-topped working bench. A curtained bow window brought light to a roller-top desk and opposite it was the centrepiece of the professional room, the examination couch.

Experienced both in medicine and in surgery, my father cared for sickly children, young adults with tuberculosis, and elderly men and women with bronchitis or pneumonia. His custom was to leave home each morning to visit his patients, driven around the town by George Best, a veteran of the First World War Western Front. The £3 that Mr Best was paid weekly was sufficient to allow him to support his wife in a modest house in Withingdean, on the outskirts of Brighton. My father's morning visits were 'domiciliary', recorded in a little black pocket diary. With sick children, one of his approaches was the offer of a 'pandrop', a white peppermint sweet carried in his waistcoat pocket. With adults, his manner was quiet and friendly, encouraging patients to talk about their family, their travels and their work and in this way promoting diagnosis. He returned home for lunch, a meal at which stewed apple was invariably served. Afterwards, he dedicated half an hour to an armchair 'siesta'. More visits followed before he came home again for a 'surgery'. Excepting Sunday, patients came each evening at six o'clock and sat in a small waiting room. Every person who came was seen – there was no appointment system – and as a result the 'surgery' often lasted until after 8 p.m.

For single-handed general practitioners, the demands of medicine in the post-First World War period were heavy. My father's skills were needed both for the administration of anaesthetics and for help in obstetric practice. Among the mothers whose children he delivered were the wives of some of the teachers from Brighton Grammar School (Chapter 3). However, there was a sprinkling of emergency cases, so that, from time to time, he would be called out late in the evening or at night to attend patients suspected of having acute appendicitis, urinary colic, pneumonia or any condition requiring immediate treatment. Occasionally, the night calls were less urgent: a neighbour telephoned at 3 o'clock one morning asking the doctor to come and see her sick dog. In 1936, M & B 693, sulphanilamide, became available.[E] It was a dramatic moment that I recall vividly, and the impact on the practice of obstetrics was immediate. Within no more than seven years, the 'wonder drug' penicillin was added to those that could be used to treat streptococcal and other infections.[F]

By 1933, the practice was becoming increasingly successful, so that, in 1938, my father's income had reached £3600. But, for a Scot, banking remained an intensely private matter in which a customer would walk to a branch of the bank, sit with the manager and conduct business in confidence. Acting on the safe Scottish premise that to keep a bank account in the town in which one lived was to invite the undesirable interest of prurient neighbours, my father kept his account with the Bank of Scotland in Bishopsgate, London. Once each month, he wrote to request sufficient cash to cover a month's demands; once each month, by return, came a registered envelope containing a £5 banknote. He often sought advice about his investments – understandably, in view of his associations with South Africa, his instinct was towards gold and diamond mines. He welcomed the suggestions of his father-in-law, Herbert Welchman (p.5) during the short times they spent together, and the term 'West Wits', the abbreviation for West Witwatersrand shares, became very familiar to us.

A family at home

After the First World War, it became increasingly common for families to own a motor car and cars were essential for medical practice, taking the place of horses and horse-drawn cabs. In 1930, my parents bought a brown Austin 12 saloon. There were running boards, a rear luggage rack, and cloth panels covering the roof and doors. The worthy vehicle was succeeded first by a similar car of dark-blue colour but with a body of metal and then, in 1936, by a £375 Austin 18, CXU1, briefly paired with a Studebaker saloon. Towards the end of the 1920s, my mother was persuaded reluctantly to learn to drive, and hazarded excursions with George Best along Brighton Front in a 1928 'bull-nosed' Morris, a name describing the oval shape of the radiator. She did not persist. The annual servicing of the cars, in particular 'decarbonizing', was in the hands of Reginald ('Reg') Dixon, who came from London once a year to spend a day on this essential work. He brought with him his young sons. While their father worked on the car, we entertained the Londoners with games that included dressing in mock Roman cloaks, with cardboard shields and paper swords. As we grew older, my brother and I began to take a technical interest in the cars that Mr Dixon was servicing, and by the age of 16 were learning to drive: it was several years before a Driving Test became obligatory.

My father was not a 'clubbable' man and did not much enjoy society meetings. As local secretary of the British Medical Association (BMA) during the Second World War, he rarely travelled to BMA House, London. Even so, there were few minutes of time when our whole family could be together and the question arose – how best to use these precious moments? A love of music ran through both sides of my family and became one of my greatest delights. My mother had shown her own joy in musical entertainment from an early age (p.7). Although not an artist, she learned to play the piano efficiently. The Brighton Pavilion was a venue for productions such as Coleridge Taylor's *Hiawatha*, while other 'musicals' were given in the Theatre Royal. My brother and I began to have piano lessons when we were no more than 6 or 7 years old. Our earliest piece was played with two fingers: it was entitled 'Buy a broom', our practice supervised kindly but firmly by Mrs Freda Bridges who sometimes brought her young daughter Sheila with her. Our music teacher was Mrs Stoner, the wife of a dental surgeon in Regency Square, Brighton. Many years later, the Stoner's daughter, Priscilla (Scilla), met and married a cellist, John Kennedy. Their son, Nigel, born in 1956, became a violin virtuoso and studied at the Yehudi Menuhin School before setting out to 'rescue classical music from the snobs'. It was at this time that I realized that the white notes on a piano appeared to have colours, so that I saw the notes C, D, E, F, G, A and B as white, light blue, pale yellow, pale brown, black, red and beige, respectively. I believe this form of visual interpretation is not uncommon; for me, it was the hint that I might later have a closer association with the nature of colour vision (p.55).

My father was blessed with a good baritone voice. As a busy doctor, he could not give time to a choir, but on Sunday evenings would often join us around the piano. My mother would play accompaniments to songs we selected from the *Scottish Student Song Book*, enjoyed in the Students Union of the University of Edinburgh. One of my father's favourites was Carolina Nairne's *Caller Herrin* published in 1846 in *Lays from Strathearn* and recorded by Clara Butt.

> *Wha'll buy my caller herrin*
> *They're bonnie fish and halesome farin'*

My mother was adept with songs from the Gilbert and Sullivan operettas, which she knew well, and we were equally at home with *The Mikado*, *Ruddigore* and *The Pirates of Penzance*. Many years later, she fell in love with *The Sound of Music*.

Sunday afternoons and evenings were the only wholly free times of my father's working week. Even during school holidays, he had few opportunities to talk with us. Sometimes the conversation turned to philately. Relaxed in a way that was not common, he would bring out his stamp albums. With Colin and me seated beside him at the dining room table, he would pick out 'duplicates' that he would give to us. In this way, I began to form a collection that continued to grow throughout my life (Figs. 24.1, 2, 3). My father occasionally acquired small collections from individuals he had befriended. One of these albums was of the Australian red 1d stamp with its infinite number of variations; another was of the early Queen Victoria 'penny red'. He also bought stamp catalogues – the annual *Stanley Gibbons Catalogue* was a prized possession and these plump blue volumes occupied prominent places on his bookshelves.

Despite his humble origins, my father was well read, and we were strongly influenced by his choice of books, which reflected his Scottish upbringing and the literature of his time. He favoured

Robert Louis Stevenson, many of whose popular writings had been published during his early life – *Kidnapped*,[3] *The Master of Ballantrae* and *Treasure Island* and other tales of Scottish history appealed particularly strongly, and contrasted with those of Galsworthy and E. M. Forster, which we also enjoyed and which were preferred by my mother. Many years later, our bookshelves carried the Waverley edition of Stevenson's entire works, obtained by subscription in 1924. My father subscribed to the *Independent*, a weekly journal of liberal views and indulged a fondness for the *Diaries* of Samuel Pepys. Beside his bed, there was invariably a volume of this seventeenth-century classic.

Holidays

When the weather was fine, we occasionally escaped with our father to the Brighton and Hove Golf Club, high on the South Downs, and it was from here that we watched the inferno that engulfed the Crystal Palace in 1936. Family holidays were devoted to Somerset in the spring, Scotland in the autumn. The spring holiday took us each year to the little town of Minehead, a place much loved both by my mother's family (Chapter 1) and by my father (Figure 2.5). Mrs. Stoat's home in 'The Parks' gave us comfortable lodgings. The journey always demanded a short call at Winchester, where my maternal grandfather, Herbert Guy Welchman (p.5) and his wife Cicely lived in retirement. As children, we found these visits tiresome, but my father always took the opportunity of picking our grandfather's astute brain: he retained a mastery of the stock market and could be relied on to give wise advice about gold shares! As we left Hampshire and drove towards the Quantock Hills, we could sense our parents' happiness: they were approaching the scenes where they had first met. We enjoyed golf on holiday and, at Minehead, came to know the local professional, Mr Goldsmith, an old-fashioned and resilient teacher who gave us memorable lessons at modest cost. It was long before *Goldfinger*, but we learned that golf is as much a game of the mind as of the body! On one occasion, a little dog could be seen running across the greens: its owner had trained it to steal golf balls from under the noses of players!

In the summer, our family holidays were generally in Scotland, although a week in the Lake District in 1934 with the 'bull-nosed' Morris (p.16) was an exception. Three people sat in the front, while a backwards-opening 'dicky' seat offered room for two or even three more. Woefully underpowered, a climb up the unmade, gravel road of Kirkstone Pass proved impossible and those in the dicky seat had to jump out and push! There were no motorways and, even with an overnight break *en route*, the journey to Scotland occupied two full days. My father retained a deep love for Connell Ferry and the Highlands. Looking back, it seems strange that we should not have spent more time in the West of Scotland. One exception

Figure 2.5 *Dunster village, near Minehead.*

was in 1938, when a small diversion enabled a visit to the Empire Exhibition in Glasgow, the place where many of us first tasted pure orange juice as a commercial beverage! But it was usually convenient to pause in Edinburgh, giving a welcome chance to meet my aunt Annie[G] and her cousin, Nancy Rankin.[H] In the North, our favourite family destinations were Rosemarkie in the Black Isle, Fortrose, and Lossiemouth, the home of the former Prime Minister, Ramsay MacDonald. The reasons for our love of the little town were not far to seek. A modest hotel, *Laverock Bank*, was comfortable and welcoming. Strolling down towards the sea, we could watch the fishing boats as they came in and out of the harbour. Close to the beach was a splendid 18-hole golf course. The sands were sites for picnics and the bathing huts encouraged brave souls, including my mother, to plunge into the icy waters of the Moray Firth. On one occasion, she was alone with a pack of some twenty friendly seals.

A glance at Hitler's Germany

The year of the Berlin Olympic Games, 1936, was an extraordinary exception. Suddenly our holidays took a European turn!

As schoolchildren, we were not to know of the rise to autocratic power of Adolf Hitler, but years later we became familiar with Germany's descent into chaos through writings such as those of Albert Speer, Hitler's architect and Minister for Munitions.[4] At school in Putney, one of my mother's lifelong friends had been Magda Schönhals, a native of the industrial city of Mannheim, a centre for the flourishing German chemicals industry and Speer's home town. Mannheim was within easy reach of the Black Forest (the Schwarzwald) and of the University town of Heidelburg.

My mother persuaded my father to take our heavily laden Austin 18 car (Figure 2.6) across the English Channel to visit Magda. We set off by steamer from Dover, arriving at Ostend before driving through Bruges to Brussels. A short journey across the Aix la Chapelle (Aachen) frontier into Germany was followed by a longer drive leading to the new concrete motorways, the *Autobahnen*, along the spectacular dual lanes of which roared great motor trucks with trailers.

In Mannheim, we found our way to the flat owned by Magda and her sister, Freya. Magda, a skilled musician, was a piano teacher and almost at once we began to hear her fine rendering of Greig's *Wedding Day*. Magda's flat stood in a high, black, late Victorian block of six-storey city houses where every inhabitant already had a place allocated in air-raid shelters in the double basements. Each autumn evening, we watched the fire services practising their skills while columns of 'brownshirts', the *Sturmabteilung* or SA, marched by: they were well established by 1931. One evening my father commented: 'Yes, of course it must have been difficult for you after you lost the war.' Immediately, Magda retorted in her perfect English: 'But we did not lose the war!'

Figure 2.6 *On holiday in Germany in 1936: (left to right) Magda Schönhals, Marjorie Gardner, the author, Colin Gardner, Thomas Gardner.*

The Mannheim cafés proved irresistible to adults, the toy shops fairy palaces for children. But fate was occasionally against us. Given an expensive, beautifully made penknife of the kind that would now be called a Swiss knife, I carelessly dropped it through the iron grid that covered a basement 'well'. I was distraught! But there were rewards. As young boys, we were easily seduced by the enormous bowls of ice cream that graced German restaurant dining room tables, dwarfing anything that we had seen coming from Wall's & Co in Britain.

After two nights in Mannheim, we drove to the Black Forest. On the roads we saw the machine-gun-carrying motorcycle sidecars of the Luftwaffe. Our hotel, 'Rote Lache' (Figure 2.7), was popular with Himmler's elite corps, the *Sturmstaffel* or SS, feared and despised as the guards of the concentration camps. There were many foreign guests in the hotel, French and British, but few chose to speak to the 'blackshirts' as they stood at the bar, revolvers protruding from

Figure 2.7 *Hotel Rote Lache in the Black Forest, 1936.*

their hip pockets. The nearby country was densely forested and most beautiful. Among the unusual wildlife was a population of enormous, brightly coloured, red, green and yellow snails unlike any we had seen in Britain. In the company of a director of a local telephone exchange and his family, we set off one evening for a stroll through the trees. We were soon lost but 'Boy Scout' ingenuity with compass and torch guided us safely back to the bright lights of the hotel. There were other shared interests, golf among them, as a game in Baden Baden proved.

The end of the beginning

My mother was vigorously healthy throughout her long life and, as she said, 'hardly knew what a cold was'. However, letters I received from her and from my father early in 1946 showed that she had been found to have suffered a fracture of the head of one of her arm bones, the radius. In later years, her only illness was an infection of one finger. My father (Figure 2.8) was less fortunate. He enjoyed good health over many years, but behind his façade of vigorous medical practice lay a story of medical difficulty. Not only had he suffered from dysentery during his time in Africa, but he had also developed the common condition of 'duodenal ulcer'. Seeking the cause of ulceration in the early part of the twentieth century, suspicion fell heavily upon anxiety and stress, on cigarette smoking, on hurried meals, and on hyperacidity of the stomach. The association between gastric disease and infection with the microorganism *Helicobacter pylori*, rediscovered in 1979, was not suspected until 1981. Like so many in the wars of the twentieth century, my father smoked cigarettes, preferring Churchman's Number 1 but occasionally finding solace in a pipe in which Erinmore mixture was placed at one shilling (5 pence in decimal currency) an ounce. Poor digestion was also blamed upon faulty dentition: he had had his remaining teeth extracted in early adult life.

In the spring of 1947, my father was clearly not well and sat at his desk recording his own blood pressure. He spoke little of his illness, but he and my mother decided that the best course of action was their customary holiday. Soon after their arrival in Minehead, on 14th April, my father wrote an unusually long letter to me in his minuscule handwriting. Having decided to retire, he wrote another letter eight days later, but this time it was addressed to the office of the British

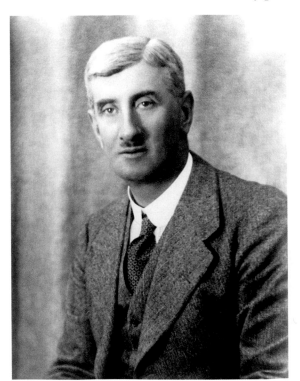

Figure 2.8 *My father, Thomas Gardner, 1937.*

Medical Association that advised practitioners buying or selling medical practices. In his letter, he explained in frail and cramped handwriting that ' he …'. The letter was never completed. It appears likely that he stopped writing to rest but never awoke. A certificate recorded the cause of his sudden death as coronary artery disease, but the details were not established with certainty. He was buried in Minehead Cemetery, where my mother was to be laid to rest nearly 40 years later. His gravestone was inscribed with words that I was allowed to choose from the title of McNair Wilson's (1926) biography of Sir James Mackenzie:[5] 'Thomas Gardner, the Beloved Physician'.

After my father's death, my mother was left with a very small income. Three-quarters of the annual return from my father's investments were paid to her by the trustees, the Bank of Scotland, the remaining one-quarter invested in a Thomas Gardner Trust.[1] She moved to the house that she and my father had bought for his possible retirement, Cranham Cottage, Minehead, a charming bungalow barely half a mile from the centre of the town. However, my mother had no car and the bus service was infrequent so that this distance was frustrating even to a vigorous walker. After some years, she decided to sell her bungalow and to buy the upper flat of a house belonging to her friend, Thersie Jackman (p.6). Later (p.156) her continued close friendship with the family of Derek Peters (p.28) led to an invitation to join the elderly Mrs Gladys Peters in Derek's home, St Anne's House, High Street, Lewes. When Derek and his wife separated, my mother moved to Place House, Patcham, near Preston Park where Gladys now lived and eventually, in 1979, moved to Manchester (p.156).

CHAPTER 3

An English schoolboy

On the South Downs

'Then the whining school-boy, with his satchel and shining morning face, creeping like snail unwillingly to school'

Shakespeare[1]

It has been said that everyone entering the medical or nursing professions should have experienced ill health. Suffering influences artistic creativity,[2] and the sickness of politicians can be an explanation for impetuous or dangerous decisions.[3] Many distinguished physicians, surgeons and pathologists have practised successfully despite ill health, but it is impossible for the individual to judge whether disease has changed their capacity to respond to the demands of life.

Chapter summary
- St Wilfred's School, Brighton
- Brighton, Hove and Sussex Grammar School

In 1928, aged four, I developed bilateral otitis media, an infection of both ears. The disease spread to the mastoid bones, and abscesses formed. It was long before the introduction of chemotherapy. To reduce the risk of meningitis, an immediate operation was needed and my father asked for the help of his Brighton surgical colleague, Mr Crow.[A] The procedure was performed under chloroform anaesthesia in a nearby nursing home. A mask was placed over my face and I was told to breathe deeply. I felt as though I was moving down a long, dark tunnel and remembered nothing more.

I was lucky in my father's choice of surgeon and in the success of my first operation. Recovering in the nursing home, with my anxious mother sleeping in the same room, there was a long period of convalescence. I recall being taken to visit another sick young boy and we consoled each other by comparing teddy bears! The kindly nurses seemed enormous and of ferocious strength, skilled at removing my clothes not only to bathe me but also to inflict that ultimate indignity, an enema.

I often suffered from toothache, my pain eased by blocks of ice cream bought for two pennies (less than one pence in decimal currency) from a Lyons tea shop at the nearby corner of St James Street. In 1931, after fearsome struggles with well-intentioned dentists who came to the house with their containers of laughing gas (nitrous oxide), I developed rheumatic fever. The disease followed a throat infection. By chance, it was a moment when my father had invited a consultant from London to give a second opinion on the condition of one of his Brighton patients. The physician was Sir Thomas Horder of St Bartholomew's Hospital, consultant to the Royal Household. Before leaving, the great man, an authority on rheumatic fever and its occasional but dreaded complication, endocarditis, agreed to see me. I shall never forget his reassuring manner. He confirmed that I should continue to receive the accepted treatment, aspirin (acetylsalicylic acid): when I became a medical student in 1942, I realized that there could have been no other possible decision. The diagnosis of rheumatic fever was received with relief by my parents, who, it might be supposed, feared that I might have contracted the common and much more deadly condition of tuberculosis, the infection that may have killed my maternal grandmother in 1890 (p.5).

St Wilfred's School, Brighton

At a very early age, as the days of Nurse Pemberton ended, our domestic staff came to include Nettie Harris, a tall and kindly Aberdonian helper. It was soon time to be sent to a 'primary' school, St Wilfred's. We still lived at 6 Pavilion Parade and the journey to Dyke Road was made by tramcar. At first, I was taken to St Wilfred's by Nettie, but I learned to travel by myself, crossing the wide Parade with a penny clutched in my hand. Carried uphill past Brighton Station to the Seven Dials, it was a short walk to the detached Georgian schoolhouse, where the pupils ranged from 7 to 14 years, the older girls gigantic. The younger children wore pale grey shirts and grey trousers, their jumpers edged in blue, their little grey caps embroidered with a large 'W'. There was an appropriate emphasis on the teachings of the Christian Church and each day there were prayers and a hymn. The Headmistress, Miss Blaine, a generously built but benign and kindly lady, taught her classes to chant the ambiguous words 'There is a green hill far away, without a city wall'. Why did the city not have a wall?

In the following year, my brother Colin (p.10) joined me. Like so many youngsters in the 1930s, we were introduced to a weekly magazine, the *Modern Boy*, on which two pennies of our pocket money was spent happily. Nettie Harris, our 'carer', pored over the pages as enthusiastically as we did. One of my mother's relations had an association with the *Boy's Own Paper*, but Colin and I found this magazine 'stuffy', its objectives too ecclesiastical. When *Picture Post* first appeared, its strong political flavour caught our attention at once. We loved *The Illustrated London News* for its splendid illustrations and scanned the monthly *National Geographic Magazine* with amazement. At home, the *Daily Telegraph* was my father's preferred choice, but my great-uncle Frank, who escaped the terrors of the London 'blitz' by living with us during the war years, read *The Times*.

 Winnie the Pooh and *The Water Babies* featured in our earliest reading days, but Richmal Compton soon overtook these childish interests and *Just William*, *William the Conqueror*, *William in Trouble* and *William the Rebel* were among our large collection of her stories. *The Wind in the Willows* remained a longstanding favourite. After reading it, I recall writing to Kenneth Grahame, the author, and receiving a kindly letter of thanks. When his widow was preparing a memoir of his life years later, she asked if I could pass the letter to her and I did so. For me, the little Nelson's *Classics* soon offered a simple, cheap way into the world of literature and I learned to love Dumas and Harrison Ainsworth at an early age.

Brighton, Hove and Sussex Grammar School

Whether by luck or by parental good management, 24 Windlesham Road, where we had moved in 1933, was within a mile of the renowned Brighton Grammar School (Figure 3.1), founded in 1861.

Figure 3.1 *Brighton Grammar School. Since 1975, it has been the Brighton, Hove and Sussex Sixth Form College.*

Figure 3.2 *Garden at 24 Windlesham Road, Brighton. (Back row, left to right) A friend; Madge Murray (neé Garroway), Thomas Gardner's cousin; Mrs and Mr Young (patients); Marjorie Gardner, my mother. (At front) Jean Murray, my cousin; Colin Gardner.*

St Wilfred's was only a few hundred yards from the Grammar School gates but on the opposite side of the road, and I found myself whisked from its calm domesticity to the imposing boy's school, a 1913 red-brick institute with swathes of green, gently undulating playing fields. I remained a pupil at the Grammar School until 1937; Colin joined me in 1934 (Figure 3.2) and stayed until 1939.

We had much to learn. Early on, I was asked to stand up in class and read a passage that included a mention of 'pneumonia'. I'd never seen such a word before and I said 'per-noi-mon-I-are'. The whole class laughed. But Colin and I soon made new friends. My particular 'buddy' was Richards. One day, he and I incurred the wrath of the Headmaster, Mr Baron. We were occupying our lunchtime minutes with a game of room soccer, played in a large basement area, using a tin can as a football. Unfortunately, the large room was immediately below the Headmaster's study. Red-faced, his wrathful figure descended on us like Zeus from the Gods and his flexible cane brought us to our youthful senses! Another companion, Ralph Lester, had an older brother, John, easily identifiable because of a deformity of one arm. In 1936, Colin formed an enduring friendship with a younger Derek F. Peters[B] (Figure 3.3): Derek's father, one of my father's patients, was manager of the branch of Barclays Bank at the Seven Dials.

Several of the Grammar School masters – there were few female teachers – were also patients of my father, and it is possible that this was a factor in his choice of a school for his sons. Mr Baron, a formidable figure, ruled his establishment firmly but efficiently, with his son as one of his pupils. The classrooms of the Grammar School were spacious and well equipped and there were good laboratories where practical aspects of science were taught effectively. W. H. Rider instructed us in history; his wife was in my father's care during a pregnancy. W. H. Stansfield taught physics, while R. E. Palmer, who introduced us to mathematics, suffered occasionally from the spirited character of his pupils, one of whom threw an open penknife at him in the course of a rumbustious session. Monsieur Jules Robiony, a Frenchman nicknamed 'Robot' or 'Rover', practised linguistics without any great success. R. J. Milton, another neighbour, advanced my early knowledge of Stone Age history: he died during the Second World War. A. B. Clements was a classicist who used his slight

Figure 3.3 *My brother, Colin (at left), with his friend Derek Peters.*

educational guiles upon me when, in 1937, I was entered for the Common Entrance Examination, success in which, it was said without foundation, was essential for my possible later attempt to gain entry to Loretto School, Musselburgh (p.33). During the examination, I found that my knowledge of 'scripture', confined to the Old Testament, was of scant assistance in answering questions on the journeys of St Paul.

A large school hall with a well-built stage accommodated morning prayers and was the venue for an annual Gilbert and Sullivan opera. *The Pirates of Penzance*, *The Mikado* and *Ruddigore* were among those I remember best. For the performance in December 1933, the end of the hall opposite the stage formed a platform on which sat the more distinguished guests, my father and mother in the front row, Colin and I beside them. The platform was draughty – in retrospect, it was not wise for my mother to insist that we should wear our kilts: I had recently recovered from rheumatic fever. Partly because of its name, but partly because the principal boy died not many months later from lymphoma, my recollection of *Ruddigore* is vivid.

Membership of the Boy Scouts organization, formed by Baden-Powell after the 'Boer' war of 1899–1902, was a stimulating part of our school activities. I became a 'Cub', the junior equivalent of a Boy Scout. Like the Scouts, the Cubs were formed into 'patrols' of six boys. The patrols were in turn organized into 'troops', each with a leader.

Our troop leader, dressed in short trousers but with an elegant tunic, was Mr Rider, his appearance contrasting with our usual impression of a formally clad teacher. Neither he nor his colleagues seemed conscious of the incongruity of their uniforms! We met each week and learnt about ropes and knots, compasses and maps, the Morse code, and signalling with flags, an introduction to semaphore. In the summer months, we put our new skills to practical use by camping on the South Downs. To gain a 'badge', a sign of proficiency shown by a small symbol stitched to our tunics, we were tested: a fire of paper and twigs had to be lit with no more than two matches; sausages had to be fried on an open camp fire; 'injured' arms were suspended in slings; and bandages were applied to supposedly cut fingers.

Although foreign travel was exceptional, there were activities beyond Brighton and, from time to time, the school took us to London. I recall a day when we visited Croydon Airport (Figure 3.4), where we saw the enormous biplanes of Imperial Airways taking off on their way to Paris. From Croydon, our bus carried us to Dagenham (Figure 3.5), where we watched Ford cars being assembled.

Armistice Day, 11th November, was a solemn annual occasion. It was not many years since the First World War ended, to be followed by the Peace Treaty of 1919, and the school memorials were a daily reminder of the great losses that had been suffered. There was always a formal parade in which the Headmaster, his entire staff, the cadet forces and the scouts stood to attention as the last post was sounded, a one-minute silence observed.

Sunday afternoons were not exciting. The small Brighton and Hove Natural History Museum was a short walk from the Grammar School and was a favourite venue, but the time was usually spent at zealous meetings of a religious organization, the Crusaders, one of whose aims was to interest schoolboys in Christianity and to keep them off the streets. Two or three of us, Colin included, were dispatched to walk to Church Road, where we met in a small hall. All was well until the gatherings ended. Then, on the way home, we were often seduced by building sites. The scaffolding was irresist-

Figure 3.4 *Croydon Airport in 1936.*

ible – we clambered among the beams and brickworks, ran around the rough grounds, and became noisy and grimy. Back home, no-one seemed to notice: my mother was busy with her knitting, my father with his appointment book.

In view of his early years spent in industry and the mines, it was understandable that my father should have had an interest in carpentry and mechanics. He arranged for a skilled carpenter to come to the house and teach us the rudiments of woodwork. An elderly and kindly Mr Robinson appeared each week and introduced us to chisels, set

Figure 3.5 *The Ford factory at Dagenham in the 1930s.*

squares and a variety of saws and to the intricate task of making joints in planking to be converted into boxes. He constructed the cabinet that housed our growing collection of Meccano, the girders, metal plates, screws, washers, nuts and bolts of which gave us an early understanding of metalwork long before the introduction of Lego. Mr Robinson helped with the repair of the ancient Victorian doll's house given to my father by a patient – it served as a plaything for the Mickey Mice we had named by the colour of their trousers and collected during our very early years.

I soon came to love photography. After seeing an advertisement for a tiny 'box' camera in 1934, I was determined to have one. The price was 3 shillings and 10 pence (19 pence in decimal currency). The problem was that I had only the 6 pennies (2.5 new pence) of pocket money we were given each week. But I knew that my mother kept some coins in her treasured bureau. One day, when her back was turned, I went to a drawer and took out four shillings in the form of two florins.[C] My mother gave no sign that she had mislaid the coins – but whether this was a reflection of ignorance or a possibly wise decision not to acknowledge my theft, I never discovered!

There were good reasons why my parents worried about the effects of illness on my physique. To avoid any effect on our general growth and development, our father called for the help of a physiotherapist, Miss Rothera, who he employed in his practice. She chose the richly patterned Persian carpeted floor of the 'consulting room' (p.13) as an arena where we practised her exercises. There were other, less happy forms of physical activity! One Christmas, a well-intentioned relative gave us boxing gloves. Since there were no convenient sparring partners, I began to use my long-suffering young brother as a 'punchbag'. Wisely, he arranged for the gloves to be 'lost'.

The cinema was a magnet for schoolchildren, sometimes by themselves, sometimes with an adult. Uncle Frank (p.5) shared this liking and we occasionally went together to see films such as *The Count of Monte Cristo* and *Lost Horizon*. There was one snag: I often developed migraine, so the cinema became synonymous with headache!

But the world was becoming a darker place. As the wireless brought us daily news of growing trouble in Europe, as our school friends and members of the family disappeared into the Armed Forces, so our reading tastes changed. Humfrey Jordan caught my eye and I dived into *Sea Way Only*, *Mauritania*, *The Commander Shall* and *Tide Still Flowing*. Several relations were members of the Royal Navy and we felt close to the dramas that unfolded on the Atlantic and Pacific Oceans, in the North Sea and on the route to Murmansk.

At the end of 1936, during which we had our memorable visit to Hitler's Germany (p.19), the scene changed dramatically. Whether the approach of war influenced their decision, I do not know, but my parents decided that I should be sent to school in Scotland. My father was convinced, not without reason, that the Scottish education from which he had himself benefited was 'the best that money could buy'. He was a far-sighted person, although his knowledge and understanding of English schools was probably limited and the possibility of remaining in the South was not mentioned. The prospect of journeying to Scotland did not worry me – we had frequently been to Edinburgh and had enjoyed holidays on the Black Isle – but the idea of living in a Scottish school was disturbing.

The first step was to prepare me for leaving home, and I returned to the Brighton and Hove Grammar School, not as the day pupil that I had been for the previous 5 years, but as a 'boarder'. The Brighton Grammar School boarding house was a block within the school grounds, a short walk from the main buildings. We slept in long, spacious dormitories, 12 or 14 boys to a room. There was no particular discomfort, but each night the sight of a glowing cigarette end reminded us that a master, Eric Dickinson, was on the alert. He was right to be on the outlook! From time to time, there were 'midnight feasts' during which we crowded silently into the bathroom and opened tins of pilchards, cans of beans and bottles of lemonade.

CHAPTER 4

A Scottish schoolboy

On the banks of the Esk

'Mensa, O table, is the vocative case,' he replied. 'But why "O table"?' I persisted in genuine curiosity. 'O table – you would use that in addressing a table, in invoking a table.' And then seeing he was not carrying me with him, 'You would use it in speaking to a table.' 'But I never do,' I blurted out in astonishment. 'If you are impertinent, you will be punished, and punished, let me tell you, very severely,' was his conclusive rejoinder.

Churchill[1]

In September 1937, aged 13, I was introduced to a new friend, the London and North Eastern Railway, the LNER. Sent to Loretto School,[A] 400 miles north of my home, I made the return journey from Brighton to Musselburgh 15 times during the next five years.

Accompanied by my mother, I left Brighton for Victoria Station, London. The Southern Railway line was one of the earliest to be electrified and the journey took exactly 60 minutes. Even when wartime bombs began to fall, travel was rarely interrupted, although my train once collided with a stationary wagon, hurling a suitcase onto the vacant seat opposite me.

We took the Underground railway, 'the Tube', to King's Cross, where breakfast was followed by a tearful farewell. For £1.6s (£1.30 in decimal currency), the Flying Scotsman bore me northwards for seven hours,[B] the bridge across the River Tweed at Berwick offering a first sight of what seemed to be a foreign country. I marvelled at the coalmines near the Longniddry power station and spied Edinburgh when Arthur's Seat came into view. Struggling off the train at Waverley Station, I was met by my Aunt Nancy (p.19). She knew nothing of Loretto but delivered me to a bus that took me five miles eastwards to Musselburgh for the cost of a ticket that I paid from the two shillings that represented my first term's pocket money.

> *Chapter summary*
> - The three 'R's'
> - Friends
> - The sound of music
> - Sport
> - Religion
> - The approach of war
> - Casualties
> - Holidays and home

I reached Loretto School alone. By contrast, many new boys already knew each other and came from Scottish communities, while others, 'Nippers', moved from the nearby Loretto Preparatory School. I was directed to Holm House, one of five residences scattered around Schoolhouse, an old building decorated in the pale yellow ochre so beloved of eighteenth-century architects. Clive of India was said to have lived there when he returned to this country in 1760. Linkfield House adjoined the A1 highway and faced the ancient nine-hole Musselburgh Links, the golf course on which King Charles I played in 1640. Newfield House lay in the direction of the sea. Each room in Holm House accommodated three, four or more boys and had a designated 'head boy' responsible for discipline. Our House Master was the heavily built J.D. Andrews, an older man with no overt interest in sport or athletics. He taught History and French and was tolerated rather than liked, perhaps because of his ingratiating manner. Some years later, he became a priest at St Peter's Episcopal Church, Newington, Edinburgh.

The ethos of Loretto School originated with Arnold of Rugby, who had inspired the famous headmaster, Dr Hely Hutchinson Almond.[C] The school motto – *Spartam nactus es, hanc exorna* – explained a great deal.[2] Translated literally, it meant 'Sparta is what you have obtained: this is what you must embellish'[D] Success at Loretto centred on modest academic achievement, physical fitness, excellence at sport (in particular, rugby football), fair play and honour.

There were problems for 'southerners'. My Sussex accent was the target for ribald joking. In Brighton, I had played association football, 'soccer', and had, in fact, never seen a rugby ball. At the Grammar School, corporal punishment was exceptional (p.28): by contrast, 'beating' was standard practice at Loretto and within a few days of arriving as a 'new boy', I was given three strokes of a cane for leaving my music case in a shoe locker.

> Loretto history demonstrated vividly that the character of a Headmaster was likely to determine the whole style of a school. In no instance was this better illustrated than by the appointment in 1926 of Dr J. R. C. Greenlees, a Glasgow medical practitioner, international rugby player and hero. Awarded the DSO and bar during the First World War, Greenlees dominated the school firmly, kindly and courteously. He supported his teaching staff with loyalty and took a personal interest in our progress, often sharing with us his interest in history.

A bell rang at 7 each morning. Summoned from bed, I was astonished to find my friends leaping out of baths of cold water. Dressed and in proper order, a roll call was taken at 7.30. Whatever the weather, we ran first towards the Gas Works, then to the dining hall in Schoolhouse. In the eyes of Almond, it seemed that an early shock to the system followed by a brisk run and a large plate of porridge was an excellent way of ensuring academic activity. At first, I found it had the opposite effect!

We wore dark blue shorts, not long trousers, but on formal occasions we dressed in a red jacket (the notorious 'red coat') and short white trousers. To the economic benefit of the School laundry, underclothes were not worn, although a clean flannel shirt was encouraged weekly. On Sundays, the approach to dress was strikingly different, and a kilt with a formal black jacket and silver buttons was *de rigueur*. The choice of kilt offered the chance of displaying one's heritage, so that the Frasers, the MacDonalds, the Camerons and the Mackenzies could show their clan origins to the world. It was less easy for those with names like Smith and Jones. My family tree pointed to MacIntyre, although the Lindsay tartan (p.2) might be preferred.

Porridge for breakfast, meat or white 'puddings' with potatoes and green vegetables for lunch, and herring or black pudding for tea were staple components of our diet. At breakfast, the pale face of Miss Gray, the domestic supervisor, could be seen ladling out the porridge. We sat at long tables, a senior boy at the end, the youngest in the middle. A masters' table, the Headmaster sometimes in the centre, lay across the windows of the dining hall. The arrangement did not prevent cheating – in spite of the presence of the senior boy, greedy classmates could empty the whole of a vegetable dish onto their own plates. On Sunday, boiled eggs were in such demand that voracious individuals might stay and eat two, three or even four. Until wartime rationing began, a Tuck Shop in the charge of a kindly but firm Mrs Tinsley, widow of the School's cricket professional, enabled us to buy sweetmeats, jams, fruit, gym shoes and other necessities.

The health of his pupils was closely monitored by Greenlees. By the time I reached Loretto, Balcarres House, next to Trafalgar Lodge garden, was a proper sanatorium, by contrast with the box-like building erected by Almond in 1897. The care of the sick was the responsibility of a qualified nurse, but discipline was sometimes lax. There was a daily demand for the treatment of minor complaints. Each day, at 10.30 a.m., the Matron, a Miss Jackson,[E] conducted a 'clinic' at which we could present ourselves with complaints ranging from sore throats, boils and athletes' foot to bruises, strains and even fractures for the attentions of this quiet and composed little lady. The decision to give exemption from morning gym or afternoon rugby was in her hands, but where there were signs of more serious disorder, she had the support of a local general practitioner, Dr A. Cleland, whose surgery was in Musselburgh High Street. School Doctor from 1926 to 1961, Dr Cleland remains associated in my mind with his frequent prescription of a medicine called *Byniamara*. Mysterious healing properties were attributed to this 'tonic'. In the light of what is now known of placebos, it is entirely likely that Dr Cleland's panacea was genuinely effective.

I had need of dental care on a number of occasions, my treatment given by a tall, kilt-wearing Mr Robertson in his High Street surgery. Owing to the growing scarcity of assistants as war approached, he

Figure 4.1 *Colin Gardner (at left) and the author preparing for school in 1940, with our mother, Marjorie Gardner.*

recruited a Polish dentist, whose training, it seemed to me, might have lain in a veterinary rather than in a dental school.

One quiet day, anxious to taste a cigarette, three of us climbed down under the loose floorboards of an empty classroom. I was lucky, because I found the cigarette so unpleasant that I never smoked one again. However, at University (p.49), I bought a pipe and, like a later Prime Minister, Harold Wilson, found that simply holding it in my hand promoted an air of calm in those near me.

I was joined by my brother, Colin (p.10), in the autumn of 1939 (Figure 4.1). He was not interested in sport and found life at Loretto difficult. Accomplished in literature, with a talent for drama, our paths crossed relatively infrequently – the two years difference in our ages determined that our school activities seldom coincided.

The three 'R's'

Each class had 15–20 boys. We sat at old-fashioned metal-framed, wooden desks, the 'eager beavers' near the front. For my first three years, I was taught French, some classics and the rudiments of science. I learned a little Latin from J.A. Pateman, who was in his element as an officer in the Cadet Force. Asking for a translation of a Latin quotation one day and expecting the answer 'Don't be afraid', he seemed surprised when I answered 'Fear not' and sent a school report to my parents that read 'He is a young dilettante.'

But we had to concentrate on more serious concerns! Sadly, the teaching of mathematics did not inspire us. My first instructor, P. H. F. Mermagen, did not 'tolerate fools gladly'. Each Monday morning in the fourth form, three of us – Thomas ('Tommy') Morgan, Ronald Gilchrist and I – were called to the front of an expectant class and told that our performances in the previous week's tests in algebra were 'unacceptably poor'. There was only one solution: three strokes of the cane, and each week we bent over without complaint. Our sufferings did not noticeably increase our mathematical ability and, in later life, we were sorry for the pupils of Ipswich School when we heard that Mermagen had become their Headmaster. F. ('Freddie') Morrison retained the perceptible brogue that he had used as a student of Trinity College, Dublin. He had an easy manner, and sympathy for those who, like himself, were not entirely happy with expressions such as $E = mc^2$. A. J. Mornard, a clever man, found it difficult to communicate with less able boys, but this did not prevent him from being an exacting Commanding Officer of the Cadet Force. Considerable interest was aroused one day when it became known that he was to marry the sister of our classmates, the Newton brothers.

In science, W. A. J. Musson, taught physics. He was a slightly built, diffident man at home as a hockey umpire but less able to control unruly classes. I recall vividly his demonstrations of particle physics with the Wilson cloud chamber, a factor contributing to my later fascination with the use of isotopes in medical research (p.159). An elderly P. J. Lancelot Smith taught chemistry, but the same strictures applied and his attitude was towards the enforcement of discipline rather than any emphasis on Avogadro's hypothesis. We relied heavily on Sherwood Taylor.[3] Nevertheless, like Oliver Sacks,[4] I was intrigued by Mendeleev's table of the elements. D. S. Oscroft introduced us to microscopes in his unusual classes in biology. Oscroft demanded the precise use of words and there was, he insisted, no place on biology for vague terms such as 'goodness' or 'brightness'. He left to recuperate from tuberculosis, but the disease recurred and he died not many years later, in 1944. His place was taken by an amiable, young but short-sighted locum, Mr Cowan. One day, the internal windings of a golf ball were hung inside a water-filled glass cylinder and a classmate asked the poor man for his opinion on 'this recently discovered tapeworm'.

By the time I reached the fifth form, I had become accustomed to the rigours of Loretto life and was beginning to enjoy some of the teaching, in particular English, under the guidance of the inspired A. H. Mahler. As his class advanced, he tempted us into Shakespearean theatre. In *As You Like It*, I was cast as the melancholy Jacques, while in *Twelfth Night*, I wore black cloth bands over my yellow trouser legs as I performed Malvolio. My enthusiastic friend James Thin (p.39) played Sir Andrew Aguecheek and Alistair Forrest (below) acted as Sir Toby Belch.

But as I grew up, my view of school life changed and, by 1940, I had developed a feeling of 'belonging', a sense of *esprit de corps*. I became the head of a room, with a first experience of proper responsibility, and then, in 1941, a House Prefect. My simple interests were helped by a small sixth-form library with a modest collection of classical works. I was presented with a book by Sir James Jeans[5] as a General Science Prize and reaped the benefit of a present of £5 I had been given by a kindly uncle. With this money, I bought the four volumes of Winston Churchill's life of his ancestor, Marlborough.[6] By chance, the history of the early eighteenth-century wars was selected as the subject for a competitive examination for boys studying history. Because I had read Marlborough so recently, I decided to enter the fray and was fortunate to be awarded the consequential Sinclair Thomson History Essay Prize. Richard Dark, a scholarly man who returned from retirement to serve the School during the war, was the adjudicator. The real reward, however, was my lifelong interest in Winston Churchill's life and the desire to acquire copies of all of his many books.

After passing the examinations for School Certificate, the old equivalent of 'O' levels, I decided to follow my father and great uncle Frank and to pursue a career in medicine. My father took the wise advice of Dr Greenlees, who had been a Cambridge student himself, and he recommended that I follow his example. In place of reading for a Higher Certificate (A levels), I began to study the subjects that formed part of the examinations for the First MB. In particular, it was essential to work longer hours in the modest Biology, Chemistry and Physics Laboratories, where wartime stringency limited the quality of the reagents and the sophistication of the apparatus.

Friends

As the years passed, I came to form close friendships with some of the boys in my class.

John (Jock) Allan Dalrymple Anderson became Professor of Community Medicine of the University of London. Many years later, we met in Japan (Figure 16.2).

Geoffrey Arthur Robinson, a leading figure in the business of shipping repairs in north-east England, was for 20 years a Governor of Loretto School.

Henry Colin Brown, not a conspicuous figure in either the academic or the athletic fields, had a distinguished record in the Second World War, surviving naval duty in the North Atlantic, convoys to Russia, mine sweeping and the Normandy landings on D-day.

Alistair Douglas Forrest was a burly sportsman blessed with meticulous handwriting that served him well in examinations. With a natural talent for games, he played rugby and hockey for the University of St Andrews, graduating in Medicine and becoming Physician Superintendent of Gogarburn Hospital, Edinburgh and subsequently, Professor of Psychiatry at the University of Saskatoon, Canada, where he died in 1979.

David James Marshall and I came to know each other very well, and he took me to visit his widowed mother in Kilmacolm. He was not an athlete, but I admired the stoicism with which he endured corporal punishment and, later, the spirit with which he became a naval officer, serving in the Mediterranean field of war. During his naval training, he attended the King Alfred Royal Navy training school at Brighton, where he met my parents.

James Thin was a grandson of the founder of the well-known Edinburgh bookshop that bore his name until very recent times. Jimmy was not interested in games or sport. He was highly literate and found his niche as librarian of the sixth-form Library. Nor was he musical, and we observed that he and a small number of others did not attend the Chapel choir practices but appeared as though by magic after these lively occasions ended. Many years later, we renewed our acquaintanceship when I went to search for books at his grandfather's shop. Jimmy died in 1997.

The sound of music

It was a delight to find that music played a large part in school life. The senior boys put together a Christmas pantomime in which the words 'Hearts' ('heearts') and 'Hibs' were repeated. I learnt the language of Scottish football! Soon after reaching Loretto, I was shepherded into the front row of a choir for a performance of Handel's *Messiah*. Beside me stood a new friend, Anthony Charles Kidd, later to distinguish himself during service in the Royal Navy. I began piano lessons again, at first with the chapel organist, C. H. Stuart Duncan,[F] but soon under the talented and sympathetic guidance of H. W. P. McLean. 'Squeaker' McLean shared my love of poetry, and our piano lessons often became discussions of iambic pentameters and sonnets. Not long afterwards, he was conscripted into the Royal Navy (p.47).

Sport

I learned rugby the hard way. I was recruited to a 'scratch' side, my companions and the referee aware that I did not understand the game. They told me to be the full-back. I was astonished to see a boy pick up the egg-shaped ball and run with it under his arm – in Brighton, he would have been severely reprimanded! He came straight towards me and I stood to one side to allow him to pass. Since he had handled the ball, I judged that the game would be suspended. I was therefore surprised to watch him place the ovoid ball on the ground beneath strange goal posts from which negli-

Figure 4.2 *The Loretto Rugby Third XV of 1941–42. Left to right: (back row) R. C. Murray, J. G. Wakelin, A. G. Laing, T. J. Boyd, F. E. Booth, G. S. Mackenzie; (middle row) W. J. C. Little, R. Gilchrist, D. L. Gardner, G. L. L. de Moubray, O. H. Taylor; (front row) J. Robinson, I. A. Ross, H. C. Brown, W. I. Stewart.*

gent carpenters had omitted to trim the uprights. In later years, I made amends and learned enough of the game to captain the Third Fifteen (Figure 4.2) and on one occasion played for the Second.

I enjoyed hockey greatly, a game played only in the spring term. Although a supporter of Sussex County in the world of cricket, I was neither a capable batsman nor bowler and did not reach any school eleven. Golf was another matter, but it was not a formal 'school game' and there was little time for playing on the ancient Links. There were unusual moments, especially when one of my classmates began to hide the ball of an opponent by burying it in a bunker. But when he started to take pieces of apparatus from the laboratories, the hand of the law sprang into action and his time at Loretto came to a premature end, his thefts brought to light when he left stolen goods on a night train to London. There was little encouragement to play tennis, although the school grounds included a good hard court. By contrast, fives, a game resembling squash but played with a gloved hand, not a racquet, was popular and masters often competed against senior boys in courts near the gymnasium

As part of the physical training essential for success in rugby, we were often directed to run on the nearby country roads. The runs, of varying length, were named after local landmarks. Wallyford was only two miles from the school, so there was both a 'short wally' and a 'long wally'. The circuit, returning along the shorefront through Prestonpans, was of five miles and there was competition to see who could finish without pausing. On Sunday afternoons, if it was too wet to walk, we changed into football clothes for yet another run!

From time to time, the entire school would set off by bus for a village at the foot of the Lammermuir Hills. With little preparation and no maps or compasses, we were told to cross the heights, a distance of some miles, and find our way back to Gifford, where we would meet for tea. It was not a difficult physical challenge for older boys, but for youngsters who did not know the way it was such a severe test, that on one occasion I was so exhausted that I found I could no longer eat and was promptly admitted to the Sanatorium.

We were encouraged to take our bicycles to school. By 1938, I was old enough to have a Halford Sports fitted with Sturmey Archer three-speed gears and costing £4.12s.6d (£4.63 in decimal currency). It was sent each term by train from King's Cross for 3s (15 new pence). From time to time, we were allowed to cycle eastwards, down the Great North Road past the Musselburgh Links, the wind at our backs, the sun shining in our faces. Hurrying up to Wallyford, we joined the Gullane road and were soon past Tranent and flying down to Longniddrie. Exhilarated by an unusual sense of freedom, the ride back from North Berwick offered an unforgettable skyline, a panorama interrupted by the tall chimney of the old, red-brick Portobello power station, the sun sinking behind the Pentland hills. As Arthur's Seat and the buildings of the 'Auld Toone' came into view, they combined to give a massif, looming through the grey atmosphere of smoke that commonly shrouded the ancient city.

Religion

A formal service at 11 o'clock every Sunday morning was followed by another at 6 o'clock each Sunday evening. The chapel (Figure 4.3) was affiliated to the Episcopal Church of Scotland. In addition to the School Chaplain, there were three Chapel Wardens, boys whose duties included meeting visitors as they arrived, tidying the pews and the chapel itself, and laying out hymn and prayer books. It was the custom for the most junior Warden to be from the third form and the second Warden from the fifth form, while the Senior Warden was a house or school prefect. Soon after reaching Loretto, I was surprised to be told that I was to be the Junior Warden. Later, I succeeded to the more senior positions. The price paid for these privileges was the need to prepare for each service long before the other boys; the reward was a degree of freedom unusual in this tightly regulated community.

Figure 4.3 *Loretto School chapel.*

In 1937, the Chaplain was the Reverend R. A. Goodwin.[G] During the week, he taught classics with mannerisms that would have appealed to the producers of today's television comedy programmes. He was succeeded by the Reverend B. C. ('Blahsy') Snell, who served Loretto from 1940 to 1941 and again from 1944 to 1946. His roots lay in East Anglia, and the quality of the chapel services quickly rose as the sermons became more thoughtful, the services of confirmation more conventional. It was the custom for the school to invite senior clerics from Edinburgh to come as visiting preachers, and we listened to Dr Selby Wright from the Canongate Kirk, to the Bishop of Edinburgh and to another speaker whose words stay with me to this day. Reminding us of Mallory and Irvine, who had lost their lives near the summit of Mount Everest in 1925, he said they were 'last seen going strong for the top'.

The approach of war

I had grown up in the shadows of the First World War, with family talk of the Somme, of food rationing, of air-raid balloons and of Sopwith Camels. At Loretto, the *Daily Telegraph* alerted us to the threat of renewed hostilities (Figure 4.4). The School took sensible precautions to protect both staff and pupils. The air raid shelters to which Dr Greenlees had devoted much thought were used only occa-

Figure 4.4 *The Home Fleet anchored below the Forth Bridge – a photograph taken by the author in 1938.*

sionally. They were sufficiently comfortable to allow us to sit with our books for one or two hours, but I do not recall that we ever had to spend a whole night in one, even when air raids on Glasgow brought German bombers overhead. With the 'blackout', the darkened skies took on a new meaning. Walking through the grounds at night, I gazed in amazement at the constellations of stars, which, like the Northern Lights, were visible in all their grandeur for the first time. Periodically, a meteor disrupted the panorama, while the new moon, like a searchlight, interrupted every other astronomical thought.

The valiant efforts of J. R. C. Greenlees to maintain standards in athletics, games and physical training bore fruit, although competition with other schools was sometimes restricted by limitations of travel and transport. The health of boys did not suffer and a sensible approach to food rationing was successful. When necessary, immunization was practised and the periodic inspection of our skin minimized the spread of communicable diseases.

For a short time, the school staff remained largely unchanged, but, even before 1939, younger teachers had begun to volunteer for active military service. They were gradually replaced by older men who were either unfit for army duties or had retired. One consequence was an erosion of the standards of academic work. Another, indirect, result was a diminishing opportunity for education in music, art, drama, literature and sociology, subjects not central to the conventional curriculum. To counteract these changes, Greenlees maintained his contacts with senior figures in his old university, Cambridge, ensuring that there was a warm welcome for boys who chose to follow in their masters' footsteps.

Every boy at Loretto School became a member of the cadet force – the Junior Training Corps or JTC – an organization based upon Army tradition and discipline. The khaki uniform of the Corps centred on the kilt. The officers were members of the teaching staff. The Corps maintained a pipe band and carried out regular drills and exercises. The boys of Loretto School entered the Second World War with one further advantage not shared by all British schools: the School maintained an indoor rifle range and there were frequent competitions. We all had the opportunity of mastering the skills of firing 0.22-inch calibre rifles accurately, in the prone position. As the Second World War moved into an increasingly active and dangerous phase, the JTC underwent a dramatic change when a civilian national defence force was formed.

In the early summer of 1940, as the Battle of Britain was fought by the Spitfires and Hurricanes of the Royal Air Force, the threat of an invasion by the German Army became very real. On the evening of 14th May, the Secretary of State for War, Anthony Eden, asked for volunteers for a new organisation, the Local Defence Volunteers, the LDV. All British men aged between 17 and 65 years were invited to join. Within a short time, hundreds of thousands had offered their services. British schools responded at once, and those older cadets in the Loretto School JTC became members. Soon, Winston Churchill proposed a shorter name for the LDV: they became the Home Guard.

At Loretto, the task of the Home Guard was to protect the A1 motorway, the main road between England and Scotland, against attack by airborne forces. The defences centred on Wallyford, an important junction on the A1 route to Edinburgh. The junction was guarded by huge concrete blocks, similar to those still seen beside Gullane Golf Course. From time-to-time, we slept, fully dressed, on the floor of the Miners' Institute. Trenches were dug and here we were sometimes engaged in mock raids made by a University cadet force carried from Edinburgh in trucks to 'attack' the junction.

School Home Guard recruits had to be taught to load and fire conventional infantry weapons. Accuracy with large-calibre weapons came less easily than with the 0.22-calibre rifles of the School rifle range. Arming the Home Guard was a slow process. At first, we were issued with 0.300-inch calibre rifles, brought from the United

States. Unfortunately, most of the available ammunition was for 0.303-calibre weapons. When supplies of the correct weapons reached us, we were taken for firing practice to Hunter's Bog on the slopes of Edinburgh's Arthur's Seat. 'Tommy' (Sten) guns then arrived and vivid images of Al Capone were in my mind as I stood firing the little automatic weapon, deafened by the noise of the explosions. There was also the need to throw hand grenades, and it became second nature to remember not to release the pin until it was time to hurl the bomb!

It was not many months later before some of us were drawn into another new organisation – the Air Training Corps or ATC.

> An Air Defence Cadet Corps had been set up in 1938. In order to give part-time training to young men destined for the Royal Air Force, the RAF. The ATC was established under a Royal Warrant of February 1941.

Since it was my intention to join the RAF, I left the JTC and joined the ATC. I was appointed Flight Sergeant and it became one of my tasks to supervise our contingent at camps held at Drem, the RAF Station in East Lothian. On one occasion, the venture was shared with Merchiston School and there was some discontent among the Merchistonians when they were commanded to march by a Lorettonian sergeant! But we worked together successfully, learned how to fire Vickers machine guns and were taught navigation and aircraft recognition. There were bumpy flights with inexperienced Canadian pilots in Bristol Beaufort torpedo bombers and gentle views of the East Lothian landscape in a Tiger Moth, a little plane that was so slow that I could look through my goggles over the side of the passenger's cockpit and watch cars on the ground moving only slightly more slowly than the aircraft.

During wartime school terms, free afternoons were given to weeding and hoeing at an agricultural estate near Musselburgh. When the summer holiday came in 1941, my young friend Ralph Ross Russell and I were part of a group organised by S. T. Hutchinson[H] to help farmers and their Land Girl Army near Ancrum, in the Scottish Borders.

Casualties

There was a less happy aspect of the war years. I could not help thinking of my friends and teachers fighting in Normandy, in North Africa, on the Atlantic and in the air over Germany. There was an atmosphere of vigilance and apprehension: no-one knew when news of the next defeat or victory would be broadcast on the 'wireless'. As hostilities progressed, we became used to the announcement of increasing numbers of casualties. Major G. Hedderwick, the Deputy Headmaster or Vicegerent, had made a lasting impression as a firm, forthright teacher. He had the delightful habit of bringing his bull terrier into our classes, during which the dog lay quietly under his master's desk. Called to the army, there was great sadness when it was reported that he had been killed in action during the retreat to Dunkirk in the summer of 1940. Dr Greenlees used his periodic morning talks ('Doubles'), which followed morning prayers, to tell the School of those who had been killed or wounded. In these moving and poignant moments, he would recall the personality and achievements of the dead in a style that left an indelible memory in the minds of us all. When young Graham Rolland was lost over the English Channel, we mourned with his older brother. Later, when Ronald Gillespie, James Henderson and Angus Colquhoun were killed, I felt a profound sadness for the disappearance of my classmates.

But school losses were not limited to those due to the war. One day, when I was head of a room in Linkfield House, we were told that one of our friends, Joseph Robinson, had drowned in an accident at Gladsmuir Reservoir. He and others had taken their lunch beside the water and had unwisely gone swimming. Robinson was seized with cramp and could not be rescued.

Holidays and home

A school holiday meant a journey to Brighton. On one occasion, in 1938, I found myself on the Silver Jubilee express, a streamlined train with a rear observation coach in which rotating armchairs allowed splendid views of the railway line receding at 90 miles per hour. The train reached London from Edinburgh in six hours without stopping. Comfortably seated, I was conscious that an older man and his wife were watching me with kindly interest: apparently he was a Governor of Loretto School, concerned for my security. Later, wartime journeys were less pleasant. By 1939, the blackout was in force, food and drink rare luxuries, the trains packed with soldiers, sailors and airmen. Seats designed for three people accommodated four. There was incessant cigarette smoking, criminal behaviour was commonplace, theft frequent and I lost an attaché case and a suitcase.

In 1940, Brighton was central to the planned German invasion of Britain. The long shingle beaches, so loved by weekend holidaymakers from London, were mined and covered by barbed wire. Anti-aircraft guns were sited at intervals along the esplanade that stretched from Shoreham to Rottingdean and Peacehaven. I enjoyed walking along the beautiful coast, but I was almost always alone, with no other civilian in sight. One morning, a wandering Messerschmitt fighter flew so low above our home that I could easily see the pilot's head. One night, I heard a noise like a powerful machine gun passing overhead; looking out I caught a glimpse of the fiery pulse-jet engine of one of the first V1 missiles heading for London.

But these challenging days were coming to an end. On 13th September 1940, J. R. C. Greenlees had written to me in his own hand to tell me that I had obtained 'credits in 8 School Certificate examinations'. As he said: 'It is a good result and you deserved it. Now what next?' The answer came when I was told that because of the shortage of Medical Officers for the Armed Forces, I would not be permitted to enlist in the RAF but must pursue my peacetime choice, Medicine. There followed conversations between my father and Dr Greenlees, who recommended an attempt to gain admission to the University of Cambridge. I visited Clare College in 1941 for a welcoming interview with the Master, Henry Thirkill, and have a clear recollection of the score of a Mozart sonata open on his grand piano! There followed arduous preparations for First MB examinations in Physics, Inorganic Chemistry and Biology, with Organic Chemistry to follow later.

Even in this academic world, there was no escape from the ravages of war. Walking past Heffer's bookshop in Cambridge, to which I had travelled for a Part 1 MB examination, I saw a placard 'HOOD SUNK'. It was a moment I shall never forget. At 6 am on 24th May 1941, the battlecruiser *Hood* had been sunk by a shell from the German battleship *Bismarck*. The loss of the *Hood* and all save three members of the 1400 crew struck a personal blow.[1] Among the dead was my former music teacher, 'Squeaker' McLean (p.39).

II.

To East Anglia,
the Water Of Leith and
Lincolnshire

CHAPTER 5

An English student

Beside the Cam

'Faith' is a fine invention
When Gentlemen can see
But Microscopes are prudent
In an Emergency

Emily Elizabeth Dickinson[1]

As the Second World War entered its fourth year, life in Cambridge flowed on as it had done for centuries. Markets, cinemas and public houses were busy, but the battles raging in Europe and Africa cast a blight over normal life. Each day, the papers brought news of military and naval disasters. Each night, during the 'blackout', all lights were rigorously shielded as Lancaster bombers from nearby airfields roared overhead. Travel was restricted, petrol and food rationed. Shortages of coal and gas, the many men and women absent in the Services, and the threat of air raids and invasion were ever-present reminders of the conflict. The contrast with Scotland, I learnt later, was significant. In parts like West Lothian, where my future father- and mother-in law lived, food rationing was less strict. There were air raids on Glasgow and attacks on the Forth Bridge but, overall, there were fewer air raid alarms.

> **Chapter summary**
> - College life
> - Chapel
> - Music
> - Sport
> - Classes
> - Part II Pathology
> - Towards the war's end

College life

I became a medical student at Clare College,[A] Cambridge[2,3] (Figure 5.1) in September 1942. My first clear recollection is of Memorial Court (Figure 5.2). The building, in front of the new University Library, was on the far side of the River Cam. I was fortunate to be allowed to stay in the College throughout my three years there and did not have to move into lodgings in the town. We were given dinner each evening in the College dining hall, but for other meals we fended for ourselves. My father, whose general practice in Brighton was increasingly successful, remained intensely conscious of the poverty in which he had been brought up and made me a strict

Figure 5.1 *Clare College and the Backs.*

Figure 5.2 *Memorial Court, Clare College.*

allowance of £10 for each term, twice the amount he drew monthly, from his London bank, for himself. There was no possibility of asking for more, and at lunchtime I often called at a 'British Restaurant', the eating houses set up by the Government to alleviate the problems of food rationing. At one of these busy places I could buy a meal for one shilling (5 pence in decimal currency), leaving sufficient in the bank to pay for a newspaper, textbooks and an occasional concert.

At first, my rooms were on the ground floor. I had a sitting room with a sofa, a dining table and bookshelves where *Gray's Anatomy*[4] and a textbook of physiology jostled for space between Jane Austen,[5] Sir James Jeans,[6,7] Winston Churchill,[8] Sigmund Freud,[9] William James[10] and a Bible.[11] I appreciated the spacious bedroom and shared a kitchen and a bathroom with my mathematician neighbour, Bryan Thwaites.[B] I recall how, sitting at his table, armed with a pencil, paper, a jar of malt and honey, and a spoon, he grappled with his equations in a style reminding me of Albert Einstein. One day, asked which new apparatus he required for the Institute of Physics in Berlin, Einstein is said to have reached in his pocket for a pencil and said: 'Thank you but I have all that I need here.' With Bryan, I faced the challenge of making wartime suppers with egg powder. But, very occasionally, we would creep out after dark and make our way to the pool at Grantchester, where we took off our clothes and jumped in for a nocturnal swim. In my third year, I was able to move upstairs to brighter, first-floor rooms vacated by Ian Stoddart,[C] who had gone to London (p.59) for his clinical studies.

Immediately above Bryan lived David Hacking, whose generous parents – his father was a man of the church – made him a financial allowance that was much greater than mine and which he liked to spend in the many Cambridge public houses. A school friend of mine, Bruce Robertson, had rooms in the same block. We worked together in the practical classes of the medical school, but his firm religious beliefs, which he tested on me each afternoon, led him to the Cambridge Intercollegiate Christian Union, the CICCU – the 'Kick You'. After one year, he left to study for the Church, eventually becoming Minister of the Scots Kirk, Rue Baynard, Paris.

Another good friend was David Morley.[D] On 8th September 1944, we went with other friends to North Wales to explore the mountainsides of Snowdonia. I recall the day vividly. I was sitting in a railway carriage at Euston station, on my way to Liverpool and then to Chester, to join the adventure. It was the moment when the Germans launched the first of their V2 rockets at London. Suddenly there was a huge explosion in the distance. Everyone thought that a gas main had blown up, but it was the arrival of the first missile.

During the Second World War, student life was, of course, very restricted when compared with peacetime. Nevertheless, life in Memorial Court was preferable to that in the rooms of Old Court, which had few modern facilities and where students and Fellows scurried in their dressing gowns across the very public quadrangle towards the communal bathrooms, which lay in the basement of the ancient building.

Each day, as I walked over Clare Bridge towards the town centre, I noticed the ancient, sculptured stone spheres that decorated the upper parapet of the bridge. From one stone, a segment on its far side had been cut out as though it were a slice of cake. It was widely believed that to touch this recess in passing would bring good luck. I kept to the custom 'just in case'.

An advantage of Memorial Court for the adventurous was that it was possible to creep into the building 'after hours'. In the 1940s, the gates of all University buildings were locked at 10 p.m. and no visitors were admitted after this time without a written permit from a tutor. However, the stonework of Memorial Court offered step-like projections that could be used as a ladder – by climbing the wall it was possible to escape the eagle eyes of the night porter, although it was necessary to be certain that a friend had left one of his windows unfastened!

In 1942, Memorial Court contained a water tank built for the wartime College Fire Squad, of which I was part. We had a mobile fire pump drawn by an Essex *Terraplane* car. One Sunday, as I was driving my fellow firemen through the town, I learnt that the brakes were weak – the car collided with a sack of potatoes on the back of a greengrocer's lorry in Sidney Street! The enraged shop owner waved his fists as we sped off. The Fire Squad remained in the College throughout Christmas; one year, my mother sent me a haggis to cheer me up and I invited fellow members of the Squad to share the delicacy. Unfortunately, I had not realised that a haggis, within its skin, should be heated slowly. I boiled mine: the skin burst, but my fellow firemen were too polite to object to the soup that was the savoury result.

Figure 5.3 *The Reverend Charles ('Charlie') Francis Digby Moule CBE FBA, Lady Margaret's Professor of Divinity.*

Chapel

I had enjoyed my experience as a Chapel Warden at Loretto School (p.41) and offered to assist the College Chapel. It was in this way that I met the Dean, the Reverend William Telfer. The position brought us together, arranging the details of services and meeting for Sunday breakfasts. The fact that I had been confirmed at school into the Episcopal Church of Scotland was not allowed to stand in our way. It was not long afterwards that he became Bishop of Ely. His successor was C. F. D. ('Charlie') Moule[E] (Figure 5.3). Charlie, one of the leading New Testament scholars of his day, became a dear friend. He maintained an enormous correspondence with his many friends around the world and I kept in touch year-by-year, always on his birthday and at Christmas. Charlie died on 30th September 2007 in his 99th year.

Music

Hostilities did not stop or even reduce the music that had always been an important part of Cambridge life, and I often went to piano recitals and to oratorios. The finest occasions were performances of Bach's Mass in B minor in the Cambridge Town Hall and of Verdi's Requiem in King's College Chapel, when Isobel Baillie and Kathleen Ferrier were outstanding soloists. Piano recitals were given on Sunday afternoons in the Cambridge Arts Theatre. The stage was small and, on one occasion, when the performance was to be by Louis Kentner, the famous pianist, the audience was so large that seats had to be placed very near the instrument. I was given the chair closest to the soloist and learnt the huge physical effort that recitals demanded. By the end of the afternoon, Kentner, the sweat pouring down his face, seemed exhausted. From more comfortable seats, I heard Solomon and Myra Hess.

Sport

Sporting activities during the war were restricted to an even greater extent than academic. However, college rivalry on the rugby and football pitches continued, and the larger colleges encouraged competition in rowing, tennis and golf. I played in the Clare College rugby team during 1942–44. Tennis was a social activity, and my friend Russell persuaded me to help him with his girlfriend one afternoon when he could not honour an arrangement to play a game with her. She quickly learned that I had not been taught tennis at school: I was a 'rabbit'! However, there was one memorable encounter on the court when I was paired with a golfing 'blue' in a match against Corpus Christi College. For a few minutes, our opponents were misled – from a distance, they could not see that the pale blue letters on my friend's sweater were not CUTC (Cambridge University Tennis Club) but CUGC (Cambridge University Golf Club). A few swift strokes were enough to disprove this fallacy and we were swept to a crushing but good-natured defeat.

Classes

Our challenge was how best to prepare for the examinations for the Honours degree of BA, part of the Natural Sciences Tripos.[F] In peacetime, examinations for Part I of the Tripos were taken after three years' study. Every summer, 'long' vacations extended from the beginning of July until the end of September. The war reduced the three years to two and the 'long' vacations were largely replaced by coursework.

Our course demanded a whole working day, each day. I smiled when a student of Economics told me that he had to attend only one lecture each week! Our lectures were in buildings on the University's Downing Street site, such a short distance from Clare that a 15-minute walk each morning past King's College Chapel was sufficient to take me there. At first, my lectures were in Anatomy, Physiology and Biochemistry. In the afternoons, I went to the laboratories for practical classes, and, in my second year, started Pathology and Pharmacology. On many other occasions, like almost every Cambridge student, I used a bicycle. There was a vigorous market in stolen bicycles and, in spite of being chained to the College railings, two of mine were stolen.

The forthright teaching of Professor H. A. Harris, Head of the **Anatomy** School, occasionally led to provocative exchanges. One Clare student, Linklater, told how, during an oral examination, Harris threw a human femur to him across the table, demanding: 'What's that?' Characteristically, Linklater set the scene for his brief medical career when he threw the bone back, saying 'Tell me yourself!' In another episode, Walter Spector and his fellow student Cremona sat in the front row of the Anatomy Lecture Theatre. Professor Harris made a joke about Cremona custard and Cremona walked out. Wally Spector was later to be Professor of Pathology at St Bartholomew's Hospital Medical School.

H. A. Harris was ably supported by Dr D. V. Davies, later Professor of Anatomy at St Thomas's Hospital Medical School and by Drs H. L. H. Green and G. W. Harris. Geoffrey Harris's subsequent studies of pituitary gland structure and function gained international recognition. Davies was an intimidating demonstrator in the practical classes. He retained a flavour of his own Welsh accent, and his penetrating eye and vigorous inspection of idle students readily exposed those who were indolent or lacking understanding of the comparative anatomy of the primates. Despite his oratory, the distinction between phylogeny and ontogeny was never entirely clear to me and for this ignorance I paid a price in my examinations!

Practical anatomy centred on the dissecting room and on a large classroom where a great variety of specimens and artwork was displayed. The vast dissection room accommodated the preserved bodies used for 'anatomization'. Around each table, two, three, four or more students clustered as they dissected an arm, a leg or the viscera while demonstrators hovered in the background, ready to offer explanations and guidance. Not surprisingly, the dissecting room tables were foci for social as well as for scientific activity and here friendships were made, assignations arranged.

> In the course of months labouring over the structure of human bones and the attachments of innumerable muscles, tendons and ligaments, I accumulated many handwritten notebooks[G] in which I recorded the words of the lecturers and the results of innumerable practical classes. My practice was to take rough notes during lectures and then to transcribe them in the evenings with the aid of textbooks and drawings. The notes recorded the principles of developmental anatomy, the sex organs, the embryo and the placenta, the developing innervation of the skin and muscles of the limbs, reflex arcs, the autonomic nervous system, and the origins of the circulatory and lymphatic systems. Detailed reviews of the central nervous system were followed by the phylogeny of the brain. Insanity was touched on and comments on motor and sensory pathways followed by observations on the functions of selected parts of the cerebral cortex and of the spinal cord.

We also enjoyed anatomy tutorials conducted by Professor J. D. Boyd, whose tutorials were unusual because he was an 'immigrant'! He held the Chair of Anatomy at the London Hospital School of Medicine in Whitechapel, but the war brought his department away from London. His Cambridge base was the Sedgwick Museum of Geology. Here, little groups of Anatomy students would sit discussing the vasculature of the human gut amidst the statues, rocks and other displays of Palaeolithic times. Later, I came to know Professor

Boyd well when he wrote a generous introduction to the first edition of *Human Histology*.[12]

The academic atmosphere in **Physiology** was entirely different. The study of the function, as opposed to the structure, of the mammalian body was led by the Nobel Laureate Professor E. D. Adrian FRS. His prize had come early in life, in studies close to those of Charles Sherrington,[H] who wrote of his work in the *Integrative Action of the Nervous System*.[13] Sherrington lived to a great age and we occasionally saw him as he passed along Sidney Street. Adrian was fond of hill walking and during my time at Cambridge had famously slipped on one of his walks in the Lake District, accidentally falling on and breaking his wife's leg.

With Adrian was the amiable Dr Tunnicliffe, who excelled in giving lectures that were so easy to understand that those with little experience of public speaking were inclined to dismiss them as simplistic. Dr Gilbert Adair taught the properties of the blood pigment haemoglobin. Practical histology classes, each student with a tray of slides and a microscope, were directed with great skill by the artistic E. N. Willmer[14] (p.57), famed for his work on tissue culture and for his interest in colour vision. He was a dry speaker, not known for his sense of humour but revered for his encyclopaedic knowledge.

Our teachers enjoyed priceless support from a group of expatriate Europeans. For the first two years after he had escaped from Nazi Germany, Hans Krebs was among others welcomed to Cambridge, and his autobiography[15] tells the moving story of how scientists, regarded officially as 'enemy aliens', came to be British citizens. Among others who reached Cambridge before the war were W. U. Jacobson, Hermann (Hugh) Blaschko and Wilhelm Feldberg. After graduating in Germany, Feldberg spent some years in England before returning to his homeland. He left Germany again at the time of the Jewish persecution in 1933. He excelled in experiments with live animals, and his demonstrations to small student groups of pancreatic secretion, of the actions of acetylcholine and of gastric secretion held his audiences spellbound. I once had the opportunity of proposing a vote of thanks for a talk he gave to the Clare Medical Society.

Practical physiology was taught in classes where we would sit with microscopes, examining living preparations of cells and tissues, and in demonstrations that often followed individual lectures. Tunnicliffe, for example, showed the oxygen-binding curves of haemoglobin. Adrian preferred the drama of electronics. On one occasion, he inserted a microelectrode into the auditory (internal ear) nerve of a live monkey so that the nerve impulses generated by simple sounds could be shown on cathode-ray oscilloscopes, to the amazement of an entranced class.

Much time was devoted to **Biochemistry**, one of the University's most prominent subjects.[I] The Department of Biochemistry was directed by Sir Frederick Gowland Hopkins,[J] the first to describe a vitamin, ascorbic acid, vitamin C. As J. D. Bernal wrote,[16] 'the

Biochemistry Laboratory, after the Cavendish', was 'the centre of scientific advance in that University'. By the time I reached his department, Hopkins was an elderly figure who passed us without speaking as he clambered up his stairs. The research programmes in bacterial biochemistry were ably supported by Dr D. Stephenson. However, the greatest part of the burden of teaching the wartime medical class fell on the shoulders of Ernest Baldwin, who was both a talented teacher and an expert in his own field of comparative biochemistry, where there was a special interest in the characteristics of primitive vertebrates such as sharks. It was a time when the citric acid cycle discovered by Hans Krebs (p.55) was 'the talk of the town', and Baldwin often referred to it. Looking back, I believe we would have appreciated the significance of the discovery better had our teachers explained more fully how pioneers like Krebs had come to their Nobel Prize-winning conclusions. In 1942–43, Baldwin would often appear for his afternoon lectures dressed in the uniform of an air-raid warden, since the country, and in particular London, was being subjected to the full might of the Luftwaffe's bombing attacks.

The building occupied by Biochemistry welcomed students to a large practical classroom on the top floor. Considering the number of students – many non-medical undergraduates joined the group – and in view of the ravages of war, the practical classes were highly organized, with members of the staff in constant attendance. One day, as we walked up to a practical examination, one of these kindly European teachers reassured me, saying, 'Don't worry! You will find that you know the answers!'

In October 1943, we entered the mysterious world of disease, **Pathology**.[17] I had had the good fortune to be introduced to the subject while at school in Brighton, where my father's friend and colleague Dr Janes,[K] a former colleague of Professor Lionel Whitby[L] at the Middlesex Hospital, was the Clinical Pathologist to the Sussex County Hospital. Before I left school, my father asked him to advise me on the choice of a student microscope. Dr Janes showed me a sparkling new Beck monocular instrument and compared it with a second-hand Leitz instrument. Both were to cost £50. Naively, I chose the new instrument; it came from Welbeck Street, London and is still in my possession.

The Cambridge classes in Pathology were in the inspired hands of Professor H. R. Dean[M] (Figure 5.4). Henry Roy Dean had studied with Robert Koch in Berlin and contributed greatly

Figure 5.4 *H. R. Dean, Professor of Pathology.*

to establishing the new science of immunology. He became Professor of Pathology in Sheffield, where one of his 'boys' was Howard Florey[N] (p.163), before moving to the Chair of Pathology in Manchester. It was here, during the First World War, that he completed his pioneering work on anti-tetanus immunization. Dean was admired and even worshipped by those closest to him. He believed, correctly, that many of the most difficult problems in life are lightened by humour.

'Daddy' Dean was an inveterate pipe-smoker and members of his staff were accustomed to being stopped in the corridor and asked for a little tobacco. Whereupon, the great man – he was a large figure – without a moment's hesitation would empty the contents of a tobacco pouch into the cavernous bowl of his professorial pipe and disappear down the corridor, a twinkle in his eye. On another, later, occasion, a large lecture hall, packed with members of the Pathological Society of Great Britain and Ireland, had been darkened for the demonstration of a lantern slide showing the faint outline of a fluorescent reaction. Turning to the audience with a mischievous smile, Dean struck two matches at the same time: to his evident delight, the audience was momentarily blinded! His eccentricities, well described in the *Journal of Pathology and Bacteriology* by Henry Dible, were widely known. From time to time, with a broad grin, he would exclaim to us that, as a large man, he insisted on large pieces of apparatus, so that he liked a boiling tube rather than a test tube, a Kahn tube rather than a precipitin tube.

In the practical classroom, every student enjoyed a share of a bench where small but serious practical work was conducted on a surprisingly liberal scale. Students were expected to make preparations of bacterial cultures on glass slides or coverslips, and to stain them carefully. We were closely and actively supervised. Among the demonstrators was Colonel Whittaker, late of the Indian Army. He had suffered from rectal cancer and his tumour had been removed surgically. He kept the specimen in a glass jar and enjoyed displaying it to groups of fascinated students.

Our academic progress was supervised in College tutorials, which complemented the formal teaching of the University and were held in the tutors' own rooms. I was lucky to come under the spell of E. N. Willmer (p.55). Willmer taught me the significance of the work of the French scientist Claude Bernard, who described *le milieu interieur* (the internal environment) of the living body, that is, the fluids and substances bathing the cells of which the tissues and organs are composed. Many years later, we visited the vineyard in France named after Bernard and tasted one of the wines.

Part II Pathology

In 1944, I joined the class for Part II of the Natural Sciences Tripos, a privilege that demanded a further year at the University. There were ten students in this little group, nine of them men.[O] To spend an entire year in the close study of the laboratory sciences proved

Figure 5.5 *A. M. Barrett, University Morbid Anatomist.*

to be an unforgettable experience and one that influenced the whole course of my professional life. Under H. R. Dean's masterly direction, a bevy of teachers – many scientists of international repute, others younger and aspiring research workers – laboured to instil in us the principles of scientific thought, enquiry and practice.

Among the senior teachers was A. M. Barrett (Figure 5.5), who contributed his teaching skills in pathological anatomy and histopathology; J. R. Marack, busy formulating the structure of antibodies; and R. R. Race and G. L. Taylor, extending the horizons of new knowledge in the field of blood groups and, in particular, in the area of the recently discovered rhesus (Rh) factor. E. T. C. Spooner[p] injected a strong core of contemporary microbiology; Raymond Williamson gave special instruction in the behaviour of lymphocytes; and a class on Tropical Medicine instilled a lifelong interest in the numerous disorders of the 'Third World'. Practical skills were acquired by practising techniques such as the titration of antibodies and the study of bacterial plates. Spooner was assisted by Dr Tomlinson, a person of musical culture and interest but a cigarette addict. So intense were the clouds of smoke that enveloped him as he manipulated his bacterial culture plates that he had to pause every few minutes to rub the brown film from his glasses!

Even the most experienced teachers sometimes face unexpected challenges for which they are not prepared. One day, 'Teddy' Spooner, lecturing on the principles of autoclaves, the vessels used to sterilize instruments in surgery, admitted to us that his mind had become a blank. Overcome by the vacuum that occasionally clouds even the finest intellect, he gave up halfway through his talk and admitted that he could not explain the subject to us that day! In my third year, Spooner became my tutor. He was a wonderfully clear thinker but, when in doubt, took refuge in his pipe with which he consumed one ounce (28 g) of tobacco each day. Spooner was an authority on viral and rickettsial diseases, and in the early summer of 1944, as the allied armies advanced into Europe, news of the Nazi concentration camps spread like wildfire. There was a call for additional medical help, and our small group of students was told that we were to be sent to Belsen, to help with the medical officers struggling with an outbreak of typhus. In the event, this plan was countermanded, but it was of extraordinary interest to see the remains of Belsen when, some years later, I lived briefly in the SS headquarters building (p.105).

Towards the war's end

In the few summer weeks remaining after the completion of my last third-year term, I was able to attend the informal teaching, in Addenbrooke's Hospital, of Professor R. A. McCance,[Q] a world authority on tissue metabolism and nutrition. So memorable were his words, so skilled his teaching that, when I met him again, 31 years later, in Professor Ford's office in Manchester (p.239), I was able to remind him of a young woman with a crippling bone disease about which he had taught me in 1945. Without a moment's hesitation he responded: 'She did very well.'

Despite the war, we still enjoyed short vacations during which I journeyed back to Brighton. In the spring of 1944, as the British and American armies concentrated for the invasion of Normandy, my father sent his chauffeur, George Best, to drive me home, fearing for the safety of the railways. As we travelled down the main roads leading to the south coast, we passed mile upon mile of armoured cars, trucks, guns and tanks. Reaching the coast, I remember seeing the great concentrations of barges and small ships filling the harbours at Shoreham and Worthing.

It was at this time that Sir Thomas Horder (p.26) visited Brighton again. He travelled early and came to breakfast. Food rationing was only one of many restrictions imposed on the civilian population. Well prepared, the King's Physician brought his own lumps of sugar tucked into a waistcoat pocket, behind a gold watch chain! It was at this time that I was confronted by another life-threatening bacterial infection. I pricked my finger in the garden and, within a few hours, a thin red line appeared at my wrist, spreading up my forearm. The condition was lymphangitis, evidence that bacteria were being carried from the skin towards the bloodstream and a warning of septicaemia. The invading streptococci were stopped in their tracks by the first injection of penicillin.

In 1945, it was still not possible to complete the hospital studies essential for a qualification in Medicine in Cambridge.[R] The University held examinations for the degrees of Bachelor of Medicine (MB) and Bachelor of Surgery (ChB), but the Medical School with its teaching hospital, Addenbrooke's, could not yet provide the systematic clinical teaching, teaching with patients, a necessary preparation for students attempting these tests. The majority of the students in the class of which I had been part during my first two years therefore moved to London: many went to the Medical School of St Thomas' Hospital, some to the corresponding Schools of King's College Hospital, St Bartholomew's or Guy's However, my father believed in the teaching traditions of his *alma mater*, the

University of Edinburgh (p.2). He therefore sought the advice both of Dr Spooner and of Dr Frederick Price, the distinguished physician, before advising me where to go. I did not know at the time that Price was a candidate for the Chair of Medicine at Edinburgh, a position soon to be filled by Stanley Davidson (p.67), who had himself been a Cambridge undergraduate. Price had no difficulty in persuading my father that I should return to 'The Athens of the North'. I graduated BA (Hons) in June 1945 and proceeded MA in 1950. My ScD degree came many years later, in 1986.

The war ended with the surrender of the Japanese on 15th August 1945 (VJ Day), and I soon resumed my familiarity with the London and North Eastern Railway Company!

CHAPTER 6

A Scottish student

Near Dunsepie Loch

Why have women Passion, intellect, moral
activity – these three – and a place in society
where no one of the three can be exercised?

Florence Nightingale[1]

My aunt Annie Gardner (p.7) had been a nurse who became a hospital matron. I was soon to learn that nursing would 'run in the family'!

But first, my problem on reaching Edinburgh in 1945 was to find somewhere to live. In 1824, Edinburgh, 'Auld Reekie', was 'a picturesque, odorous, inconvenient, old-fashioned town, of about seventy thousand inhabitants.'[2] In September 1945 I formed the same impression. Students' money, not their comfort, was what mattered. At first, I was fortunate. Ralph Ross Russell's (p.45) mother lived in Merchiston Gardens and offered me a room for a modest rent. Their house was a short walk from the tramline that ran from Morningside, first to the Royal Infirmary of Edinburgh in Lauriston Place and then, a short distance further, to the Medical School, at Teviot Place. The tram service was frequent, the fare one penny (1d, less than half a decimal penny). Mrs Ross Russell gave me breakfast and supper; lunch took the form of a sandwich or a pie bought from a café or from the Students' Union.

Mrs Ross Russell was an enthusiastic musician and among her friends were professional pianists, including a Ms Buchanan. I had the benefit, therefore, not only of a comfortable bed but also of living in a world of song, pianoforte and ballet. From time-to-time, Ross Russell parties included Scottish country dancing. In sharp contrast to my friend James Thin (p.39), an accomplished dancer, my school days had taught me nothing of this skill and I watched with amazement the gyrations of the foursome and eightsome reels until, after three months, I sensed it was time to move.

My first attempt at finding new lodgings, 'digs', led me to a third-floor room above the Post Office in Teviot Place, where the only bed

Chapter summary
- **The Livingstone Dispensary**
- **In the footsteps of Conan Doyle**
- **Classes and constraints**
- **Learning practical medicine and surgery**
- **Every cloud has a silver lining**
- **Nearly a doctor!**

was a folding sofa, the centre of which coincided with the lower part of my spine. After five sleepless nights, I moved again, this time to an attic flat in Warrender Park Road, access to which, from the top floor of the house, was by wooden ladder. The little room had a skylight but no window. If the skylight was opened, the rain fell on me; if it stayed closed, I suffocated. Another week was the limit of my tenancy, and a letter from my father showed that my parents were concerned.

Not long after this salutary experience, I found a third-floor room at 139 Dalkeith Road. The owners, a Mr and Mrs Gibson, had two schoolchildren, a daughter of 13 and a son of 11. I shared the flat with Michael Mills, a classmate.[A] Dalkeith Road was only a mile from my classes at Teviot Place, and a brisk walk each day taught me the geography of south Edinburgh. Mr Gibson was a skilled amateur golfer who had been a wartime mess sergeant. However, he had a volatile temperament. Returning from an evening of conviviality at Prestonfield Golf Club, he would hurl abuse at 'those students' who were 'cluttering up' his house. Violence was just avoided: Mrs Gibson was calm and sensible, and when my father and mother made one of their rare visits to Edinburgh, she entertained them generously.

The Livingstone Dispensary

In the later months of 1946, I learnt of the Livingstone Dispensary (Figure 6.1) in the Cowgate.[3,B] It turned out to be the most unusual lodging of my student days. The Magdalene Chapel,[C] adjoining the Dispensary, had enjoyed the patronage of the ancient Incorporation of Hammermakers. The armorial shields and name scrolls that hung on the walls dated back to the formation of the Incorporation in 1490.

I joined the clinical students who were providing the medical and dental care for the poor who lived in the ancient Edinburgh tenements of the Grassmarket and the surrounding wynds. The National Health Service had not yet been inaugurated and local people had no regular medical attendant. Maternity care was provided by nurses from the Simpson Memorial Hospital, but it was left to us to deal with obstetric problems such as breech presentations, dystocia and toxaemia. We became accustomed to having newborn children named after us! Called to visit the sick, we found that many of the stone buildings had changed little for 400 years: it was usual to clamber up flights of crumbling wooden stairways to reach the small, ancient rooms. On one occasion, I found a family with four children, two of whom had measles. The only furniture, apart from the bed in which they and their parents were lying, was an orange box.

The ground floor of the Dispensary contained a crowded out-patient clinic and waiting room. Old soldiers with neglected, suppurating wounds and amyloidosis; malnourished adults with

Figure 6.1 *This drawing of the Cowgate shows the Chapel of the Hammermakers Incorporation (left), the Livingstone Dispensary (centre) and the building termed 'The Rock', added in 1903. My room was near the top right-hand corner of this last block. (Reproduced by courtesy of EMMS International.)*

the productive cough of chronic pulmonary tuberculosis; young children with tonsillitis, rheumatic fever or diphtheria; and others with dental caries or toothache were among the patients testing our elementary skills. Dr Price, a retired medical missionary, was the Superintendent and Resident Medical Officer. We met him at meals, times when the lodgers came to know each other well. They included Bob Gillies, who I encountered again in Belfast in 1971 (p.194). The domestic arrangements of the Dispensary were in the hands of Miss Jackson, who I remembered in her former capacity as Matron of Loretto School (p.35).

One advantage of the Livingstone Dispensary was the modest cost, another its location, within a short distance of the Medical School. Each morning, I reached my classes by walking up Candlemaker Row, the ancient thoroughfare at the top of which sat the much-loved statue of Greyfriars Bobby, the little dog (Figure 6.2) made famous by his loyalty to his master John Gray, a tale reminiscent of Dr John Brown's[D] *Rab and His Friends*.[4] The winter of 1947 was particularly cold and heavy snow called for extra time to reach my nine o'clock lectures. In the opposite direction, a short walk along the

Figure 6.2 *The statue of Greyfriars Bobby at the top of Candlemaker Row, Edinburgh.*

Grassmarket took me to Heriot's Wynd, the steps of which passed the walls of Heriot's School, giving easy access to the West Gate of the Royal Infirmary of Edinburgh.

The living accommodation of the Livingstone Dispensary was in the upper part of the old building. My third-floor room was blessed with a small window that allowed me a view across the Grassmarket to the city spires. Looking up from pages of lecture notes, I could see a pall of smoke enveloping the old town, much of it emitted by the tall chimney that marked the site of the boiler house of the 1879 Infirmary. I was in this room on the evening of 27th April 1947 when a deeply troubled Dr Price came to tell me of a telephone call from Somerset to say that my father had died suddenly while on holiday (p.22). I left Edinburgh at once to join a night train to London. The next few days passed in a haze as my mother, my brother and I met our relatives in Minehead in preparation for the funeral. Returning to classes in Edinburgh, I was struck by the kindness of fellow students who gazed at me anxiously and asked whether I was well.

In the footsteps of Conan Doyle

I soon moved again, this time to 12 Lonsdale Terrace, a row of nine-teenth-century villas facing the Meadows. Three other students had rooms in the same flat: Colin Hay,[E] his friend Ann and another girl. Years later, reading of the life of Arthur Conan Doyle, I discovered that the author's family had lived next door, at 11 Lonsdale Terrace. My landlady in 1947–48 was a miserly Mrs Hare. Breakfast took the form of half a tomato and a single piece of bread. Recalling past times, I was reminded of the murderers, William Burke and William Hare!

Among the British students attending the Edinburgh Medical School at that time there was a greater degree of comradeship than I had found in England. One reason was the effect of the war – many students at Clare had been young officers in training, attending University courses of instruction as they waited for their call to the armed forces. In 1945, many Edinburgh medical students had been at school together, had entered the University at the same time, belonged to the Officers' Training Corps and were enthusiastic members of the Students Union.[F] Thrown together by wartime companion-ship, many of those who had come to the Medical School in 1943 were close friends, sharing interests not only in their studies but also in golf, the theatre and music. Quite naturally, they viewed newcomers, especially those from England, the 'Auld Enemy', with some uncertainty!

I soon met three others in a position similar to my own. They were James (later Sir James) Fraser,[G] Harry Coll[H] and Colin Hay. We shared many interests, especially golf. Taking advantage of the very small cost to students of playing on any of the 23 private courses of which Edinburgh was proud, we were allowed a 'round' for as little as one or two shillings (5–10 decimal pence). Gullane, Bruntsfield, Barnton and Mortonhall were among the courses we favoured and there was friendly rivalry to find who could equal James Fraser's skills. We soon found that he had an unusual sense of humour and was liable to pitch my golf clubs into a puddle if the course was wet. On another occasion, when we were walking along the surgical corridor of the Royal Infirmary, we saw Sir James Learmonth[I] approaching with his assistants. James Fraser waited until we were within a few yards of the great man and then knocked my heels together so that I fell flat on my face in front of the King's Surgeon!

Although Colin and James were inclined to give their lunch hours to the billiard table in the Students' Union, this was not a game I enjoyed. I do not remember that any of us went to the Saturday evening dances ('hops') held in the Union 'Palais de dance', very much part of the Edinburgh student social scene. Our class included a small number of Dutch students who had come to this country to ease post-war pressures on medical schools like those of Amsterdam and Leiden. Our Dutch friends were, on average, older, their maturity matched by high intelligence and dedication. After graduating in Medicine, most returned to the Netherlands, but some, including my friend Bram Gieben, stayed in this country.[J]

Classes and constraints

The reason I had come to Edinburgh was to learn the practice of medicine and surgery (p.60), but, joining the third year, I was obliged to attend not only the clinics but also all the classes of that year. The principal subjects were Pathology, Microbiology and Pharmacology, in each of which lectures, from 9 to 11 o'clock each morning, were followed by practical classes from 2 to 4 every afternoon. My frustration at having to repeat these subjects was soon relieved, since the teaching could not have been more different from the style adopted in the south. The imaginative brilliance of the Cambridge teachers contrasted with the dull classrooms of Edinburgh!

The lecture theatres, where a large proportion of the conventional instruction was given, consisted of serried rows of wooden benches. Speakers were rarely given a microphone, their lectures still illustrated with enormous glass lantern slides inserted by a technician into a huge 'projector'. Attendance at lectures was obligatory. We were compelled to hand attendance cards to a uniformed Faculty 'officer' as we entered the lecture theatre. The names on the cards were transcribed to a systematic list, allowing the Dean's office to keep a record of those who had not attended the proportion of lectures judged to be sufficient. At the end of each term, every student was given a certificate of attendance, which was termed a DP ('duly performed'). The possession of such a certificate in each subject was a condition for being allowed to attempt the term's class examinations and, of course, the professional examinations held at the end of each academic year.

In **pathology**, Professor Alexander Murray Drennan[K] was a kindly person but a dreary speaker. Because the classes were obligatory, his lectures attracted a full complement of students. As soon as the lights were dimmed to allow slides to be shown, there was a noise like the rushing of wind. When the lights were turned on again, it was clear that the class had shrunk to no more than 30 or 40 hardened veterans: the remainder had escaped quietly through the rear doors. Drennan never gave any sign that he was aware of this exodus and continued his monologues as though nothing had happened. By contrast, some of Drennan's colleagues were such compelling teachers that their words remain with me to this day. William Blackwood's descriptions of the jelly-like human brain, easily damaged when the skull is struck, are examples.

The practical pathology classes in Edinburgh were as different from those in Cambridge as the lectures. Each day, after lunch, we were addressed by Dr Robertson Fotheringham Ogilvie,[L] a man of serious purpose (p.156). His postprandial talks were interminable: when Ogilvie spoke on the subject of pathological histology, he read from his own book, rarely changing a phrase. One day a student called out 'You've missed out a word!' Ogilvie was not amused. However, his illustrations were of the highest quality, prepared by Thomas Cairns Dodds.[M] The practical work that followed was held in Sir William Turner's enormous old Teviot Place building. We sat at teak benches, faced by clusters of glass jars containing anatomical specimens preserved in formalin. Each collection of specimens represented a 'case', the residue of a single autopsy, and was accompanied by a copy of the hospital record. Ogilvie's intention and that of his assistants William Forbes and James Davidson, was to persuade us to write a detailed description of the specimens and to explain the diseases that had led to death. Our notebooks, collected and marked, contributed to an assessment of our progress but gave no real evidence of how much or how little we understood of pathology: those who wrote most legibly and drew most artistically scored better than those whose handwriting recalled the illegible scrawl of Isaac Newton.

Thomas Jones Mackie, Professor of Microbiology, of grave mien but immense knowledge, bore the responsibility not only for educating the student classes in the rapidly developing subjects of **bacteriology** and virology but also of serving as Bacteriologist to the Royal Infirmary of Edinburgh. Microbiology lectures were often illustrated not with projected lantern slides but with gigantic coloured drawings that hung in great sheets above the blackboard. Mackie was a kindly man but impetuous, castigating students who performed poorly in his class examinations. One day, when it chanced that I felt pleased with my results, Mackie sent for me. Without allowing me to speak, he snarled: 'Gardner, your answers are disgraceful!' I explained that he had mistaken my name for that of another student. Mackie was generous with his apology.

However unimaginative the teaching of pathology in the late 1940s, no such complaint could be directed at **pharmacology**, where John Henry Gaddum FRS, one of Feldberg's collaborators (p.55), had gathered a galaxy of teachers and investigators, among them Marthe Louise Vogt, one of the world's most distinguished neuroscientists. Many of the practical classes depended on collaboration between groups of us, and Colin Hay and I joined forces with Jocelyn Sandison and Katherine Carmichael.

Teaching the principles, as opposed to the practice, of **medicine** centred on excellent lectures given by Professor Stanley (later Sir Stanley) Davidson and his associates. The lectures were accompanied by a series of cyclostyled sheets, the forerunners of his book.[5] I kept my own notes[N] as well as his.

Many of the lectures on **surgery** were given by James Learmonth. Speaking to a large class, his manner often appeared gruff and unfriendly. He would pause and growl: 'Now boys and girls, I'll give you three minutes to blow your noses and cough before I resume.' But he was a kindly man and surprisingly diffident; the style he adopted in public did not show when one day he stopped me as I passed Middle Meadow walk and asked how I was getting on, knowing I was a friend of James Fraser (p.65).

We were instructed in the theory of **obstetrics and gynaecology** by Professor RJ Kellar, who had recently come from Hammersmith, London with a great academic reputation. One of the Dutch students laughed aloud when Kellar made a remark about the contraceptive named a 'Dutch cap'. The professor was furiously angry and called the student to the rostrum when the class ended. Kellar's lectures were dull – he appeared to read from the textbook written by his predecessor, R. W. Johnstone[6] – and I dozed gently through many of them. When I read the results of the class examination and saw that I had scored no more than 36%, I realized I had paid a heavy price for my inattention. Failing an examination, even a class test, was a demoralizing experience. I imagined having to explain my failure to my father who, I knew, was not well.

Learning practical medicine and surgery

To learn the clinical skills needed for hospital medicine or surgery, as opposed to the theories of these subjects, my class was divided into seven or eight groups of 20 or more students, each group the responsibility of a senior physician or surgeon in charge of a hospital unit. The 'Chief' as he was called – there were at that time no women consultants – still held the old title 'Physician-in-Ordinary' or 'Surgeon-in-Ordinary', positions tenable for only 15 years. The majority of the Chiefs were responsible for one and one-half hospital wards; in modern terms, they and their Associate Physicians would be designated Consultants and were assisted by a Clinical Tutor, a position analogous to a Specialist Registrar.[O] In the Royal Infirmary, there were eight medical units, seven surgical units and others of varied size. A medical unit generally cared for a whole ward of 30 male or female patients and half a further ward accommodating 15 female or male patients. These were the places where I began to learn how to examine patients, how to diagnose their illnesses and how to treat them.

In 1945, to learn the practice of **medicine** (Internal Medicine), I was directed to the clinic of Dr Fergus Hewat,[P] located in Wards 32 and 33 of the Infirmary, where his Associate Physician was Dr Kelman Robertson. Dr Hewat's speciality was diseases of the chest and lungs – respiratory medicine. Each morning, we reached the wards after our lectures, at a time when the physicians and surgeons had ended their daily private practice.[Q] First, we were given an informal talk. We were then taken into the wards to follow the Chief as he spoke to selected patients before examining them, using a stethoscope to listen to the heart and lungs. If we were lucky, he might pass his instrument to one of us, encouraging us to hear the diagnostic signs such as lung crepitations or heart murmurs that he had already detected. After each consultation, Dr Hewat would ask us questions to test our understanding of what we had heard and seen. On one occasion, he questioned our diagnosis of a patient with chronic lung disease. It chanced that I gave the correct answer, bronchiectasis, and I believe this was one of the reasons why he soon offered me the privilege of becoming his Resident House Physician after I qualified (p.75).

A few of us chose to return to the wards on the once-weekly evenings on which our unit was responsible for the admission of emergency cases from Casualty (Accident and Emergency). We served as unqualified assistants, but might be fortunate enough to be asked to perform more skilled duties such as blood transfusion, lumbar puncture or cardiography. I found these evening visits of especial value, partly because there was direct contact with acutely ill patients but also because of the informal discussions we could enjoy with the attending physician, usually the Clinical Tutor. On Dr Hewat's wards, our Tutor was Henry Matthew.

For me, the attendance at the hospital on evenings when my ward unit was 'on take' was exhilarating: the challenge of seeing, speaking to and examining a new patient, often suffering from a condition demanding immediate treatment, always tested my understanding of medicine to its limits. On one occasion, a young man was admitted complaining of severe, sudden headache. His temperature was slightly raised and meningitis was suspected.

However, the cerebrospinal fluid, obtained by lumbar puncture, contained increased numbers of red blood cells, and we concluded that he had suffered from bleeding into the spinal fluid, subarachnoid haemorrhage. The explanation lay in his pulse: it measured only nine beats per minute! I was able to use an old instrument to record the pulse. It was a McKenzie polygraph, found on the shelves of the ward side room. The cause of the slow pulse, bradycardia, and of the sudden bleeding, was congenital heart disease.

My first and salutary experience of the potentially hazardous technique of lumbar (spinal) puncture came one day during a clinical class, when, without warning, Dr Matthew said: 'Gardner, I'd like you to demonstrate to these dental students how to do a spinal "tap"'. I had no choice but to 'scrub up', the term used to prepare hands for surgery by washing meticulously. I then had to apply antiseptic to the lower part of the patient's back, to anaesthetize his skin by means of a local injection of lignocaine (lidocaine) and to attempt to pass the long, sterile needle into his spinal canal. I knew, as did Dr Matthew, that the procedure was not one that would normally be delegated to a student! But 'Fortune favours the brave' and my attempt met with success, a sample of fluid was obtained and the dental students seemed content.

In the following year, to learn **surgery**, I found myself in a clinical group (Figure 6.3) under the tutelage of Mr W. Quarry Wood, who, together with his associate, W. A. D. Adamson, had charge of Wards 9 and 10. The surgical operating theatres had viewing galleries where we sat and periodically watched operations or listened to tutorials. Occasionally, I was able to attend very similar clinics in Wards 7 and 8 (Mr Thomas McWalter Millar and Sir James Learmonth). It was not possible to learn much of the practice of surgery in this way, but we understood a little more of these skills when we attended the wards during nights when a unit was 'on call', caring for emergencies.

Determined to master **obstetrics and gynaecology**, I could not have imagined that an examination failure (p.67) would change the whole course of my life!

I was determined to make amends for my failure in the class examination and to master this important field of practice. With the consent of the consultant in charge of the Antenatal Clinic in the Livingstone Dispensary (p.62), Dr W. D. A. Callam, my friend Jock Keenan and I volunteered to help the examination of the great numbers of expectant mothers who came from the impoverished tenement buildings of the Cowgate. It was the beginning of a time that had startling consequences! In the Clinic, Dr Callam sat quietly at his desk while we took the mothers' histories. We learned quickly. One afternoon I asked a mother: 'And how many (pregnancies) is this?' In a few seconds, her reply told me more than I could have learned from a chapter of Johnstone's textbook: 'This is the nineteenth, sir.'

Figure 6.3 *Mr W. Quarry Wood's staff and students in his clinic of early 1947. In the front row, left to right, are Dr C. D. (Dale) Falconer, Dr D. S. Middleton, Mr W. A. D. Adamson, Mr W. Quarry Wood, Sister Black, Dr L. S. Smith and Mr J. R. Frank. Harry Coll is third from the left, back row. I was absent because of illness*

Jock and I then decided to devote our Sunday mornings to the gynaecological wards of the Royal Infirmary. With Jock, I went to see the redoubtable Dr Chalmers Fahmy in Ward 34. He agreed that we might join his weekend ward 'rounds', the times when he and his assistants visited and spoke to each of their patients to make sure that those who had been operated on were recovering satisfactorily. Dr Fahmy's charming colleague, John Sturrock, was the Associate Gynaecologist. He was assisted by a less amiable registrar, Dr Brown! One day the boisterous Brown decided that it would be fun to put a nurse in the ward laundry basket. Jock demurred, and I rushed to the rescue. Only the threat of a 'punch-up' deterred the aggressor. However, Brown's hostility was more than matched by the kindness of the ward Sister, 'Tottie' Mackay, who made sure that the students, her 'young laddies', were properly fed and watered.

An unexpected consequence of my time on Ward 34 was that Dr Fahmy, whose son had been at Loretto School (p.33), asked me whether, after graduating, I would consider joining him as his House Surgeon. With real regret – I had already accepted an invitation from Dr Fergus Hewat – I had to decline. Much later, I heard that Fahmy's son had been posted missing while serving during the war with the Royal Air Force.

Every cloud has a silver lining

One day I asked the staff nurse on Ward 34 whether there were any among her colleagues who would enjoy a game of tennis. Next to the hospital Red Home[R] (Figure 6.4), there was a tennis court where summer days allowed staff to play. One of the nurses on Ward 34 was a strikingly beautiful Helen Harrower, who was serving the third

Figure 6.4 *The Red Home of the 1879 Royal Infirmary of Edinburgh as it was in 1906.*

of her four years in training. Nurse Harrower offered to play, but we soon found that to be watched by all passing hospital staff and patients was distracting. We therefore arranged to meet on public tennis courts, in the Meadows, a short distance away. I soon realized that Helen was a far more skilled tennis player than I was, but I also quickly learned of her sense of humour – the rather lengthy white rugby shorts I wore attracted especial merriment, but it was not until much later that she confided to me that at the time she wondered whether I had 'knock knees'.

Helen's parents lived in Bo'ness, West Lothian, where her father, a well-known and much respected local figure, had inherited a business importing wooden pit props from Scandinavia, for the coal mines. Bo'ness had an old established dockyard where ships from Finland and Sweden could berth. The timber was stacked beside the railway linked to the main Edinburgh-to-Glasgow line. The yards were within sight of Grangemouth, an important industrial town at the eastern end of the Clyde–Forth canal. The Harrower home was 'Elmpark', Earngarth Road. It was a prominent Victorian mansion, built in 1864 (Figure 6.5). It lay in spacious grounds, the front garden shaded by tall trees, the rear garden, with sheds and a greenhouse, large enough to accommodate a much loved grass tennis court. The residential area was known to the Romans – the Antonine wall ran within a mile of Earngarth Road and the name Earngarth was mentioned by Gibbon.[7]

Figure 6.5 *'Elmpark', the home of the Harrower family, Bo'ness, West Lothian, photographed before a later addition to the building.*

I soon gathered that Helen had been at St Margaret's School, Polmont. Shortly after the Second World War began, the school, united with St Anne's School, Edinburgh, was evacuated to MucKairn Castle, Taynuilt, on the shores of Loch Etive. The castle was the home of Sir William Thompson, one of whose family had been a pupil at St Anne's. When war came in 1939, Helen was sent to Taynuilt. In 1942, the school was forced to close for financial reasons and, at the age of 16, Helen spent some months at home before deciding that, with nursing as her ultimate aim, training in domestic science would be of value. She enrolled at the School of Domestic Science, Atholl Crescent, Edinburgh. She and her mother were interviewed at the Royal Infirmary of Edinburgh by the Matron, Miss Smaile, who had little hesitation in accepting Helen as a probationer nurse. She completed her training in 1948 and joined an elite band entitled to wear the coveted 'Pelican', a badge valued and respected nationwide and signifying nurses fully qualified to practise their profession.

Helen and I shared a deep love for music. In no way was this better demonstrated than in 1947, soon after the Edinburgh Festival of Music and Drama had begun, when I was lucky to obtain free tickets for a dress rehearsal of Verdi's *Masked Ball*. As the months went by, we went to concerts by the Scottish National Orchestra in the Usher Hall, Edinburgh, to occasional performances of the ballet, and, of course, to the cinema. On one occasion, a deeply suspicious Colin Hay came with us to the King's Theatre. He had no interest in classical music and it was fascinating to see his face light up as he became drawn into scenes from the ballet.

At MucKairn Castle, Helen inherited the task of playing the harmonium for the Sunday services at the local church. During 1947, after my father's death, as I continued to live in the Livingstone Dispensary (p.62), Helen practised the harmonium in the ancient chapel of the Hammermakers' Guild. I found it difficult to talk of our recent family tragedy, and Helen endured long silences. But I was not tongue-tied, and it was at this time that we became engaged (Figure 6.6). I had little money, and a first visit to a jeweller in Princes' Street, searching for an engagement ring, was frustrating. However, a second attempt in Shandwick Place led us to a second-hand diamond ring that cost £25, one-quarter of my life's savings. The ring was placed on a receptive finger on a suitable moment when we happened to be walking under the Dean Bridge!

Nearly a doctor!

As the summer of 1948 slid past, my Final Examinations approached. They took the form both of written papers and of the examination of hospital patients under the scrutiny of internal and of external examiners. My 'external' examiner in Medicine was the eminent and considerate Professor Cohen from Liverpool. I was worried that

Figure 6.6 *The author with Helen at the time of our engagement in 1948.*

I might not be able to sleep before the most important of the written papers, and picked up my copy of *Ivanhoe*,[8] thinking it would be a long, tedious tale. At three o'clock in the morning, I was still engrossed in its pages!

As soon as the examinations were ended, I left Edinburgh for a few days in Windermere at the home of my mother's friend, Alcie Dobson (p.6). After reading the graduation list of those who had passed, Helen telephoned to tell me that I had been called for an Honours examination in Clinical Surgery, a subject in which I appeared to have done well. I went back to Edinburgh as quickly as possible. Another candidate was Bram Gieben. We were tested by the redoubtable surgeon, Thomas ('Tommy') Millar. Bram showed his superior skills and knowledge and was the winner. However, I was delighted to have passed the Finals and to be on the way to graduating in Medicine, my lifelong ambition. It was a step forward, perhaps even to paid employment!

CHAPTER 7

The National Health

In sight of Arthur's Seat

> To us whose work is with the sick and suffering,
> the great boon of this wonderful century ... is
> the fact that the leaves of the tree of Science
> have been for the healing of the nations.
>
> William Osler[1]

The fifth of July 1948 dawned bright and clear, an auspicious sign for the launch of the National Health Service, the NHS.[A] But 180 of us, elegantly dressed and gowned and crowded into the McEwan Hall of the University of Edinburgh, were thinking not of this revolution but of the fact that we were to be given our first medical degree,[B] a step towards a 'license to practise'.

Chapter summary
- **The Hospital Residency**
- **Caring for medical patients**
- **Clinical care**
- **Caring for surgical patients**

As I nervously approached the platform where the acting University Principal and Vice Chancellor, Sir Edward Appleton,[C] stood majestically, it was difficult to believe what was happening. The excited mood of the great numbers of relatives and friends gathered to witness the graduation of their sons and daughters, their brothers and sisters, was captured by the flashlights of innumerable cameras. Each time one of us stepped forward, rapturous applause broke out. Sir Edward murmured a few words in my ear – were they in English or Latin? – and tapped me on the head with the Geneva bonnet that, tradition claimed, had been made from the breeches of John Knox. I felt relief, but no sudden sense of euphoria. Was it too good to be true?

Jean Grieve, my cousin, and Helen Harrower (p.71) were among those present. I was saddened by the sudden thought that my father had not lived to see this day. Within a few minutes, we escaped into the summer sun only to be confronted by a representative of an insurance company who wanted me to buy one of his policies.[D] Without such a safeguard, he warned, I would be ill-advised to attempt to practise medicine! Soon, a persuasive representative of the BMA, the British Medical Association, asked me to join the ranks of their medical 'trade union'.

To be allowed to practise medicine, we had to have a recognized degree or diploma. In 1950, it was determined by the General Medical Council that new graduates must train for at least a year as a Resident House Physician or House Surgeon in a recognized hospital. Although this regulation had not yet come into effect, we were advised to obtain this experience. We knew that there were great differences in the quality of training to be gained in different centres. The most sought-after positions lay in the teaching hospitals, where the large numbers and range of patients offered a rich variety of education, where the senior staff represented the cream of the profession, and where the levels of staffing and the supportive services were of the highest. In Edinburgh, these criteria were met by the Royal Infirmary of Edinburgh, the RIE, until July 1948 a charitable hospital supported, not by the State, but by voluntary subscription.

Sixty-four years later, it is easy to forget the enormous public effort required to collect the money necessary to maintain such a hospital. Charitable donations from corporations, companies, churches, stores, banks and local communities; annual carnivals held throughout the region; and legacies – all of these were recorded in the annual Reports of the Infirmary Management Committee. With the advent of the NHS, the scene changed dramatically: where the hospital had been guided and directed by a Superintendent and a Secretary together with nine assistants, within months this staff had risen fivefold! There was little sign that this influenced the Management, and under the Chairmanship of Professor George Romanes, no Annual Reports were issued until 1960.

The question now was: 'What should I do next?' I had no doubt that my future lay in the new Health Service, although my father, like many of the doctors questioned by the BMA, was not in favour of Aneurin Bevan's scheme. Thomas Gardner did not want to be 'an employee of the State'. I knew that Resident House Physicians and Surgeons were still selected personally by the Physicians- and Surgeons-in-Ordinary, the consultants in charge of ward units. There were no formal applications for appointment to the teaching hospital, no selection committees, no referees and no interviews. The name of an individual chosen by a consultant was placed before the Management Committee and rarely questioned. Appointments to the maternity hospital, the Simpson Memorial Maternity Pavilion of the RIE, were made in the same way.

As it happened, my immediate future had already been decided. I was very fortunate since, during my first year as a clinical student, I had been asked by Dr Fergus Hewat to become his Resident House Physician (p.68). At the time – it was 1946 – I did not appreciate the significance of this unusually early offer until I mentioned it to my father. He exclaimed: 'Good gracious! You have been lucky!' In retrospect, I wondered whether this wonderful offer owed something to the fact that both Dr Hewat and my father had served in the RAMC during the First World War: there was an understandable rapport between ex-servicemen.

The Hospital Residency

In the autumn of 1948, my life changed dramatically. After a short holiday at my mother's new home in Somerset, I moved my few clothes and books to the residential block of the Royal Infirmary of Edinburgh, the Residency. The massive stone building (Figure 7.1) in which I was to live for many months was an integral part of the original 1879 Infirmary, its Victorian stone walls reassuringly secure. An outer door in the block provided access to the road that led down from the East Gate of the hospital, past the entrance to the Surgical Out Patient Department, the SOPD, where accidents and emergencies were received. An inner door communicated directly with the main corridor of the surgical half of the hospital, allowing us to reach the wards without disturbing our neighbours. But this door had a second, less obvious advantage: it was the route by which visitors of either sex could enter the Residency at any time of day or night!

In 1948, the lifestyle of a House Physician or House Surgeon, or of a Resident Anaesthetist or Casualty Officer, was very different from that of newly qualified hospital doctors in the twenty-first century.

Figure 7.1 *The 1879 Royal Infirmary of Edinburgh. The East gate to the hospital lies to the left of the illustration, the Residency block is not far from Middle Meadow Walk, which extends up the left side of the figure.*

My appointment began at 9 am on the morning of 1ˢᵗ October 1948 and extended until 12 midnight on 30ᵗʰ March 1949. I was expected to be ready to attend my patients, to be 'on call', 24 hours each day, every day and every night. Resident posts, whether as House Physician, House Surgeon or Resident Anaesthetist, demanded physical fitness and mental stamina. Our duties included the one day each week when it was the responsibility of each ward unit in turn to accept emergencies, a challenge that I learned by experience was more demanding in surgery than in medicine. When I came to be a Resident House Surgeon (p.84), I found that our 'Waiting Day' was Saturday, so that my working 'day' extended from nine o'clock on Saturday morning to late on Sunday evening.

There were no statutory holidays and no 'days off', although during quiet times it was sometimes possible to escape from the hospital and to seek a few minutes peace in De Marco's café in Forest Road or in 'Ma Hogg's', a little shop near the West Gate of the Royal Infirmary. On the days when Helen could find time from her own demanding duties, we met in one of these havens. However, we had so little money that it was a question of choosing one cup of coffee and two biscuits or one biscuit and two cups of coffee! Like my father when he graduated in 1908, I was penniless! Without a moment's hesitation, I had accepted six months employment for a salary[E] of £70 per annum, so that my monthly pay cheque was £5/12/8d, equivalent today to £5.63. It would have been impossible to subsist on this salary

Figure 7.2 *The Residents of the RIE in the early spring of 1949. In the back row, left to right, are Michael Mills, Sir James Fraser, the author and Alan Reay.*

outside the hospital, but the Managers of the Infirmary had for many years provided accommodation in the Residency. The kitchens sent good meals three times daily to the dining room, where the food was served and supervised by a long-serving butler, Morris, well versed in the foibles and habits of the young graduates thrust into his care. With me were 21 other young doctors (Figure 7.2), many recently qualified.[F] All were male.

Caring for medical patients

Fergus Hewat (p.68) was in charge of Ward 32, where there were 30 male patients, and of 15 of the patients in Ward 33, which was reserved for females. There was never any question of the modern 'mixed-sex ward'. On my first morning, I was welcomed to Ward 32 by Sister Williamson. After the 'Chief', she was the most important of the wise and tolerant people caring for the sick. Her associate in Ward 33, Sister Chisholm, was equally supportive. Like the other ward sisters, Ms Williamson lived in the hospital, with a bedroom and a sitting room immediately beside her ward. The advantage of this traditional arrangement was that she knew, from minute to minute, all that was happening to her patients. The disadvantages were her own lack of privacy and a tendency for senior medical staff to call for her help at any time of day or night. Sister Williamson was assisted by a staff nurse and several other trained nurses, and one or two 'probationers' who had not yet completed six months' duty. Sister Williamson became a good friend and helped to protect me from the personal advances of some of her nurses!

The standards of nursing were extremely high, recalling the pioneering ideas of Florence Nightingale.

The education, training and discipline of the Infirmary nurses, under the direction of Miss Smaile, a Matron of distinction, were outstandingly good, the quality of the nursing of the best. From Helen, I learnt much of their way of life. It was long before the days when nurses were permitted to live outside the hospital, and, as a probationer nurse, starting work in 1944, she had a tiny room in the Red Home (Figure 6.4) before she moved to the nearby new Nurses Home. During the war, with food rationing in place, nurses on night duty lived in Canaan Lane, South Edinburgh. Reaching the RIE by bus, they were given a breakfast consisting of the dinner from the previous night. A Nursing Tutor imposed strict discipline: there was little free time, and each week nurses in training were only allowed to have Sunday morning or Sunday afternoon to themselves.

There were major differences between the catering organization of the RIE in 1948 and those seen today. Prior to 1948, the Royal Infirmary kitchens prepared food that was carried to the wards and divided between patients by the ward staff under the supervision of the Sister. Breakfast and lunch were apportioned in this way. Unless a patient's relatives had brought eggs, immediately inscribed with a patient's name, evening meals comprised no more than tea, bread and jam. As soon as the NHS began, the quality of hospital food, both for patients and staff, improved dramatically. The nursing staff watched carefully over their patients' diet, helping those who could not feed themselves and ensuring that articles of food brought by visitors were safely stored or, when necessary, destroyed! The advice of dieticians was sought and they were responsible for important decisions such as the dose of insulin required by a diabetic patient.

Clinical care

Like his colleagues, Dr Hewat had the responsibility for the clinical instruction of both senior and junior students (Figure 7.3). The teaching offered to third-year students was identical to my own, earlier experience (p.68). A smaller number of senior students attended the same ward 'rounds', but were expected to display their greater knowledge when patients were examined.

My early experience suggested surprising differences in the

Figure 7.3 *Dr Fergus Hewat's staff and students of Wards 32 and 33 of the RIE in the spring of 1949. Dr Hewat is in the centre; on his right are Sister Williamson, the author and, next but one, Dr Randolph Russell. On Dr Hewat's left are Sister Chisholm and Dr Kelman Robertson.*

response of patients and their families to the attention they received. I found that quite often those patients who were gravely ill and for whom we could do little, were most grateful for their care. By contrast, patients who were less ill and perhaps more vigorous were sometimes less appreciative or even critical.

One evening, an elderly man was admitted to Ward 32 in a moribund state. Waxen and pale, he was suffering from pernicious anaemia, the haemoglobin in his blood little more than one-tenth of its normal level. Sitting on the hard benches at the entrance to the ward was a group of relatives, many already dressed in funereal black. Calling on the Blood Transfusion Service, I transfused him with several bottles[G] of concentrated red blood cells. The following morning, the old man was sitting up cheerfully, his face a healthy pink glow. The relatives who had come back prepared to collect a death certificate were disconsolate: they had lost their inheritance!

By contrast, in the female ward, there lay an elderly lady dying from cancer. I could do little for her other than taking fluid from around her diseased lung, using the metal and glass syringes that are now museum pieces. But she and her relatives, like another man with lymphoma affecting his chest, pressed gifts upon me while thanking me profusely for the little treatment we had been able to offer.

Supporting Fergus Hewat was a second consultant, an Assistant Physician, Dr Kelman Robertson. The most senior of the non-consultant staff was the Clinical Tutor or Registrar, Dr Randolph Russell. With him were a number of ex-servicemen who had returned from the war and were seeking employment and the opportunity to take higher examinations such as those for Membership of the Royal Colleges of Physicians of Edinburgh, the MRCPEd. That part of Ward 33 not in Dr Hewat's charge was in the care of Dr T. R. R. ('Tarara') Todd, an experienced physician but a victim of the First World War, which had left indelible scars upon his character. One day, as the long-suffering Sister Chisholm was leaving for her day off, in civilian clothes but wearing a simple hat, he shouted at her down the length of the ward: 'Sister, Dress properly before you go out!'

Fergus Hewat was a chest physician, so it was no surprise to find that many patients admitted to his care suffered from chronic bronchitis, pulmonary tuberculosis (phthisis), lung cancer or occupational disorders such as pneumoconiosis. Many patients with underlying tuberculosis were first recognized when they developed a pleural effusion and it was my task to relieve the pressure on the affected lung by drawing off the fluid. Streptomycin had become available for the treatment of tuberculosis, but was not yet widely used. Patients with phthisis were still taken to the sanatorium at Southfields Hospital, where prolonged rest and good food in beds on the open verandas offered treatment similar to that described by Thomas Mann[2] and employed in Davos in 1890 when Dr Arthur Conan Doyle took his ailing wife to Switzerland.[3]

Treating patients with medical disorders was largely based on the use of a remarkably small number of effective compounds, prescribed in 'elegant' prescriptions that had, until recently, been written in Latin with the doses given in an 'Apothecaries System' in which drachms and ounces had not yet yielded to a metric form. Digitalis, atropine, morphine and heroin had been in use since Victorian times, and some drugs such as quinine traced their origins back for hundreds of years. Heart failure due to myocardial infarction, hyperthyroidism or mitral or aortic valve diseases was generally treated by the administration of digitalis, an old-fashioned remedy obtained from foxgloves. Other compounds, such as arsphenamine, an agent for the treatment of syphilis, originated before the First World War. But in the 1930s, as Chapter 2 has described, a revolution had begun when the first sulpha drugs, the sulphonamides, came on to the commercial market. At once, deadly skin infections such as erysipelas, puerperal sepsis, some forms of pneumonia, and septicaemia began to lose their danger. Then, with the advent of war and the search for even better remedies, penicillin, a product of Fleming's research (p.15), was brought into large-scale production. To the benefit of the war-wounded and later of millions of sufferers, including myself (p.59), the era of modern antibiosis had begun. As a Resident House Physician, I had the privilege of prescribing all these compounds, as well as sedatives, hypnotics and anticonvulsants.

There was not always a sharp distinction between medical and surgical treatment. For many patients, however, there was no choice, and the opinion of a consultant surgeon was needed as soon as a first diagnosis had been suggested. It was in this way that I met some of the leading surgeons of the time – called to give an opinion on the possibility of surgical care, they would come with Dr Hewat to his ward, where I would watch as they examined a patient and listen to their conclusions, which would often take the form of a request for preliminary X-rays.

The surgical treatment of primary lung cancer and the use of radiotherapy were being developed, but had not yet reached a stage where cure could be anticipated. In a proportion of fortunate individuals suffering from renal failure, the cause might be obstruction to the urinary output caused by a stone, a calculus, that could be removed surgically, or disorders of the bladder or the prostate gland that were also amenable to surgery. However, in a large proportion of those whose kidney defect was the result of inflammatory diseases such as nephritis, a loss of appetite and debility could only be treated medically.[H] In one unusual instance, there was vigorous debate among postgraduate students concerning the diagnosis of a patient with a variety of unexplained signs and symptoms. The evidence pointed strongly to polyarteritis nodosa. When he came to surgical operation, the answer was peptic ulcer!

Many of the patients admitted to the wards on the weekly 'receiving day', the day when Fergus Hewat's charge was responsible for the care of emergencies, were dangerously ill. A substantial proportion did not survive: during my first 16 days on his wards, there were 16 deaths. It was the sensible practice at that time for the exact cause of every hospital death to be investigated by autopsy, provided that the deceased patient's relatives had given signed permission. My interest in pathology, encouraged by my time in Cambridge (Chapter 5), led me to the autopsy room each time our wards suffered a fatality. There were so many deaths in such a short time that Dr Hewat became concerned for the morale of his staff, and one evening he took us all to the theatre to see a performance of a Gilbert and Sullivan opera. He had a particular sympathy for the many hundreds of ex-Service medical men who still sought employment after the war's end.

In 1948, the Resident Physicians and Resident Surgeons performed many of the simple, routine diagnostic tests that are today the province of central laboratories. Among the procedures that I was called upon to undertake day-by-day were examination of the urine for sugar and albumin; measurement of blood haemoglobin, red and white cell numbers and the erythrocyte sedimentation rate, the ESR; and tests of the faeces for blood. The central laboratory facilities available in even the largest hospital were primitive by today's standards. An Edinburgh public Blood Transfusion Service had been established in 1936, but blood counts and the measurement of constituents of the plasma such as sodium, potassium, chloride and urea were made painstakingly by manual techniques. None of these methods was automated and it would be some years before the auto-analyser (p.137) became available. Consequently, the results that we were sent by the clinical chemical laboratory, some written by hand, came slowly and were requested relatively infrequently.

In one instance, soon after taking up my new responsibilities, I was left in sole charge of an unconscious man, in diabetic coma. Dr Randolph Russell bade me a cheerful goodnight before going home saying, 'I hope everything goes well'. By contemporary standards, the patient's treatment during the night was rudimentary. In the case of this poor man, only two assays of blood sugar were possible in the course of the next 10 hours: I had no other means of determining how much insulin he should be given, and it was no surprise when he died. In another case, an elderly farmer suffered from delirium tremens, became violently abusive and had to be restrained by the intravenous injection of paraldehyde. In such instances, or where there was evidence of serious mental disorder, patients were taken to Ward 3, which was reserved for psychiatric cases and for those in police custody.

There was very little time for research or even for reading. However, one day, I happened to notice that a patient with chronic lymphocytic leukaemia improved when he developed lobar pneumonia. I followed the white blood cell counts carefully and saw that as the lung infection developed, the number of leukaemic cells in the blood fell. I was able to pursue this interest later when I was in the haematology laboratory of Addenbrooke's Hospital, Cambridge (p.115).

Caring for surgical patients

My second Resident House Officer appointment, in surgery, began on 1st April 1949. My predecessor had been Dr Robert Mahler,[1] with whom I kept in contact over many years. My position was in Wards 9 and 10, with the redoubtable W. Quarry Wood,[J] at that time President of the Royal College of Surgeons of Edinburgh (p.328). Quarry Wood, a gold medallist in Anatomy, was a surgeon of great skill. He reached the hospital each morning in a modest Triumph car and my duties included opening his car door when he arrived and showing him to his car when he left. Quarry wore small, 'half-moon' glasses. His quiet manner belied great reserves of physical strength and mental endurance.

One day, towards the end of a long and exhausting series of operations that had started with his private surgical patients at 7 am in one of the several Edinburgh nursing homes, he made a serious error, ligating the lower end of a patient's oesophagus instead of the left gastric artery. It was 1.30 pm. Looking up over his glasses, he said 'Tut Tut'. The theatre staff lapsed into astonished silence. It was as though the Moderator of the Church of Scotland had sworn coarsely at the General Assembly!

Quarry Wood's associate, the second consultant to Wards 9 and 10, was Mr W. A. D. Adamson, after whom the Adamson Building of the Royal College of Surgeons of Edinburgh came to be named many years later. The nursing sister in charge of Wards 9 and 10 was Miss Black (Figure 6.3), *une femme formidable* whose authoritative manner, one result of many years of nursing experience, concealed great kindness both to patients and to junior medical staff.

Among the patients admitted to Mr Quarry Wood's care was an army officer who had sustained a compound fracture of his lower leg when he fell from an Edinburgh tramcar. At that time, there was a rule that each patient in whom there was judged to be a risk of tetanus or gas gangrene, conditions associated with tissue death and destruction, should be given injections of the specific sera against the toxins of these organisms. In spite of our care and to our astonishment, the officer developed the ominous signs of tetanus. At once, the consultants and an Assistant, Mr Ian Campbell, searched my notes to make sure that I had administered the antitoxins correctly. I was greatly relieved to be assured that everything was in order. It was, however, only a matter of days before the patient died.

On another occasion, a road traffic accident had torn open a young man's knee joint. The Clinical Tutor of Wards 9 and 10, Mr Dale Falconer, was quite uncertain what to do and it fell to me to tell him that he had no choice but to amputate the leg.

When a nurse became suddenly ill, she was examined in the Casualty Department in the same way as any other emergency patient. However, ethical responsibilities were taken seriously, and the ward sisters were at pains never to allow a male resident medical or surgical officer to be left alone with any sick young lady.

One day, a medical student came to my office in Ward 9 and asked for help. He said that some time previously, he had had an accident and felt ill. He asked whether I could give him something for the pain and mentioned the drug pethidine, used quite often at that time in surgical patients recovering from an operation. I had no reason to doubt his story and gave him what he needed. I began to feel suspicious when he came back the next week with the same request. After that, it was quite clear that he was addicted to the drug. He told me that his problem had started when he was in the army and he had not been able to control it. I had to refuse any further help. At that time, the support for, and treatment of addicts was not well organized and I didn't know of any advice he could obtain in the RIE. Many years later, when I was in charge of a laboratory in Manchester, a young man who had applied for a technician's post confessed that he had been a heroin addict but had been treated successfully. I recognized a moral dilemma, but decided that, in fairness to the other applicants, he should not be employed.

After a year of astonishingly interesting but exhausting labour, my resident appointments ended in September 1949 (Figure 7.4). In

Figure 7.4 *The RIE Residents in the autumn of 1949. In the front row, left to right, are the author, AN Other, J. K. Davidson and Lindsay Wilkie. Burke, a Resident Anaesthetist (centre), is President of the mess. John Gould sits second from the right.*

Wards 32 and 33 I was followed by Michael Mills (p.62) (Figure 7.5), and in Wards 9 and 10 by Dr David Tulloch[K]. During this arduous year, Helen, preoccupied with her own demanding job, had been closely aware of mine. But now, we agreed, it was time to break free and look to the future!

Figure 7.5 *Dr Fergus Hewat's retirement dinner, 1950. Among others with him are his colleagues Drs J. K. Slater, Kelman Robertson, Randolph Russell and Henry Matthew and many of his former Resident House Physicians.*
In the upper illustration, I am facing Dr Hewat (to his left), with Michael Mills at my right. Randolph Russell sits at Dr Hewat's left, Randolph's face turned towards him.
In the lower illustration, James Elliot Murray stands at the far left while a presentation is made.

CHAPTER 8

Marriage, then medicine

By the Spaarn and the Witham

Am Brunnen vor dem Tore
Da steht ein Lindenbaum:
Ich träumt' in seinem Schatten
So manchen süssen Traum

Wilhelm Müller[1]

As the days of my resident appointments in the Royal Infirmary of Edinburgh moved towards their end, our plans changed dramatically. Helen and I had come to know each other better and better, so that few of our friends and none of our families were surprised when we decided that the time had come for our wedding.

Chapter summary
- A sojourn in Holland
- To be a physician?
- Life in Louth
- The County Infirmary, Louth

It was a bold decision on Helen's part: I was virtually penniless and had no settled employment. After much thought and discussion, we decided that the wedding should be in September, as soon as possible after my resident House Surgeon's appointment ended. My friends joked that this was to avoid paying the fine that the Residency Mess Association[A] treasurer would have imposed if we had married during my time in post.

Helen's father, D. B. (Davie) Harrower (Figure 8.1), wise and kindly, knew that my father, Thomas Gardner, had died in 1947 and that I had little money; with great generosity, Davie decided to accept the entire cost of the wedding. It was a decision strongly endorsed by Emily Harrower (Figure 8.2), Helen's mother.

There were important preliminary matters to attend to. The Harrowers knew the Reverend Dr W. White Anderson, Minister of St Cuthbert's Church, Edinburgh, and he agreed to conduct the ceremony there. He was assisted by the Reverend William Bryce Johnston, at that time Minister to St Andrew's Church, Bo'ness. Helen designed her own wedding dress and it was made up with the help of a Miss Brockie of Shandwick Place, Edinburgh. Helen's school friend Judy Main, who she had known from the age of two, agreed to be the Bridesmaid and my brother Colin was the Best Man.

Figure 8.1 *David Balfour Harrower, Helen's father.*

Figure 8.2 *Emily Harrower, Helen's mother.*

The occasion could not have been happier – the ceremony was held in the early afternoon of 29th September 1949. The church adjoined Castle Terrace and lay at the west end of Princes Street in spacious grounds below the level of the main road. Colin had lived in England for some years and it was amusing to see him struggle into the kilt, sporran, dress jacket and cravat we had selected for the occasion! Our reception was held in the Roxburgh Hotel, Charlotte Square, Edinburgh and we were delighted to have among the guests Margaret, Helen's aunt, and her artist husband, Ashley Havinden.[B] But there were many other relations, close friends and hospital colleagues, including Sister Williamson and nurses from the Infirmary. At the dinner that followed the reception, Ashley, more at home in Oxford Street than Princes Street, joked to the other guests that when he saw Colin and me entering St Cuthbert's Church, he assumed we were some kind of quaint Scottish entertainers – we were resplendent in McIntyre tartan!

A sojourn in Holland

Our honeymoon was spent in Holland at Haarlem,[C] the capital of North Holland, a choice suggested by a friend of Helen's mother, Miss Springer, an 'exchange visitor' in the Women's Voluntary Service of Bo'ness. Miss Springer's inspired proposal led to the first of our many foreign travels. We flew to London from the little

Turnhouse Airport, Edinburgh, where the ravages of war were still clearly visible. The passenger lounge was a Nissan hut and another wooden building served as a cafeteria. The aircraft was a twin-engined Dakota, a DC3. During the flight, the smiling captain noticed flecks of confetti on my shoulders and arranged for us to have a glass of champagne. The train took us to Harwich and we sailed to the Hook of Holland, and then by rail through Rotterdam, Delft and Leiden to Haarlem (Figure 8.3), where we stayed not far from the Zuyder Zee at a small but friendly Hotel Rosenthal. The rooms were simple and comfortable but without *en suite* facilities, so that it cost the equivalent of two shillings (10 pence in decimal currency) to have a bath. We visited the kind Ms Springer at Zandvoort, famous for its road racing circuit and only eight kilometres from Haarlem, and thanked her for introducing us to her beautiful country.

Figure 8.3 *The Amsterdam Gate, Haarlem. (From the US Library of Congress Collection.)*

Two weeks and many encounters with the friendly local people were enough to remind us of how the Dutch had suffered during the wartime German occupation.[2] But the Dutch are a resilient people, and as we walked beside the canals, past fields of bulbs and mountains of cheese, spectacular signs of recovery showed how the customs of peace were returning. Much of the flat landscape, around Aalsmeer for example, where there was a flourishing fruit and flower market, was occupied by carefully cultivated fields, interspersed with the canals that carry so much of the local farm products. In the course of the next few days, we visited St Bavo's cathedral and took meals at Vroom and Dreesmann's store, bought a Penguin novel for the equivalent of 19 (modern) pence, saw Spaarndam, a fishing village, and travelled several times to Amsterdam.

Helen soon learnt of the price to be paid for marrying a laboratory enthusiast! An introduction to the hospital at Overvroom offered a chance to see some excellent Dutch research laboratories and to hear of their sophisticated work, which came to mind again when we toured the Leeuwenhoek cancer research laboratories in Amsterdam. With selfish enthusiasm, I persuaded Helen to come with me on a visit to the spacious Wilhelmina Hospital, modern in style by contrast with the 1879 Edinburgh Royal Infirmary. Impetuously setting on one side any reservations that my young bride might feel, I asked if we might see the new mortuary with its sophisticated refrigeration facilities. Amsterdam was notorious for its drug dealers, and bodies were often recovered from the canals: one was brought out for our inspection.

But we quickly returned to activities more usual for honeymoon couples! At the Rijksmuseum, we were fascinated by Rembrandt's

Night Watch. We saw his house and listened spellbound to the Concertgebouw Orchestra – it was a time when the Scottish National Orchestra had not yet returned to its peacetime excellence. Another concert at Haarlem and visits to a number of films provided evening entertainment. In Leiden, we saw St Peter's Church, where Winston Churchill had received his honorary degree in 1946. On the way back to Britain, our journey took us to The Hague, Den Haag, where we visited the Peace Palace, a building made possible by Carnegie during the years 1907–13.

To be a physician?

Back in Scotland, the task of finding a job could no longer be postponed. When the Second World War ended, the rush by ex-servicemen and -women to find employment meant that there were sometimes 200 or more applicants for a single appointment. But these hectic days were ending and there were now opportunities for training to become a consultant in each of the three main hospital fields of Medicine (Internal Medicine, as it was termed in the United States), Surgery, and Obstetrics and Gynaecology. Much of the advantage of having worked in a large, central teaching hospital lay in the influence that its reputation and that of its consultant staff could exert on behalf of young graduates searching for promotion and experience. The prospects for advancement were good.

My interests were in the first of the three main fields, Medicine. For any hope of success in this competitive medical world, it was essential to have a higher qualification. The challenge was to become a Member of one of the Colleges of Physicians.[D] By 1950, as Medicine became increasingly divided into narrower sub-specialities, it was necessary to express a particular field of interest. The physician in charge of the medical wards in which I worked in Edinburgh, Fergus Hewat, specialized in diseases of the chest and lungs, Respiratory Medicine. Under his wise tutelage, it was in his field that I had gained any particular experience to which I could lay claim. I therefore decided to attempt the Edinburgh MRCP examination in this speciality. To prepare for this challenge, it would have been possible to stay in Edinburgh and study in or close to the Royal Infirmary. However, I judged that a period of independent clinical experience would be of value and sought a position in a smaller, non-teaching hospital where there should also be time for periods of study. I was fortunate to come across an advertisement for a position as Clinical Assistant in Medicine at the Louth County Infirmary, a district hospital in Lincolnshire (Figure 8.4). It is now the County Hospital, Louth.

Interviews for the appointment were held in the Hospital Boardroom. Among those forming the committee was Mr Nicholson, the senior consultant surgeon and Medical Superintendent. 'Nick' was so well known locally that the County Infirmary was often called 'Nicholson's Hospital'. Together with Christopher Cummins

Figure 8.4 *The County Infirmary, Louth, as it was in the 1950s. (Courtesy of Peter Kerman, Support Services Team Leader, Louth Hospital, NHS Lincolnshire.)*

FRCSEd, an older, ex-service applicant for a corresponding position in Surgery (p.285), I was accepted and agreed to start at an early date. Later that day, I suspected that I had been the only applicant!

Life in Louth

Before taking up my new position, we visited my mother in Minehead, Somerset. It was during one of these visits that we decided to buy a car – we had to make visits not only to Scotland but also to Helen's sister, to Cambridge, and to Ipswich for the wedding of my cousin Jean (Figure 3.2). In a local commercial garage in Minehead, we found a 1936 Austin 7, a 'baby' Austin saloon (Figure 8.5). We bought it for £250. It proved a reliable if cramped little friend.

Figure 8.5 *An Austin 7 car, a so-called 'baby' Austin. (Courtesy of the Motoring Picture Library of the National Motor Museum.)*

There was no 'self-starter' and the motor was stirred into action by cranking a handle, nor were there any direction signals. At that time, there was no compulsory driving test and I followed the driver's manual by lowering my window and sticking out my arm to indicate turns to left or right. In the same old-fashioned way, I warned drivers following us of a change of speed by flapping my arm up and down and encouraged them to overtake by a rotary movement of my hand. Capable of a cruising speed of 38 miles an hour, the tiny saloon, with a folding luggage grid and a petrol tank that hung from the back, could accelerate to 45 miles an hour if pointed downhill with a favourable wind behind it. The floor beside the driver was not a complete covering, so that I could see the surface of the road as we passed over it.

On a visit to Scotland, with two suitcases strapped to the luggage rack at the back of the car, we had difficulty climbing the steep hill into Carlisle in bottom gear. In the main street, we stopped to buy a newspaper. I detected a smell of petrol and found a drip from the tank falling directly on to the exhaust pipe. Urgent action was demanded! A packet of chewing gum proved the answer. Before I left for Germany (Chapter 9), I was able to sell the car for only £25 less than I gave for it, the chewing gum still in place!

Helen and I realized that we would quickly have to find accommodation in Lincolnshire, a part of the country where neither of us had friends or relations. We were fortunate in being able to stay two nights with Dr and Mrs Horace Wilmot, friends of one of Helen's cousins. Tom and Bessie were very generous and we came to know them well. Searching the *Louth Chronicle*, we came across rented accommodation in Charles Street, within half a mile of the hospital. Mr and Mrs Marshall, Bun and Lill, offered to provide two rooms – a sitting room and a bedroom – together with the use of the bathroom, at a modest charge. Thursday was 'bath night'. The toilet was immaculate, but was in a garden outhouse and to reach it we had to pass through the Marshall's kitchen. Bun, with a lovely Yorkshire accent, was, as he put it, 'shunter on railway'. His work took him to the line to Lincoln and thence to the main railway to Doncaster. He and Lill were simple but kindly folk, often astonished at some of our habits. One day, Lill asked Helen how long we had been married. On learning that this was our first home, Lill remarked 'I thought you was just beginners. You don't av much kissin, does you?' We were never certain that Lill could read – she explained that she enjoyed 'reading' the pictures in the Daily Mirror. Bun and Lill had a terrier, a poor dog kept strictly in a kennel in the back garden, near the toilet to which we had to make our way, by day or night. Our first living room was quiet and slightly old-fashioned. Two biblical prints faced each other on the plain walls, one inscribed '*Behold I stand at the door and knock*', the other '*Rock of Ages*'. Near them, on the mantelpiece, stood china ornaments, one a replica of Dickens' Mr Micawber, the other a cast of Sarah Gamp.

In the evenings, Helen showed great for-
bearance as I concentrated on reading textbooks and papers. Whenever possible, she
took refuge in the local music society and
in a modern language class. In spite of the
constraints, life in the little town could be
entertaining. On Sundays, we often escaped
by packing a lunch and setting off for a drive
into the countryside. Our little car allowed
us to explore beautiful parts of Lincolnshire
and to make visits to Helen's sister Florence,
settled with her husband John Pike[E] at
Stapleford Farm, near Ashridge College. At
other times, Helen journeyed by bus to
Scunthorpe to see as much as possible of the
East Anglian coast.

Figure 8.6 *St James Parish Church, Louth. (Courtesy of Stuart Sizer, guide organizer for St James.)*

The great parish church of Louth with
its vast spire (Figure 8.6), said to be the
tallest in England, enjoyed the skills of a
fine organist, Denis Townsend, later to be
organist of St Mary's Cathedral, Edinburgh.
He was keen to promote his choir of parish-
ioners, and we joined them for their weekly
practices, Helen standing in the front with
the sopranos, I at the back with the basses.
We found ourselves rehearsing Brahms's
gipsy songs, the *Zigeuner Lieder*, as well as
Bach's cantata *Wachet auf ruft uns die Stimme*
(Sleepers Wake). The cantata was to be sung in Lincoln Cathedral
some months later. When it came to the time for the performance,
it was clear that the Louth choir, joined by those from surrounding
villages and towns, was insufficiently skilled for the challenging
task, in spite of the enthusiastic direction of Mr Townsend.

The County Infirmary, Louth

My new post in this 200-bed general hospital was the equivalent
of a position that later would be termed a Senior House Officer, a
SHO, although it was soon to become clear that the responsibilities
extended far beyond those of a SHO. My work was very varied. My
'Chief' was Dr Charles Lillicrap, a graduate of Guy's Hospital.[F] I came
to know him well: we often exchanged thoughts about families and
friends and he told me that his father had been an eminent naval
architect. Charles Lillicrap, a vigorous and extremely well-informed
consultant to the large Lincoln County Hospital some 20 miles
away, enjoyed Citroen cars and attended outpatients in the Louth
County Infirmary once weekly. Faced with difficult problems in
specialities such as neurology, he referred cases to the Derby Royal

Infirmary, which had an international reputation in this and other fields. However, Dr Lillicrap was asthmatic and, travelling with him by car, it was sometimes necessary to stop to allow him to use an inhaler. One day, however, we halted not for medical reasons but to listen to a broadcast of the Grand National!

My tasks at Louth were considerable, since I shared nighttime, 'on call' duties with the small number of junior staff. Our rooms at Charles Street had no telephone, and at night I would be roused to attend an emergency by a pebble thrown at our bedroom window by a hospital porter who had cycled from his lodge. In later years, as we came to know Peebles in Scotland (p.132), we realized that this was the usual way in which a doctor could be summoned urgently before the introduction of the telephone, although in Victorian times a messenger would come on foot or on horseback.

There was no opportunity for research of any kind, nor was there time to undertake any. However, as a first step towards experience in public speaking, I was able to give a talk to the local medical society on 'Infective hepatitis', a condition of which I had had personal experience at school. Poliomyelitis was still rife, and among the tragedies I witnessed was that of the wife of an RAF officer from the nearby airfield at Manby. The virus had caused paralysis of her respiratory muscles. We placed her in an 'artificial lung', a huge cylinder resembling in size and capacity the centre of a twenty-first century CT scanner, but nothing more could be done to save her life. Another patient, a young man with pulmonary and renal tuberculosis, was more fortunate. Streptomycin had become available, and I was able to inject him daily with this antibiotic. I was grateful for the experience of spinal puncture I had had as a house physician, and I injected the antibiotic intrathecally, into the spinal fluid, on a daily basis. Six weeks after admission, he walked home.

In some cases of hospital death, an autopsy might be called for. However, the nearest consultant pathologist was at Grimsby, 20 miles away. In these cases, my fascination for pathology came to the rescue and I performed the procedures myself. I learnt of the strange condition of pseudomyxoma peritonei, an occasional complication of metastatic testicular cancer. In another case, a middle-aged man complained of a painful arm and was found to have widespread deposits from a kidney cancer. One day I had the difficult task of telling a surgical colleague that his preoperative diagnosis had been wrong when a patient, thought to have suffered from perforation of a peptic ulcer, had clearly died from lobar pneumonia.

With the encouragement of Charles Lillicrap, I entered for the Murchison Scholarship of the Royal College of Physicians of London. I was unsuccessful, but the clinical tests not only gave me experience of the kind I would face when I came to attempt an examination for a higher qualification, but also introduced me to a kindly Professor Max Rosenheim, later to be Lord Rosenheim,

President of the Royal College of Physicians of London. My experience drew me towards the examinations of this London College, but most of my medical teachers had been Fellows of the Royal College of Physicians of Edinburgh. I therefore decided that my first attempt, as I had first thought, should be directed towards the Edinburgh MRCP.

Two months before the Edinburgh examination, in the autumn of 1950, we left Louth and headed back to Scotland so that I could gain practical, hospital experience with my old teachers in the Royal Infirmary. Outstanding among them was Dr J. Halliday Croom.[G] For some weeks, we benefited from the kindness of my school friend, T. K. (Tommy) Morgan; he and his young wife[H] allowed us to live in their new house in Corstorphine before we returned to Helen's family home in Bo'ness. It was during this time that I tested the effects of a drug of potential addiction, amphetamine. I took small amounts at night to keep me awake while I was studying medical texts. The effects were remarkable and it was usually possible to stay alert until one o'clock each morning. Fortunately, I had no inclination to pursue this self-medication once my studies were over!

In preparation for the challenge I confronted, I collected old question papers from the previous five years. I kept the notebooks in which I copied the questions, and they are now in the archives of the Royal College of Surgeons of Edinburgh.[I] When it came to the oral examination, I found that I knew two of my examiners, C. Kelman Robertson and T. R. R. 'Tarara' Todd. Dr Todd asked me: 'Does alcohol play any part in alleviating angina of effort? I had to think quickly. I took a chance and replied: 'In his book on *Pain*,[3] Lewis suggests that alcohol may in fact be beneficial.' It was at once obvious that neither Dr Kelman Robertson nor Dr Todd could recall enough of Thomas Lewis's writings to contradict me. All was well!

Later in the day, I read on the notice board that I had passed! Now we could look ahead with more confidence although, as it turned out, our next move was to be determined by His Majesty's Government!

III.

From The Elbe to Lake Erie

CHAPTER 9

With the army

Beside the Elbe

To everything its seasons, and for every activity
under heaven its time:
a time to be born and a time to die;
a time to plan and a time to uproot;
a time to kill and a time to heal; … a
time for war and a time for peace.

Ecclesiastes[1]

It was 1950. War had broken out in Korea on 25th June. After the end of the Second World War, all young doctors were required to spend at least two years in the Armed Forces, and it was my turn. I was at the Royal Army Medical Corps (RAMC) training centre at Crookham, Hampshire, waiting for news of my posting. 'Where do you want to go?' demanded the Colonel. I replied: 'Sir, I should prefer to remain in this country: my wife is expecting our first child.' The Colonel responded: 'I am inclined to send you to the Far East, but I think that Germany is the place for you.'

Chapter summary
- **Life in Hamburg**
- **The Military Hospital**
- **Medicine in the Army**
- **The Officers' Mess**
- **Oldenburg**
- **An epidemic**
- **Family visits**
- **On leave to Austria, the Rhine and Italy**
- **Poverty and refugees**

Germany had been divided into four occupied zones. An Allied Control Commission exercised overall authority. The Western two-thirds were shared between Britain, France and the United States, while the Russians occupied the Eastern third. In the West, a British Army of Occupation (the British Army of the Rhine, the BAOR) administered a region that extended from the Dutch border to a line that ran irregularly southwards from the Danish border and Lübeck in the North, past Lüneburg (where the Armistice had been signed) and Braunschweig towards Hanover, Hildesheim and Kassel.

Following a currency reform initiated in the West in 1948, the Soviets blockaded Berlin, but the city was saved from paralysis by an airlift. In 1949, the zones occupied by Britain, France and the United States were merged, forming the Federal Republic of Germany (West Germany). The capital was at Bonn. The Eastern, Soviet zone became the German Democratic Republic (East Germany). The three Western sectors of Berlin, an enclave separated by a distance of 180 kilometres from the East–West boundary, were dealt with in the same way.

The BAOR was a force of some 55,000 men. Together with the corresponding units of the Royal Air Force, this constituted a requirement for substantial numbers of hospitals and many medical staff. At Crookham, there was little intellectual work, some interesting physical challenges and slight instruction in weaponry. My years in the Home Guard and Air Training Corps (p.44) made it reasonably easy to accept military discipline. We trained in a gymnasium, where volleys of abuse were sometimes hurled at us as we tried to cross narrow wooden bars at great height. I was a particular object of the sergeant's derision. He would shout: 'That old man up there, *try* and behave as though you have *two* legs, not one!' But these ordeals were forgotten when I lost my copy of the *Confessions of Jean Jacques Rousseau*[2] left carelessly at the mess breakfast table. I wrote on the notice board: 'Would the person who has removed my "Confessions" please return them to Lieutenant D. L. Gardner.' They were returned and I still have them!

Part of my time was at the Royal Army Medical College, Millbank, and here I enjoyed splendid lectures on tropical diseases. From the speaker, a senior army physician, I learnt of 'diversionary answering'![A] At weekends, I drove to Ashridge,[B] where Helen was staying with her sister Florence, and in my spare time played golf at Farnham with a friend from the Middlesex Hospital. But I was soon travelling by train through Belgium and Germany to Hamburg,[C] where I joined the staff of the 39th General Hospital at Barmbek[D] (Figure 9.1). The Hospital was built in a classical style similar to the Eppendorfer Krankenhaus, the first of the 83 blocks of which were opened in 1887.[3] The British Military Hospital occupied one half of

Figure 9.1 *Barmbek Hospital, Number 39 British Military Hospital, Hamburg.*

the hospital; the other half had been returned to civilian use. For the first few weeks, I lived in the hospital. Winter was approaching, the nights extremely cold, but nearby was a frozen lake and Lieutenant Bernard Juby and I enjoyed walking down there with our skates.

Life in Hamburg

Within a few weeks of my arrival in Hamburg (Figure 9.2), Helen was able to join me. She had an exciting voyage across the North Sea. Her father, familiar with the Baltic trade, had found a convenient ship. It was only when Helen reached Leith docks that she saw that the vessel was named the *Albatross*! The little ship carried a cargo of fish and four passengers: with Helen were a German girl and two members of a motorcycle circus team. The ship lay becalmed in fog for two days off the mouth of the Elbe while I telephoned hourly to find the cause of the delay. When Helen eventually arrived, we were directed to a transit centre for officers in the prestigious, '4 star' *Die Vier Jahres Zeiten* (Four Seasons) Hotel, facing the Binnen Alster, the lake at the city centre.

We were soon granted a small modern house (Figure 9.3), 26 Floot, in a suburb only two kilometres from the Hospital.[E] We were given the services of a young German house-maid and the help of an elderly man, Herr Fenske, who stoked the coal-fired boiler and surreptitiously carried home each evening a briefcase laden with Army coal. On the BBC Forces wireless programme, a new 'soap', *The Archers*, kept us in touch with life at home. The house was relatively new, fitted with double-glazing, and well furnished, so that we enjoyed a standard of living that we were not to experience again for many years. My salary in the NHS had been £600 a year. By 1951, my pay, as a Temporary Captain, had become twice that amount. Medical military life in occupied Germany was deceptively affluent.

There was surprisingly little sign of hostility from the civilian population, but few uniformed officers wished to travel by public transport. Army families had no such reservations and used the U-bahn, the underground railway, freely. The army employed German drivers with Volkswagen cars in military colours, charging the equivalent of two pence (in modern currency) per mile for off-duty journeys. There were restrictions on

Figure 9.2 *Hamburg Town Hall, near the Binnen Alster, the lake in the centre of the city.*

Figure 9.3 *Number 26, Floot, Hamburg.*

the use of these cars, so that many of us bought second-hand cars while some regular army officers brought their own vehicles from the United Kingdom. In the early spring of 1951, I decided to buy a 1947 Volkswagen, or 'Peoples Car',[F] from a fellow officer whose tour of duty was ending. I inspected the car, covered by snow, outside *Die Vier Jahres Zeiten*, lifting the rear cover of the 'Beetle' to make sure that there was an engine, and gave him £250. I soon learned that my new purchase had cable brakes but no gearbox synchro-mesh. Driving called for practice, although the small volume of traffic eased the difficulties posed by the cobbled roads that fed the *Autobahnen*. Petrol consumption was low and the air-cooled engine proved reliable in the face of extreme changes of climate. Stuck in snow, two people could lift the rear end as easily as if it were a bicycle.

The Military Hospital

With the advantage of the Membership of the Royal College of Physicians of Edinburgh, I was graded as a Junior Medical Specialist and became responsible to my consultant, Major Peter Brown, a Senior Medical Specialist. The Officers' Mess of BMH Hamburg was an imposing red brick block. In front, stood a gaily coloured statue of *Hummel*, the famous water carrier (Figure 9.4). Working relationships between senior officers in administrative charge and junior officers who undertook much of the day-to-day medical and surgical work were not always easy. We rarely encountered the Commanding Officer, a Colonel with a splendid house in the city suburbs. We saw more of the non-medical Registrar, Captain Noble. One of my fellow officers, Geronwy Owen, was a clinical chemist from Sheffield. He was clever and well informed, but rebellious by nature and disinterested in the traditions of the RAMC. Like the other National Service officers, he was obliged to wear 'battledress'. However, Geronwy refused to don a cap in the hospital, did not fasten his belt and left his jacket unbuttoned. Another colleague was Bill Irvine, a brilliant young surgeon later to become Professor of Surgery at St Mary's Hospital Medical School. He also was a rebel who enjoyed displaying his disregard for matters military while performing exemplary surgical feats.[G]

The Hospitals of the British Army of Occupation were served by experienced British nurses, officers in Queen Alexandra's Royal Army Nursing Corps, the QARANC. The QAs, as they were called, were supported by male and female German nurses and orderlies. The QA nurses, from all parts of Britain, were gazetted Lieutenant or Captain. I was astonished and delighted to discover that the officer caring for the medical wards for which I was responsible, Lieutenant Margaret Daniel (p.125), had worked in the Edinburgh Royal Infirmary at the same time as Helen: they had been staff nurses together. As a young physician, I was particularly fortunate, since Margaret (Figure 9.5) was outstandingly experienced, trained in the treatment of infectious diseases and a strict disciplinarian. She was of small stature while several of the male German nurses were gigantic, but they, like their female counterparts, stood rigidly to attention as Margaret dictated their daily

Figure 9.4 *Statue of Hummel in front of the Officers Mess at Barmbek Hospital.*

Figure 9.5 *Lieutenant Margaret Daniel, QARANC.*

orders. Some German staff were refugees from the East: times were hard but their professional standards were high.

Medicine in the Army

My responsibilities were far in excess of those I would have expected in civilian life and extended from the Danish border in the north to Bremen in the southwest. One task was to report on the health of regular army colleagues considered for promotion or, occasionally, after their recovery from illness. To prepare an accurate and fair report was not easy, especially when it was obvious that a senior officer had adopted an intemperate lifestyle.

Casualties from Korea were returning to the UK through ports like Hamburg.

One day, a sergeant, his face and body covered by confluent pustules, was admitted to my wards. He appeared to have smallpox. The laboratory wheels were set in urgent motion and there was widespread relief when the virus was identified not as variola (smallpox) but as varicella (chickenpox). Vivid recollections of the Second World War Burma campaign came to mind when Major Michael Calvert, DSO, became a patient.[4] He had been a fearless member of Wingate's operations behind the Japanese lines. Like many, 'Mad' Mike had suffered from malaria and was experiencing a relapse. In striking contrast was a man with an Eastern name who suffered from duodenal ulcer. Prolonged pain caused him to lose his normal discretion and it became clear that he was an agent for the Eastern bloc. Another major was stationed with his unit on the border of the Russian zone, east of Hamburg. He recovered quickly from slight signs of heart disease and invited me to a mess dinner with the Dragoon Guards. This created a difficulty: my clothes included a formal 'Field Dress' made by a German tailor, but not the necessary and elegant 'Mess Dress'. However, a colleague, Captain Fleming, serving a four-year 'Short Service Commission', lent me this regimental uniform and I went off, clad in 'Blues'. The evening gave me an insight into the traditions of one of the finest units of the British Army; the Guards behaved as though they were still at war, but this time it was a Cold War.

Many officers and men had their families with them in Germany, and I was often called on to deal with the common diseases of women and children.

One afternoon the 19-year-old daughter of an army officer was rushed to the hospital from Bremen. Taken ill earlier in the day with severe headache, she was unconscious. It seemed likely that she had meningococcal meningitis, a scourge of all armies, and the diagnosis was confirmed by the laboratory. That night, Lieutenant Daniel and I struggled to save her life with the new antibiotic Aureomycin (chlortetracycline). Intravenous fluid and devoted nursing care turned the tide, and within 24 hours she was conscious in time to be visited by the senior Rhine Army Physician, Brigadier J Bennett, accompanied by Dr MacDonald Critchley from the Hospital for Nervous Diseases, London.

In Hamburg, the Allied Powers maintained diplomatic representation, and I was responsible for the medical care of consular staff. One day, there was a call to visit the young son of the French Consul. I was lucky to have as a colleague Major Berti, a delightful, multilingual officer who had worked for the British Medical Association. He admitted to understanding 16 languages but to speaking only 11! I found the boy ill with rheumatic fever, at his bedside an experienced German nurse. After my consultation, we repaired for lunch to the exquisite French dining room where Major Berti, speaking in three languages, entertained us with tales of wartime Italy.

The Officers' Mess

It was customary for the most recently arrived officer to supervise the Mess accounts. Occasional records were puzzling: I had been warned that some officers drank heavily. Yet when I examined the accounts of one lieutenant colonel at whom a finger of suspicion had been pointed, his bill appeared to be no more than £13 each month. But then a little investigation showed me that Army gin cost a mere six shillings and eight pence a bottle (33 pence in decimal currency), a good bottle of Rhine wine half that amount. The officer in charge of the hospital laboratories made a practice of arriving at the mess bar at precisely one minute before noon each day. Taking his accustomed seat, he would press a nearby bell. A white-coated German waiter would arrive, carrying the first of a series of well-filled glasses. The Colonel was aware of the hazards of his addiction, so that each Friday evening he visited a restaurant for half a kilogram of beef steak. The regime appeared to work well, but it was not many months before he had the bitter experience of recognizing the bacillus of tuberculosis, *Mycobacterium tuberculosis*, in his own sputum.

After mess dinners, 'room rugby' was sometimes played on the fine parquet floor of the officer's dining hall. Two groups, the regular army officers as one team, the National Service officers as the other, would struggle for a rolled-up sock. Tries were scored, but there was no referee and minor injuries were common. One evening, the National Service forwards devised a tactic to defeat their heavier opponents. As the 'regulars' advanced, the younger officers moved suddenly to one side: their opponents could not stop and were impaled on a radiator!

I was doubly fortunate, since two of my friends, Captain Fleming and Lieutenant Walker, were excellent pianists. The Hamburg Opera House had not yet been rebuilt, but this did not prevent the presentation of fine concerts, supported by NordWest Deutsche Rundfunk, the North West German radio station. Bach's *St Matthew Passion* was among the works we attended. On a different level, it was inevitable that some members of the Mess should join the Other Ranks, the ORs, and visit the infamous Reeperbahn, a Soho-like area in the centre of Hamburg. The street was lined by brothels where the girls sat in the windows, displaying their attributes. The street was patrolled by Military Police, but staff from the hospital wore civilian clothes and had no difficulty in buying tickets for cabarets.

Both officers and ORs enjoyed leave at Austrian ski resorts. Not surprisingly, there were many accidents, and an ambulance train was sent each week from Hamburg to Klagenfurt to bring the casualties to hospital. Early in 1951, it became my turn to act as the Medical Officer accompanying the train. Steaming out of the Hamburg Zentral Bahnhof, I found myself with a RAMC corporal and three of his mates. A jolly Cockney but ill-at ease chatting to an officer, he relaxed when we turned to chess. I woke in the shunting yards at Munich and watched the massive, black German steam engines preparing for the day's work just as they might have done in Hitler's time (p.19). In Klagenfurt, a kind RAMC officer and his wife suggested that I might like to ski. The challenge was not a success, the snow fell freely and I felt I had two left feet!

Oldenburg

One day, without warning, I was told that I had been 'posted'. Peter Brown had been a prisoner of war of the Japanese, an experience that left deep scars on his character and personality, as it did to all those who had suffered in the same way (p.194). I was a nuisance because I was inclined to dispute his diagnoses.[H] In the spring of 1951, within a few weeks of the time when Helen was expecting our first baby, I was dispatched to a Field Dressing Station, an FDS, in Oldenburg.[I] The title FDS proved misleading. I had anticipated life in a cluster of tents, water drawn from a nearby stream, cooking on open stoves and Army-style latrines. The FDS was, in fact, one wing of an excellent, modern German general hospital in which the Army occupied two wards. There was a useful working relationship with German physicians, and an elderly radiologist proved to be a skilled colleague.

We were given a furnished flat where the rooms and cupboards were festooned with spiders' webs and plagued with moths. The friendly neighbours were the families of army sergeants, and the ladies quickly told Helen: 'You should not be here! These are quarters for ORs (Other Ranks) and your husband is an officer.' I spoke to Quartermaster Major Kelly and he found us better accommodation.

Oldenburg had many attractions. Set in lands evoked by Erskine Childers,[5] the town offered good restaurants and a fine Staatstheater, where we listened to Erna Schlüter singing Strauss's *Electra* passionately. The FDS hospital in Oldenburg, with a lovely garden, turned out to be an excellent place for obstetrics. Very early on the morning of 12th May 1951, Helen called to me to find urgent transport! I phoned the dispenser, who lived nearby, and he took us in his car to the hospital, and our daughter Rosalind was born safely that day (Figure 9.6). Helen, the only patient in the maternity wards apart from the German wife of another soldier, was cared for professionally by an experienced and kindly older German nurse, Hilda Wartzman, trained before the war in Berlin. The obstetrician was my colleague, Michael Brudenell.[J] Some months later, it fell to Captain Noble to register Rosalind's birth 'under the British flag'. In error, he omitted one of her names, so, although christened Rosalind Helen Gardner, her middle name was 'mislaid'.

The FDS was commanded by Major MacGregor Robertson, a tall, laconic Glasgwegian who held a four-year 'short service' commission. I enjoyed excellent working relations with him. Sadly, he vanished, to be replaced by Major 'Bromide', a regular army officer who gave more time to Rules and Regulations than to medical matters.

Figure 9.6 *The author, Helen and Rosalind, in Oldenburg, 1951.*

The young soldiers I met on sick parades were physically fit and I was not entirely surprised that the questions asked during morning sick parades were often about venereal disease. However, finger infections were a common complaint, an important reason for loss of 'fitness for duty'. I began to collate the records, and the results formed my first published paper.[6]

With the medical staff was a young dental officer. One day I developed a dental abscess and one of my teeth had to be extracted. Lieutenant Brudenell gave me ¼ gr (about 16 mg) of morphine as premedication and injected me intravenously with the barbiturate pentothal. After the operation, Helen telephoned to ask if I had recovered. A voice answered: 'Yes, he's all right – now.' The discreet pause concealed the embarrassing information that I had briefly stopped breathing after the anaesthetic. Next day, I had thrombophlebitis of the injected arm. The extracted tooth was never found!

The notorious name Belsen came to mean a little more when I and a few of my colleagues were dispatched there for training in the work of a Field Ambulance. We lived for two weeks in the former quarters of the SS (p.21). The concentration camp itself had been demolished immediately the war ended, but the SS buildings were still there. They were comfortable and well designed, resembling the Luftwaffe hospital I came across when I visited Szczecin many years later (p.267). Our Field Ambulance training was simple. We gathered in trucks, jeeps and ambulances and drove round the district, pretending to be under battlefield conditions.

The Lieutenant Colonel commanding the Belsen unit was a man of few words but a liking for claret. One of his evening habits was walking along the nearby railway line. Some months later, I heard that one night he had been struck by a train and killed. This tragedy reenforced my view that the greatest difficulty faced by regular army medical officers in peacetime is to find sufficient, interesting employment. Boredom is a great hazard. It was on the basis of this opinion that I found it very difficult to understand why, in Germany, the Army did not work more closely with the civilian medical profession. We could have learned a great deal from each other, but in practice, rarely met.

An epidemic

In the early autumn of September 1951, I was confronted with a medical crisis. It was a bright, sunny afternoon. There was little hospital activity and I was playing tennis with Mike Brudenell when a dispatch rider arrived to ask me to come at once to the hospital. Twelve soldiers had been admitted from a nearby artillery regiment. By the time I arrived, there were 24 patients, each severely ill with acute tonsillitis. By the evening, there were 90 sick men. There were no longer sufficient beds to admit more patients and I decided to treat any further cases in the barracks. Only a day later, 232 of the Regiment of 836 men were acutely ill: none were officers. Laboratory tests showed that the epidemic was caused by a group A streptococcus. With the help of a splendid RAMC sergeant but without ethical approval, I decided to undertake a trial of different forms of treatment: at random, we gave our patients either penicillin, or sulphonamides, or aspirin and gargles. We used the entire Rhine Army stock of penicillin in three days: more was flown from England.[7] The trial showed that penicillin shortened the infection and suggested that it might prevent later complications such as rheumatic fever.[8] I suspected that the epidemic had been spread by contaminated food. During the month before the outbreak, four cooks had had infected fingers but had not been removed from duty. They prepared food for the ORs but not for officers. I discovered that the hygienic conditions within the artillery barracks were appallingly bad: every toilet was blocked, the huts dirty and neglected, yet neither the Commanding Officer, the Adjutant nor the Regimental Medical Officer appeared to be concerned.

Not many weeks later, I moved to the Royal Air Force (RAF) hospital at Rinteln, near their Headquarters at Bad Oeynhausen. My orders were to deputize for Flight Lieutenant Snell, who was on leave. The contrast between medical life in the RAF and in the Army was striking. The Air Force mess was welcoming and informal in a way I had not experienced in Hamburg. Among the patients was an airman with chronic inflammation of the surfaces of the lung, pleurisy. I felt it was unfair to prolong his care in Germany and arranged for him to be returned to the UK. When Snell came back from leave, he was annoyed at the loss of one of his favourite patients!

The epidemic of tonsillitis in Oldenburg had an unexpected sequel. At a dinner in the Army mess at Bad Oyenhausen, I was called to the Director General, Army Medical Services (DGAMS), British Army of the Rhine, Major General Cameron. Standing to attention in front of him, I felt conspicuous. He said: 'Gardner, by your insistence on treating the men with tonsillitis in their barracks, you have saved the army many days occupancy of hospital beds. What can I do for you?' Without hesitation, I replied: 'Sir, it has been a privilege. I would like to return to BMH Hamburg'. My wish was granted and Helen, Rosalind and I moved back to our previous house in the capital of the Hanseatic League, where I found that Major Brown had been posted to another unit.

The army employed many civilian drivers. I came to know one of them, Herr van Duren, very well. He was Dutch and had been conscripted into the German army when Hitler overran Holland. An officer in a tank corps, he told me how, on the Eastern front in the winter of 1943, the cold was so intense that it was necessary to light a fire under the tanks to melt the gearbox oil. He offered to look after my car and I had no hesitation in lending it to him for a holiday.

Family visits

From time to time, we enjoyed visits from our relations and friends. They were immediately astonished at the abundance of food in post-war Germany. Food rationing was still in force in Britain and a question they often asked was: 'Who won the war?' Although local people could not afford these delicacies, German restaurants offered delicious dishes of beef steak, pork, veal, sweets and gateaux. In Hamburg, we had a visit from my mother, then in her 63rd year. We took her to *Das Schiff*, a floating restaurant in the harbour. Towards the end of the meal, she settled for an extravagant strawberry concoction. I realized I did not have enough money to pay the bill. I was in uniform, and the embarrassment of my situation, among a crowd of indigent Germans, was considerable. The ladies stayed as hostages while I drove back to the house to collect the necessary marks!

On leave to Austria, the Rhine and Italy

In the spring of 1951 Helen and I took ten days leave. We travelled to Austria to see this beautiful country and to ski, staying at Lermoos, near Ehrwald, in a little hotel called *Die Drei Zigeuner*, the Three Gypsies, within sight of the Zugspitz (Figure 9.7). We arrived in warm, bright sunshine: the snow sparkled in the streets and on the house tops. Sadly, within 36 hours, the weather deteriorated and our attempts at skiing had to be abandoned. Then news came that King George VI had died and every member of the Armed Forces was ordered to wear a black armband. All social events were cancelled

Figure 9.7 *The 9700-foot-high Zugspitz.*

and the melancholy music of the zither overshadowed dinner each evening.

Early in 1952, we travelled with our good friends George Roberts and his wife Ruth[K] in their Austin A40 car to the Rhine. We saw *die Lorelei* and were astonished by the scale of the water-borne traffic using the river. We had been invited to Colin's wedding to Denise Marley which took place on 31st January but it was impracticable to journey to Somerset at that time. In the summer, we were joined by my brother-in-law, Gordon Harrower who journeyed with us by Volkswagen, through Austria, across the Brenner Pass. The journey was not without incident. The cable brakes of my 'Beetle' were not equal to the one-in-four descent into Innsbrück on an unmade, gravel-surfaced road where precipitous cliffs rising to the right were painted with skulls and cross-bones and precipices to the left fell five hundred feet. Gordon was driving, descending the pass in bottom gear but moving too quickly. Suddenly, the car slipped out of gear but instinctively I seized the lever and pushed it back into place before his hands had left the steering wheel!

Arriving in Venice, a little boy guided us to his aunt's house. She welcomed us kindly but at first insisted that my brother-in-law was Helen's husband and that I was the brother-in-law! Leaving Venice and crossing the hills, we found that meals of cheese and cherries with wine at 1/7d (8 decimal pence) a bottle made for happy journeys. Our arrival in Florence coincided with the Michelangelo Quincentenary. Helen and I enjoyed the exhibition, while Gordon sat outside in the Square, tasting cheap vino, beneath the statue of *David*. In the streets of Pisa, after dark, a mysterious female voice whispered in my ears: 'The keys of my room?'

Poverty and refugees

I had always been fascinated by the German language, and my favourite, contrived word became *teleskopische-Stossdämpfer* (telescopic shock absorber), picked up at a local garage. Anxious to improve my spoken German, I was put in touch with a middle-aged lady, who, it turned out, was the widow of a former SS colonel, anxious to earn a few deutschemarks. As the weeks went by, we noticed that the stock of toilet paper declined very sharply every time the colonel's lady came to the house and it became clear that these simple necessities of civilized society were in desperately short supply in the deprived German population.

Through this lady, we came in contact with refugees huddled in their miserable camps. The Soviet authorities had seized the German provinces east of the Oder and Neisse rivers, while the larger part of the German provinces of West Prussia, Pomerania and Silesia was passed to the Poles. Almost the entire population ceased to be German, so that millions of people fled westwards, many arriving in Hamburg, where they joined Estonians, Lithuanians and Latvians who had escaped from the Russian armies. The barren fields and ruined areas of the Hamburg suburbs were filled by wooden huts, sheds and tents, where the displaced persons eked out a precarious existence. From time to time, we visited them, taking simple gifts of tea or coffee. The warmth of our reception was embarrassing: many hoped to migrate to the United States and the recollection of their pale, anxious, haggard faces and of their impoverished environment remains deeply etched in my memory.

We saw little of the widespread corruption and crime characteristic of all defeated countries, and indeed of all countries at war but it was only to be expected that, under the prevailing conditions, there would be a flourishing black market. At our front door, we periodically encountered an elderly man who worked for Radio Hamburg and who we named *Herr Rundfunk*, 'Mr Radio'. He appeared after dark, conspiratorially but with good humour, and asked: 'Guten Abend. Wie gehts? Haben sie etwas Kaffee oder Gin?' We replied 'Bitte, kommen sie herein and we shall see what we can do'. It was in this way that we acquired a modest supply of 'black' deutschemarks, 12 to the £1. I used mine to buy a small camera, an Akaret.

An arresting portrait of one of the most degrading forms of evil that deformed medicine in Europe after the war ended was given in *The Third Man*.[9] The story was of corrupt hospital orderlies and doctors selling penicillin to a Mafia-like organisation. In the Vienna of 1945–46, penicillin was significantly more precious than gold and was pursued by relentless criminals for their own profit. There was no sign that this form of crime persisted in Hamburg in 1950, but, in earlier years, as the war ended, there was a story that the basement of the Hospital had been used as a brothel. The Army was said to have turned a blind eye to this abuse and to have provided the penicillin necessary to treat cases of syphilis and gonorrhoea. Other forms of crime were more obvious. One day, a furniture van from an accredited company approached an officers' mess and removed all the carpets for 'cleaning' from under the feet of the officers assembled for lunch. The carpets were never seen again. In BMH Hamburg, a gang of criminals entered one night and stripped large quantities of lead and copper from the roofs of the late nineteenth-century buildings.

As the end of my tour of duty approached, I was obliged to stay in Hamburg while Helen, who was expecting our second baby, moved to a hostel in Hanover where her obstetrician, Mike Brudenell, now supervised the maternity services. Our son Iain Dugald was born on 8th September 1952. George and Ruth Roberts (p.108) had been looking after young Rosalind in Münster and brought her to join Helen, but she and the children were not permitted to fly from Germany until Iain was one month old. It was early October, therefore, when the Roberts helped them onto a small plane bearing them from Düsseldorf to London. Seated in the aircraft, Helen found herself among members of the cast of the Royal Ballet who were returning from Berlin. Immediately in front of her were Margot Fonteyn and Beryl Gray. They commented on the beautiful little girl, Rosalind, behind them. Then Beryl Gray cried: 'Oh look! There's another one!' This was young Iain in his carrycot. So the children were introduced to ballet at an early age!

CHAPTER 10

Microscopes and men

A return to the Cam

There is at bottom only one genuinely scientific treatment
for all diseases, and that is to stimulate the phagocytes

George Bernard Shaw[1]

Chapter summary
- Family life in Cambridge
- Cambridge pathology
- Free time

No one who saw the impact of the ravages of war on Hamburg can ever forget the mountains of rubble and, by implication, the thousands who lay buried beneath. It was with mixed feelings that I left the ancient city.

Helen was still in Germany when I had to pack my bags and say 'Auf Wiedersehen' to Else, our young housekeeper, who had asked whether she might leave her native Schleswig-Holstein and accompany us to England. Sadly, we had to tell her that we would not have the money to make this possible. My two years of military service over, I was exceptionally lucky to have obtained an appointment as Junior Assistant Clinical Pathologist[A] to Addenbrooke's Hospital, Cambridge, where I had been as a student (Chapter 5).

Taking my trusty Volkswagen, I left 26 Floot and drove westwards. The tortuous streets of Antwerp offered some challenges, but a few hours later I reached Dunkirk. After a little discussion with the Customs authorities about the ownership of the heavily laden car – they were anxious to learn where I had obtained it – I was allowed to leave. The crossing was short, the sea calm, and disembarkation at Dover offered no difficulty. But I had forgotten that, in Britain, cars drive on the left-hand side of the road! I set off towards London and headed at an oncoming taxi! Fortunately, drivers in Dover are accustomed to this problem and we avoided a collision. I sped on in the direction of Cambridge, found a room for the night and then sought more settled accommodation.

A Mrs Williams advertised a suitable room and I accepted her terms of £3 a week. The bed was comfortable, the breakfasts good, but I soon realized that I was causing concern not only to my slightly frosty landlady but also to her other lodgers. It suddenly occurred to me that this might have something to do with my appearance – I was still in Army uniform. I then discovered my landlady was the widow of a former Professor of German. It passed through my mind that she might have ambivalent views on the legitimacy of the Allied occupation of the country to which her husband had devoted his life and I speculated that he might indeed have been German!

Four weeks later, Helen and the children arrived from Germany late in the afternoon. I met them at Northolt, the principal airport for London, helped by Alan Bicknell (p.119), who had brought his Rolls Royce to the airport. Some delay was caused by the need to feed a hungry Iain, but a valiant airport official came to our help with a glass of water and the offer of a quiet room. We helped Helen, the children and their luggage into Alan's splendid vehicle and drove to Hampstead, where Helen's aunt Florence lived. But I soon had to say farewell to my family again – it was the first time I had been called on to say *au revoir* to Iain – as the three travellers set off by train from King's Cross station for Bo'ness, where they were to stay until I found accommodation for us all in Cambridge. Met by Helen's father, they were welcomed with open arms and great rejoicing at Elmpark, the Harrower home. Little Iain was still small and weak – he suffered from postnatal jaundice – and this, together with the stress of travel, contributed to a worrying pallor.

Family life in Cambridge

Searching the advertisements, and rejecting the help of estate agents, we discovered a little semidetached house on the outskirts of Histon, four miles from the centre of Cambridge. The cost of the house, demanding our first mortgage, was £2000. There was a small front lawn but a longer back garden extended down to fields of strawberries. The discovery that they were owned by Chivers, the jam manufacturers, reminded me of the success of my grandfather, Herbert Guy Welchman, in his Norfolk fruit farming earlier in the century (p.5). The ground floor included a modest lounge with a coal fire, facing the back garden, a front dining room, and a small kitchen with a gas cooker. There was no central heating, so in the winter we warmed the house with a blue-flame paraffin heater that we carried from room to room and placed in the bathroom or at the bottom of the staircase. It was only after two months that we discovered that we were correct to suspect the frankness of the previous owners: sewage began to appear at a drain near the kitchen door. The system had been described as 'modern', but every few months the local authority had to empty the cesspit!

Our immediate neighbours were a Mr and Mrs Watts, pleasant and easy people who became good friends. They had learned how to deal with the sewage system: every few weeks, Mr Watts would appear at night with a bucket, with which he would pour the contents of the cesspit over his flourishing vegetable garden. He was a

Figure 10.1 *Helen in 1953 holding Iain, with Rosalind beside her. Standing behind are the daughters of our neighbours, the Watts.*

carpenter and joiner and made a little wheelbarrow for Iain and a dolls' cot for Rosalind, now given to her own grandchildren. The Watts had two young daughters, Joyce and Jean. As the months passed, little Rosalind grew apace and her evident charm greatly appealed to the Watts (Figure 10.1). Mrs Watts would reach across the fence that divided the properties and lift Rosalind into her own garden, where all the children could play together.

My salary in the Army had risen to £1200 per annum. However, in Cambridge, it fell again to £600. As a result, our financial situation was not strong and Helen found that the £20 a month – all that we could allow for housekeeping – demanded considerable financial stringency. However, we were lucky to have a car and two bicycles. We had bought a capacious pram from the NAAFI[B] in Hamburg – it was delivered to us in England – and it was with this fine vehicle that we took the children along the paths to the shops in Histon and for country walks

Cambridge pathology

Famed for its teaching and research in pathology since the time of Charles Smart Roy and German Sims Woodhead, the Medical

School of the University of Cambridge was a magnet for those who sought skilled teaching and training.[C] By 1952, the new National Health Service, the NHS, was well established. Teaching hospitals such as Addenbrooke's enjoyed high prestige. The laboratories that provided a diagnostic service to the hospital collaborated very closely with the medical departments of the University, so that those of us holding junior appointments benefited from the experience of working with both NHS and academic colleagues.

Our destinies were presided over by the benign, jovial but far-sighted and discriminating Professor Henry Roy Dean, who I remembered well from my student days (p.56). In addition to organizing the teaching of pathology to medical and non-medical undergraduates (p.57), Dean exerted great influence over the conduct and efficiency of the diagnostic work of the laboratories of Addenbrooke's Hospital. He extended the reputation of his already prestigious institution by recruiting scientists from a wide variety of fields.

The hospital laboratories were in four sections, each with its own dedicated space, equipment and staff. They were Morbid (pathological) Anatomy, Microbiology, Clinical Chemistry and Haematology. Each section was under the direction of a consultant who held both a NHS appointment and an honorary University title. Arthur Max Barrett[D] (p.116) was University Morbid Anatomist, M. H. Gleeson White[E] University Bacteriologist, N. R. Laurie[F] University Clinical Chemist and John Marks[G] University Haematologist. They were our teachers.

I was one of six Junior Assistant Clinical Pathologists, allocated to the four principal subjects.[H] Our appointments were for two years, and every six months we moved to a new section. At the end of my first year, two of my colleagues left and we were joined by Austin Gresham[I] and John Rack.[J] Our duties were undertaken partly in the laboratories of Addenbrooke's Hospital, partly in the University Department of Pathology. Those in the former location included Clinical Chemistry, Haematology and Microbiology. Our time in Pathological Anatomy was divided between the University Department and the mortuary that adjoined the main hospital block.

Among the technical staff who played a large part in our training in diagnostic technology were Percy Powells and a younger assistant, Peter Haslam. Percy reminded me of some of the sergeants I had encountered in my years with the Army. He was often the object of some amusement since one of his tasks was to supervise the collection of specimens of semen from patients who were under investigation for infertility. Percy and the patient would disappear mysteriously into a small side-room, whence the patient would emerge triumphant some time later. Peter spent much of his time telling us of his love-life – he married after I had left.

My work began in **Microbiology**. My days started when I inspected the bacterial cultures set up the previous day. I then had to examine the many new specimens that had come overnight both from the Hospital and from medical practitioners in the district. I found it of absorbing interest, partly because I had some experience of epidemic infective disease in clinical practice (p.106) but also because it was an opportunity for learning the techniques that enabled modern treatment to be rapid and effective. There was a slight but real risk that the workbenches and our hands could bear the pathogenic bacteria with which we were working. Anticipating the days when outbreaks of methicillin-resistant *Staphylococcus aureus* (MRSA) would dominate discussions of hospital politics, it was decided one day to find whether any parts of the laboratory were contaminated. We took swabs from every part of the room – benches, floor, and windowsill – and from our hands and clothes. The benches and floors were clean and the only site found to be infected was the roller towel on which every staff member dried their hands after washing them on the way to lunch or tea!

In **Morbid Anatomy**, the day's autopsies, supervised by Dr Barrett, were central to our experience. He was meticulous and cautious, and little escaped his eagle eyes. Even at that time, there was particular concern about the unexplained deaths of infants, co-called 'cot deaths', particularly when they were recognized in the children of well-educated parents. It was occasionally necessary for some fatalities to be reported to HM Coroner. The legal complexity of certain cases called for a second opinion, and Home Office Pathologists, among them Keith Simpson, might be asked for their views. In one such case, the event was memorable because Dr Simpson brought with him not a portable tape recorder of the kind that was becoming commonplace but an elegant young blonde, his secretary, who stood unperturbed in the mortuary as Simpson dictated his notes.

In **Clinical Chemistry**, these were the days immediately before the introduction of the revolutionary 'autoanalyser' (p.137). Every test, for example of the concentration in the blood of glucose or of urea, was made by hand, a time-consuming task calling for the measurement of coloured reagents with the aid of glass tubes and vessels. Because the tests were slow, they were requested much less often than is the practice today and the numbers undertaken in laboratories as large as those of Addenbrooke's Hospital were small by modern criteria.

In **Haematology**, the tasks were time-consuming but physically undemanding. The common tests were blood counts, made by hand, using small glass pipettes and counting chambers that had changed little within living memory. Like measurements of chemical values, these procedures were soon to be superseded by automatic counting and measuring devices. In a small proportion of patients, hospital physicians requested the examination of bone marrow samples, taken by needle from the sternal bone.[K] In later years I encountered a case where the test had gone disastrously wrong. The 'puncture', a form of biopsy, had been left in the hands of an inexperienced House Physician. The needle had slipped over the edge of the sternal bone, penetrating the chest wall and the right atrium of the heart, which lay a short distance beneath the bone. Bleeding had taken place into the pericardial 'sac' that surrounded the heart, the return of blood to the heart had been prevented and the circulation obstructed. The patient, a young woman, died of heart failure.

From my earliest moments as a medical student, I instinctively sought explanations for the diseases I saw and reasons for the suffering that patients endured. In the army, hand infections among the soldiers, an epidemic of tonsillitis in an artillery regiment and a few cases of exceptional interest in civilian personnel or families were my only opportunities for research. In Addenbrooke's Hospital, chance led me to new and unexpected phenomena.

One of my tasks was to count the blood platelets in cancer patients being treated in the Department of Radiotherapy. I recorded the platelet numbers in 100 of Professor Mitchell's cases. I was reminded of the behaviour of the cells in a patient with leukaemia whose white blood cell count had fallen as a result of developing bacterial pneumonia (p.83). My interest in blood platelets formed the basis of investigations of rheumatoid arthritis that I followed when I moved to Edinburgh in 1954 (p.121).

It fell to me one day to conduct an autopsy on a young mother who had successfully given birth to a child but had died suddenly in the course of a second pregnancy. Throughout her life, she had had an unusual blue tinge to her skin: she had been what is often termed a 'blue baby'. The cause of her death we found to be pulmonary embolism – a thrombus (a 'blood clot') had lodged in her pulmonary artery. But we were astonished to discover that the principal vein carrying blood from the body back to the lungs, the inferior vena cava, drained not into the right atrium but into the left[L] (Figure 10.2).

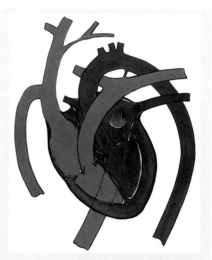

Figure 10.2 *Diagram showing the inferior vena cava draining into the left atrium.*

My observations of the anomalous inferior vena cava, confirmed by Dr A. M. Barrett, were of such rarity[L] that I was asked by the senior consultant cardiologist, Dr Leslie Cole, to describe the case to a meeting in Cambridge of the British Cardiac Society. This was to be a new experience, the first opportunity I had had of speaking to an internationally renowned body. I decided to take the plunge and follow an unwritten law of the Pathological Society of Great Britain and Ireland:[M] 'No paper may be read.' In other words, the speaker must not use notes or a script and must speak unaided. I set to work at once. The script was written quickly. But then, during each coffee and tea break, I escaped to a large cupboard where I could rehearse my talk without disturbing anyone else. There was a risk that, if I were overheard, talking to myself, I might be regarded as 'of unsound mind'. But I took this risk. The day of the meeting came. The lantern slides were ready, the talk went smoothly and, in the course of time, my observations were published.[2]

Soon afterwards, we decided to offer the case to the Pathological Society itself. This time the presentation was to be a 'poster', a display of text and illustrations mounted on large cards so that they could be easily seen. It was my introduction to meetings of the Society. The winter meeting was in Birmingham and wartime conditions still prevailed. I was not in a position to pay for hotel accommodation, so, together with other young trainees, I was given a bed in a Nissan hut, a temporary hutted building of a kind still widely used during these postwar years. Each morning, we made our way through the wintry snow to the lecture theatres and halls where the Society talks and posters were publicized, careful to make ourselves known to our professors and, in particular, to the members of the Society Committee.

The routine tasks of the laboratory were occasionally interrupted by sudden, unexpected events. In 1953, a patient with an infective arterial aneurysm of the leg proved to be the source of the bacterium *Salmonella enteriditis* that led to a small epidemic and the closure of an entire surgical ward. In quite separate incidents, I encountered two fatal cases of enterocolitis in orthopaedic patients treated with the new 'broad-spectrum' antibiotics aureomycin (chlortetracycline) and chloramphenicol. The intestinal infections were attributable to antibiotic-resistant staphylococci that had 'overgrown' the normal gut flora. My report[3] was one of the first in a field that now confronts the problems of MRSA and the challenge of *Clostridium difficile*.

Our duties included responsibility for night calls. 'On call', we had our evening meal in the hospital and slept in a room that had the benefit of a television set. Here, between moments of activities that could be frenetic, programmes such as boxing matches, test match cricket and interviews could be seen in relative comfort. It was in this way that I saw Dick Turpin boxing his way to a championship, Brown captaining an English eleven against the Australians and John Freeman conducting his notorious *Face to Face* exchanges with characters as diverse as John Reith, Gilbert Harding and Tony Hancock. The nocturnal work included preparing blood for transfusion by cross-matching.

The blood of an individual known to be group A might be selected as a suitable source for donation to a surgical patient due for operation the following morning. The surgical patient was known also to be of group A, but it was still an essential matter of safety to test the compatibility of donor and recipient.

Tony Ackerley was particularly careful, even obsessive, in this work. Sitting at supper in the hospital dining room, he would suddenly say: 'I have just cross-matched a number of bloods but I can't be certain in my own mind that I did the tests accurately.' He would leave the table, return to the laboratory, and repeat the whole of his earlier work. We did not know at the time that another colleague had developed an addiction. He would sit alone in the Clinical Chemistry laboratory, sniffing ether, only to stagger out at 10 o'clock in the morning asking 'Is it time for breakfast?' One day, he did not emerge and was found dead at the bench.

Free time

The laboratory hours were demanding, but life in Cambridge offered many attractions. The countryside was flat, travel by bicycle easy, so that a solitary journey into and out from the city was swift and cheap. When time permitted, I used my cycle to return home for lunch. On Friday evenings, the day's work ended, it was the Junior Assistants' custom to make their way to a public house. Faced with a four-mile cycle ride home, I usually confined myself to half a pint of 'best brew'. For the family, our trusty old Volkswagen proved invaluable in spite of its ancient cable brakes. However, one afternoon, a little dog ran out in front of my car in a narrow Cambridge street and I could not avoid the poor animal. A wrathful owner shouted abuse at me: his little friend was not killed, but the car was bruised.

On social occasions and holidays, we journeyed to Church Farm, Stapleford, near Leighton Buzzard, to visit Florence and John Pike (p.93), and to Somerset. Scotland was our destination for summer vacations. Motorways were not yet commonplace, so in the autumn of 1953 we travelled northwards on the A1, via Scotch Corner. We stopped in Edinburgh before continuing on to the Moray Firth, where we stayed in Rosemarkie and visited Lossiemouth, a favourite family haunt in the 1930s (p.19). To the west, we passed through St Fillans, a holiday resort for Helen's family, and Lochearnhead (Figure 10.3), and on one occasion listened to the Boat Race while sitting on the slopes of Ben Cruachan.

There were occasional visitors to Histon. They included my mother; Helen's parents, Emily and Davie Harrower; Helen's cousin Venice and her introspective husband Alistair Lamb; Chris Cummins (pp.90, 285); and Richard Spencer and his mother. So two happy years passed in the environs of one of Europe's most prestigious academic centres. There were special occasions, among them 30th May 1953, my birthday, when we saw the startling placard 'Everest Conquered!' Hillary and Tensing had become the first to reach the summit of the world's highest mountain. Only two days later, on 2nd June, we went to the Watts' house to see the Queen's Coronation – we could not yet afford television ourselves!

Figure 10.3 *A holiday view of Gairloch in the Scottish Highlands.*

Some years later, an unexpected problem arose in relation to Helen's elderly aunt Florence. She had married Alan Bicknell, MC. It transpired that he had hopes of inheriting her money and estate. Florence was doubly misguided. Under the influence of Bicknell, she employed a scheming Ivor Meredith as an 'adviser' and a mischievous and untruthful chauffeur, Dixon, who abused her trust in the care and use of her Bentley car. Ivor had claimed to be a graduate of the University of Cambridge and to have a DPhil degree in Forensic Science from the University of Sussex. He used his position to ingratiate himself with the elderly Florence and even managed to have his name incorporated into her will. But then John Pike and I found that there was neither evidence of an Ivor Meredith as a Cambridge graduate nor any record that the University of Sussex had awarded a DPhil to an individual of that name. Soon afterwards, Alan Bicknell died. Florence's executors included a Manager of Barclay's bank. With his aid, Meredith and Dixon were dismissed and Florence was enabled to live in the company of her sister Emily, in relative peace, until her death in March 1979.

As part of my military obligations, I was twice called back to the army for annual training. On the first of these occasions, an opinionated army instructor challenged our group to prepare plans for the medical support for a European invasion! The response, not surprisingly, was guarded. But I was determined to impale him with his own weapon and spent an entire weekend in Cambridge

Figure 10.4 *The Fellows' Garden, Clare College, Cambridge.*

preparing a detailed proposal that occupied the whole hour of his next class at Crookham. On my second annual exercise, my posting was to a parachute regiment that was training on Dartmoor, where an atomic bomb was supposed to have been dropped. The paratroop medical officers, all in red berets, were the most welcoming of hosts – unlike their senior colleagues, they generously overlooked my conventional flat army cap. Between days spent camped on the moors, shaving each morning in a mountain stream, they entertained me to tea in Tavistock and Dulverton. The 'Red Berets' clearly enjoyed mess games as much as their opposite numbers in the Rhine Army, so that it was little surprise one evening at a mess dinner to recognize General 'Boy' Browning, Daphne du Maurier's husband, presiding over a form of 'room rugby'. To readers of *Rebecca*[4] this was not an experience to be forgotten.

And so the short years in Cambridge passed quickly by. There were occasional formal dinners in Clare College (Figure 10.4), but, for the most part, our time and thoughts in Cambridge were directed to the welfare and education of the children. Blissfully unaware of the challenges posed by the outside world and not yet of school age, they were passive partners in our next adventure, a return to 'Auld Reekie'.

CHAPTER 11

Rheumatism research

By the Water of Leith

The hands are a sort of feet that serve us
in our passage towards heaven, curiously
distinguished into joints and fingers

Thomas Traherne[1]

S pinning webs and catching insects, spiders work wonders with their eight legs, each with six joints! Imagine osteoarthritis in forty-eight knees! I would soon have the chance of studying the human disease.

When my appointment in Cambridge ended in the autumn of 1954, the prospects of a career in internal medicine were still attractive, although my love for pathology remained strong. I had no wish to be a surgeon. Money was increasingly important, but to gain a consultant position in medicine demanded more years of training. I was fortunate to have the diploma of the Edinburgh MRCP (p.90) but I suspected I would have to obtain a doctorate (MD) if success was to be likely.[A]

In every field of medicine, specialization was now frequent. Should I continue with respiratory disease? There was a growing trend for trainees to concentrate on increasingly narrow fields with the aim of becoming, for example, nephrologists, cardiologists, neurologists or rheumatologists. In Addenbrooke's Hospital, I had been attracted to cardiology, the diagnosis and treatment of diseases of the heart and blood vessels. I learnt of a Senior House Officer post in this field offered by the Postgraduate Medical School at Hammersmith and carrying a slightly larger salary than I had received in Cambridge.[B] However, Helen and I liked the idea of returning to Scotland and my association with the Edinburgh Medical School remained strong.

Then, not for the last time, Fate stepped in! A Research Fellowship in the Rheumatic Diseases Unit, the RDU, of the Northern General Hospital, Edinburgh was advertised. The position was linked to the Medical School Department of Pathology so that the post would ensure continued training in the same field in which I had been

Chapter summary
- **Another new home**
- **The Rheumatic Diseases Unit**
- **The University Department of Pathology**
- **Research**
- **Escaping to the North, the Borders and Northumberland**
- **University Lecturer**

working for the previous two years. I applied and, to our delight and my real surprise, was appointed.

Another new home

Moving back to Edinburgh in 1954, with little money, we were fortunate to find a stone-built corner house at 21 Craigcrook Road. Facing a park, it had been constructed for £800 in 1905 as a manse for St Columba's Church, Blackhall; we purchased it for nearly five times as much! The large rectangular entrance (Figure 11.1) with its windowed sides and heavy oak door gave a feeling of peace and stability. Particularly in autumn, the tall trees and the quickly growing hedge threw long shadows across the little front garden.

Our new home was near the Queensferry Road shops, a bank, a garage and a bus service that took us easily to Princes Street. Groceries were delivered from a store at the end of the park. Towards the east, the road carried us to Barnton, to the beach and to the public golf course at Silverknowes. In wintertime, snow rarely fell, but the dark Scottish months of November and December were plagued by damp mists swirling in from the sea and by bleak winds. When spring came, the garden was brightened by daffodils springing up in the thin Edinburgh light, hinting at the turn of the year.

Rosalind and Iain were approaching school age. She was accepted by the Junior Department of St George's School for Girls, less than a mile from our new home. After a year at Buckingham House

Figure 11.1 *The doorway at 21 Craigcrook Road, with Marjorie Gardner (left) and Emily Harrower.*

kindergarten, Iain moved to the preparatory department of the prestigious Edinburgh Academy.

With a steadily increasing number of new friends and many of Helen's family within easy distance, there were many social occasions. Guy Fawkes's night was celebrated, but on one occasion disaster struck! Together with neighbours, I had arranged a firework display in our garden, but, while lighting a fuse, boxes containing all the other fireworks caught fire and exploded. Smoke filled the air as rockets hurtled across nearby streets. Our friends were understandably angry! Retiring into the house, I escaped into *Journey into Space* on the radio. On Christmas Day, visiting scientists were among those welcomed to lunch.

We resumed close contacts with Helen's family in Bo'ness (Figure 11.2). Although a regular bus service was valuable, at the weekends we travelled in our trusty Volkswagen 'beetle'. However, the old-fashioned mechanics and bodywork of Hitler's 'People's Car' were failing, so I bought a new model. Once again, our favourite German transport, this time with golden metallic paint, served us well and it was not until we returned from America in 1959 that we exchanged it for a capacious, dark red Morris Oxford saloon.

Figure 11.2 *D. B. (Davie) and Emily Harrower. Helen holds young Philip. Iain (left) and Rosalind Gardner are standing (at front).*

The Rheumatic Diseases Unit

I plunged into a new medical world. I was reminded that the ancient word 'rheumatism', still in universal use, came from the Old French *reume*, 'a watery discharge'. The 'rheumatic' diseases were the disorders of the musculoskeletal system: the muscles, tendons, ligaments, bones and joints. In hospital practice, they were distinguished from 'orthopaedic' diseases, conditions like fractures and dislocations, treated by an increasingly specialized class of surgeon.

At Ferry Road, the RDU was directed by Professor John James Reid (Ian) Duthie,[C] a fearless and critical clinician and investigator. I felt reasonably sure that time with him would not be wasted. Duthie's Unit comprised two wards and soon came to have laboratories and offices constructed through the generosity of the Oliver Bird Fund of the Nuffield Foundation. The Unit was opened in 1955 (Figure 11.3). The laboratories – one for biochemistry, another for immunology and microscopy – were small but well equipped. There was a staff room with a modest library and a growing display in glass jars of specimens of diseased joints. There were no facilities for tissue (histological) studies, but Duthie's plan, based on that of Professor J. Kellgren of Manchester, was to collaborate with the University Department of Pathology, and it was my responsibility to develop this part of his programme and to review any relevant biopsy and autopsy studies. Although the majority of the paraffin sections that formed the basis of virtually all my research on biopsies were prepared in the Teviot Place building of the Medical School, some were made in the Pathology laboratories of the Royal Infirmary of Edinburgh, the RIE, where Dr Ogilvie (p.66) still preferred to work, and I spent a proportion of my time there.

Duthie's co-workers were Jack Sinclair, Rowland Alexander,[D] Linda Roy and John McCormick, who moved later to join the Medical Research Council, the MRC, at Taplow. Jack had graduated both in Dentistry and in Medicine. Dr Roy and her husband were biochemists. Rowland was Duthie's clinical first assistant, a physician and laboratory scientist with an excellent understanding of immunology who had already set up a fluorescence microscope. Duthie also recruited two of my friends, John Richmond (Figure 11.4) (p.129) and Jacobus ('Jack') Potter, both outstanding graduates

Figure 11.3 *Helen Gardner on the occasion of the opening of the new Nuffield Rheumatic Diseases Unit at the Northern General Hospital, Edinburgh.*

of the Edinburgh Medical School class of 1948, and I worked closely with them. The work of the Unit would have been impossible without the dedicated labour of two remarkable ladies: Margaret Daniel (Chapter 9), who had come from Bangour Hospital to succeed Ms Bailey as Sister-in-Charge of the rheumatology wards and of the outpatient clinic, and Margaret McEwan, Duthie's loyal secretary.

A large part of the academic effort of Duthie's Unit was in the clinical field. He enjoyed the vigorous support of Professor L. S. P. Davidson (p.67), who was promoting similar approaches in other specialities at the Western General Hospital, the WGH. Duthie worked closely with his own staff, but, within the guidelines of his programme, each of us was given great freedom in the development of our own interests, often in collaboration with a laboratory colleague.

Figure 11.4 *Dr (later Professor) John Richmond.*

As part of his contribution to the Unit's investigations and using a typically direct approach, Duthie attempted to produce lesions in his own skin, in the skin of members of his staff, and in a few patients, by the injection of synovial fluid taken from the joints of patients with rheumatoid arthritis, working on the assumption that this common disease might be caused by a transmissible agent. The consequences were occasionally unfortunate: they included a small outbreak of infective hepatitis, the result of using fluid from a patient who had had this viral disease.

When Duthie and Linda Roy decided to inject themselves with the dye Evans blue in order to follow the passage of compounds through parts of the body known as 'the reticuloendothelial system', they could not have foreseen that their entire skin would remain blue–grey for months!

The University Department of Pathology

Much of my time was spent in the University Department of Pathology, which, like those of Anatomy, Physiology, Biochemistry, Forensic Medicine and Pharmacology, was still within the Turner Medical School building, opened in Teviot Place in 1880. To me, this magnificent complex with its staircases and doorways hidden mysteriously within massive stone walls, now recalls the mediaeval monastery depicted in Umberto Eco's *The Name of the Rose*.[2] The edifice housed the Faculty of Medicine office, a Senate chamber and the Erskine Medical Library. Behind the building was a brick boiler house with a tall chimney from which smoke poured and, next to it, a small animal house. The chimney had been a focus of interest in the 1920s when the BBC began wireless (radio) transmission in Scotland and used it to support an aerial, with the result that staff within the Turner building, picking up a telephone, found that they could listen to live broadcasts! The Departments of Pathology and Microbiology were on the third and fourth floors, the upper floors reached by a central lift beside an internal staircase. On the ground floor were a lecture theatre and a workshop.

The Department was not in a good state. The University had recently appointed Professor George Lightbody Montgomery[E] to the prestigious Chair of Pathology, but he had not yet had time to effect the changes urgently needed to replace the outdated practices of Professor A. Murray Drennan, his conscientious predecessor (p.66). Undergraduate teaching occupied University medical staff for much of each week, but a large proportion of their time was necessarily devoted to surgical biopsy and to autopsy (necropsy). There was little evidence of contemporary research.

I began my investigations in the huge old 'Chemi' (Chemistry) Laboratory, where the cupboards still contained microscopic sections of whole lung lobes inscribed with the name of C. S. Roy who had moved from Edinburgh to be the first Cambridge Professor of Pathology in 1882. Sharing the ancient teak benches and glancing at me between the intervening shelves was James Park, a quiet and serious colleague who left in 1957 to settle in Nova Scotia. After some months, I was given working space in a corridor that lay between the room of my senior colleague, Dr Robertson Ogilivie (p.66), and an entrance to the lift. On the opposite side of a vestibule was a small room occupied by Bruce Cruickshank,[F] a University Lecturer in Pathology. Some years later, when he moved to Glasgow, I inherited his room.

I gained an early idea of the barriers to research in Edinburgh when I investigated the diagnostic laboratory on the third floor of the Turner building. This large room, where 12 or more technicians laboured at the same teak benches enjoyed at the turn of the century, was devoted to the meticulous preparation of the tissue sections central to pathological diagnosis. There was no other provision for contemporary research and the only apparatus that could be interpreted as 'investigative' as opposed to 'diagnostic' was a single, old-fashioned balance for weighing chemicals and small specimens. The sensitivity of this ancient instrument was no more than ± 0.5 g, one-sixtieth of an ounce. There was a desperate shortage of glassware and, in the entire laboratory, there were only two glass pipettes, one of which was cracked! Plastic pipettes had not yet come into use.

The duties of the technical staff centred on hospital diagnosis. They were led by James Masson, who had come from Bangour Hospital. He was succeeded by James Waugh. Both were long-serving and of great experience in the methods of classical pathological histology, but quite unfamiliar with contemporary methods of investigation: neither had worked in the quickly growing fields of electron microscopy or histochemistry, nor did they have experience of immunological techniques. However, they were loyally supported by a young Elizabeth Ramage, who became my technician, and by James Bathgate (p.328), whose responsibility lay in the teaching classrooms and museum collections.

My programme placed an additional burden not only on the laboratory staff but also on the Department of Medical Photography. I came to know a remarkable photographer, Thomas Cairns Dodds[G,3] (Figure 11.5). Central to the work of the Department of Medical Illustration was an optical bench, differing little from the device used by the eminent German pathologist Aschoff in 1900 (Figure 11.6). With this equipment Dodds produced the superb colour photographs that illustrated the three editions of our *Human Histology*. Heavy glass slides called for huge projectors in which a beam of light came from an enormous arc lamp of the kind still in use in Belfast in 1971 (p.195): 35 mm photography and the compact, lightweight glass slides to which it gave birth, was in its infancy.

If I was fortunate enough to gain results from experiments sufficiently good to be published, why not use the same material to form part of a thesis? Within a few weeks of beginning my research fellowship, I approached the University and applied to be registered

Figure 11.5 *Thomas Cairns Dodds, Director of the Photographic Unit of the Department of Pathology.*

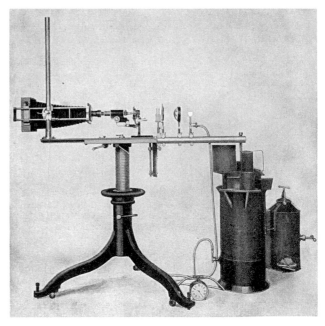

Figure 11.6 *A microscope from the time of Ludwig Aschoff (ca 1900). The optical bench and plate camera used by T. C. Dodds resembled this much older design.*

as a PhD student. The value of a PhD in medical practice was slight. However, in academic circles, a thesis could be useful and I decided that the additional work would be worthwhile. Professor Douglas Collins of Sheffield,[H] the author of a standard work on the pathology of the rheumatic diseases,[4] agreed to be my external assessor.

The early days of my PhD studentship were not without incident! Professor Montgomery had assumed his Chair at precisely the moment at which I took up my new position. Neither of us knew anything of the other, but the fact that I had been appointed without his explicit knowledge, that I came from the South and that my principle supporter was an Aberdonian, Duthie, were among factors that appeared to influence him. Within three months of my becoming a PhD student, Montgomery called me to his room and said: 'You'll have to go.' I enquired: 'Where to?' He said: 'I haven't room for you in this Department. Go down the road, wherever you like.' I went to see the Secretary of the University, who said: 'Montgomery can't do that. You are a PhD student in his Department and he must keep you there.' I stayed.

Research

I was advised to call on Bruce Cruickshank after being told that he had a strong interest in musculoskeletal diseases and that he had completed a PhD thesis on the pathological changes in the disabling condition of ankylosing spondylitis. It was a time when the painful inflammation of spondylitic spinal joints was still being treated by radiotherapy, before the risk of leukaemia had been appreciated. I explained to him that I had joined Duthie's research group and hoped to develop methods for the experimental study of arthritis. Bruce was not encouraging. He said in his amiable but blunt way: 'Well, you better get on and do it!' I added that my contributions would be to test rheumatoid synovial fluid by injection into the skin and joints of guinea pigs and to attempt to produce arthritis experimentally in animals. I continued the search for an animal model of arthritis for some years, and later, in London (p.179), I tested caragheenin[1] and other preparations as agents that might provoke synovial inflammation. Bruce's curt approach masked the conviviality of the Cruickshanks' evening parties, where guests had quotations pinned to their backs, a prize awarded when the author's name was guessed correctly.

It was against this background that my research advanced. It was not my immediate responsibility to diagnose the samples of tissue taken by Duthie and his surgical associates from the tissues of patients in the RDU: this task was in the hands of the laboratories of the WGH. However, I was given access to these tissues. Similar guidelines applied to the examination of the tissues from patients who had died in the care of the RDU. To take part in the staff autopsy rota in this way demanded an intimate understanding of the way in which this part of the hospital service operated (Chapter 13). Autopsies on patients with rheumatoid arthritis soon became my special concern, and I began the systematic collection of microscopic specimens from all patients with this disease coming to autopsy at the WGH, the RIE and hospitals ranging from Bangour in the west to East Fortune in the east.[5, 6]

One of our particular interests was the anaemia that often accompanies chronic rheumatoid arthritis. This blood disorder differs from the common iron-deficiency anaemia that results from inadequate dietary iron or excessive blood loss. John Richmond and I confirmed that, in patients with rheumatoid arthritis, iron is present in at least normal amounts in the bone marrow but is not used effectively to make new red blood cells.[7-9] I reported these results to the Pathological Society in Manchester in 1956; it was the 50th anniversary meeting of the Society (p.116). Travelling by train, I stayed with my Cambridge friend, John Rack (p.114).

Within a year, an unexpected report of a strange reaction to the drug hydralazine caught my attention.[10] The compound had been introduced in the United States for the treatment of raised blood pressure. In some patients, the response caused a syndrome with features of systemic lupus erythematosus, SLE, an uncommon disorder with some similarities to rheumatoid arthritis. I wondered: could this reaction be reproduced experimentally and, if so, how?' My first thought was to test the drug in animals. I approached Professor J. R. Learmonth (p.67), who still directed the Wilkie Research Laboratories. He quickly arranged for me to have access to 10 dogs. The treated animals became unwell but did not develop the changes of SLE or the formation in their blood of diagnostic LE cells. I described the results to an Edinburgh meeting of the Heberden Society,[11] but wondered whether, to reproduce the syndrome fully, it might be necessary to test the drug in animals with raised blood pressure.[12, 13]. The experiments that followed changed the whole direction of my subsequent research (p.137).

Every Wednesday afternoon, vigorous round table meetings were held in the Unit library. Progress reports were demanded and each of us, from the most senior consultant to the youngest research assistant, was required to defend their views in the face of Duthie's searching criticism. On the table in front of him lay a box of Swan Vesta matches, a battered pipe and an ounce of Erinmore tobacco. His pipe was filled and refilled but seldom smoked, but many matches were struck, the number reflecting the intensity of the debate! There was no respect for equivocation and speech was freely interspersed with expletives. On one occasion, a whole lunch hour was lost as Jack Potter and I, watched in silence by a more restrained John Richmond, argued with Ian over the 13th draft of a scientific paper.

At postgraduate level, Pathology Department staff meetings at Teviot Place offered opportunities for the discussion of interesting cases and research results. Once each term, these meetings were held in the Royal College of Surgeons of Edinburgh in Nicolson Street, the RCSEd (Chapter 23). Occasional meetings also took place in the little lecture theatre of the Royal Edinburgh Hospital for

Sick Children under the inspired authority of Agnes MacGregor.[J] During these years, visits to my former tutor E. T. C. Spooner, now in London, to Glasgow and to Professor Sheehan in Liverpool were interspersed with meetings of some of the Societies that I had joined: the Heberden, the Pathological Society, the Scottish Society for Experimental Medicine and the Association of Clinical Pathologists.

Escaping to the North, the Borders and Northumberland

Our second son, Philip (p.249), was born in Edinburgh on 15th January 1957 in the Chalmers Hospital. Helen and Rosalind, his sister, now six years old, cared for him devotedly. When holiday times came, we continued to enjoy visits to our old haunts in Nairn, Elgin and nearby areas. In Lossiemouth, Helen, Rosalind, Philip and I celebrated Iain's fifth birthday, 8th September, at Laverock Bank Hotel where we had been in 1939 (Figures 11.7 and 11.8).

But then, during the years from 1954 to 1958, we came to know and love the Scottish Borders. Our new neighbours on the opposite corner of Craigcrook Road, Edinburgh, were Helen and Finlay Miller. Finlay Miller's daughter by an earlier marriage, Marjorie, lived with them. Helen Miller and Finlay had a young son, Peter, whose behaviour caused them concern. They decided that he might benefit from time in the countryside and bought a little property

Figure 11.7 *Iain Gardner celebrating his fifth birthday on the beach at Lossiemouth, 1957.*

Figure 11.8 *Rosalind Gardner at Lossiemouth, 1957.*

in Peebles, an ancient Royal Burgh 22 miles south of Edinburgh. The cottage, *Tanta*, had been built during the Second World War to house Land Girls and lay on farmland opposite the steep, wooded hill that had been the old Peebles Golf Course. Some years later, with Enid Blyton's tales in mind, Philip recalled the phrase 'It isn't very good in the dark, dark wood' as he struggled with his little friend Michael up the hill. These words stayed in the family and often came to mind in later years. *Tanta* was, in fact, no more than a tin hut, but it had been lined with wood and had a kitchen and several simple rooms that could be used for spring and summer holidays. The Millers allowed us to rent it from them.

We began to discover the geography of the town and of the river Tweed and to explore the beautiful Borders countryside (Figure 11.9). However, our voices betrayed us: we were *Stooriefits*, 'foreigners', distinguished from native Peebleians, who, we discovered, were *Gutterbluids*. A pathway led down from *Tanta* to the town centre and, in the mornings, walking down with the children, we were fascinated by the wealth of shops, the cinema, the many churches and the Town Hall. One of the lanes leading from the High Street towards the river bore a wall plaque recording the capture in 1346 of King David II.

Walking along the paths that lined each side of the salmon-rich river Tweed, it was a short step to Neidpath Castle, the summit of which offered a glorious view down the valley. The Cuddy, as Eddlestone Water is named, is a tributary of the Tweed. It runs through the town from the north, and in winter times its swollen waters contribute to the joys of the gulls and storks as they hunt for food. But to local people, the rugby and football fields were often of more concern than the river banks, and, each year, local matches in Peebles and the Melrose 'Sevens' drew us to these grounds. Beyond Peebles, we often visited the magnificent gardens of Dawyck, part of the Royal Botanic Gardens, Edinburgh. Dawyck was a favourite venue for family visitors and for others who came from as far away as Japan (Chapter 16). Crossing the Border hills to St Mary's Loch, we watched yachting and water skiing. Travelling the longer route from Moffat, w enjoyed the sight of the Devil's Beef Tub. For more mundane needs, the shops and stores of Galashiels were within a few miles and the journey through Clovenfords invariably took our minds back to Walter Scott, whose Abbotsford estate lay within a comparatively short distance.

The Scottish Borders had long been a rich source of literary treasures. I had read John Buchan's *The Thirty-Nine Steps*[14] and *Greenmantle*[15] while at Loretto. A taste for Walter Scott's tales, whose volumes lined the family bookshelves in Brighton and Bo'ness, came later when time allowed me to move from *Guy Mannering*[16] to *The Surgeon's Daughter*,[17] which tells us much of the medical history of earlier centuries. In this story of the East India Company, the surgeon apothecary, Mr Gideon Gray, rides off on horseback into the dark night to attend a patient with a broken leg. His exploits

Figure 11.9 *Margaret Daniel and Helen Gardner on a visit to* Tanta *cottage, Peebles.*

were recalled by the memoirs[18] of the famous Peebles practitioner Dr Clement Bryce Gunn,[K] granted the Freedom of the Royal Borough in 1922 at the moment this honour was bestowed on Field Marshall Earl Haig. Dr Gunn wrote of how an anxious patient came to his house, *Lindores*, during the night and tried to attract his attention. Gunn had just installed a voice tube so that a patient could speak directly to him without coming into the house. Unfortunately, the caller could not use the tube and Gunn had to shout to him through the bedroom window! Fifty years later, stones were thrown at our bedroom window in Louth for much the same reason (p94).

During our subsequent times in London, Manchester and Belfast, Helen and I often journeyed back to Peebles, staying not in *Tanta* but in Venlaw Castle Hotel (Figure 11.10) or, south of the river, in Kingsmuir Hotel. We had heard of Venlaw through Helen's parents who had first stayed there in 1947 and had exclaimed 'We have been so lucky! We have found a wonderful hotel which gives us a salmon lunch, afternoon tea and grouse or pheasant for dinner!' The 1780s building retained its old style of room, with a magnificent grand piano in a lounge soon to be dedicated to television. In the dining room, the waitress sent orders to the cook by 'dumb waiter'. The call 'twa troot!' to the kitchen in the basement meant that the new guests wanted two trout! When it came to paying the hotel account at the end of our stay, the kindly owner, Alistair Cumming, was inclined to say: 'Now, I don't think you enjoyed the wine on Wednesday evening, so I won't charge you for that!'

Figure 11.10 *Venlaw Castle Hotel, Peebles (by permission of the Hotel Manager).*

We were in Venlaw on the day in 1979 when the assassination of Lord Louis Mountbatten by the Irish Republican Army, the IRA, was announced.

Kingsmuir Hotel brought its own cluster of travellers' tales! When we first enjoyed the hotel's amenities, we met the owners, Norman Kerr and his wife, who had recently moved from the Dilkusha Hotel. We particularly enjoyed the service of the barman, Keith. On our first visit after the Kerr's retirement, the new owner, a fierce, bearded man, met us in the hall and shouted: 'What do you want?' We replied that we had booked accommodation. It transpired that he had been an electron microscope technician in Germany and was accompanied by his German wife, who, we soon learnt, was an excellent cook in a Teutonic tradition. Before long, this strange couple retreated to the Highlands of Scotland and were succeeded by Mr Burn, an accountant more at home with taxation tables than with dining room practices. He became a good friend not only of our family but, later, of the Eastgate Theatre in Peebles, which he advised financially. For a number of years, in a narrow corridor behind his dining room, I had my eyes on a plaster cast of the death mask of Mary Queen of Scots that, I thought, could serve as a memento of the Hotel. And so the mask is now in the Museum of the RCSEd (Chapter 23)!

Within a mile of Kingsmuir Hotel were Kailzie Gardens,[L] where the restaurant was one of our favourite venues. Golf was a particular interest in Peebles and the public course allowed a 'round' for as little as two shillings. We were reminded that golf and football had been banned by Royal decree in 1457 when King James II called on all able-bodied men to practise archery, not games. My introduction to communal golf came when it was announced that the annual match between the University Departments of Pathology and Anatomy would take place at Gullane. The teams, led by the respective Professors, George Romanes, anatomist, and George Lightbody Montgomery, pathologist, were formed of six members of staff from each discipline. We, the Pathologists, were aware that some of the demonstrators teaching Anatomy were young surgeons supplementing their salaries by earning a little money from the University and that, 'coincidentally', a proportion of these surgeons had 'scratch' golf handicaps! In one game, I was paired against Iain Kirkland (p.321), who won the first 10 holes! Sinking his last putt, he remarked: 'Now we can relax!' However, the matches in this annual event were always played in good spirit, partly because we younger members of staff knew that the Professors would pay for the 'high tea' following the games. It was at this time that I realized that I must replace my old family golf clubs, some with wooden shafts, with a new set. The cost was staggering! A complete set of Bobby Locke clubs, with ivory inlays on the heads of the 'woods', set me back £38! It was such a large sum that, for the first time in my life, I had recourse to 'hire purchase'.

Among our closest friends during these years were Joan and Bill Hunt.[M] The first time I saw Bill was during a meeting of the Department held in the RCSEd. A talk was in progress when a small, rear door opened and a tall, elegant, bearded figure came in with Professor G. L. Montgomery. We assumed the visitor to be a distinguished foreign scientist, but it was Dr Wilfrid Estridge Hunt, who had come to Edinburgh after applying for a vacant lectureship. It was not long before Helen became friends with Joan Hunt, and we soon met their children. It was at this time that we also came to know Diana and Angus Erskine Stuart.[N] Angus, a Glasgow graduate, had joined the Edinburgh Department in 1955 and we became close friends.

University Lecturer

With the advantage of working in both the Departments of Rheumatology and of Pathology of the Edinburgh Medical School, I was hopeful that an application for a vacant Lectureship had a chance of success. And so it proved. I was appointed to a University Lectureship in Pathology in 1956. My new post, a teaching appointment, carried with it direct responsibility for a share of the hospital laboratory diagnostic work. This was technically indistinguishable from the practices I had followed during my Research Fellowship, but now I joined the other teaching staff of the University department, who formed a duty rota.

Working long hours on my PhD thesis at home each evening and at weekends, I found that half an hour's walk at 10.30 every night made writing easier. But the weekends were times for family gatherings, and on Sundays we journeyed to Bo'ness for lunch at Elmpark. By 1957, it was time to complete my thesis, typed in traditional style by Mrs Black, using a manual typewriter. Electric typewriters were coming into use, but their cost was still prohibitive. The difficulties with a conventional machine were obvious to any author: pages on which there was any form of mistake – whether a wrong word, a spelling error or even an incorrect punctuation mark – had to be retyped! The 300 completed pages of my thesis were carefully bound and sent to Sheffield.[19] It was with enormous relief that I learnt from the Dean's office in the Faculty of Medicine that Professor Collins had reported favourably on my work. I graduated in the summer only three months after the marriage of Helen's brother Gordon to Enid Brown.

Very much the same challenge arose in 1958. It was a time when the possibility had arisen of a period of research in a United States laboratory (Chapter 12). I knew that North American medical students graduated not with degrees such as MB, ChB, the qualification still adopted in Edinburgh, but as MD. I reasoned that it might be of value to fall into line with American custom if I was to work there and I decided to try to turn my most recent studies of hypertension into a thesis to be submitted quickly for the Edinburgh doctorate. Lamps filled with midnight oil were quickly relit and by April 1958 I was in time to submit three volumes, heavily illustrated in colour, to the Edinburgh Faculty of Medicine office.[20] At the summer graduation ceremony on 16th July 1958, I was pleased that my work had been regarded sufficiently well to be given two stars.

It was time for another move, and within a few weeks, as Chapter 12 explains, we were bound for North America.

CHAPTER 12

To the United States and Canada

On the banks of Lake Erie

To travel hopefully is a better thing than to
arrive, and the true success is to labour

Robert Louis Stevenson[1]

As Louis Pasteur said: 'Where observation is concerned, chance favours only the prepared mind.' We agreed that taking my studies to another country could help to 'prepare my mind' and might introduce me to new techniques and instruments, recalling the impact made by the telescope[2] and the microscope.[3]

I had had an invitation from G. C. McMillan to work at McGill University, Montreal. However, for research into the causes of raised blood pressure, my main interest in 1958, Cleveland, Ohio, stood out as a 'centre of excellence'. Pre-eminent was the laboratory of Harry Goldblatt[A] of the Beaumont Research Laboratories, Mount Sinai Hospital. I was aware that at the Veterans Administration Hospital in the same city, Leonard Skeggs had constructed an 'autoanalyser',[B] while Joseph R. Kahn pursued the pioneering work of Willem Kolff,[C] known for his wartime invention of an artificial kidney. I discovered that in the Western Reserve University (WRU)[D] Medical School, Simon Koletsky, Professor of Pathology and Associate Director, was investigating experimental hypertension, while in Physiology, George Sayers' group was studying aldosterone.

And so it was my good fortune that, early in 1958, the Chairman of the Institute of Pathology of the WRU School of Medicine, Alan Moritz,[E] visited Edinburgh. Moritz, Goldblatt's successor as Institute Director, suggested that I should come to Koletsky's laboratory. At once, I applied to the Nuffield Foundation, the Eli Lilley Foundation and the Medical Research Council for support. Eli Lilley were encouraging, but the $3000 Travelling Fellowship offered by Nuffield was more attractive. The question remained: would this grant be sufficient to support

Chapter summary
- Life in Cleveland
- The Medical School of Western Reserve University
- Boston and the Association of American Pathologists
- Vacationing in the USA
- Home again
- A return visit
- Canada once more

five of us – I could not leave my family in Scotland! Help came when Alan Moritz said that he could add $1500 for assistance with teaching, and I quickly accepted his offer. Visiting workers were granted a visa on condition that after returning to the United Kingdom, they did not come back to the United States within two years, a matter of no concern, since I had no plans to settle in North America.

To move to the United States, even for one year, posed a challenge. Fortunately, our agents found an American Air Force Master Sergeant seeking temporary accommodation and our house was leased to him. It was necessary to arrange a year's leave of absence from school for Rosalind, now aged seven years, and for Iain, who was six, and to ensure that they would be accepted by schools in the United States. Little Philip was not yet of school age. The US Consul arranged visas for us, while Nuffield applied for an allocation of $12 per day and agreed to cover the cost of our travel within America. I was allowed to carry travellers' cheques, £10 in Sterling notes and $200 in US notes.

Through Wakefield Fortune, a travel company, we reserved passages on a ship of the Hamburg Atlantic Line, the SS *Hanseatic*, formerly the *Empress of Scotland*! The ship was to sail from Southampton on 4th September 1958.

Armed with rail tickets costing £4.3s.6d (£4.18 in decimal currency), we arrived at Waverley Station late on 3rd September, surprised but delighted to find Margaret Daniel, who, together with Helen's mother and father, had come to see us off. We realized that this was only the start of a challenging journey when we found ourselves in an old-fashioned four-berth compartment without reading lamps or water. Rosalind sat for a long time watching the passing lights, but the children eventually settled for a long but disturbed night. We were relieved to reach King's Cross Station shortly before 7 am, delighted to be met by our friends, Silvia and Fred Dische (p.114; note 10[H]), who devoted the whole of the day showing us parts of London with which we were not familiar before delivering us in the evening to a late train for Southampton. One sudden, unexpected difficulty arose. The children had recently been exposed to chickenpox and Philip still bore a few, inconspicuous pocks. Helen concealed the skin lesions with face cream as we made our heavily laden way through HM Customs at one o'clock in the morning.

Reaching our cabin, we found four bunks and a cot! A notice, reminding us that discipline was Teutonic, read 'Breakfast 7.30–9.30 a.m. Breakfast for children 6.30 a.m.' The voyage passed calmly. The huge ship sailed the waves smoothly (Figure 12.1), although a swell caused slight signs of seasickness. The 8th of September was Iain's birthday and as we sat down to our evening meal, the band struck up *Happy Birthday to You* and a beautifully decorated cake was brought to the table, where Iain seemed suspicious of this unexpected attention.

In New York (Figure 12.2), we collected our baggage and walked to the Customs. When the officers saw Philip in Helen's arms,

Figure 12.1 *Rosalind and Iain Gardner on the SS* Hanseatic, *1958.*

Figure 12.2 *Approaching New York.*

they took us to the front of the queue. John and Jenny Richmond (p.124), already in New York, had invited us for dinner, but there was barely time to reach Grand Central Station for the overnight train to Cleveland. Our carriage had bunks but no restaurant car. Sugary sweets comforted Philip through a restless night and a kindly American businessman in the saloon coach talked to the older children, gave them glasses of fruit juice and slipped a silver dollar into each little hand.

Life in Cleveland

We reached Cleveland[F] in the early morning and found a café for our first American breakfast. The proprietor welcomed us with characteristic American warmth and we tasted our first North American food. Alan Moritz's secretary sent a car to collect us and we sped off into the Ohio countryside. He had written on 23rd May 1958 to say:

> I think that the simplest way to deal with the housing and school problems will be to make no definite arrangements until after you arrive. We have a cottage in our place in the country which we will be glad to have you use until you can find something in town in the neighborhood of the Institute. During that time you and Mrs Gardner can use my car as much as you need to find living quarters and to make school arrangements.

He was as good as his word. Mrs Moritz greeted us at their country house and took to the children as though they were her own. We soon learnt that her 21-year-old daughter had been killed in a road accident not many months before our arrival. The Moritz cottage was only a short distance from their house and lay within a large garden.

The size of our grant called for strict economy but was enough to rent a property belonging to a Mr and Mrs Knopf, whose daughter Barbara had married a medical student, John J. (Jeff) Nicholas.[G] John and Barbara occupied one half of a semidetached ('duplex') timber-framed house on Belfield, a street in Cleveland Heights less than a mile from the Medical School. The white-painted building had three floors and capacious cellars. Still fully furnished, the property had become available because the tenant had been evicted, charged with beating his wife. She had fled to Mexico, leaving all their possessions in their home. Members of a local church partly cleared the house, but some days after we moved in, the miscreant came to search for his belongings: I was at work, the two older children at school, and Helen wisely took Philip into the garden until the 'wife-beater' left.

The enthusiasm with which we were welcomed by our new neighbours was startling! On our first evening, one of them, Don Glover, walked through our open French windows without a moment's hesitation, saying: 'Hi, folks! I'm Don and I like chocolate milk so I've brought some with me!' Don and his wife Sue became good friends and introduced us to other neighbours, some associated with the Cleveland Orchestra. One evening, at a concert under the guidance of the eminent conductor Georg (later Sir Georg) Szell, a woman sitting near us had to be helped from the hall. I went with her, thinking that there might be no other doctor nearby. She was not seriously ill, but I used my handkerchief to wipe her brow. The next day, a handwritten note from Szell thanked me for preventing an interruption to his performance and enclosing a new handkerchief!

Life in Belfield pursued an even course, but our calm was disturbed when we heard that a man had been shot dead at the end of the street while robbing a liquor store! Each day, a milkman brought milk and a range of goods to the back door; each day, the mail carrier called. The contrast between housekeeping costs in Scotland and those in Cleveland proved interesting. Helen had quickly found her way to our first 'supermarket', and she and Barbara compared notes. The American household budget included paper towels, toiletries and other 'non-essential' items and was much greater than the Scottish.

Rosalind and Iain were welcomed into Shaker Heights primary school, Roxboro. Rosalind was greeted kindly and introduced to her classmates. Iain's welcome was less happy: when his teacher remarked, 'You must be missing your little friends in Scotland', the tears began to fall! However, the children soon grew used each morning to swearing allegiance to the United States flag.

After some weeks, I realized that, without a car, life in the United States is difficult. A kindly secretary told me that her son had a black 4½-litre Oldsmobile for sale. I paid her $150 before finding that insurance would cost a further $170! The Moritz's suggested that we might like a short break, leaving the children in their care. They mentioned Niagara Falls and we leapt at the idea. Some days later, we drove northwards and reached Niagara in the early evening. Moving slowly, I encountered an elderly man on a pedestrian crossing and pressed the foot brake. Nothing happened. At a garage, we were told that the hydraulic brake cylinder was cracked, but we soon forgot this scare when we saw the awe-inspiring sight of the Falls (Figure 12.3).

Back in Cleveland, we were dismayed to hear that Iain had been rushed to Lakeside

Figure 12.3 *Niagara Falls in the autumn of 1958.*

Hospital. Some tablets had been left in a cupboard in the garden cottage and one day, after playing in the bathroom, Iain had complained of sickness. Dr Moritz assumed that he had swallowed some of the pills. Iain was not clear that he had taken any, but the anxiety caused to the Moritz's was beyond belief, the cost of emergency care considerable.

We had arrived in the Mid-West as the 'Fall' approached, the time when the maple trees display their most brilliant colours before the leaves drop. Suddenly, on Thanksgiving Day, 25th November 1958, the temperature plunged, the first snow covered the roads and we heard the noise of gigantic snowploughs. When Helen and the children went to the supermarket in their warm, Scottish clothes, shop assistants, accustomed to the sallow complexion of the automobile-loving locals, would ask: 'Where are you from? We just love your pink cheeks!' (Figure 12.4). It was to be a long, hard winter, and the snow did not disappear until the first days of April 1959. Spring lasted barely three weeks and suddenly there was an intensely hot summer. One day in June 1959 while I was away, visiting New Orleans (p.150), a fierce thunderstorm broke out. A phone call from the school warned that serious flooding had occurred, that a bus had been swept down a main road and that children should be escorted home.

Figure 12.4 *A family winter walk.*

The Medical School of Western Reserve University

Lakeside, the University Hospital, was in Euclid Avenue (Figure 12.5). Within a few days of our arrival, I began my research, the background set out in a letter written to Simon (Si) Koletsky on 17th May 1958. I explained my attempt to reproduce the so-called 'hydralazine syndrome' (p.129), how I had come to realize that to mimic systemic lupus erythematosus I might have to study animals with raised blood pressure, and how this had led me to learn how to produce hypertension in animals. I described my recent studies of the effects of raised blood pressure and outlined the glomerular changes that accompanied treatment with hydralazine. I explained that giving potent antihypertensive drugs such as hydralazine *intermittently* to rats with severe hypertension could prevent damage to visceral arterioles in spite of very large fluxes of blood pressure, to which the visceral arterioles seemed immune. In reply, Dr Koletsky sent me a list of his published papers and offered help and guidance. His experimental work in animals with hypertension had begun in 1947, while in 1957 he had taken part in collaborative investigations of aldosterone secretion.

Figure 12.5 *Western University Medical School buildings at Lakeside Hospital, Cleveland.*

Within two days of reaching Cleveland, I started my work in his laboratory by establishing a group of rats in which I caused raised blood pressure by placing a minute silver clip around a single renal artery, the technique introduced in London by Byrom[H] and Wilson. To undertake this work required the use of instruments lent to me by Si Koletsky's two pleasant young technicians who were assisting him in his studies of raised blood pressure induced by feeding animals with excess salt (sodium chloride) solution, saline. I visited the laboratory every day, including Sundays. I noticed that Koletsky's own animals – my investigations were in the same rooms as his – were treated at weekends by a medical student who, often in a hurry, sometimes used tap water in place of saline. I told Koletsky of this irregularity without realizing that, if the validity of his investigations was questioned, his scientific reputation might be threatened, his ability to attract financial support prejudiced. He snarled: 'You'll have to go!' I asked: 'Where to?' He said: 'Back where you came from or wherever you like'. I responded 'But I've only just arrived!' He said: 'That's your problem. You're upsetting my technicians'. There was no choice but to ask Alan Moritz for guidance. Kindly and with sympathy and understanding, he said: 'I tell you what. I'll ask Si if he would mind if I moved you to another laboratory'.

And so I was dispatched to a room on the fourth floor of the Institute, the office of Dr Irving Lepow ('Lee'), Associate Professor of Biochemical Pathology, where one of the two desks was vacant. Lee explained that the empty desk had been that of Louis Pillemer, well known in immunology for describing the 'second component of complement': he had recently committed suicide. In this strange way, a long-lasting friendship with Lee began. He told me how he had graduated as a biochemist before his first wife died from multiple sclerosis and how he had decided to study medicine, working as a full-time biochemist while simultaneously studying medicine. He admitted: 'For several years, I went to bed every other night!' He had married again and we soon came to know Martha (Marty), a paediatrician. Some months later, she looked after Rosalind when she developed mumps. Lee was an inveterate cigarette smoker, but for a short time I managed to persuade him to stop and even to buy a bicycle. But abstinence, he said, was destroying his ability to concentrate and he resumed his habit.

I soon met Neil Solomon,[I] a mature MD/PhD student working with Sayers, whose large staff laboured 24 hours a day in eight-hour shifts, seven days each week. At 5 o'clock each afternoon, he led them down to the gymnasium for a 'workout'. Sadly, this enthusiasm failed to gain him the accolade he sought, a Nobel Prize. Neil, married with a young family, covered his costs by running a small laundry. He proved to be very helpful by introducing me to E. H. Bloch, Associate Professor of Anatomy, who generously allowed me to use his sophisticated equipment to test the responses of live animals to changes in blood pressure.

With his apparatus, I was able to show that the small mesenteric arteries of normal rats tolerated very large changes in blood pressure without harm. I applied pressures of up to 1000 mm Hg without any demonstrable damage – evidence supporting my theory that high blood pressure by itself is not damaging to normal small blood vessels and that the lesions seen in malignant (accelerated) hypertension form in vessels the cells of which are predisposed to injury by metabolic changes. Further evidence came later when I showed significant alterations in the enzyme activities of vessels in animals subjected to a regime in which hypertension was developing but in which microscopic lesions were not yet demonstrable.[J]

To visit Harry Goldblatt (Figure 12.6) was a high priority. One cold day, I walked to his Mount Sinai Hospital office. Very quickly, we began to talk about measuring blood pressure. 'Would you like to see how I do it?', he asked, 'No one who is not fond of animals should work with them.' Moving to the door, he let out a shrill whistle. A large dog ran down the corridor, jumped onto Goldblatt's table and lay down on its back. Without a word, Goldblatt inserted a cannula into one of its femoral arteries and watched a column of mercury rise in his manometer. A gentle word and his canine friend hurried back to its room.

It was important to get to know the staff of the Institute and, in particular, the younger members.[K] There was an educational session for Pathology Residents in Training at 8 o'clock each morning, at which hospital cases were discussed, and biopsies and autopsies reviewed.[L] I took an active part and occasionally presented cases

Figure 12.6 *(left to right) Harry Goldblattt, Alan Moritz and Thomas D. Kinney.*

that I had myself encountered in the hospital. Among them were two examples of systemic nocardiosis in patients with rheumatoid arthritis who had been treated with large doses of steroids.[4] On a number of occasions I was asked to talk to the Residents and chose to speak to them on *Rheumatoid arthritis*, on *Experimental hypertension* and about *British training in pathology*. I enjoyed research discussions with Drs R. Moore and M. Schoenberg, both Assistant Professors of Pathology, and many other members of the Institute staff.

I was soon invited to meet Drs Kahn and Skeggs at the Crile Veterans Administration Hospital, an opportunity to discuss the mode of action of renin and the synthesis of hypertensin (later angiotensin) I and II. My visit to Dr Kahn began at 7.30 am. His astonishing first question was: 'What do you think about Winston Churchill?' And so for an hour we talked about Marlborough and the South African and Second World Wars before turning to hypertension! I also visited the Cleveland Clinic and discussed our mutual interests in hydralazine and vascular disease with Lawrence McCormack and the mechanisms of adrenal regeneration hypertension with Georges Masson.

I could not help observing the long hours worked in US laboratories. It was not uncommon for staff to have two occupations. In WRU, the Pathology Institute photographer would labour from 8 am to 4 pm, return home and then resume his own private business. The departmental engineer rented his services: the longer he worked, the more he earned, so he chose to arrive at 7 am and finish at midnight!

The teaching programmes of the Medical School and its affiliated hospitals were highly organized. Each week, a printed schedule was circulated, and monthly Bulletins came from the private Cleveland Clinic. Clinicopathological conferences had become common and in Cleveland, as in Edinburgh, consultants took turns to present cases of interest. On 21st October 1958, I conducted the discussion of a case presented by Dr George J. Gabuzda.

I attended meetings of the Cleveland Pathology Society, the Cleveland branch of the Society for Experimental Biology and Medicine, and the American Association for the History of Medicine, a gathering in the Cleveland Medical Library. Chauncey D. Leake presided over a symposium on 'The heart' and Victor A. McKusick spoke on 'The historical development of methods for diagnosing heart disease'. A few days later I watched a televised clinical symposium on 'Hypertension', my first experience of 'video-conferencing'.

Boston and the Association of American Pathologists

In the spring of 1959, I welcomed the chance of attending a Boston meeting of the American Association of Pathologists to be held in association with the International Academy of Pathology.[M] Leaving the family for a few days, I travelled to Massachusetts with a group of enthusiastic young members of Alan Moritz's staff. With the opportunity of addressing one of the most prestigious American Societies, I spoke about my research. In my paper,[5,6] I concluded:

> The results suggest that subtle changes in cardiovascular metabolism, not detected by conventional microscopy, occur in the earliest stages of rat hypertension at a time when arterioles appear intact structurally.

At the Congress, Barnett conducted a discussion on 'Histochemistry for electron microscopy' in the Anatomy Department of Harvard University and J. Gross held another in the Massachusetts General Hospital. One morning, I saw a poor speaker drop the box with all his enormous 3¼ × 4¼ inch (8.1 × 10.6 cm) glass slides as he walked to the podium. In the evening, a dinner at the Market Restaurant opened my eyes to some American feeding habits. In place of a chicken leg, one young pathologist ate a whole chicken, while another consumed a whole duck. A steak was the size of a dinner plate, a slice of blueberry pie sufficient for four British diners.

After a seminar on lymphoid diseases[N], I joined a tour of the city. We saw the ancient façade of Harvard University, the good ship *Constitution* moored in the harbour (Figure 12.7), and the site where five Boston citizens had been shot by 'redcoats' in 1770, the episode described as *The Bloody Massacre in King Street* by Paul Revere, whose house we passed. A view across the Charles River allowed a glimpse

Figure 12.7 *The USS* Constitution *in Boston Harbour.*

of the Massachusetts Institute of Technology, the nearby avenues lined by magnolia blooms.

In June 1959, I agreed to lecture on experimental hypertension in the Pathology Department of Louisiana State University Medical School. My visit was a first opportunity to see the Mississippi River and savour the unique atmosphere of the old city, but much of my two days in New Orleans was spent with Floyd Skelton, Director of the Urban Maes Research Laboratory and Associate Professor of Pathology. He showed me his techniques for producing adrenal regeneration hypertension.

Some weeks later, I was able to visit Dr Hamilton, Professor of Pathology, Banting Pathology Institute, Toronto, and Robert More, Professor of Pathology, Department of Pathology, Queen's University, Kingston, Ontario. I was fortunate also to be able to meet C. G. Macmillan, Professor of Pathology, Department of Pathology, McGill University, Montreal, C. A. Stetson, Director, Department of Pathology, New York University, Bellevue Medical Center, New York, and Homer-Smith of the Bellevue Department of Physiology.

Vacationing in the USA

Not all my time was spent at meetings! On our first holiday in 1959, we drove from Cleveland to Washington, across the Adirondack Mountains (Figure 12.8), visited the Gettysburg battlefield (Figure 12.9) and saw General Lee's Headquarters. As we gazed at the Lincoln memorial, the children played on the grass below the Washington Monument, from the top of which we saw the Capitol and the White House.

Figure 12.8 *A picnic in the Appalachians.*

In the early summer, we had a visit from my enterprising 70-year-old mother, on her way to see friends in California. She had sailed to Montreal, and we drove north to meet her, our first chance of seeing this lovely city and an opportunity of introducing her to the Niagara Falls. Back in Cleveland, she spent four weeks with us, enduring the humid heat but relishing the chance of seeing her three grandchildren.

As the autumn of 1959 approached, we decided to sell our trusty Oldsmobile for $40 to a scrap yard. Only then did I find that the main frame was cracked! Travelling to Montreal by rail, we embarked on an eagerly awaited tour to the West and boarded the Trans-Canada express to Vancouver, carrying our provisions with us. We were helped by two kindly nuns, who shared their food with the children. The train travelled slowly but purposefully through some of the most vivid and arresting country in the world, our nights eased by comfortable sleeping bunks, our days enlivened by observation windows in the upper part of the coach. Sitting with Philip, watching the lights changing at each level crossing, his few comments were: 'Red light! Green light! Red light'. Traversing the Great Plains, an occasional moose could be seen standing in the waters. The Rocky Mountains came in sight and at one point, the front of the train, with its two gigantic engines, could be seen emerging from an enormously long U-shaped tunnel as the end of the train was entering it.

Figure 12.9 *Our family on the Gettysburg battlefield.*

In Vancouver, we hired a Plymouth car and set off southwards, across Oregon, sighting chipmunks on the edge of Crater Lake. Near Fresno, the temperature reached 105°F (41°C) and it was too hot to hold the steering wheel of the car. At Los Angeles, an early morning breakfast of a 'short stack' (of pancakes) and two eggs 'over easy' led us to Disney Land. For the children, this was the reason we had come to the United States! We spent the whole day exploring the ancient sailing ship, the submarine and the overhead railway, watching Indians dancing and a wonderful background of flowers and shrubs.

Home again

We sailed home on the SS *Homeric* from Montreal on 31ˢᵗ August 1959. The voyage allowed Iain another opportunity for celebrating his birthday on the Atlantic! Arriving at Southampton, we collected our car and drove to Minehead to visit my mother. There was much rejoicing at the return of the travellers, but we could not stay long and were soon on our way northwards. Arriving back in Edinburgh, we found our house in good order, although our American tenants, as well as stealing electricity from the street mains supply, had used our garage for their enormous deep-freeze cabinets and had installed wiring and switches for this purpose. We soon visited Bo'ness, where Emily Harrower's delight at seeing her grandchildren again was overwhelming.

Within a few days, I was back at work. I planned to continue my research, and approached the University for money. After 3 months, I was granted £25. But then I recalled that at Duke University, North Carolina, I had met Dr Thomas D. Kinney (Figure 12.6), Editor of the *American Journal of Pathology*, who enquired: 'Do you need support for your work? Why not ask the US Public Health Service for help?' With this encouragement, I submitted a lengthy application to Washington and was delighted when $12,000 arrived in 1960. Three years later, I was granted a further $35,000, enough to form a very effective group of scientists.

A return visit

In 1965, I learnt of a meeting of the American Heart Association to be held on 15th–17th October in Miami Beach, Florida. I submitted a paper and was pleased when it was accepted. The children were at school but we decided that it would be possible for me to leave Edinburgh for four weeks. My plan was to visit old friends and colleagues as well as calling on Helen's cousin Muffet and her husband, Lionel Frost, in Toronto.

I travelled uncomfortably from Heathrow with a planeload of Danish soldiers who were on a training exercise. Every one of them smoked cigarettes continuously, but I consoled myself with *Lady Chatterley's Lover*, although even this was barely enough to ease the discomfort. Arriving in New York late in the evening of 1st October, I was met by our friend Jacobus (Jack) Potter (p.124), whose wife Elizabeth had generously offered hospitality. I stayed two nights with them at their home on the Hudson River. I had arranged to visit Cornell University Medical School, where Whitley Branwood (p.161) was now a Professor of Pathology, and to speak there about our recent experiments on the experimental effects of raised blood pressure. Later that day, I went to see Hans Popper at Mount Sinai Hospital, and to give another short talk. It was a Friday evening, and I found myself drawn into the weekly staff meeting, which started at 6 p.m. and ended at midnight. Leaving the hospital at that time of night and walking to the darkened Metro station, I sensed that this was not a good time to be exploring Harlem!

In Buffalo, I had arranged to see Floyd Skelton, who had moved there from New Orleans. However, the rain was pouring down and I was obliged to buy a plastic 'Mac' costing $1. I travelled on to our former hometown, Cleveland, where I had told Drs Goldblatt, Moritz and Lepow of my visit. Their welcome was embarrassingly warm. I stayed with the Lepows and enjoyed a breakfast of strong coffee and bagels. Si Koletsky had arranged for me to lecture, and the next day I described to the assembled Medical School the surprising chemical changes that occur in small arteries as animals begin to develop raised blood pressure.[7] Harry Goldblatt kindly came round to the Lepow's house in the evening and we talked long into the night.

The flight to Miami ran into tempestuous weather. The rain grew heavier and heavier and we landed with some difficulty in several inches of water. It was the beginning of the hurricane season and my hotel near the sea front was intolerably hot and humid. The humidity was so great, the air conditioning so poor, that I could eat nothing at breakfast. Looking out of the windows, I saw pelicans diving for fish, but on the horizon (some hundreds of miles away I was told), great banks of copper-coloured clouds presaged the approaching storm. Fortunately, the conference hotel, a mile or so away, was much better equipped and despite the presence of no less than 5000 enthusiastic cardiologists and their associates, the halls were cool and comfortable. However, the crowds were so great that, after giving my prepared talk[8] and a perfunctory attempt to study some displays, I decided to cut short my stay. I quickly took a flight to St Louis, where I hoped to see Dr Loury. My hotel in St Louis was like none I had encountered in Europe. My room had a gigantic, king-size, double bed and was decorated in an Elizabethan style. Then I recalled that I was in the Tudor Hotel. The waiters, black men, were dressed in doublets and hose!

And so to visit my old friend and colleague, Dr Donald F.M. Bunce Jr[o] (Figure 12.10), who had been with us in Edinburgh and who later spent some months in London. He was a member of the staff of the School of Osteopathic Medicine and Surgery, Des Moines, Iowa, and retained a major interest in the structure of blood vessels, a subject

Figure 12.10 *The author at Des Moines with Donald Bunce (seated, at right) and his colleagues.*

on which he had published a well-illustrated atlas.[9] Thanks to him, on 23rd May 1966, I was elected a Fellow of the International College of Angiology. At his invitation, I gave a talk to the local medical society and was then entertained to a splendid repast at a local restaurant. For the first time, I encountered a vast buffet-style meal in which huge numbers of dishes, ranging from turkeys and chickens to sides of beef and ducklings, were accompanied by dozens of sweet delicacies. It was a style of eating that would soon spread to Europe.

Arriving in Denver, on a delayed flight via Chicago, I received an unexpected telephone call from a member of the staff of the University Department of Pathology, who was expecting me as a guest. The voice asked: 'Hi! Are you all set to be picked up in the morning?' I said 'Yes, of course.' The voice replied: 'Fine. I'll call by at 7 am to take you to the Departmental breakfast.' I had never heard of any such academic occasion, but suppressed my surprise and weakly muttered: 'Fine'.

The breakfast was chaired by the eminent Head of the Department, Dr Donald West King.[P] Halfway through the meal, without warning, he stood up and said: 'We're sure glad to have Dr Dugald Gardner here, from Edinboro', Scotland. He's going to take 10 minutes to give us a summary of the work of the British National Health Service' and sat down. I did my unprepared best. Soon afterwards, we moved to a large lecture theatre, where it was announced that 'Dr Gardner has agreed to be the discussant at the Clinico-Pathological Conference, which now begins.' I concealed my surprise as best I could – I had had no warning! As it happened, I need not have worried. It turned out that the case under discussion was one of lung disease. I was able to introduce the subject of dust disease of the lung, pneumoconiosis, but, in view of the altitude of Denver, Colorado, I fortunately remembered to take altitude sickness into account. One of Donald King's staff generously entertained me to dinner and I was interested to see that he was driving a British Jaguar car.

From Denver, a lovely city where winter skiing comes as second nature, a plane took me to Kingston, Ontario. I renewed my friendship and acquaintance with the Head of the Medical School Department of Pathology, Dr Robert More. We dined and wined together. He was a most charming and persuasive person, but all his guiles, and the offer of a salary two or three times greater than the amounts paid in Scotland, could not convince me that I should leave Edinburgh and settle as Chief Pathologist to the Hotel Dieu Hospital in Kingston.

It was only a short distance along the St Lawrence River to Toronto and I was soon in the company of Muffet and Lionel Frost. They were characteristically kindly and, after long family recollections, generously accompanied me to the airport for a return to New York, whence I was due to fly back to Scotland. A sad visit to Dr Patrick Fitzgerald of the Downstate Medical Center of the University of New York found him in some distress. He was courteous in his proposal that I might return to New York but desperately worried that his wife, who I met at his home, was seriously ill with cancer. After my return to Scotland, as he explained in a handwritten letter enclosing an honorarium to cover my travel costs, she died a short time later.

Before the journey, there was a serious matter to attend to: presents for the family! Rosalind was now 14 years old, and a colourful doll offered no difficulty. Iain was 13 and was happy with a new watch. Philip was eight and enjoyed a children's annual. David (Chapter 13) was nearly five, and a colourful metal toy truck was a delight. They were all seized upon as soon as I set foot in Craigleith View and opened my large, black case.

Canada once more

We renewed our acquaintance with Canada when on Monday 9th October 1982, Helen and I set out to attend a conference in Kingston, Ontario. The subject was to be 'Clinical Patterns and Pathological Features in Osteoarthritis', the organizer T. D. V. Cooke, Associate Professor of Orthopaedic Surgery of the Queen's University, Kingston. I had been invited to present a contribution on osteoarthritis[10] and to take part in the discussions.

> There were to be 50 or more participants from Europe and North America. We knew many of them well, in particular Cecil Armstrong (New York), who had been taught mechanical engineering by Professor Crossland in Belfast and had been a highly successful PhD student in my Department of the Queen's University (Chapter 15). The speakers included J. G. Peyron (Paris), René Lagier (Geneva), Aubrey Hough (Little Rock, Arkansas), Louis Solomon (Johannesburg), Watson Buchanan (McMaster University, Hamilton, Ontario), Henry Mankin (Boston, Massachusetts), Hubert Sissons (New York), Hugh Smythe (Toronto), Eric Radin (Morgantown, West Virginia) and David Howell (Miami). Among those from the United Kingdom were Verna Wright, George Nuki, D. A. Brewerton, John Ball, P. D. Byers and Phillip Wood.

Although the University of Manchester helped with travel costs, the arrangements for our visit were in the hands of Ciba-Geigy (Novartis), the Swiss international pharmaceutical company (p.291), who arranged our accommodation at the Donald Gordon Centre in Kingston.

After the conference, we flew to Toronto and took the opportunity of visiting Lionel and Muffet Frost again. After a night in their splendid flat, we visited Hamilton, Ontario, and were reunited with Alun and Anita Wynn-Williams, who had left Edinburgh in 1964. Alun had been drawn into a complex medico-legal debate. The mother of a deceased child was demanding the return of the microscopic slides made from her son's tissues and was pursuing legal action. Alun was worried about the effects this might have on his pension should his appointment be threatened. Alun and Anita were very generous of their time and took us to the Niagara Falls, which we had last seen in 1959. Afterwards, we had the chance of viewing the new teaching programmes that McMaster University Medical School had pioneered and made a note to draw them to the attention of the Faculty of Medicine in Manchester. The Medical School was within walking distance of the Wynn-Williams home.

Some days later, the conference ended, we took advantage of an invitation to visit a friend and colleague, Feroze N. Ghadially,[Q] Professor of Pathology at the University of Saskatchewan at Saskatoon. We stayed at the splendid Bessborough Hotel, with the Governor General as a fellow guest. One of Feroze's technicians owned 20 acres of land some miles outside the city and ran a prosperous honeybee business in his spare hours. He had 400 hives scattered across 10–15 miles of country and exported his products to Europe. He and his 'buddies' provided our first western Canadian 'cook-out', with one pound of steak allotted for each of us.

Feroze was a prolific writer. One explanation for his prodigious output was the climate in Saskatoon. The winters were long, the snowfalls heavy and frequent. The cold was so bitter that, for the first time in our lives, we saw how cars, driven to a shopping centre, had to be connected to electric warming devices to prevent the stationary engines from freezing. As Feroze said cheerfully, there was little to be gained from emerging into the open air, and his laboratories offered a warm sanctuary. A second explanation for his endless activity was the fact that, like Joseph (Lord) Lister, his wife acted as his secretary. Feroze had invited a cluster of his friends and co-workers to a barbecue held in his garden. As was the custom, the men undertook the cooking while the womenfolk sat indoors exchanging news and views. We soon found that the arrangement had disadvantages: the air was laden with mosquitoes. To escape their bites, the cooks soon had to join the ladies.

From Saskatoon, we travelled 1000 miles back to the east and spent two nights in Montreal. With time to spare, we took a bus to Quebec and discovered that it was one of the most beautiful cities we had ever seen. We had an unusual flight back to the United Kingdom since I found myself sitting next to a young, fair-haired, drug-taking Canadian dressed in a moose coat, who told me of his Arabian grandfather. He explained that he lived with the Quebec Indians and gained strength by speaking to the trees, around which he liked to clasp his arms. He travelled to Europe every three months to sell the leather coats made by the tribe. As we conversed, he offered us some of his opiates, but I explained that we were too old for that kind of pharmacology. We arrived home on 25th October.

CHAPTER 13

A Scottish university hospital

A return to the Firth of Forth

Language is only the instrument of science,
and words are but the signs of ideas

Samuel Johnson[1]

On 1st October 1961, I became a Senior Lecturer in the Department of Pathology of the University of Edinburgh[A] and Honorary Consultant Pathologist to the South Eastern Region Hospital Board, Scotland. Andrew Shivas[B] had been appointed to a similar position and I was surprised but delighted that another vacancy had arisen.

Chapter summary
- Hospital consultant
- Research
- The new Medical School building
- Teaching
- Examining
- Communications and committees
- The countryside
- Visitors
- Looking ahead

In the meantime it had not taken long to re-establish our roots in Craigcrook Road, but the house demanded attention. Clambering through the skylight onto a flat roof, I painted the windows, but there was more work to do. An unexpected legacy from Helen's great uncle, J. Miller Thomson (Uncle Jim) helped with the construction of a garage. I laid concrete foundations beside the garden wall and used timber brought from Bo'ness by Harrower Welsh & Co. to add a fence so that passers-by could no longer peer into our dining room. The painful price I paid was a 'tennis elbow'! The house had no central heating, but a solid fuel-fired kitchen boiler and a paraffin heater came to the rescue, while coal fires warmed the sitting room. We could now afford television, allowing us to watch views of the first manned spacecraft in 1961 and NASA's successful Mercury – Atlas ventures in 1962.

Once more, Number 21 became our busy, happy home. Rosalind returned to a senior class at St George's School for Girls, Iain to the Edinburgh Academy, where Philip went to the Preparatory School, while David, born on 23rd December 1960, was introduced to a convenient kindergarten. After taking the family to school each morning, I walked up the Mound to Forest Road, returning home late each evening as experience reminded me that research takes little account of domestic convenience.

But the children were growing quickly, making new friends and widening their interests, and in 1962 we moved to a larger house in Craigleith View, a ring road near Ravelstone Dykes. The bungalow cost £6500 and had the advantage of a large attic room giving bedroom space for the older boys, their table tennis and model railway. The owner, about to move to America, was most reluctant to part with his rose bushes and gave us his notebook to explain how they should be cared for! From our kitchen window, a fine northwards view towards the Firth of Forth was a delight. In the early morning, I would sometimes take David from his cot so that we could gaze at the scene together. To the west of our house lived Lewis and Heather Aitken, with their son, George, and their two daughters, Mary and Diana. Lewis had served as a 'Desert Rat' during the Second World War and worked for Ferranti. Across the crescent, my laboratory colleague, Nigel Harcourt-Webster,[C] who had come from Charing Cross Hospital, was a new neighbour. Unfortunately, accidents happen, and one day in 1965, Iain and Harvey Harris, son of Phillip Harris, a neurosurgeon, were being taken by car to play golf when the car struck another vehicle. Iain was thrown forward and his knee hit a parcel shelf. He was cared for by George Mitchell, an orthopaedic surgeon, who reported that Iain had made a complete recovery but warned later that he should avoid rugby that season.

> During our early years in Edinburgh, Helen's parents, David and Emily Harrower, continued to live in their large, Victorian mansion, 'Elmpark', in Earngarth Road, Bo'ness.[D] We often visited them at weekends. By this time, Helen's brother, Gordon and his wife Enid had established their home, 'Craigdhu', in Grange Terrace, Bo'ness. Eventually it became clear that 'Elmpark' was too large for Helen's parents and they bought a flat in Panbrae Road. In 1967, Helen's father suffered a stroke and after two weeks in Bangour Hospital, West Lothian, he died. Emily wisely accepted the invitation of her sister Florence to join her in 'Burchetts', a large house in Sussex.
>
> My widowed mother Marjorie (p.23) kept in touch with us wherever we went. She moved from 'Cranham Cottage', Minehead, in August 1961 to a flat in 'Rosemount', a house at Whitegate Road belonging to her friend Thersie Jackman on the other side of the town. However, there were disagreements. Marjorie sold her half of the house back to her friend and in the spring of 1962 returned to Hove, where she rented a flat at Fonthill Road. Soon she was tempted by Derek Peters' (p.28) offer of accommodation at St Ann's, his house in Lewes. When the Peters moved to Place House, Patcham, Marjorie joined them and found herself close to Derek's mother, Gladys, another old friend. In 1965, aged 76 and as vigorous as ever, Marjorie visited Freya, Magda Schönhals' sister, in Mannheim, where we had been in 1936 (p.19).

Hospital consultant

As an honorary consultant in the University Department of Pathology (Chapter 11), it was now a central part of my duties to share the supervision of the diagnostic biopsy and autopsy work of the departmental Registrars and Lecturers. Samples of tissue removed during surgical operations in the Royal Infirmary itself were sent as quickly as possible to the Infirmary laboratories, which were under the direction of R. F. Ogilvie (p.66). The hospital responsibilities of the University Department extended many miles beyond Edinburgh, and the surgical specimens from other hospitals were 'processed' in the Medical School building, where they were studied by pathologists in training and examined meticulously by the consultant staff. In this incessantly demanding work, I benefited greatly from the skill and experience of wise colleagues, particularly John D. MacGregor, with whom we shared responsibility for the precision of the reports. I was also fortunate in the wise guidance I received from the technical staff: the Laboratory Superintendent, T. C. Dodds[E] (p.127), had been succeeded by James Masson, and he was followed by James (Jimmy) Waugh (p.126).

From time to time, I was asked by a consultant to visit a patient for whom they were caring or by a surgeon to see someone on whom he had operated. It was in this way that I first met Professor Michael (later Sir Michael) Woodruff,[F] who had come to Edinburgh as Professor of Surgical Science. Michael soon achieved worldwide fame for his pioneering introduction into this country of kidney transplantation.[2, 3] He was not accustomed to having his opinions contradicted. One day, I reported that a small black lesion on a patient's knee was the condition of intradermal naevus. Standing in his Royal Infirmary ward, he said firmly: 'This is a malignant melanoma.' 'No, sir', I said, 'It is a simple lesion'. 'No', he said 'it is a melanoma because I say it is!' Dogmatism, a reflection of the confidence of seniority, was not confined to Sir Michael and I recognized it again when I encountered Sir John Biggart in Belfast (p.191). It was at this time that I met John Crofton,[G] who had taken up the Chair of Respiratory Medicine. Professor Crofton held weekly staff meetings at the City Hospital; learning of my special interest in diseases of the heart and lungs, he encouraged me to take part.

In the Royal Infirmary of Edinburgh, autopsies were conducted in a mortuary near the chapel, the boiler house and the west gate (Figure 13.1). More than a thousand examinations were performed each year and it was not uncommon to be asked to undertake two or even three in a single morning. On the door, a notice warned inquisitive passers-by: *sectio cadaveris hodie* (there will be an autopsy today)! Inside, there were three stone tables in an amphitheatre where a tier of benches enabled student classes to see our work and to listen to our teaching. Bodies brought from the chapel or a

Figure 13.1 *The Pathology building of the Royal Infirmary of Edinburgh, beside the East gate of the hospital*

refrigerated store were laid on the tables while we would remove our jackets in a small changing room and put on white rubber boots. On the desk an ominous note reminded us that in 1936, a time when gloves were not often worn during autopsies, a pathologist had died from septicaemia after accidentally cutting his hand. We were assisted by two skilled and cheerful attendants, Jim and Frank, but occasionally distracted by an older, uniformed porter who enjoyed creeping up behind us and tying additional knots in our aprons, a practice of which he was particularly fond on New Year's Day!

It was accepted that organs showing interesting examples of disease should be retained for teaching. Occasionally, this led to bizarre consequences. One day, I noticed that the lower leg of an elderly woman who had died in the Royal Infirmary contained not one knee joint but two. She had fractured her tibia when young; the fracture had healed but had left an extremely unusual feature, a pseudarthrosis or false joint. I advised the mortuary attendants that the lower leg should be passed to the pathology museum. Some days later, I was accosted in the street by the enraged family doctor, David Tulloch (p.86), who told me that the woman had been one of two identical twins and that the only way the family could identify their deceased relative was by looking at her leg! But the leg was no longer there!

We were also responsible for the autopsies requested in many parts of what became the East Lothian Health Authority, so that, according to a rota of duties, I drove periodically to the City Hospital, to the Southern General Hospital, to Bangour Hospital, West Lothian, to Peel Hospital and to East Fortune Hospital, near Haddington.[H] The condition of some of the hospital mortuaries was primitive. In the Bruntsfield Hospital, Edinburgh, there was so little space that I had to hang my jacket on the crucifix! At the Northern General Hospital, the mortuary was unheated: at intervals during my dissections, I had to plunge my gloved hands into a bucket of hot water.

Unlike the Coroners who regulated enquiries into unexplained deaths in other parts of the country, the Procurator Fiscal in Scotland made no payments for the reports he required from us. We therefore received no financial returns from our time-consuming and physically demanding journeys, but there were less obvious rewards! A call to Bangour would offer the chance of enjoying coffee with our old friend Sister Margaret Daniel (p.101) in the years before she moved to the Northern General Hospital, Edinburgh. On the way back from East Fortune, a glimpse of the beautiful bird sanctuary at Aberlady Bay could be followed by a brief stop in Musselburgh to buy ice cream from Luca's famous shop.

Research

Returning from Cleveland, I resumed the investigations I had been making with Ian Duthie and his team into the causes and pathological features of rheumatoid arthritis, RA.

It remained possible that this common condition might be caused by an infective agent. With J. M. K. Mackay and Barry Marmion, we attempted to pass the disease from man to monkeys by injecting animals with live cells from arthritic human joints, work conducted at Inveresk Research International. This programme of research continued after I moved to Belfast, but ended in 1972 (p.198). Duthie judged that when the experimental animals were killed, I should return to Edinburgh to conduct the autopsies and collect the histological material. My journey had its lighter moments, as I describe in Chapter 15! The results of three years' observation[4] were negative, but the study must be judged inconclusive, since it was terminated by the Arthritis and Rheumatism Council, the ARC, for financial, not scientific, reasons.

In the Medical School animal house, the attendant, Bill Robb, tended to speak more of his new Ford Anglia car in his broad, Lothian dialect than of the rabbits, rats and guinea pigs for which he cared. Our son Iain sometimes came with me on weekend mornings to help Bill, but caused concern by finishing in one hour work that might take the animal house staff half a day.

Surgical operations on patients with rheumatoid arthritis presented particular hazards,[5] including the complications of anaesthesia and of postoperative infection.[6] We had come to recognize the predisposition of patients with rheumatoid arthritis to bacterial and viral diseases, and were aware that mycoses – fungal diseases – might complicate steroid treatment (p.146). During this work, we encountered a case of viral leukoencephalitis[7] and a patient with asthma treated with corticosteroids who died from staphylococcal endocarditis.

Raised blood pressure and the effects of hydralazine continued to be of intense interest. I visited the London Hospital to meet Dr M. A. Floyer, Dr F. B. Byrom and Professor Clifford Wilson. Wilson and Byrom's pioneering work had shown that, by contrast with the dog, it was not necessary to remove one kidney from a rat in order to cause persistent raised blood pressure by constricting the contralateral renal artery. I told them of my results,[8] in essence the same as those that I had described to the American Pathological Association at their Boston meeting in 1959 (p.147) and repeated in a talk to the Edinburgh Pathological Club.[9] My interests continued to centre on the behaviour of arterioles, the very small blood vessels linking the arteries that convey blood from the heart to the capillaries, the minute channels taking blood to individual tissues and cells. During the 1950s, a new subject, enzyme histochemistry, had emerged.[10] Most of the earlier studies of enzyme histochemistry were with coloured reagents, used to show where the enzyme reactions were taking place, not how much activity existed. Investigations using this form of <u>qualitative histochemistry</u> could be of value in the diagnosis of some diseases, but the degree of enzyme activity could only be estimated roughly. To understand the difference in enzyme activity between different tissues or even between different cells, a more sophisticated approach was necessary, using measuring techniques in <u>quantitative histochemistry</u>. In this work, I was greatly helped by a young organic chemist, Christine Laing.[l] Our interests turned also to the culture of live arterioles, and for this work I was joined by Michael Faed from Professor Swan's Edinburgh Department. Michael developed the technique of interference microscopy[11] to view the living tissues.

It was during these years that I was drawn to the use of radioactive isotopes. My interest had arisen when, in 1958, Dr Ogilvie (p.157) and I conducted autopsies on two patients who had been under the care of the eminent neurosurgeon Norman Dott. During cerebral angiography in the 1930s, using a novel technique for demonstrating the arteries of the brain, he had injected these patients with thorium dioxide in a colloidal suspension called Thorotrast.[J] Twenty or so years later, both patients died from cancer and came to autopsy. Using the technique of autoradiography, we demonstrated radioactive thorium in their splenic and hepatic cells and concluded that the malignancies were attributable to the earlier administration of thorium. I described the cases to the Pathological Society of Great Britain and Ireland. The paper, subsequently published,[12] attracted an astonishing response from my audience. The lantern slides had been prepared with the help of T. C. Dodds (p.127) and were of such exceptional quality that the audience broke into a round of applause led by Professor A. C. Lendrum of Dundee.

My interest in thorium took me to the literature on the undesirable long-term effects of radioactive substances on animal and human tissues. I decided to attend a course on radiation biology given at Strathclyde University in Glasgow.

My new understanding soon proved of practical value when I began to use a novel form of balance to weigh the minute portions of arteriolar tissue that I had taken from small animals in which I had induced raised blood pressure. The instrument was a 'decimicro' balance, signifying that it was capable of being used to weigh accurately samples many times smaller than those employed in conventional biochemistry. Because the balance was so sensitive, very small changes in electric charge in the space around the weighing pan were liable to distort the results. To overcome this problem, I placed a small quantity of the radioactive element americium-95 (^{95}Am) close to the moving parts of the balance, which was kept in a locked room on the fifth floor of the Department.

Figure 13.2 *The 1962 Medical School building at the corner of George Square with (at front) the added Chrystal Macmillan building of 2008.*

The new Medical School building

Following the Second World War, controversial plans had been afoot in Edinburgh for a reconstruction of George Square. One of the proposals was for a Medical School building at the northwest corner of the Square. Even with the impetus of Professor Michael Swann, now the Vice-Chancellor, it took eight years, including five of public controversy, before the development was complete (Figure 13.2). The official opening, by Professor Sir Roy Cameron, FRS, took place on 4th June 1962.

On the eve of the opening, my friend Angus Stuart[K] and I toured the new Department (Figure 13.3) to view the equipment, the provision of which had been the responsibility of the resourceful T. C. Dodds. We visited the splendidly equipped diagnostic laboratories and put the facilities to a simple test, slipping a packet of warm fish and chips into a new incubator!

I chose an excellent room on the fifth floor, from the large windows of which I could enjoy a panoramic view across Blackford Hill to the Pentlands. We quickly found the building too cold in winter and too hot in summer. The explanation was that the City Council had instructed the architect to face the western aspect of the building with hand-cut stone to match the Victorian style of the 1879 Royal Infirmary of Edinburgh, which lay at the opposite side of Middle Meadow Walk. To find the money to meet the Council's demand, the installation of double glazing and air-conditioning was cancelled. Worse was to follow. Central heating came from a rebuilt boiler house and the new corridors and walls were insulated with asbestos, work completed before the dangers of this mineral were fully recognized. Some years later, the demanding work of stripping it out took many months.

Figure 13.3 *The author in the new staff room of the Department of Pathology, University of Edinburgh, in 1964.*

During this period of modernization there were changes in the departmental staff, recorded by Angus Stuart in the *Festschrift* that he compiled to commemorate George Montgomery's retirement. Robertson Ogilvie (p.66) continued his laboratory duties in the Royal Infirmary until instructed by Professor Montgomery to move to the new building in George Square, where Whitely Branwood[L] pursued the professorial research on coronary artery disease. In 1956, Alun Wynn-Williams (p.153) came from Aberdeen to a senior lectureship and Neil McLean[M] obtained a consultant position at the Western General Hospital. Walter Coulson moved to North America, as did Hamish Turner, while Robert (Bob) Nagle joined the Department of Forensic Medicine. I collaborated with W. E. Hunt (p.134), came to know Stanley Barrett and John Macgregor well, and made occasional visits to Douglas Bain[N] in the Hospital for Sick Children. Kathryn MacLaren[O] led much of the diagnostic histopathology, Mary MacDonald[P] was a pioneer in electron microscopy, Ian Inglis Smith[Q] joined the Department as an Assistant Lecturer, and I occasionally encountered James Black, W. S. A. Allan, Sandy Parkinson and Peter Yates. During the 1960s the health of the staff was of concern. I recollect that each year, on average, there was one new case of tuberculosis. The cause of this endemic could be traced not to contact with specimens of tuberculous tissues but to the presence of a lecturer who had open pulmonary tuberculosis, for which he had a lung lobe successfully removed after he left Edinburgh.

Teaching

I have always loved teaching. There is no greater privilege and pleasure than telling a young class of the wonders of nature shown through biology and then, in terms of pathology, of the perversions that affect normality. In the late 1950s, there were few signs that the style of education in the Edinburgh Faculty of Medicine had altered significantly within living memory. However, the new building changed our approach. There were spacious classrooms large enough for at least one half of a class to sit together. They had before them microscopes and boxes of glass slides representing a wide range of diseases. From time to time, our students were tested by projecting images of these slides onto a screen – computers were not yet in vogue – and were asked to identify them. Those who scored well returned to the classroom; those who scored poorly were invited to identify further pictures until only a rump of 'under-performers' remained. Their fate was to attend an additional tutorial!

The new building provided two museum floors: one devoted to undergraduate and one to postgraduate teaching. In these new rooms, students could study by themselves or be taken into small groups with individual tutors. Student teaching continued to be helped by the displays of pathological specimens in the museums, collections amassed over many years. Other specimens were stored in a basement, together with oil drums holding the lungs of coal miners whose deaths were the subject of legal claims for industrial silicosis.

During the years in which Walter Perry was Dean of the Faculty of Medicine, he made far-reaching changes in the structure of the teaching programmes. With my colleagues John Richmond, George Boyd, Alan Muir and Gerald Collee, I was heavily involved in these changes, and in May 1965 I became one of a number of Directors of Studies, an appointment that carried an annual honorarium of £125. Some years later, in June 1968, after Walter had completed a term as Vice Principal of the University of Edinburgh, he became Vice Chancellor of the Open University. I wrote to congratulate him and received a note of thanks and a thoughtful reply in which he surmised that medical education was not an option for his new institution. However, he regarded 'in-post' training in the medical field by means of computer-based techniques, 'over-the-air' as he expressed it, as a possibility. The Royal Society of Medicine organized a meeting at which Perry's views were widely discussed and I presented a paper supporting his proposals.[13]

Examining

At the end of each term, our students sat a 'class' examination, followed by a professional examination at the close of each academic year. At the end of every second term, I arranged an additional, practical 'class' examination. With the help of Nigel Harcourt-Webster, 50 pathological specimens, microscope slides, photographs and diagrams were laid upon the classroom benches. Students were allowed 60 minutes to identify these items. Marks were given for the test and added to those granted for the corresponding simultaneous theoretical (written) examination. At that time, the rights of the individual did not preclude these results being shown publicly, and their display on departmental notice boards delighted the successful.

When first asked to be an examiner, no guidance or instruction was given, no formal syllabus presented. Examining medical or dental students was a responsibility required of those of University Senior Lecturer or of Consultant status. My experience began with the testing of students of Dentistry. It was a dreary task, not because of any lack of quality of the students themselves – all had passed rigorous examinations before admission to the Edinburgh School of Dentistry, one of the oldest and most prestigious in the country – but because those teaching my subject had clearly failed to inspire their classes. One explanation may have been the practice of delegating the education of dental students to the less senior staff.

Postgraduate examinations were another matter altogether. In 1960, a letter came asking whether I could act as an examiner for the Fellowship of the Royal College of Surgeons of Edinburgh, the FRCSEd. I never regretted accepting, and continued until 1994, as I describe in Chapter 23. In addition, I enjoyed examining MD, PhD and other theses submitted from a variety of British Universities, including Cambridge, Oxford, Liverpool and London, and from occasional overseas institutions.

Communications and committees

We made vigorous attempts to publish the results of our research as soon as they became available. To complement our scientific papers, I decided to put together my growing experience in the fields of rheumatic and connective tissue disease.[14, 15] My books received a friendly reception from Professor Zaimis in London and from Alan Moritz in Cleveland. I was invited by E. G. L. (Eric) Bywaters to join the Pathology Committee of the European League Against Rheumatism, EULAR, of which he was chairman. EULAR was emerging as an influential body, bringing together the activities of those investigating the rheumatic diseases in many of the 33 European countries.

During these years, I was often called on to present our results at local and national meetings.[R] But there was time to attend the Lister Memorial Lecture given by Professor Sir Howard Florey in the Royal Infirmary, Glasgow – it was 1965, 100 years since Joseph Lister had described his first success in the use of carbolic acid in the prevention of wound infection. Tongue in cheek, Florey spoke of his interest in small blood vessels, commenting 'I am a man of limited intelligence and have to choose topics for my research that are within my comprehension. This is why I am examining the simple problem of how water crosses the walls of capillaries.' After the lecture, together with a large number of associates, I found myself in the University of Glasgow Staff Club, where we had been taken for a drink. Without thinking, standing among a group of colleagues, I took my pipe and a box of matches out of my pocket. Filling the pipe with tobacco, I rather carelessly lit a match and applied it to the bowl of the pipe. There was no ashtray in sight, so I put the used match back in its box. But the match was still hot. At once, an explosion startled the delegates and a cloud of smoke filled the hall!

The countryside

As the children grew up, we came to know and love the little town of Bamburgh (Figure 13.4), ancient capital of Northumbria, and we continued to visit the beautiful coast after settling in London in 1966. My cousin Jean and her husband Jim Grieve owned a small house, '*Cumthawaysin*', in the village. It faced the sand dunes and they allowed us to use it for holidays. To the right, half a mile away, we could see the magnificent profile of Bamburgh Castle, restored during the eighteenth and nineteenth centuries and finally bought by William Armstrong, the Victorian industrialist, who completed the restoration.

Barely 15 miles to the north was Holy Island, Lindisfarne, with its castle and the ruins of the priory founded by St Aidan in AD 635. The island, we were told, could only be reached safely via a causeway, accessible at low tide. We were all anxious to test this advice! Soon we heard of Grace Darling, who, with her father, a keeper of two lighthouses, had set out in a rowing boat on a stormy night in 1838 and rescued 13 people from among the 63 on board the SS *Forfarshire*. Near the sandy Bamburgh beach were outcrops of rocks with pools

Figure 13.4 *Rosalind, Iain, Philip and David at Bamburgh.*

Figure 13.5 *Helen, David, Rosalind, Philip and the author at Seahouses.*

where anemones and crabs could be watched. Occasionally, a little fish might be caught. We often visited Seahouses (Figure 13.5), a nearby fishing village, where kippers could be bought cheaply. A toyshop was an irresistible attraction for young Philip.

Not far from Bamburgh was Hadrian's Roman Wall, built in AD 122. Much of the Wall could be traced on foot. We were fascinated by the stones that were the remains of the fort at Chesters, Hexham, Northumberland. The fort was the best preserved of the Roman cavalry forts in this country and a great source of fun and inspiration for the children, who loved tracing the outlines of the baths and searching the nearby museum.

Visitors

We often enjoyed visits from members of our family who lived in Edinburgh but, less frequently, from those who lived 'south of the Border' (Figure. 13.6). Among the scientists who came to see us was Ted Gillman[16] who had left Natal to join the Agricultural Research Council when the South African government imposed oppressive restrictions on the coloured students he was teaching. Ted stayed with us and as we sat at the dining room table; it was evident that he was charmed by the children, entertaining them with stories of his baboons. He and I travelled together to the 1963 Pathological Society meeting in Aberdeen. The Forth Road Bridge did not open until 1964 so we enjoyed crossing the Firth of Forth by ferry, from Queensferry to Inverkeithing.

Figure 13.6 *(left to right) Florence Pike; Iain, Helen and Philip Gardner; and Susie Pike. David Gardner stands in front of them.*

One day I learned that Professor Sir Howard Florey was visiting a former colleague, David Whitteridge, Professor of Physiology in Edinburgh. They had known each other well in Oxford. Hearing of this, I asked Whitteridge whether Florey might be persuaded to give me advice on my studies of arterioles – Florey had a particular interest in capillaries. Whitteridge agreed to raise the question with his friend and one day, shortly after lunch, there was a knock at my door – my visitors had arrived. A perceptible scent of gin wafted into my little room where I had a microscope and slides ready. I invited Professor Florey to sit down at my microscope. However, he immediately recognized that the instrument, with its two eyepieces, had been adjusted for my height, not his. Trying to reach up and look at my slides, he growled: 'What the bloody 'ell is wrong with this instrument?' And that was the entire contribution the Nobel Laureate was able to make to my research!

Looking ahead

By 1964, it had become clear that to enhance my position and to obtain a larger and much needed income, I would have to move. I had become a Founder Member of the new College of Pathologists in July 1963 and a Fellow of the Royal College of Physicians of Edinburgh in November of that year. George Montgomery was not due to retire for another seven years, so my search would have to turn from Edinburgh to other institutions. I therefore applied for the vacant Chair of Pathology in the University of Sheffield. The events that followed can only be described as a pantomime!

I travelled to Sheffield on the day prior to the interview. Immediately before the gathering, a lunch had been arranged for the five selected candidates, who included Dr W. J. (Bill) Crane, the Department's Senior Lecturer. To my surprise, the meal was attended by all the members of the interviewing panel itself. As the lunch progressed, the conversation, which had understandably been somewhat stilted, became freer. Across the table, a consultant who I later found to have been the senior Clinical Chemist, spoke to Crane. 'Bill', he said without any attempt to soften his voice, 'When you are appointed to this Chair, how will you deal with St James Hospital?' There was a sudden silence as the other four candidates realized that the position for which they had applied had been 'rigged'. It was no surprise when, late in the afternoon, Bill's appointment was announced. The experience did not deter me and in January 1965 I made an enquiry concerning the Chair of Pathology at Guy's Hospital Medical and Dental School, London.

In May 1965, a letter from the Ministry of Defence Microbiological Research Establishment at Porton Down, the MRE, asked me whether I was interested in applying for the position of Deputy Chief Scientific Officer. I declined this offer largely because I did not wish either to become a Government employee or to leave an academic teaching institution with the freedom to choose my own avenue of research. However, a less formal association with the MRE offered no such constraint and it was at that time that the Director of the Research Establishment, Dr Graham Smith, resigned to become Dean of the London School of Hygiene and Tropical Medicine. The Chief Scientific Adviser, Professor Evans, began the search for a successor and asked me whether I would be interested. I declined again, but one consequence was an invitation to join the Biological Research Advisory Board (BRAB), the non-executive committee that provided guidance to the many scientists working at Porton (p.182). I accepted the offer and my association with the Board continued for some years, while for a short period I had the responsibility of acting as Chairman of a subcommittee of the Board.

There was no alternative but to look overseas. I had never seriously considered living in the United States, although the opportunity had arisen several times during our stay there. But the Commonwealth was a different matter, and in 1966 I sought the vacant second Chair of Pathology in Melbourne, Australia. Sir Roy Cameron generously agreed to act as a referee. However, it was at this precise moment that the Directorship of the new Kennedy Institute of Rheumatology was advertised (p.169). By the time the Australian High Commission had been in touch to tell me that the Melbourne position had been filled by Professor Christie of Brisbane, I had applied for and accepted the London appointment.

It was in this way that our lives changed again. I resigned from the University of Edinburgh on 28th February 1966 and on 31st May left the Department where I had spent so many years.

IV.

From the Thames and the Lagan to the oceans of the World

CHAPTER 14

A London first

By the banks of the Thames

Discovery consists of seeing what everybody has
seen and thinking what nobody has thought

Albert von Szent-Györgyi[1]

In the spring of 1966, I visited my South African friend, Ted Gillman (p.165). Sitting in his office at Babraham, I chanced upon an advertisement seeking a Director for a new Research Institute associated with the Charing Cross Hospital Medical School. The Institute was to be for the study of the rheumatic diseases.

In the face of this exciting news, I sought Ian Duthie's (p.124) advice and with his support, applied for the appointment. Called for interview with the Charing Cross Dean, Seymour Reynolds, and a group of advisors, among them W. S. C. Copeman,[A] President of the Arthritis and Rheumatism Council, the ARC,[B] I was genuinely surprised to be told I had been appointed with effect from 1st June.

I travelled to London on 31st May and found temporary accommodation in a guest house in Castelnau, a main thoroughfare leading to the Hammersmith roundabout. The walls were so thin that I thought I could hear the occupant of the adjacent room squeezing his toothpaste onto a brush. But Castlenau served its purpose until Helen and the children arrived at the beginning of their holidays.

Meanwhile, we began a search for new schools. My instinct was to approach St Paul's. The High Master, T. E. B. Howarth, proved extraordinarily understanding: Iain was invited to sit examination papers in subjects of his own choice and was immediately accepted. The Headmistress of St Paul's School for Girls, Alison Monro, responded with equal generosity, and Rosalind was taken into a competitive group of young ladies rather different from those she had come to know in Edinburgh. Mr Collis, Head of Colet Court, St Paul's Junior School, proposed that Philip, now nine, come from Edinburgh for interview, and one day he and I set off for London by train. As we crossed the border between Scotland and England, little Philip stared out of the window and asked in an incredulous voice:

Chapter summary

- Looking for a house
- The Institute
- The opening of the new Institute
- The Royal Patron
- Research
- Committee, Society and other memberships
- Visitors
- Meetings and conferences
- The end of one road
- A change is in sight

'Are those people really *English*?' – he could not believe he was moving into a country that, he had been taught, was 'The Auld Enemy'. However, once admitted, Philip joined a group of new boys, several of whom had come from overseas. Unhappily, they were bullied, but Philip, born with a naturally strong right arm, sprang to their defence. Among his new friends was Harold Pinter's son, Daniel. David, now aged six, was welcomed at Mortlake Primary School.

Looking for a house

We had sold our Edinburgh house to a fellow medical practitioner for £6800. Twice as much was needed to secure a substantial semi-detached house in East Sheen, London. Twenty-Eight York Avenue had a beautiful oak front door, an ample garage and a garden that brought us close to unusual neighbours, Mr and Mrs Radziwell. They were of the Polish aristocracy, fortunate to have escaped Hitler's Europe. His family was related to that of President John F. Kennedy's wife, Jackie. Mr Radziwell had become an art dealer. Generous to a fault, he offered us fine watercolours of Naples very cheaply but gave us other paintings when his wife was not looking!

A short walk down a gentle hill brought us to the Upper Richmond Road, while, in the opposite direction, the Sheen Gate of Richmond Park lay no more than half a mile away. There were surprising encounters. One day, as we were having a picnic, a figure in Wellington boots paused for a chat; it was Lord Hailsham. On another occasion, James Mason walked past and a figure on horseback turned out to be David Jacobs. As Rosalind discovered when she took advantage of her grandfather's old Austin saloon, the road around the Park was ideal for young people learning to drive, although the sheep and deer wandering across the grasslands led hazardous lives! The flight path from Heathrow Airport was almost overhead, but a more distracting noise came from a nearby house belonging to bakers who set off for work in a sports car at half past five each morning. Our house was not far from the home of Helen's uncle and aunt, the Moyses-Stevens, who lived at Roehampton, an area named 'Cash Kingdom'. Uncle Harold devoted as much care to his garden lawn as he did to his florist business, from which he supplied the Royal household.

Construction of the new Institute building was nearing completion. I drove each morning to the site, behind the West London Hospital at Bute Gardens, Hammersmith, but found that to leave my car south of the river Thames was quicker than taking it to the Institute. For many journeys in and across London, I grew accustomed to the convenience of the underground railway, but was amazed to find that to reach Whitechapel from Hammersmith took as long as the rail journey from Edinburgh to Glasgow, giving ample time to study *Current Contents*![C]

The Royal Festival Hall was within easy reach and we could afford to go occasionally to the opera at Covent Garden. Rosalind learnt the piano, Iain the oboe and Philip, absorbed with The Beatles, took to percussion. At school, a performance of *Joseph and the Amazing Technicolor Dreamcoat* allowed him to use his talented voice. He visited a family in France, and later his French friend came to stay with us, journeying to Hampton Court and down the Thames to see the Crown Jewels and the *Cutty Sark*. At the Hammersmith Odeon, we all watched *One Hundred and One Dalmatians* and *Goldfinger* with great delight, while in Richmond we visited the theatre and occasional concerts. Each of the children's schools had a vigorous interest in sport. St Paul's encouraged Iain and Philip to show their athleticism – both played in the position of wing on the rugby field. Iain argued: 'What's the point of being mangled in the scrum?'

As the years passed, the children were faced with decisions about their future. In 1968, Rosalind decided to follow her mother's example and enrol in the School of Nursing of the Edinburgh Royal Infirmary. After becoming a Registered General Nurse (RGN), she went further and embarked on ophthalmic training. By 1969, after success in his A-level examinations and his achievement in gaining the Montgomery of Alamein Science Prize, Iain was drawn towards Medicine. He prepared a project on '*The growth of neonatal mouse bone*' with the skill that would later bring him such success in ophthalmology. It was already evident that St Mary's Hospital Medical School was prepared to accept him, but the prospect of life in London was not appealing. Edinburgh was a natural choice, but the city was a long way from his friends. He chose Birmingham, and in 1973 was joined by Philip, whose very different scholarly interests were in literature, poetry and history, leading him to become a student of Law and to his LL.B. degree in 1978.

Our children's first year in London was marred by ill health. Philip developed a debilitating illness in which fever was followed by a loss of muscle power, so that for some weeks he could move very little. We remembered that, in 1955, an outbreak of a similar illness had affected 200 nurses at the Royal Free Hospital, London. At first, it was thought that they had a form of epidemic hysteria, but it came to be accepted that the disease, myalgic encephalomyelitis or ME, was probably of viral origin. We were introduced to a very helpful and kindly paediatrician, Herbert Barrie, who not only visited Philip but also examined Rosalind, who had simultaneously contracted a sore throat. Herbert became a good friend and we met later when he took part in the assessment of candidates for the Fellowship examinations of the Royal College of Surgeons of Edinburgh. To make matters worse, it was at this time that Iain began to suffer more discomfort from his injured knee. An operation was unavoidable, and the torn medial meniscus was repaired at the West London Hospital.

But there was time for well-earned holidays. On one occasion, we rented a little cottage in west Wales. Although it was near a lighthouse with an incessant foghorn, this mattered little by contrast with our delight when, quite suddenly, we watched Philip, restored to better health, climbing a steep grass-covered slope on the Pembrokeshire coast. Later that year, with the help of 'JYM 455D', our Austin Westminster car, we made the next of many long journeys northwards that led us to Bamburgh, Edinburgh and Lossiemouth.

In November 1969, we celebrated my mother's 80th birthday by taking her to the restaurant at the top of the new Telephone Tower. Enthusiastic about our move to London, she had agreed to become Chairman of the Brighton and Hove branch of the ARC.

The Institute

The story of the new Institute arose from the marriage of Mathilda Marks, a daughter of Michael Marks, founder of Marks & Spencer, and an American former ballet dancer, Terence Frank Kennedy. Mathilda Marks-Kennedy developed osteoarthritis, but received invaluable help from her doctor, Leslie Lankester. One day, it is said, Mathilda Kennedy asked him: 'What can I do to repay you?' He replied 'Establish a centre to search for the causes of the disorder from which you suffer'.[D] Dr Lankester's proposal was to offer money to St Thomas's Hospital Medical School. St Thomas's, without the necessary space, was unable to accept the bequest and the offer was taken to the Charing Cross Hospital Medical School, the CCHMS, which was in the throes of moving to Fulham. The intention was to design new laboratories to occupy one of the 22 floors in the new building. Then money began to run out, and five stories of the planned building, together with the floor reserved for the Marks/Kennedy laboratories, were sacrificed. Fortunately, there was sufficient space behind the West London Hospital, Hammersmith, to construct a new building, and it was here that the Kennedy Institute was born.

In 1961, the Mathilda and Terence Kennedy Charitable Trust offered £530,000 for the cost of the new building together with £10,000 annually for 10 years, for essential services. As the anticipated costs rose, the ARC added £36,000 and agreed to donate £200,000 over 10 years to cover research. The Scientific Adviser to the Council, Dr L. E. Glynn,[E] argued that preliminary studies could begin, so by June 1966 less than two-thirds of the original grant remained. The ARC confronted this further challenge and underwrote the first three years of what proved to be a very rapid period of growth. Dr Copeman became the Chairman of the Executive Committee of the new Institute and, by 1967, as research programmes developed, grants began to come from the Medical Research Council, the Nuffield Foundation, the Cystic Fibrosis Foundation, the Wellcome Trust, Ciba Laboratories, Syntex Pharmaceuticals and the Dan Mason Research Foundation.

The Institute building[F] (Figure 14.1) in Bute Gardens had been designed by Alan Stubbs and Partners. A spacious entrance hall led up a polished oak stairway to a common room and offices, to rooms accessible to patients and hospital staff and to a library (Figure 14.2), which was divisible into two large but separate rooms, by

Figure 14.1 *The Kennedy Institute seen from Bute Gardens, West London.*

Figure 14.2 *The library of the Institute.*

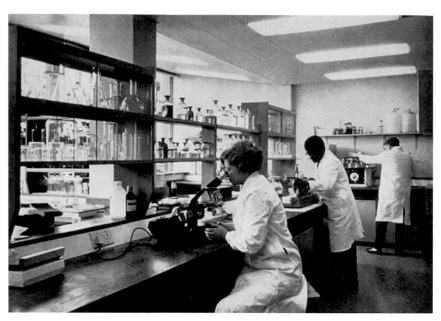

Figure 14.3 *An Institute laboratory.*

folding partitions. Each of the succeeding five floors accommodated research laboratories (Figure 14.3), while the sixth was the animal house, and the seventh space for lift motors and ventilation plant. From the front of the building, a horizontal extension was raised above an open court, within which was a fountain pool and a small, landscaped garden leading to a car park. Behind, a residential or staff block was positioned above a rear exit into Wolverton Gardens.

The opening of the new Institute

The Institute was the first of its kind devoted solely to the study of the rheumatic diseases. It was opened by the Duke and Duchess of Gloucester on the afternoon of 5th October 1966 (Figure 14.4). Lord Porritt, Chairman of the ARC, presided. The Mayor of Hammersmith, 150 politicians, scientists, medical experts and their families and friends watched as the Duchess was presented with a bouquet of flowers by our daughter Rosalind. Very quickly, Dr Copeman called on his friends and colleagues to join the Management Committee.[G]

I had to recruit staff swiftly. My most immediate need was for an experienced secretary. I placed an advertisement in the Press and was surprised almost at once to receive a telephone call: it was from Lord Reith,[H] who told me how much he owed to a young Barbara Hickman. He wished to recommend her highly. Widely respected by staff and management alike, Barbara served the Institute with devotion until 1969. The second most essential post was for a Laboratory

Superintendent. I selected Douglas Irvine, an experienced laboratory scientist whose interests included horology. I placed the Animal House in the capable hands of Paul J. Warden and the workshop in those of W. A. Briggs.

The Charing Cross Hospital staff responsible for the laboratories of the adjoining West London Hospital included W. St C. Symmers,[I] John Sloper and Harold Winner. They had no responsibility for the work of the Institute, but were concerned that its interests might conflict with their own. Professor Sloper in particular, a close associate of Professor Symmers, was not enthusiastic. Adding to this slight air of suspicion was the fact that, without authority, L. E. Glynn had offered Winner access to any electron microscope that might be installed in the Institute. When the moment came and the Sir Edward Lewis Foundation made it possible to purchase such an instrument, Winner invited me to lunch. To his chagrin, I had to tell him that I could not commit the use of the microscope to a laboratory that was not part of the Institute. Angry at the cost of the meal, he quite literally danced with rage.

Figure 14.4 *The opening of the Institute by the Duke and Duchess of Gloucester.*

But there were others on whose personal friendship and professional advice Helen and I depended heavily. They included J. T. (Tom) Scott, Consultant Physician in General Medicine to Charing Cross Hospital and in Rheumatology to the West London Hospital.

Tom became Head of the Institute's Clinical Research Division and my Deputy Director, and Oswald Savage, Editor of the *Annals of the Rheumatic Diseases*, acted in an advisory role. Tom had worked with Eric Bywaters at the Hammersmith Hospital. He was ably assisted by A. B. Myles, Paul Bacon and Rodney Grahame, and later by Dr (now Sir Ravinder) R. N. (Tiny) Maini.[J]

Immunology came to be directed by Dudley Dumonde.[K] The laboratories of the Division were in constant use by his assistant David Morley, whose associates included Gabriel Panayi. In establishing a Division of Biochemistry, I was fortunate in persuading Helen Muir[L] to move from her laboratories at St Mary's Hospital Medical School, where she was collaborating with Professor Neuberger, FRS. She enjoyed the assistance of K. Brandt and M. F. Dale, and was joined later by Tim Hardingham. We decided that the Head of a Division of Cellular Biology was to be Joseph Chayen,[M] and I agreed that he should bring Lucille Bitensky as his Deputy. They were aided by F. P. Altmann, R. G. Butcher and Len Poulter.

I assumed the responsibility for Experimental Pathology myself, ably supported by Franco Quagliata and by my technician, Roy Gillett. Among my research assistants was Phillippa Sanders, who I knew from her excellent student record in Edinburgh; Anne Wyke, who had studied the structure of the spinal vertebrae; Margaret Matthews, who joined my group to investigate the ultrastructure of small blood vessels; and Margaret Wicks, who undertook the measurement of arterial enzymes.

Clinicians and scientists quickly joined us from many parts of the world. They included Hajime ('Jimmy') Inoue[N] (Okayama, Japan), M. A. H. A. ('Mac') El-Maghraby (Egypt), Art Gryfe (Canada), Carlos Soria Herrera (Mexico) and D. C. MacGillivray[O] (Canada). Peter D. Gorevic worked with us on the properties of arterioles and the use of carbon labelling. He subsequently moved to the Mount Sinai Hospital, New York. In a letter to me in 1968, he told me how he had had the extraordinary opportunity of surveying the histological material left by the late Paul Klemperer, the 'father of connective tissue disease'.

The Royal Patron

In December 1967, Princess Margaret opened the Lewis Electron Microscope Laboratory. Not long afterwards, Dr Copeman persuaded her to become the Patron of the Institute, helping the work of the ARC. She made another formal visit in 1968. Welcomed by the Mayor of Hammersmith, by Lord Kindersley and by Dr

Figure 14.5 *Princess Margaret is greeted by Terence Kennedy when visiting the Institute in 1968 with (left to right) J. T. Scott, the author and W. S. C. Copeman.*

Copeman, the Princess arrived in a sparkling apricot-coloured dress with an eye-catching short skirt (Figure 14.5). She made a tour of the Institute, asking well-informed questions and not easily persuaded to accept answers she thought glib or superficial. She looked at our results on articular disease and asked: 'Have you made any *real* progress?' and was obviously fascinated by David Morley's studies of inflammation in experimental arthritis, in which he used radio-active isotopes. So intense was her concentration that when the Lady-in-Waiting reminded her that a distinguished company was awaiting her arrival at their tea tables, the Princess replied: 'Let them wait!' As she sat down with members of the Board, I could not help noticing her long cigarette-holder as she was plied with cucumber sandwiches by Dudley Dumonde.

In 1970, Princess Margaret was present when we all attended the premiere of a slightly improbable adventure film set in Albania, to raise money for the ARC. Rosalind Russell, the star of the film, had developed arthritis and was readily persuaded to support the Appeal. My last audience with Princess Margaret was on 11th March 1971, when I was invited to cocktails in the dark and intimidating rooms of Kensington Palace.[P]

Research

As soon as possible, I resumed my research into arthritis.[2]

With John Chalmers, we had described aspects of the bone disorder, osteo-malacia,[3] but abnormalities of the cells and tissues of arterioles had occupied much of my time in Edinburgh and Cleveland and this work continued for some months in London. Consequently, while studies more directly relevant to the rheumatic diseases were getting underway, we were able once again to reproduce hypertension in laboratory rats and to show that injury to the arterioles associated with high blood pressure could be prevented by the administration of the immunosuppressive compound rubidomycin (now more widely known as daunorubicin).

Dr El-Maghraby, who had moved to the Institute from St George's Hospital Medical School, contributed original observations on blood vessel compo-nents.[4-6] It was during his time at the Institute that an accident occurred that threatened the whole building. 'Mac' had placed a small dish of acetone in a domestic-type refrigerator. The dish contained part of a hen's egg that he was studying. Early one Sunday morning, there was an explosion – the acetone had been ignited by a spark from the refrigerator motor – and the whole contents of the little laboratory room was destroyed, with fragments of glass from above the door embedded in the concrete wall. The fire alarms sounded, but by the time the fire brigade arrived, the stairway and every corridor of the Institute were filled with smoke, the walls blackened. Almost the whole of the public parts of the building required repainting! It was at this time that I read of a report from Australia of a biochemical laboratory demolished, and individuals killed, when a large bottle of ether had exploded after falling to the floor.

Unharmed, Mac returned to Egypt, first to the Institute of Pathology of the Al Azhar University in Cairo, then as consultant pathologist, to the El Maadi Military Hospital.

Dr Franco Quagliata preferred to work at night. He sought to learn a rabbit ear-chamber technique from Dr P. A. G. Monro, an active member of the British Microcirculation Society in Professor J. D. Boyd's Cambridge Department of Anatomy. It was during this time that Anna Kadar (p.256), who had come from Hungary (Chapter 19), used her interest in the elastic tissue of blood vessels to develop new, electron-microscopic techniques for the study of this material. Her work merged closely with my interest in the structure and function of arterioles and their contribution both to hypertension and to connective tissue disease. Her investigations complemented the electron-microscopic studies of Dr Margaret Matthews. When Anna presented her results to the Pathological Society, she added a new word to the English language! Knowing the English word 'roughened', she argued that it would be reasonable to describe some of the appearances she had found as 'smoothened'. Another Research Fellow was Joan Feldman. She struggled to complete her PhD thesis and returned to South Africa for 5 weeks while it was being considered.

In the belief that a better understanding of the microscopic structure of articular cartilage might help to explain why it disintegrates in osteoarthritis, I embarked on microscopic studies of specimens from human and animal joints. I began to investigate the calcium content of cartilage matrix in avian tissue and came across a report in *Nature* of the results of measurements of the mineral content of bone made by the new technique of electron-probe X-ray microanalysis. The author was a Dr T. A. (Ted) Hall of the Cavendish Laboratory, Cambridge. I arranged to visit Dr Hall in the hope that I might learn of his methods at first hand, taking with me microscopic sections from developing chickens' eggs. I found Ted in a compact laboratory with a gigantic Geoscan IV microanalyser. As a collaborator, Ted was a quietly spoken, courteous man with whom it was a pleasure to work. His intellect was revealed one day, after we had completed a series of measurements of calcium and phosphorus.[7] He remarked: 'Now I must pass these figures to one of my research students who can complete the calculations by computer.' Pausing for a moment, he added: 'On reflection, it will be quicker if I do them in my head.'

It was many years later that I discovered that, inadvertently, I had stumbled into scientific collaboration with an American who had acted as a Russian agent during the Second World War. In 1996 the *Washington Post* broke the news that Ted Hall (born Theodore Alvin Holtzberg) had been a man who had given secrets of American nuclear technology to the Soviet Union.[8] A brilliant mathematician, Hall helped to determine the critical mass of uranium required for the Hiroshima bomb. In essence, the information revealed by Ted Hall described the new principle of the plutonium bomb, dropped on the Japanese city of Nagasaki on 9th August 1945. It was in this way that the Russians were able to develop and test an atomic bomb some years before the Americans thought it possible. Inevitably, this startling story raised the question: who was T. A. Hall and what were his motives? It became clear that Hall's father had been an immigrant Russian. Hall was an idealist who had graduated with distinction from Harvard at the precociously early age of 18 and had at once been invited to join the Manhattan Project at Los Alamos. He came to believe that it was not right that only America should have a monopoly of atomic secrets. He thought that he would be doing humanity a favour by ensuring that America's knowledge was shared with their wartime ally, Soviet Russia.

But even the most brilliant physicists, the cleverest agents, are susceptible to human weaknesses! One day, our work at the Cavendish Laboratory was delayed because the Geoscan could not be made to work. A whole morning went by as Ted, his senior technicians and assistants struggled to persuade the electrons to flow. Then, just before lunch, an assistant went round the back of the enormous machine and discovered that a single 13-amp plug was not in its socket! It was the source of power for a monitor without which images from the scanner could not be viewed!

Seen during surgery or at autopsy, cartilage surfaces appeared remarkably smooth. However, looking more closely, with instruments such as the immersion incident light microscope,[9,10] such surfaces display a series of delicate undulations, often related to the presence near the surface of cartilage cells, chondrocytes. These surface irregularities could be viewed with the electron microscope, but in 1966 the preparation of the extremely thin tissue sections needed for this instrument required preliminary immersion in a preservative, a fixative, which might cause artefactual distortion of the surface cells and matrix. Together with my colleague Dr MacGillivray, we collected animal tissue for examination. We chose to investigate pig joints from the Progeny Testing Station of T. Walls & Sons, Tring, knowing that in this animal not only the limb joints but other parts such as the kidney bear a close resemblance to those of man.

It was a time when the scanning electron microscope, the SEM, was becoming available.[11–14] Alice Maroudas (Chapter 21) arranged for me to use the instrument of the Department of Botany at Imperial College, London, and we obtained pictures of cartilage surfaces demonstrating that normal, unloaded articular cartilage surfaces are not smooth but are indeed characterized by microscopic undulations. The results formed the central theme of my 1971 Heberden Oration.[15] Scanning electron microscopy also enabled us to survey the surfaces of synovia[16,17] and helped Hajime Inoue (p.176) gain the experience that led to his scientific progress in Japan (p.204).

A large proportion of my Edinburgh studies had been directed to the anatomical and microscopical changes of rheumatoid arthritis.[18] It was less easy to continue these enquiries in London, because I did not have immediate access to the autopsy service of Charing Cross Hospital. Nevertheless, our results continued to be published,[19] together with comments on the epidemiology and treatment of the disease.[20–25] We had shown that a useful model of arthritis could be provoked by injecting turpentine[26] or caragheenin into rat knee joints (Chapter 11). Alternatively, arthritis could be caused by the injection of an adjuvant, a mixture of the residues of mycobacteria, the organisms that cause tuberculosis, with an oil. At first, the addition of the protein collagen seemed to be necessary[27] and it appeared significant that the arthritis could be inhibited by administering rubidomycin (daunorubicin),[28,29] the immunosuppressive agent that could prevent arteriolar disease in hypertension.

There were, of course, opportunities for reporting technical advances.[30] Many pathologists had begun to sense that attempts should be made to modernize histopathology, a science still resting on techniques originating in the nineteenth century. The manual use of the light microscope to examine sections of tissue stained with coloured dyes remained crucial to hospital diagnosis, but was being overtaken by newer methods. I drafted a paper[31] on this theme for Gordon Signy, Editor of the *Journal of Clinical Pathology*, who was thinking along the same lines and investigating automation in haematology.

Committee, Society and other memberships

I attended the Scientific Coordinating and other Committees of the ARC, primarily to present the Annual Reports of the Institute but also to propose each annual budget. I met many distinguished colleagues at a Physiological Systems Committees of the Medical Research Council and through the Heberden Society, but my membership of an advisory committee of the Nuffield Foundation was brief. In December 1969, W. S. C. Copeman enlisted the support of Lord Reith to propose my name for election to the Athenaeum. Membership of the Pathological Society (p.116) was an essential part of my professional life, and in due course I joined the editorial board of the *Journal of Pathology*.[Q] Inevitably, I was drawn into the meetings of a wide range of societies,[R] and in 1966 was elected to the American Association of Anatomists and to the International College of Angiology.

Visitors

Our contacts with friends and colleagues in Scotland continued and we attended many family gatherings. In the spring of 1970, John Richmond (p.124) wrote to tell us of the illness of one of Helen's old friends, Jenny Woodburn. Helen had stayed with the Woodburns while attending Atholl Crescent, Edinburgh in 1942. She came to know Mrs ('Ma') Woodburn, her daughter Sarah, married to a general practitioner, Dr Turnbull, and her other daughter Jenny. Margaret Daniel came from Edinburgh in January 1971, the month in which Mary Stevens, Edwin Stevens's elder daughter (p.232), married Patrick McGaughey, and on 21st May, we attended the marriage in Berhamstead of Helen's niece, Susan Margaret (Susie) Pike, to Sean Travers-Healy (Figure 13.6).

We welcomed clinicians and scientists to the Institute and to our home. One evening, Ian Duthie (p.124) and Kenneth Walton[S] came for dinner. It would be hard to imagine two colleagues less alike in manner, background and temperament! Among other scientific visitors were Richy Nairn (p.280) from Melbourne, Dr Nanna Svartz and Professor Kodama, who came from Tokyo as head of a Japanese delegation considering the construction of a similar rheumatology institute in Tokyo. His first question was: 'Excuse me, but how far is it to Harrods?' His second enquiry was to ask how long it would take to reach the golf course at St Andrew's. Harry Jellinek, Director of the Second Department of Pathology, Semmelweiss University, visited the Institute from Budapest. Harry (p.254) asked whether we would accept one of his leading research workers, Anna Kadar (p.256), and she joined the Kennedy Institute of Rheumatology on 26th May 1969, returning to Hungary in July 1970. V. T. Tzonchev arrived from Bulgaria, and Donald Bunce Jr from the Osteopathic School of Medicine of the University of Iowa. Dr J. J. Morrison came from the Esso Petroleum Company, while Ken Muirden from Australia, Sir Ashley Miles, FRS, Peter Medawar, FRS, and Barrie Tait were other welcome guests.

Meetings and conferences

Throughout the years 1966–71, one of my obvious responsibilities was to ensure that our research was made known as widely as possible. Our first overseas commitment was to the 10th Congress of Rheumatology in Lisbon on 8th October 1967. In the following year, I attended the Hungarian Society of Rheumatology meeting in Budapest. Both visits are described in Chapter 19. I had been asked by Eric Bywaters, Chairman of the Pathology Committee of the European League Against Rheumatism (EULAR) (p.268), to become secretary of the Committee, and this led to friendships with professional colleagues in Denmark, Switzerland, Germany, Belgium, Poland and Hungary.

I was admitted to Membership of the Royal College of Physicians of London in November 1968, but continued to lecture in the Internal Medicine postgraduate course of the sister College in Edinburgh. I remained an examiner for the Royal College of Surgeons of Edinburgh and, from time to time, an external examiner for degrees such as the DPhil and MSc of the University of Oxford, where my fellow examiners included Dr C. R. Rizza and Dame Janet Vaughan (p.197).

The end of one road

Will Copeman became ill in the autumn of 1970 and was admitted to the Middlesex Hospital. I wrote to Oswald Savage to tell him of the situation, mentioning that I would shortly be attending a meeting in Zurich. Oswald and his wife, an author, lived in Nice. He responded to my news by inviting me to visit them (Figure 14.6).

Figure 14.6 *Dr Oswald Savage at his home in Nice, 1970.*

Leaving the Swiss meeting, I flew to France on 10th September and spent two nights on the Riviera.

Will Copeman's death in November marked a turning point in the development of the Institute. At a commemoration of his life, I read from the Old Testament and said:

> Like all humanists, Will Copeman set a high value on friendship. A physician with a strong inheritance of scholarship, by his own personal efforts he established the single most important concentration of laboratory and scientific staff ever to be devoted to (a search for) the causes of the rheumatic diseases. With his death, an epoch in the history of these crippling ailments has ended.

In spite of the pleasure of working in London, with relatively easy access to theatres, concert halls, galleries and museums, and of many privileges I had been granted, we came to feel that a change both of employment and of location was necessary. Bob Nagle, a good friend, wrote from Edinburgh on 13th January 1970 to say that he was anxiously looking forward to my full-time return to Edinburgh in perhaps two years' time. Bob, like Andrew Shivas (p.155), Angus E. Stuart, Anderson (Glasgow) and Gibson (Hong Kong) were speculating on the succession to G.L. Montgomery (p.126), who was due to retire in 1971.

A change is in sight

It gradually became clear that the loss from the Management Committee of the Kennedy Institute of Will Copeman would complicate my position. Authority became vested in the hands of Sir Brian Windeyer, the influential Dean of the Middlesex Hospital Medical School but not a rheumatologist. I sensed the loss of a university environment and wished to return to an established academic department. There was another, unexpected problem: finance. My salary, equivalent to that of a NHS consultant, remained as it had been at the time of my appointment. I had no private practice and the cost of living in West London while paying school fees was great.

By chance, the approach from Professor Evans, Chairman of the Biological Research Advisory Board (BRAB) of the Microbiological Research Establishment (MRE) had briefly renewed my interest in moving to the directorship of that national institute (pp. 167 and 200). I knew that the University of Southampton was considering Pathology as a new subject in its curriculum and that, in Dundee, A. C. Lendrum was approaching retirement. However, Sir John Henry Biggart was also about to retire after 30 years in the Queen's University of Belfast Chair of Pathology, and my thoughts turned in this direction. Henry Biggart was known internationally for the skill with which he had established an influential department and added lustre to a famous medical school. In my approach to all these institutions, I received warm and sometimes unexpectedly strong support in letters from Brian Windeyer and from Michael Woodruff. I had become a Member of the Royal College of Physicians of London in 1969, a distinction which led to the Fellowship in 1975, the year in which I was also elected to the Fellowship of the Royal College of Pathologists.

Helen and I realized that to accept a position in Belfast would call for far-reaching changes in every aspect of our domestic life and that such a move would take us further away from my mother, my brother and our daughter and eldest son. Once again, we would have to seek not only a new home but, of critical importance, new schools for Philip and David. Our friends and medical colleagues were doubtful of the wisdom of leaving London, with all its associations, to cross the water to a troubled Ulster.

However, after the most careful thought, we agreed that I should seize this unexpected opportunity. We knew well that it was the year in which Professor George Montgomery was due to end his substantial contributions to the Edinburgh Chair of Pathology. He and I had continued an active correspondence throughout the years I had been in London, but I decided not to pursue the opportunity of succeeding him and, when it came to the time for him to leave, Angus Stuart, Andrew Shivas and I had the privilege of speaking at his farewell dinner, an occasion that brought together many of those with whom I had worked over the years.

CHAPTER 15

Across the water

To the Lagan

There are more things in heaven and earth, Horatio,
Than are dreamt of in your philosophy

Shakespeare[1]

From the Mull of Kintyre to the rugged coast of Antrim is no more than 16 miles. Yet in 1971, to Londoners, Ulster and mainland Britain appeared different worlds. When I said that I was moving to the Province, some friends declared: 'You are mad!' Others asked: 'But where will the children go to school?'[A]

My answer was that the educational system in Ulster was of the highest quality, the population, in spite of social disturbance, remarkably stable, so that the skills of graduate and technical staff were excellent. I added that the Medical School of the Queen's University of Belfast was the sixth largest in the country and that students came from all parts of the world.[B] I said that I had discussed my move with an enthusiastic Sir Eric Ashby, a former Vice Chancellor of the Queen's University of Belfast and now Master of Clare College, Cambridge.[C, 2]

But neither we nor our London friends were fully aware of the extent of the 'Troubles' now afflicting Ulster or of the impact that the disorders were having on daily life. The *Observer* journalist Robert Chesshyre aptly described life in Belfast as 'like living in a city in a state of siege', with 'many people – especially Catholics – never venturing from their areas, certainly not after dark'. We were about to learn!

A new home

During an exploratory visit I paid to Belfast (Figure 15.1), I had found valuable accommodation at the Wellington Park Hotel, but, settling in the city on 1st December, I accepted the advice of R. T. (Bob) Spence:[D] he recommended a small flat in Biggart House, a modern residential block conveniently near the Institute of Pathology but close to a part of the city where gunfire could be heard each evening.

Chapter summary
- A new home
- The hospitals
- The social scene
- The University Department of Pathology
- The Faculty of Medicine
- Meeting my students
- Teaching
- Research
- Countryside, games, schools and visitors
- Meetings and travel
- Family

Figure 15.1 *A Townsend Thoresen ferry approaching Belfast.*

When Helen, Philip and David came from London, we rented accommodation for some weeks in Garranard Park, Circular Road. Before long, however, we found 2 Woodland Avenue (Figure 15.2) in the beautiful area of Helen's Bay, near the shores of the Belfast Loch, a short drive from Holywood and within easy reach of Bangor and Strangford Loch (Figure 15.3). Desmond Archer[E] soon became a neighbour.

Our daughter, Rosalind, busy with her nursing studies in Edinburgh, was engaged to Iain Norman Fanshawe McQueen, a final-year medi-

Figure 15.2 *Woodland Avenue, Helen's Bay.*

Figure 15.3 *A view of the coast of County Down.*

cal student and son of an Edinburgh general practitioner. Their wedding, on 3rd September 1971, took place in the Greyfriars Church, Edinburgh and was conducted by the Minister, the Reverend Stuart Loudon. In the celebrations that followed in the Calais Hotel, Professor George Montgomery was among the guests and my friend Angus Stuart, toasting the bride, made an eloquent speech.

Our son Iain, a medical student in Birmingham, had developed an interest in diseases of the eye and, on the advice of Professor Archer, spent some months at Moorfields Eye Hospital, London, a factor influencing his decision to specialize in this field after his graduation in 1976.

Our second son, Philip, reluctantly leaving St Paul's School, London, was accepted by Campbell College, Belfast where the Headmaster was Robin Morgan.[F] Philip was a considerable athlete, gifted with the skills of sprinting and invited to run for the Irish Schools. He was particularly well-read, with a liking for T. S. Elliot and Harold Pinter's *Caretaker*.

David, now aged 11, moved to Rockport School, Cragavad, a beautiful wooded site near the coast. He enjoyed cricket and football, but did not find the Headmaster, Eric Tucker, sympathetic to his particular needs. In 1973, on the recommendation of Helen Miller, we decided he would benefit from a move to Abbotsholme School, Derbyshire.

The hospitals

The Royal Victoria Hospital, Belfast, the RVH, traced its origins back for more than 200 years.[3] By 1971, the campus was much larger than that of the Edinburgh Royal Infirmary and included the Maternity and Children's Hospitals, the Dental School and the University Departments of Pathology and Microbiology. There were 165 consultants.

The hospital benefited from a large dining room, a useful venue for informal chats with younger staff, and a consultant club where I could meet my colleagues in the early evenings for informal conversations that would often turn to the day's news – the firing of a bazooka rocket against the walls of the Children's Hospital, an explosion in the town or the shooting of a consultant's son on his way to school. It was a surprise to me to find that the Belfast surgeon who repaired defects in skulls injured by accident or explosion was also a consultant to the Eire Army, while one gynaecologist did not hesitate to drive his Rolls Royce to Dublin to see his stabled race-horses.

The Institute of Pathology, a 1933 five-storey brick building, incorporated a lecture theatre, classrooms, a museum and the laboratories that provided diagnostic services for the District. I became Director of the Institute, and a bold noticeboard proclaimed this fact to the disquiet of Dr (later Professor) M. Gerald (Gerry) Nelson, consultant haematologist and many years my senior. As an honorary consultant, I was quickly drawn into the very busy biopsy and autopsy services of the hospital. The workload was high and my working week during my first six months in Belfast averaged 105 hours. It was a time when new methods were coming into use and we began to consider computers as a means of sending laboratory reports quickly to areas distant from Belfast

One of my responsibilities was for the mortuary of the RVH. Near the Falls Road, it held the organs and tissues of the victims of the shootings and explosions that characterized the 'Troubles'. The forensic investigation of these miserable victims was the intensive and unremitting responsibility of Professor Tom Marshall[G] and his skilled assistants. When I made my daily visit to the little building and its devoted attendants it was not unusual to find the body of a victim of a terrorist atrocity on a mortuary table. On one occasion, a hundred or more limb bones, hands, feet and heads, retrieved in sackloads from the site of a bomb blast, were arranged grotesquely in heaps. In the case of a young woman foolish enough to peer from her front door one night, a minute entrance wound on her left temple was the fatal result of the 0.22 calibre bullet of an assassin who had mistaken her drab dress for an army uniform.

The corridors of the RVH included a bank, near the coronary care unit, and a post office. The cardiac patients were occasionally disturbed! One day, armed militants attempted to rob the bank. Suddenly, paratroopers came round the corner and shot them dead. The car park opposite the Institute was guarded by a uniformed officer responsible for closing the gates leading to the Falls Road. He unlocked them for me each evening. After 5 pm, the sound of a whistle would often be heard, a sign for rifle fire to reverberate around the area. One evening, a small car leaving the rear entrance to the hospital grounds was crushed by an armoured car responding to an emergency call.

On another occasion, the long-serving technician who projected slides during teaching came to me and said: 'I have to leave.' He explained: 'I'm a volunteer in the Ulster Defence Force [the UDF]. All of us have revolvers. The IRA don't like it and told me that I'd have to stop carrying a gun or they'd shoot me.' I said: I'm very sorry to hear this, Les. What are you going to do?' He said: 'I'm lucky. The mortuary attendant at Forster Green Hospital has just been assassinated for not paying his dues, and I'm going to take his place.' It was a vivid reminder of the large part played in Belfast life by 'protection money'.

My association with the City Hospital, Lisburn Road, was close. The hospital had its own diagnostic laboratories, but shared in undergraduate and postgraduate teaching. I was fortunate to enjoy the help of the senior consultant and Head of Department, Professor John Edgar Morison, an internationally recognized expert in children's pathology, respected for his wise opinions but, on his own admission, not by nature a public speaker.

I was privileged to be a consultant to the Catholic Mater Hospital as well as to the RVH. I decided to break with Protestant tradition and learn of the Mater by conducting autopsies there myself. I found a state of neglect, the little mortuary infested by rats, uncollected refuse littering the floor. By contrast, the medical and surgical care and the teaching were of the highest quality. Any consultant whose patient had died would come to the mortuary to discuss the clinical problem and then invite me to an intensive care ward, where we would sit in a window bay drinking tea. I was told that it was a room from which a notorious but critically injured prisoner had one day sprung to life, cast off his bandages, thrown aside his transfusion tubes, leapt through the window and run away! I was sympathetic to the hospital's needs and asked Dr Mullaly, Chairman of the Medical Staff Committee, to speed efforts to modernize the mortuary building and to accelerate the supply of instruments.

The social scene

We soon made good friends in Helen's Bay. Among them were Doreen and Derek Eves. A fervent follower of the church, she was confronted with disaster when Derek was drowned accidentally in Strangford Loch while attempting to board his yacht.

We took advantage of the countryside, drove from time to time to the coastal villages and towards the Mourne Mountains, and occasionally northwards to Coleraine and the Giant's Causeway. However, the 'Troubles' were at their height and evidence of the disorders could not be avoided. During our early weeks in Helen's Bay,

I took a morning train to the city centre. Walking up the Falls Road to the RVH, I was careful to avoid the rifles of soldiers stretched on the ground, at street corners. The road was a frequent venue for marches by demonstrators and it was not easy to predict when crowds would gather. I soon learned to use my Austin car, although its name, Westminster, was not popular, even at army road blocks!

The Troubles influenced our family life directly and indirectly. On one occasion when there was a general strike, masked agitators prevented cars from passing so that supplies could not be brought. Medical and nursing staff were unable to reach their work and the possibility arose of having to fly blood for transfusion from Liverpool. But blocked roads did not stop Helen from cycling to Bangor with her shopping basket: masked demonstrators waved her past with cheery words! In Helen's Bay, the house opposite was occupied by an irascible businessman. One Sunday afternoon, he shouted that he could not stand the noise of Philip's drums any longer – Philip practised in our garage – and had sent for the police. I asked him whether, in the middle of the insurgency, this was a reasonable call upon their time.

We learned quickly that, in Ulster, religion and politics were not subjects for amusement and I was reminded of the advice I received before travelling in 1958 to the United States, where, I was told: 'Never discuss politics, sex or religion.' In the United States, and in Belfast, this advice was seldom heeded! One day, Helen and I were invited to join four others for lunch with a consultant gynaecologist and his wife. As we settled to coffee, one lady, a stern-faced woman, asked stridently: 'I'm a liberal Protestant. What do we have here?' Astonished, I realized she was questioning our religious affiliations. Without appreciating that she was also asking us whether we were loyalists or republicans, I replied: 'For my part, I'm a Scottish Buddhist.' There was a stony silence.

Some months later, when Helen, Philip, David and I travelled to Dublin together (Figure 15.4), we were able to visit the National Gallery and to watch a play at the Abbey Theatre. Philip had pursued his fascination with pop music and wished to have a full drum kit comprising a bass drum, tenor drums and cymbals. We bought these in a music shop, where they were packed in a large cardboard case. However, because of the continual cross-border 'incidents' and political sensitivities, security measures were tight on the train service between Dublin and Belfast. At one point, the train drew to a halt. A guard walked through the train, calling out 'Does anyone own a large cardboard packing case that is in the luggage compartment?' (It might have contained a bomb). We had to confess to the drum kit, and all was well.

Our holidays were often spent in Scotland. A memorable visit to the Glenogle Sailing School at Lochearnhead allowed Philip to take a first lesson in sailing and to be given the National Elementary Dayboat Certificate. I joined the venture, but had a narrow escape

Figure 15.4 *Philip, Helen, David and the author, Dublin, 1973.*

when our little boat capsized and I had to swim ashore – the rescue craft was at the other end of the Loch.

The University Department of Pathology[4]

The influence of the Troubles on the practice of pathology was very obvious (p.188). Teaching was much less affected. Disturbances in University life were relatively slight, although the road from the RVH to the University passed through areas where shooting and abduction were not rare, and a tradesman called to our home to repair a sofa carried a revolver. I received great support from the University Vice Chancellor, Arthur Vick. He learnt that I had been given no Merit Award, part of a graded NHS system for remunerating senior clinical staff. Sir Arthur pursued this anomaly on my behalf, but it was not until late in my time at the University of Manchester that I was granted this advantage.

My predecessor, Professor John Henry Biggart,[H] now Sir John, had retired before I reached Belfast and I encountered him only occasionally. My immediate colleague and deputy was Professor Florence McKeown.[I] Next in line was Dr (later Professor) Ingrid Allen,[J] a neuropathologist. Frank O'Brien held a Chair in Dental Pathology and was a good friend as well as an able colleague. He greatly helped and advised Bill Hunt (p.134). The Medical School staff included Sir

John's son, Dennis Biggart, who subsequently moved to a consultant position at the City Hospital, James Sloan, Denis O'Hara and Hoshang Bharucha. Claire M. Hill, a young physician appointed as a Research Registrar in August 1972, became a consultant pathologist in 1980; she had worked closely with Dr Mollie McGeown (p.194).

In spite of the excellence of these colleagues and of our trainees, John McClure, Rosemary Shillington and Philip McKee, it was clear that there was a shortage both of diagnostic and of teaching staff, and I conveyed my anxieties to Arthur Vick. I told him that to cover the North of Ireland there appeared to be only seven consultant pathologists, but that, compared with the national average, and taking into account the involvement of the City Hospital laboratory in teaching, there should be many more. I proposed that Dr W. E. Hunt[K] be invited to come as a locum consultant (Figure 15.5) and that Dr Sloan, a Belfast graduate now working in Sheffield, be considered as a candidate for a consultancy at the Ulster Hospital. As a means of adding to the number of those in training, I investigated the possibility of a rotating Senior Registrar appointment to be held jointly with the Norfolk and Norwich Hospital, where my friend John Rack (p.114) was a consultant.

Figure 15.5 *Helen amuses W. E. (Bill) Hunt during a visit to Coleraine*

The technical staff was led by Bert Russell, Chief Technician, who had joined J. H. Biggart from Edinburgh in 1940. He was an invariably loyal colleague and devoted servant of the Department. He was succeeded by his close colleague Cecil Bennett, who retired in 1989. Jack Reid was Chief Technician in charge of the preparation laboratory. I relied equally heavily on Stuart Cameron, who cared for the electron microscope laboratory, and David Mahaffey, photographer and general factotum, an irrepressible 'character' who was sorely missed when he retired in January 1974 (Figure 15.6). I depended heavily on the skills of my secretaries, of whom the first sought to prove her worth by arriving each morning before me! For some weeks, we played a little game: the earlier I arrived, the earlier she came. Eventually, the trial ended, but her obsessive character drove her to keep her own diary of every visitor, every appointment and every commitment until 1973, when she was succeeded by a lady whose husband was serving with the Parachute Regiment in Belfast and whose characteristic was to bring with her a late breakfast of chocolate biscuits.

Figure 15.6 *At the retirement of David Mehaffey: (front, left to right) Sir John Henry Biggart, Mr Mehaffey, the author. Florence McKeown is at centre, back row, Bert Russell at her left.*

The Faculty of Medicine

The Medical School Dean, Professor Peter (later Sir Peter) Leslie Froggatt, a man of great talent, was supportive in almost everything I planned. In 1976, he succeeded to the University Vice Chancellorship. The medical staff of the Royal Victoria Hospital of Belfast included many well-known physicians, among whom it was impossible to overlook the unique personality and clinical contributions of James Francis (Frank) Pantridge, MC.[5] Like other former prisoners of the Japanese during the Second World War,[L] he did not suffer fools gladly and combined originality of ideas with a provocative manner of expressing them. In his original research, first welcomed in the United States, he showed that by using high-speed ambulances to reach patients suffering 'heart attacks' quickly and to carry them rapidly to hospital, he could greatly reduce their mortality. I enjoyed a close working relationship with John Vallance Owen, Professor of Medicine and renowned for his studies of diabetes mellitus. His son was a fellow student of Iain's in Birmingham. J. J. Pritchard, Professor of Anatomy and Editor of the *Journal of Anatomy*, was another respected colleague.

I knew Harold W. Rodgers, Professor of Surgery less well. He retired in 1973 and was succeeded by Arthur Douglas Roy. I soon discovered that Terence Leslie Kennedy, a gastroenterological surgeon, demonstrated an unique knowledge of- and skill in the diagnosis and treatment of diseases of the stomach, intestines and related organs. In microbiology, I shared many interests with Kenny Fraser, who held the University Chair, helped by the fact that his 'right-hand man' was Robert (Bob) Gillies, with whom I had collaborated in Edinburgh. I came to have a similar partnership with Dr Desmond Neill,[M] Head of the Clinical Chemistry Laboratories. In the City Hospital, Dr Mary Graham (Mollie) McGeown was a recognized authority in renal disease; she and her husband became good friends. Through Dr Stanley Roberts, consultant in rheumatology, I learned much of the Musgrave Park Hospital.

Meeting my students

My new position presented unusual challenges. I had to accept the great influence that my predecessor, John Henry Biggart, had exerted over many years on the pattern of medical teaching. Pathological anatomy and histology retained a dominance, reflected in the competitive annual student debates between Belfast and Dublin, a tradition no longer obvious in other medical schools, where molecular biology, cytogenetics, immunology and virology were among a host of increasingly important disciplines.

Then there was the character of the students, a majority from the North of Ireland but many from other parts of the United Kingdom and from Europe. What mattered more than the students' nationality, I soon discovered, was their high academic quality, their freedom of expression, their tolerance of reasonable academic criticism, and their delight in sport, music and theatre. It was the custom to hold a 'Dean's Birthday Party' at which a pantomime was performed, and the identity and character of the Faculty staff caricatured. So it was no surprise to find that my classes expected vigour, clarity, stimulus and a proper grasp of contemporary medical and scientific knowledge from their lecturers.

I learned the hard way! Within a few days of arriving in Belfast, a call from Peter Elmes, Professor of Therapeutics, explained that he was not well and asked whether I could take his place at a student dinner. He warned that I would be expected to speak – few evening functions in Ulster, whether medical, academic or student, ended without speeches! I agreed – as a newcomer I could do no less – and enjoyed a friendly meal in the company of a large body of young people. But I made a serious misjudgement. Assuming that the gathering would not want dull words from someone who they knew by that time to be a 'mere research worker from that unfriendly place, London', I contented myself with: 'I am Professor Gardner. Thank you for asking me to this, my first Belfast student dinner. We shall see much of each other during the next few months so I shall say no more now.' It was clear that there was disappointment and frustration: the students were expecting jokes, repartee and an entertaining reminder of how they were part of one of Europe's finest medical schools. I realized that I should have seized the opportunity of impressing on the class that I was not what they feared – a foreign 'backroom worker' from a research institute 'across the water' – but that I shared their hope that together we could develop the most modern and vigorous style of medical education, offering them a bright and prosperous future of opportunity.

Teaching

New plans to modernize teaching were clearly essential. I held early meetings with all my medical colleagues and with the senior technical staff to explain my ideas. I hoped to persuade the Faculty of Medicine to add to the number of lecturers and to extend the programmes. To begin with, my classes were spread over four terms, the first in the summer term of the third year, centring on the 'Principles of pathology', the following three (the fourth year) devoted to 'Systematic pathology'. However, it became possible to extend the time devoted to the 'Principles' by adding classes in the second, spring term of the third year.

To allow two practical classes to be taught simultaneously, I planned to divide the large classroom in two, using moveable soundproof partitions of the kind I had found so successful in the library of the Kennedy Institute. Part of my plan was to modernize the mortuary demonstrations held at lunchtime each day: they were rarely attended by more than six or seven students, but more, I guessed, might be attracted by the use of television. The Open University had shown that television could revolutionize the impact of lectures and demonstrations, and I decided to test this new technique already used in Aberdeen lecture theatres.

Dr Colhoun and his staff of the Queen's University Audiovisual Department were skilled and enthusiastic. Together, we assembled in the mortuary a black-and-white television camera and two monitors, and with this cheap equipment – the initial cost was equivalent to 20d per day per student (a little over 8p in decimal currency) – I began to demonstrate the anatomical details of each day's autopsies to the lunchtime classes. At once, the attendance rose. In place of a handful of enthusiasts, as many as 50 or more students poured in. Every day, I invited the consultant whose case we were analysing to describe the clinical problems he had encountered. With colour cameras and monitors, attendance soared to more than 100. John McClure and I reported our experiences to the Pathological Society in Newcastle, England.

Humour always has a part to play in effective teaching, and on one occasion I turned to Mathew Baillie.[6] In 1812, one of his engravings was of a poor man who had rashly placed a William III crown in his mouth. It slipped: impacted in his throat, he suffered a 'flux of blood' and died. The coin, bearing the King's head, was shown in the drawing, protruding from the pharynx. No image could be better suited to Belfast humour: knowledge of the Battle of the Boyne[N] was ingrained within the minds of Ulster students and this was a sure way of capturing the attention of a class who might not otherwise be interested in diseases of the mouth, pharynx and oesophagus. But the shoe could be on the other foot. On another day, while lecturing on tissue transplantation, the class seemed unusually restive. Snorts, giggles and laughter accompanied my attempts to explain aspects of autoimmune disease. Only at the end of the lecture did I notice a pair of trousers hanging above the screen. It was the birthday of one of the youngsters and his friends had celebrated by removing his garments before my talk started.

Class (termly) and professional (annual) examinations were part of the system. It was essential to find a senior colleague to act as External Examiner. Professor Alastair (later Sir Alastair) Currie accepted the invitation but was never able to 'cross the water'. However, I was fortunate in being able to replace him with my enthusiastic Liverpool friend, Donald Heath.[O] Strange problems, some related to social disturbances, arose during both oral and written examinations. Marking papers submitted for the third professional examination, I saw that one young man, answering the question 'Discuss the causes and pathological features of leukaemia', had written abject nonsense. The question was: had he been taking drugs? Both his parents were general practitioners who could shed no light on his problem. He denied any addiction, but admitted

Figure 15.7 *Examiners for the Honours BSc in Pathology: (front, left to right) the author, Professor Dermot Hourihane, Dr Ingrid Allen.*

that for days before the examination he had drunk a pint of strong coffee every hour. In another instance, a girl was in tears before an examination and would not enter the hall: her father, who owned a pub, had been threatened by the IRA.

In addition to the large numbers preparing for the professional examinations in pathology, there was a small but highly selective class sitting an Honours BSc, a programme calling for an additional 'intercalated' year of work. My colleague Professor Dermot Hourihane (Figure 15.7) came from Dublin to assist in examining these students, and in time I returned the favour.

During these years, I continued to examine for the Fellowship of the Royal College of Surgeons of Edinburgh and was called upon to examine in Oxford and other universities. In Oxford, Dame Janet Vaughan, DBE, Principal of Somerville College, Oxford, was a fellow examiner (p.181) and we shared long discussions when she came to Belfast.

Research

Behind these changes in teaching lay the demand to develop vigorous research programmes and to publish original work, enhancing the Institute's international reputation and bringing much-needed money from Research Councils and other funding bodies. Nor might I allow any serious pause in my earlier research, in the publication of original papers and books,[7] in the welcoming of visitors or in attendance at conferences. In the competitive world of medical and biological research, there could be no prolonged interruption. With support from the ARC (p.169) and the help of occasional studentships and fellowships, it proved possible to build a new team of investigators dedicated to the search for the nature and causes of arthritis and rheumatism.

As one necessary step, taking my studies towards the physical properties of cartilage, I formed a valuable association with the Department of Mechanical Engineering, the Head of which was the distinguished Professor Crossland. One day, I encountered him at the airport as we were both journeying to mainland Britain. I asked him the purpose of his visit. He said: 'I am going to Dounreay to seal a crack in a nuclear reactor.' Thereupon, he reached for his wallet, brought out a sliver of material the size of a postage stamp and explained: 'This is all the explosive I need.'

Crossland recommended Cecil Armstrong, a PhD student, for a named Fellowship given for the investigation of rheumatism but, until my arrival, never used. I met Cecil on 2nd July 1973: his project was for the direct mechanical study of human hip joints. Specimens were placed in a rig, the original purpose of which had been the testing of Ford motor car axles! With an X-ray plant beside the rig, Cecil measured the deformation of the joint cartilage as increasing loads were applied. He presented the results in a paper given at the Hammersmith Postgraduate Medical School.[8] It was the start of an association that culminated in his publication of a number of highly original scientific papers, leading in turn, to the resumption of much further research, in Manchester (Chapter 18) in the same field.

We were joined by Roy Elliot, a biochemist who had completed his PhD in Belfast on collagen hydrolysis, and by Ruth Gilmore, a niece of Professor W. St C. Symmers (p.175). When I moved from Belfast to Manchester, Roy came with us, but soon returned to his native Ulster. Another active research fellow was Barrie Longmore. By 1974, C. J. Kirkpatrick,[P] already an international athlete, was well established as one of my PhD students. He benefited greatly from the wise advice of Dame Honor Fell of the Strangeways Laboratory, Cambridge, who agreed to act as his external supervisor. CJ, as he was often called, became an influential figure in European pathology. I was also approached by a young dental surgeon, Nairn H. F. Wilson,[Q] who wished to learn our techniques for studying surface structures. His subsequent MSc and PhD theses and studies of the temporomandibular joint were the start of a long period of collaboration (p.243).

To continue the use of scanning electron microscopy in the investigation of cartilage surfaces, I depended heavily on the goodwill of Professor Alwyn (later Sir Alwyn) Williams of the Queen's University of Belfast Department of Geology. However, he left in December 1973 and I was concerned that the instrument might be moved from his department. Fortunately, I was still able to use the instruments of the Cavendish Laboratory, Cambridge and, in 1974, I called on Peter Marriott at the Kennedy Institute, for help with quartz slides for the examination of new material.

Professor J. J. R. Duthie asked me to come to Edinburgh to complete the studies of rheumatoid arthritis that he had initiated in collaboration with the Inveresk Research Laboratories (Chapter 13). He wanted me to perform the autopsies on his baboons to which live synovial cells from patients with rheumatoid arthritis had been given three years previously.[9] I agreed and left Belfast on a Sunday morning. The airport was unusually quiet. At the security checkpoint, the staff, inspecting my case with its array of scalpels, knives and saws, was incredulous when I explained that the reason for my journey was to perform autopsies in Edinburgh on 25 baboons. Clearly, I had spent too long in the bar!

Countryside, games, schools and visitors

A simple account of professional life in Ulster cannot do justice to all the joys of this startlingly beautiful country or to the stability, steadfastness and reliability of the great majority of its people even in times of great trouble. It was inevitable that political dissension, crime and violence should hog the headlines. But I found, as so many others have done, that on the shores or in the hills, on the golf courses and rugby fields, and in the concert halls and academic centres, few parts of the United Kingdom could better express the attributes of a people. Golf, like rugby football, was taken very seriously. One day, I was invited by a senior consultant, the captain of the Royal County Down Club, near Newcastle, to join him and his friends in a game. It was obviously an indirect assessment of my suitability for the Chair of Pathology! The game occupied a whole day, since we started with coffee at the captain's house before a 30-mile drive southwards. An excellent lunch preceded a serious match, in which I played badly. After returning to the city, I was not surprised by an invitation to dinner, so this single game represented an entire day of genial social exchange! Watching rugby took less time, but games involving the Ulster team were of the highest quality.

We made journeys to Rockport School, conveniently near the shops in Hollywood and Bangor. Until Philip began his undergraduate studies in Birmingham, we joined parents' meetings at Campbell College to discuss with his teachers his progress in the subjects he preferred, especially History and English Literature. Iain visited us regularly and enjoyed the use of our little Fiat car to prepare for his driving test. Rosalind and Iain McQueen came less often. My mother did not choose to venture 'across the water', but Helen drove her mother, Emily Harrower, from Edinburgh to Stranraer so that they could catch the ferry to Belfast.

It was not surprising that I received fewer professional visitors than had been the case in London. However, among those who came was Dr R. F. Robertson, Honorary Secretary of the Royal College of Physicians of Edinburgh, who stayed with us during a scientific meeting, as did Donald Heath, our external examiner. My contacts with overseas colleagues continued when Professor Salter came from Canada.

Meetings and travel

My research programmes led to invitations to overseas conferences, described in later chapters.

In 1973, I was invited to deliver the Watson Smith Lecture to the Royal College of Physicians of London.[10] At almost the same moment, I became an Honorary Member of the Hungarian Society of Anatomy and Pathology and continued to attend meetings of the Arthritis and Rheumatism Council, the Medical Research Society and the Bone and Tooth Society. Another task in 1974 was to join a group representing the Medical Research Council on an inspection of the Kennedy Institute.

Meetings of the Biological Research Advisory Board (BRAB) of the Ministry of Defence (pp. 167 and 182) continued to take place at Porton. While in London, the journey to the Centre was a simple drive. However, to reach Porton from Ulster required either air or sea as well as rail travel. Of particular interest were visits when special topics such as the techniques of satellite surveys were demonstrated. Virology and immunology occupied much time and a visit to the Meteorological Centre at Bracknell was revealing. In the North of Ireland, where the security of the Board proceedings was paramount, Governmental communications were mainly by letter or telephone, but could sometimes be by military channels. One day, sitting in my office in the Institute of Pathology, there was a knock at the door and a rifle barrel appeared. To my relief, the unexpected visitor was not a frustrated student but a uniformed soldier carrying a document from BRAB.

One price paid for being administrative head of a university department is attendance at innumerable committees. When the responsibility extends to include the National Health Service, the challenge is even greater. At Queen's, I attended the Academic Council and was a member of the Faculty of Medicine, while hospital medical staff meetings occupied further time. There was much correspondence. In October 1974, Winfried Mohr, from Ülm, told me that Professor Beneke had died: I had been hoping to visit him and Professor Sandritter, authors of a fine German text. George Meachim wrote from Liverpool about our shared interests and I heard from Dr Malik, now in Khartoum, that he had been advanced to a Readership. I kept in touch with Dr Paul Byers and continued my long association with my dear friend Charlie Moule (p.52): in December 1972, I visited him in Cambridge shortly before I became a Fellow of the Royal College of Pathologists.

Family

While all these varied events were taking place, as the conflicting politics of Ulster were emerging from their dark shadows, our family began to grow! On 17th January 1974, Rosalind's eldest son David Iain Lindsay McQueen was born in Edinburgh. Helen travelled to join them and to help to care for our first grandchild. By 1976, when our granddaughter Jane was born on 9th March, Dr and Mrs McQueen had moved to Glasgow, where Iain worked with Professor Simpson in neurology, at the Southern General Hospital. Again Helen journeyed to be with them and helped in Jane's care. It was only a few weeks after the death, on 26th February, of Helen's brother-in-law, John Pike, DFC and bar. Later in the year, we had the great pleasure of attending Iain's graduation ceremony in Birmingham (Figure 15.8).

Towards the end of 1976, it was clear to me that Rosalind, Iain, Philip and David would all be happier if their parents were again in mainland Britain. No one who has not enjoyed the experience of life in Ulster and time in Dublin can ever forget their unique attractions. In spite of this, I decided that the experience of the North of Ireland with its breathtakingly beautiful countryside and the privilege of working in the scholarly avenues of the Queen's University of Belfast were not fully balanced by the time and the cost of travelling 'across the water' and the challenges imposed by the political and social problems of the Province.

I explored the possibility of returning to London, of an appointment in Sheffield and other cities, and considered an earlier option of moving to North America or Australia. But family ties and common sense prevailed, so that when an opening arose in Manchester (Chapter 18), I quickly expressed my interest. On my departure from Belfast, I was given a most generous Departmental dinner, as well as particularly fine gifts from the consultant staff of the Mater Hospital. I was succeeded by Florence McKeown, and she in turn by Peter Toner (1984–2001).

Figure 15.8 *Iain Gardner at his graduation in Birmingham, 1976.*

CHAPTER 16

Japan and a view of China

Tokyo Bay and the Yellow Sea

Japan offers as much novelty ... as an
excursion to another planet.

Isabella Bird[1]

Walking off the plane in the huge, barren landscape of Alaska bespattered with lakes and sparse forests, my hand was seized by a complete stranger. It was a German physician, Herr Dr Ott.[A] Without any introduction, he said: 'I have much enjoyed your book!' We were friends at once.

A FIRST VISIT TO THE FAR EAST

We were travelling to Tokyo, on the way to Kyoto. It was September 1973, the occasion of our initial visit to Asia and the first of two junctures when we were able to leave Belfast to attend international meetings. The reason for travelling to the Far East was to take part in a Congress of Rheumatology. We had flown from London, across Greenland, landing to refuel in Anchorage. Our first sight of Japan was of Tokyo Bay (Figure 16.1), with gigantic oil tankers approaching the port. We flew on, landed at Osaka and were taken by coach to the Grand Hotel, Kyoto, where we met Ian Duthie (p.124) (Figure 16.2). Travelling alone, he was delighted to be offered a little whisky in our room. He had prepared for the evening by exchanging his clothes for the kimono provided for each guest!

The meeting[B] started on Sunday, 30th September, with more than 1200 participants from all parts of the world gathered at the Expo 70 conference centre (Figure 16.3). The beauty of the Japanese gardens, where huge, brightly coloured carp swam towards the edge of the lake, contrasted with the concrete and steel building. Many speakers had with them 'accompanying persons' of widely different cultures, the conspicuous formality of our Japanese hosts in sharp contrast to the brusque behaviour of the Americans and Australians. At the first evening reception, before any speech of welcome, the Americans rushed towards the tables laden with food and square, wooden cups containing sake.

Chapter summary
- A first visit to the Far East
- Kyoto City
- Osaka and Nara
- Bangkok
- In the Orient again
- Okayama
- A formal occasion
- To China
- Xian
- Suzhou
- Shanghai
- Guilin
- Hong Kong

Figure 16.1 *Tokyo Bay from the air.*

Figure 16.2 *Ian Duthie, (right) J. A. D. (Jock) Anderson (seated, at back) and another delegate.*

Next day, the formal presentation of more than 600 scientific papers began. Our London friend, Dr Hajime Inoue (p.176) (Figure 16.4), gave two talks on the work he had started at the Kennedy Institute and was a participant in a third presentation. It was research that, he believed, played a large part in the University of Okayama's decision to appoint him some years later to the Chair of Orthopaedic Surgery.

> In a symposium on the biochemistry of connective tissue, I described Roy Elliott's studies of the measurement of cartilage collagen.[2] Later in the meeting, I spoke of the experiments we had done using a reflected-light interference microscope.[3] It was a method permitting a direct approach to the problem of cartilage changes in osteoarthritis.

Kyoto City

While I attended the congress sessions, Helen explored the ancient city of Kyoto. She found the back streets narrow and crowded, the trees green but with surprisingly few flowers. There was a kaleidoscopic mixture of native and foreign races,

Figure 16.3 *Expo 70 conference centre gardens.*

Figure 16.4 *Helen with Dr Hajime Inoue.*

although the presence of Coca-Cola and Fanta machines indicated the predominant influence of the post-war American occupation. Walking through a shopping centre, the street sweepers were busy, the pedestrians orderly. Fruit was being sold from vans: a large, red apple cost 100 yen, the same price as a bag of rice cookies or a packet of chocolate. Mothers pushed infants in padded, square prams, and schoolgirls in uniforms with long, navy pleated skirts (Figure 16.5) lingered between small, dark stalls where old men with bicycles wore round hats, flowing black robes and white socks. Helen chose lunch at a small restaurant where the menus could be seen beside window displays of plastic models of each dish. Inside, the chefs were occupied with unravelling their fishing nets. The local people seemed surprised to see Helen, probably assuming that she was American. At the end of their meals, each diner was given a hot, wet towel and carefully wiped their hands and mouth, their face and ears, a ritual so thorough that it seemed like a daily bath!

An evening performance of the ancient art of Bunraku was strikingly original. Helen was entertained by the eminent American rheumatologist Dr Currier McEwan, whose enthusiasm contrasted with the boredom of a group of nearby French physicians. The puppets were half life-size, each operated by three black-hooded figures. While the puppets moved, a 'narrator' chanted a story with subtle variations in tone and expression, to the accompaniment of a shamisen, an instrument resembling an elongated loop, played with pot-scourers.

Formal Congress proceedings were interspersed with carefully planned tours for all participants and 'accompanying persons'. Hajime Inoue took us to a sandwich lunch and we left for a city

Figure 16.5 *Schoolchildren walking through the temple gardens in Kyoto.*

excursion, visiting the famous *Shishinden*, where the Emperor Hirohito had been enthroned. It was the season for one of the biannual school excursions, and orderly groups of schoolchildren in white shirts and coloured sun hats were often surprised to be photographed beside foreign visitors. In the polite, Japanese style, they giggled behind hands held over their mouths. Passing to the Golden Pavilion, we were enthralled by the vast and splendid gardens. By chance, we met an Egyptian who knew our London colleague M. A. H. El-Maghraby (p.176). We tried to explain the 'green tea ceremony' to him – we had been taught its intricacies in London by Dr and Mrs Inoue – and then moved to the symbolic rock gardens.

After dark, we walked to the station area and dined cheaply on a mixed platter of fish and rice and a cold salad with half a bottle of sake. Characteristically, the waitress refused any tip. We declined coffee at 200 yen per cup, but the offer reminded us that we needed instant coffee for our hotel room. Walking past the brightly lit shops, Helen saw a window display of coffee jars. Not hesitating, she went in but noticed unusually large crowds of people gathered in curious groups, around tables. It was only after an assistant had courteously sold her a jar of coffee that Helen realized that what she thought was a shop was in fact a pinball alley: the jars were prizes!

A visit to see cloisonné jewellery was disappointing, but an excursion to Yuzen was more exciting and took us to a kimono factory at the Nishiji Museum, where there was a fascinating array of materials, principally silk, hand-painted, dyed and sometimes hand-woven 'for special occasions'. The materials, we were told, could last for up to 20 years, during which there might be clever changes of pattern and re-dyeing. A fashion show of kimonos followed and then a display of pottery manufactured in the Kiyomizu Centre. The evening ended with a wonderful view from the top of the Kyoto Tower, before a supper of milk and rolls bought from exceedingly polite, elderly ladies at a small stall. The simple meal was supplemented by a Japanese 'pear', a large, yellow apple-shaped fruit (Figure 16.6) at its best at this time of year and good value at 100 yen.

Osaka and Nara

We travelled to Osaka, an industrial city, twice the size of Kyoto. It was the month of the harvest, and small fields of rice between the outlying houses extended up the hillside

Figure 16.6 *Helen holding a Japanese pear in our hotel room.*

and took the place of trees or forests. Apartment blocks rose side by side with private buildings covered with impractical blue glazed tiles so different from the brown clay exteriors of older structures. At the famous Amusement Centre, we were entertained by the Takarazuka Revue. For the first half of this traditional Japanese-style 'song and dance' performance, the chorus was entirely of unmarried females who performed in costumes and against scenery of multicoloured brilliance. The second half of the entertainment was a modern west-ern-style 'floor show', with a cast entirely of tall girls with bleached hair and deep voices dressed as men and wearing wigs of various hues. The show was wildly popular but, for us, repetitive.

A taxi then took us to the ancient capital, Nara, where we saw the largest Buddha in the world, with a weight of 450 tons. Together with the hundreds of other visitors, we burned a joss stick and said a prayer. Helen paid for a fortune teller, who sold a 'Fortune for 50 years' script to be pinned on a tree entitled 'Moderately Good Fortune'. We bought bottled iced coffee and another Japanese 'pear'.

On 3rd October, we enjoyed a continental-style breakfast in the company of Dr McEwan. He compared the pancakes and syrup unfavourably with those he was accustomed to at home! But then, next day, back to business!

> I found myself as a co-chairman of a scientific session together with a Mexi-can consultant. The following morning, Friday 5th October, began with an early lecture by Michael Freeman, the London orthopaedic surgeon. I pre-sented a short report of our recent work with Barrie Longmore and Ruth Gil-more (p.198). There was a stimulating discussion[4, 5] during a long and varied session with Dr McEwan, a relaxed and efficient 'moderator'.

It was soon time to prepare for the Congress banquet in the Kyoto Hotel, where we were placed between Drs L. E. Glynn (p.172) and Zuki among a vast, hot conglomeration of people. Our friend Hajime Inoue arrived wearing western-style evening dress! There were speeches in various languages and a display of Japanese cul-ture, with dancers and drums, Geisha girls, and a tea ceremony, although the noise of the throng precluded easy listening. We had become reasonably accomplished in the necessary art of bowing and, after many obeisances, made our way back to the Grand Hotel and soft drinks in the company of Madeline Grueter, our Swiss Cook's guide. The sixth of October was largely occupied with final meetings of Congress Chairpersons, with packing and the dispatch of cards and letters to family and friends.

The Congress over, we went to Kyoto station and by Kintetsu railways, a local express line, to Uji Yamada and thence by coach to Kobe, visiting en route the Grand Shrine and the Futamigaura beach. At Kobe, we travelled to Mikimoto Pearl Island (Figure 16.7) to see the process of making cultured pearls. Later that day, we went, again

Figure 16.7 *Pearl fishing near Mikimoto Pearl Island.*

by train and bus, to the Miyako Hotel, Nagoya. The next morning, 8th October, we set off by Japanese National Railways 'bullet' train to Tokyo, where we stayed at the New Otani Hotel. After two hours of sightseeing – the Imperial Palace East Garden, the National Diet Building and the Meiji Park with its facilities for the Olympiad – our final destination was the airport en route for Thailand.

Bangkok

In the luxurious Garden Hotel, a Secretary Bird (*Sagittarius serpentarius*) paraded among the tropical plants. Swimming lazily in the hotel pool, I found I could summon a white-coated attendant to bring a glass of gin by reaching up to strike a huge gong. Helen sat with Professor Fassbender and fellow Congress members watching me (Figure 16.8), and it was only later that she woke with intolerable itching and swelling of her legs – she had been bitten by hundreds of ants! I was fortunate to find a modern pharmacist who sold antihistamine cream. While she rested, I joined a small group visiting the klongs, where I was amazed to see how local people lived perilously close to the water, their young children swimming dangerously near the motor launches that carried sightseers (Figure 16.9). At the water's edge, the little elephant that featured in *The Man with the Golden Gun* mingled with the spectators (Figure 16.10). For Helen, flying home was a painful test of endurance as she rested

Figure 16.8 *Congress members beside the swimming pool in Bangkok.*

Figure 16.9 *The Chao Praya river in Bangkok.*

her swollen legs. At Heathrow, however, we were entertained by watching one of our British consultant colleagues persuading the Customs authorities that he had 'nothing to declare' when we knew that concealed in his cases was a significant collection of jewellery he had purchased in the Far East!

Figure 16.10 *The little elephant welcomes visitors beside the river, Bangkok.*

IN THE ORIENT AGAIN

It was many years later. The evening light threw strange shadows on the funeral procession. From the heights of the Tokyo Tower, snake-like columns of gowned mourners could be seen winding their way through the temple gates as great crowds accompanied the priests to the solemn rites that marked the passing of one of Japan's most eminent citizens.

Towards the end of 1992, I had had a letter from Professor Hajime Inoue asking whether I would join the celebrations of the 40th anniversary of the Department of Orthopaedic Surgery of Okayama University. He invited Helen to come with me, assured me that all our costs would be covered and explained that I would be expected to give a formal address. It was a remarkable offer. I realized that much preparation would be needed, but the chance of another visit to Japan was too tempting to refuse.

Knowing of the Japanese temperament and of the tremendous emphasis placed on etiquette and formality, I judged it would appeal if I were to give at least part of my talk in their language. I took the plunge and signed on for one of the classes at the Edinburgh Language School at Hill Place, near the Edinburgh College of Surgeons. It was a salutary experience! I found myself with a happy but very much younger group of students, evidently with quicker ears for the subtleties of Japanese than mine! I soon learned the significance of 'sa', 'si' and 'ka' as postpositions (in contrast to our prepositions) and of the intriguing way in which questions were asked not by an inflection of the voice but by the simple addition of 'ka' to the end of a sentence. I realized that one reason why some Japanese sounded so abrupt and assertive – I thought of the guards in *Bridge on the River Kwai* – was the subtlety of the language.

A little thought suggested that we could take advantage of a visit to Japan to arrange our first tour in China – the journey to Asia was notoriously long and it seemed wasteful to go so far simply to deliver one lecture. David was enthusiastic about joining us. We contacted Bales, a company experienced in conducting groups around the Orient. They arranged for David to fly with them directly to Beijing. At the end of our days in Okayama, Helen and I would fly from Japan to China to join a group of 14, guided by Pamela Hammond of Bales.

Okayama

We set off from Heathrow on Sunday 5th June 1994. In 1973, our journey to Tokyo had taken us over Greenland. This time, the range of the aircraft had increased, the route changed and we flew eastwards, across the Middle East and Asia, a journey that occupied barely half the time taken in 1973. Landing in Tokyo, we were met by a small reception committee: it became clear that, with characteristic Japanese care and foresight and as a token of the importance of the occasion, Hajime had instructed two of his lecturers to 'watch over' us. One of these young doctors was Dr Takashi Hyashi, whose father owned a private hospital near Okayama. Later, Takashi came to Edinburgh for postgraduate training in orthopaedic surgery and lived in the nurses home of the Princes Margaret Rose Orthopaedic Hospital (Note 14[P]). Before he left, he confessed to the bottles of Scotch whisky that he had relished during his two-month stay!

We travelled by 'bullet' express to Okayama, impressed by the speed of the train and the precision of the timetable. We were regaled by the story of how one day, a driver, ashamed of being two minutes late in reaching his destination, had committed suicide. Taken to our large suite in the luxury hotel where, we were told, US President Reagan had stayed, we found that the bathroom toilet was electrically operated. Beside it were controls for telephone and television. One evening, we made the mistake of sampling the packets of green tea laid out on the lounge table. The effects were disastrous – we found that we could not sleep at all! Awake all night, we still enjoyed the splendid breakfast brought to us before we joined the Japanese surgeons preparing for their conference.

I had decided to centre my lecture on the investigations we had carried out with a great range of microscopes in the analysis of cartilage, subjects outlined in Chapters 11, 13 and 22. I argued to myself that since the Japanese were notoriously interested in technology, our recent work on low-temperature scanning electron microscopy and on the new methods of laser confocal microscopy might appeal to an audience of surgeons whose work often focused on the effects of the rheumatic diseases.

To illustrate my talk,[6] I had chosen to use two projectors, allowing two pictures to be displayed simultaneously. When I explained to Hajime that I needed two instruments, he ordered his technical staff to come and help. I was astonished to find that there were to be two assistants for each projector: one in charge, the second a reserve operator, present in case the first young man was overcome by the gravity of the occasion! Since there was, in addition, a senior technician, I found that, for an operation that would have been handled by one person in Edinburgh, five individuals were required! Once again, I was reminded of the infinite Japanese capacity for painstaking work, a characteristic showing itself in their scientific and medical research.

A formal occasion

My lecture on 11th June proceeded without interruption. No one hissed or booed when I gave my first paragraph in Japanese! Looking back, perhaps one reason why the large audience was so quiet was that they found microscopes a good deal less interesting than I did! When I finished, there was a statutory round of applause and Hajime, from his position as chairman, thanked me formally and presented me with an inscribed, wrapped book. I had been taught how to respond: bowing in turn, I presented him with a silver 'quaich', engraved with the arms of the University of Edinburgh, one of the many gifts we had brought from Scotland in preparation for the occasion.

That evening, a formal dinner required that we sit at the top table, beside the Dean of the University of Okayama Medical School and other dignitaries. We were helped through many delicious dishes by an orchestra that, to our astonishment, played works by Mozart and other European composers. At one point, several of those sitting near us burst out laughing – the jollity of the evening had already been helped by large rounds of spirits as well as wine – and Hajime explained that the Dean, intending to pay to Helen what he thought was a compliment of the highest order, had said: 'You are just like Mrs Thatcher!' When the words were explained, Helen felt obliged to thank our hosts for their gracious remarks. On returning to our suite, she became a little more outspoken and said she thought the compliment could be regarded as 'double-edged'!

We were honoured by being taken to Professor Inoue's own home, an unusual distinction for foreign guests. Japanese professional and businessmen were notorious in their choice of an evening's entertainment – meeting after work at an inn or restaurant, karaoke was commonplace – but, for most Japanese, home life was very private and personal, their residencies ordered, meticulously clean and disciplined. We left our shoes at Hajime's doorway, put on 'house slippers' and were guided carefully away from a beautiful new carpet. At once, we noticed one of the largest television sets we had ever seen. After the exchange of formal courtesies with Mrs Inoue, who we remembered from her time in London in 1971, we sat down to cups of coffee and elegant pieces of cake and biscuit. It had been a long day and, after some conversation, I asked to be shown to the toilet. Here it proved necessary to exchange the 'house slippers' for a pair of 'bathroom slippers' – house shoes may not enter the bathroom! Later, Hajime took me upstairs to show me his small but organized study. He was equally proud of his little garden – land was at a premium in this mountainous and volcanic country where 90% of the population was packed into the 20% of the land bordering the sea.

Next day, we visited another temple before driving to the coast on the way to a shopping market in Tokyo, where the railway station, much of it underground, seemed as large as Heathrow.

To China

Released from the formalities of Japan, we left Tokyo (Figure 16.11) by Nippon Airways on Monday 13th June and flew to Beijing,[C] arriving after lunch. The formalities of entering China were tiresome and slow, so it was late in the afternoon before a taxi delivered us to the Lido Holiday Inn. Here we were very relieved to recognize David among the Bales touring group. After their first day in Beijing, some of the travellers had visited the Forbidden City. David's cheerful face gave no sign of fatigue after his long flight from Britain. Almost at once, a young lady, Miss Tyler, asked whether we would like to join her that evening in a visit to the Chinese opera. David and I declined, but Helen accepted with alacrity and she and Ms Tyler went off by taxi. They came back some hours later – we were a little concerned for their safety – having had what E. M. Forster in his *Room With A View* would have described as 'an adventure'! Enthralled by the Chinese singers and dancers but with little sign of public transport, they decided to walk back to the hotel. In the winding streets and back alleys of the enormous city, they soon lost their way. Walking along the narrow roads, they were fascinated to find many local people cooking their evening meals on braziers on the pavements. At last a passing taxi came to their rescue.

Figure 16.11 *A glimpse of Mount Fujiyama from the air.*

On Tuesday 14th, a bus carried us northwards to the Great Wall. On the way, we stopped at a silk factory, where we were struck by the crowded conditions under which hordes of workers struggled to make cloth, clothes, scarves and other adornments. The Wall lived up to every expectation. From its heights, we looked northwards into Mongolia, while, to the west, the interminable, winding structure reached as far as the eye could see.

Xian

The next day, we visited the Summer Palace on Kunming Lake before flying to the ancient walled city of Xian, where we stayed at the modest but comfortable Wan Nian Hotel. Late in the evening, Fate stepped in! After dinner, we went to look for David, who had gone upstairs to his own room. I tried his door, but could not turn the handle. He attempted to open the door from inside, without success. We asked the receptionists for assistance, but neither of them could help. I suggested breaking in, but this caused consternation – damage could not be accepted by the management, probably because of cost. An engineer from the University was sent for. He made little progress, and by this time – it was after 10 pm – uniformed security guards had arrived together with a little crowd of our fellow tourists. One of our friends, a rather impetuous young farmer, reached the scene with his video camera. Attempting to film what had by now become a pantomime of some 11 or 12 people, he was abruptly stopped by the guards. 'Filming is not permitted!' It was late at night when the door was finally opened and we were re-united with David.

Thursday morning was the occasion for one of the most amazing scenes that we encountered: It was a visit to the third-century burial site of the Emperor Qin Shi Huangdi. Passing through the countryside, we were shown the huge mountain of earth that represented the man-made mausoleum. Some years previously, 8000 life-size terracotta warriors (Figure 16.12) had been discovered in a gigantic underground cavern. At the carefully controlled doorways, large notices stressed that photography was forbidden. Going inside, we saw the arrays of warriors whose appearance has become familiar to many who have not been lucky enough to have visited China but have seen the more recent exhibition at the British Museum.

It was at this time that we were encouraged to go to a local hospital, where we watched white-coated practitioners engaged in the art of acupuncture. A volunteer was asked for and our farmer friend stepped forward, rather impetuously I thought, and allowed needles to be inserted into his wrist. I could not help thinking of the hazards of hepatitis – there was no attempt to sterilize either the skin or the needles.

Figure 16.12 *The model we bought of a Chinese warrior from the collection of terracotta sculptures depicting the armies of Qin Shi Huangdi, the first Emperor of China.*

Suzhou

On Friday 17th June, we flew to Shanghai, where we stayed at the Yangtze Hotel. The next day, our little group visited Suzhou. The town is situated on the Imperial Grand Canal and we were delighted to see the classical Chinese gardens and a silk-producing centre. Working conditions for the large numbers who were dyeing silk and making clothes, gowns and sheets were poor, and the degree of overcrowding recalled the textile trade in Britain during the early years of the Industrial Revolution. Looking out from a comfortable hotel bedroom each morning, one of the most remarkable sights was of thousands of cyclists on their way to work. By Western standards of the time, there was relatively little motor traffic, but at busier road junctions the usual appearance was of 'organized chaos' – an occasional traffic policeman but no electric signals – and it was clearly a question of 'first come, first served'. Lorries laden with farm produce and building materials seemed always to be in a hurry, paying little attention to pedestrians and cyclists in their paths.

Shanghai

Back in Shanghai on Sunday 19th June, the city lived up to our expectations as one of the largest in the industrial East. The day proved very hot. We passed through leafy streets lined by large houses and crowded with bicycles, taxis and coaches, on our way to see the jade Buddha, a figure from Burma with soft features, designed, we were told, to influence women. Nearby were other, vast gold figures. We saw the Wu Gardens, with porous rocks like those of the Suzhou City of Jiangsu Province, built during the Emperor Jiajin period of the Ming Dynasty. In a jade-cutting works, we bought Chinese cloisonné eggs. We enjoyed a lunch 'in the round' at the Rainbow Hotel, where the facilities were good and the price – 50 yuan a head – modest. Later, the busy, crowded lanes lined with stalls selling trinkets, dishes and jewellery proved less attractive – piles of evil-smelling rubbish, some covered with sacking, were festering in the hot sunshine in spite of the official view that Shanghai streets are swept 12 times daily. We had been warned about thieves and guarded our bags carefully. We were told that the Queen had stopped for refreshment at one famous old tea house – we hoped that she enjoyed the green weed that we were to hear about the next day. We walked back through the same lanes and gardens, but to our consternation the tourist bus containing many of our personal belongings, including passports, money and tickets, was nowhere to be seen – the car park was full. We had twenty anxious minutes in which to consider what Bales would do if the bus failed to return! But it turned up, making an unscheduled stop on the edge of the crowded road, which we had to cross, dodging bicycles and cars and aware of the continual war waged between drivers and the over-stretched police.

I looked across the waterfront to the famous Bund, shielding my eyes and trying to block out the hundreds of skyscrapers and office blocks that formed a skyline and to imagine the scene as it had been at the time of the opium wars. I have often attempted to explain the scale of Chinese roads to my friends. Princes Street, in Edinburgh, I judge to be about one mile long with 5000–10,000 people on the pavements at any moment. The Nanking Road in Shanghai, with its immense variety of shops, is 10 miles long and at any time about 2 million people can be found on it. In striking contrast to the industrial city were the beautiful Yuan Gardens, which we saw before travelling by train to Hangzhou for two nights at the Dragon Hotel and a cruise on the West Lake.

Guilin

I had been looking forward eagerly to a sight of the mountainous area around Guilin where we flew on Tuesday 21th June. But our visit also gave us the chance of a cruise on the River Li and the opportunity of seeing the fishermen using their skills with their assistants, the trained cormorants, catching fish for sale. A gentle noose was passed around each bird's neck. When the animal had effected a catch, the ensnared fish was taken out of the bird's mouth and the noose was released.

Hong Kong

Yet another flight took us to Hong Kong and the City Garden Hotel. Stupendous skyscrapers dominated the horizon, but the crowded market streets made a welcome contrast and we saw every form and variety of food on sale at busy stalls. It has been said that Chinese people are content to eat anything that moves: our experience, both in restaurants and on the streets, certainly confirmed that chickens, birds of all kinds, snakes, molluscs, snails and fish were snapped up eagerly by passers-by. It was impossible to resist the shopping malls, and here enthusiastic salesmen offered to make me a 'Harrison Tweed' suit overnight. I knew that one of my colleagues had accepted such an offer. I asked about the golf course that lies near the centre of the city and was told that the fee for membership of this private nine-hole club was $1,000,000! Tempting as the idea was to some of the party, we did not have either the time or the inclination to visit any of the Hong Kong gambling casinos! Our time was up and within a few hours we were winging it back to the United Kingdom. Leaving Hong Kong late on 24th June, we were at Heathrow early the next morning.

CHAPTER 17

A sight of Brazil

Towards the Amazon

Go rolling down to Rio
(Roll down – roll down to Rio!)
And I'd like to roll to Rio
Some day before I'm old!

Rudyard Kipling[1]

I n July 1975, I was astonished to receive a letter from Professor Israel Bonomo[A] of Rio de Janeiro, inviting me to lecture to the 1976 South American Congress of Rheumatology in Fortaleza.[B] The invitation offered us an introduction to a part of the New World we had not seen before.

Attendance at the Fortaleza Conference, Bonomo explained, was to enable young doctors to join the South American Society of Rheumatology, a step towards specialization in this branch of medicine. Morris Ziff, David Howell and John Talbott[C] were coming from the United States and F. Delbarre from France (Figure 17.1). Helen and I discussed this unusual opportunity carefully, knowing that Rosalind now lived in Glasgow, while Iain continued his studies in Birmingham. We were satisfied that Philip and David could care for themselves safely. I told the British Council of the invitation and they suggested that I add a lecture tour to the Congress visit. In return for support for my travel, they asked for a full report on the state of Brazilian Pathology, and the present chapter reflects my observations.

After a long transatlantic flight, we landed at Recife early on 23rd July. Welcomed by Robin Evans, the British Council Regional Director, we were taken to the Hotel Boa Viagem, near the beach. Its splendid appearance was not matched by the offer of accommodation in a shed-like annex where dusky figures squatted in the dark and beetles swarmed. We preferred to spend the rest of the night in the lounge, gazing spellbound at the magnificent southern Atlantic Ocean and eating breakfast before joining a noisy crowd jostling for a flight northwards.

Chapter summary
- Fortaleza
- Brasilia
- Goiania
- Belo Horizonte
- Sabara and Minas Gerais
- Rio de Janeiro
- São Paulo

Figure 17.1 *(left to right) Helen Gardner, David Howell, the Congress chairman and his wife, John Talbott, Dugald Gardner.*

Fortaleza

Landing at Fortaleza, we were met by the Secretary-General to the Congress, Dr Francisco Vieira, who accompanied us to our hotel, the Beira Mar. Next day, we found the lecture theatre near the sea, its roof of plastic. Each time a gust of wind swept in, the roof roared like thunder, drowning any speaker. Of the 200 who had registered, fewer than 30 or 40 of the young physicians were present, and I realized that many had escaped to the sunny beaches.

My Congress lectures were on 'The pathology of rheumatoid arthritis', 'Cartilage and osteoarthritis', 'Infection in joint disease' and 'Systemic diseases of connective tissue'. In free moments, we joined the participants on the shore (Figure 17.2). Aware that 15 minutes' exposure to the tropical sun was enough to cause sunburn, we measured our times carefully. In spite of our precautions, I suffered badly and for the rest of the meeting was nicknamed 'the red doctor'!

At the end of the meeting, a social gathering (Figure 17.3) in the Brazilian Medical Association centre included a lottery, and we came away with a hammock. A midnight Congress dinner and

Figure 17.2 *The beach at Fortaleza.*

Figure 17.3 *Helen Gardner with Dr John Talbott at a social gathering in Fortaleza.*

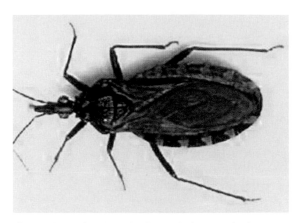

Figure 17.4 *The triatomine bug, which transmits the trypanosome that causes Chagas' disease.*

dance followed. John Talbott observed that a young Brazilian doctor was attempting to teach me the samba and remarked to Helen: 'Looks as though Dugald has got more than he bargained for!'

I was anxious to see as much as I could of medical teaching in Ceará. The Dean of the Medical Faculty kindly showed me round the Fortaleza Medical School buildings. I was not surprised to see that the student boxes of microscopic slides contained many examples of tropical diseases, since I had been told that in Fortaleza and the surrounding countryside, 20% of the population had schistosomiasis.[D] Chagas' disease[E,2] was a recognized national problem (Figure 17.4) and in Fortaleza 10% of the population suffered from amoebiasis,[F] while chloroquine-resistant malaria and leprosy were rife[G] and tuberculosis common. I noticed few examples of cancer among the slides and was astonished when the Dean said: 'Cancer is not a problem here!' He added: 'The expectation of life is only 40 years.'[3]

Brasilia

We began our lecture tour the next day. There was no early flight to the new capital city, Brasilia, and we were fortunate to battle through the crowds at Salvador to join a plane bound for the capital. In Brasilia, we were collected from the Hotel Das Americanos by Professor Alberto Raick, a reserved and courteous pathologist who had trained in North America. As we travelled through the capital, we marvelled at the dark-red earth of the countryside and saw a panorama of new buildings with skyscrapers and socially segregated apartment blocks, the concept of a 'people's city' with building on an egalitarian basis superseded by the need to put diplomacy and administration before manual labour.

In Brasilia, a new University, but not a University hospital, was complete, so patient-based (clinical) teaching was at the Sobridino District General Hospital. Driving us past the enormous city lake in Brasilia, Professor Raick told us that the water was already contaminated with the worm of schistosomiasis. The hospitals in Brazil, he said, tended to be private, federal, state or Catholic, so the word 'hospital' was applied to the many small private clinics as well as to larger hospitals, and Raick reminded us that community care in Goias was spread widely, divided between 60 different centres. At Sobridino, he explained, most patients were from the poor rather than from the better-endowed people who represented the core of the half-million who lived in the new capital.

Passing through the guarded gates, we came to the Pathology Department, an enormous, single-floor concrete structure. I was interested to see the style of Brazilian laboratory practice. The histology laboratories were clean and tidy, the diagnostic work careful, the preparations, examined by Zeiss microscope, exemplary. On the autopsy table, I saw the body of a middle-aged woman who had died with Chagas' disease. Professor Raick had devised a good filing system and a splendid collection of teaching photographs. He told us that when he arrived in Brasilia, he had only one qualified assistant but now had six. He explained that illiteracy was common, skilled secretarial help difficult to find. Children went to schools, when they were available, at the age of 7, but by the age of 10 only one in five remained in formal education.

I met Dr Howard, formerly Professor of Paediatrics in Dallas, Texas. He admitted that in dealing with the great numbers of sick and malnourished children he faced a challenge: he could not control infection by isolation and there was a shortage of trained nurses. He showed us cases of rapid-onset diarrhoea requiring intravenous fluids. There was good equipment but insufficient educated staff. The families of the sick often stayed beside their children in the wards, sleeping on chairs or the floor.

The consultant in charge of perinatal care had spent two years in London. She worked closely with Howard and with the Italian consultant obstetrician, who had come from Chicago. Their task was enormous: their wards dealt with 10,000 antenatal visits each year. The obstetrician said that within one year in this hospital alone she had seen a greater variety of problems than she would expect to see in the whole of Chicago. There was a sufficient number of resident medical staff. The younger Brazilians loved speciality training – it led to lucrative private practice – but they seemed to shun responsibility. I gave a talk about British systems of undergraduate and postgraduate education and at lunch was joined by the Oxford-trained consultant anaesthetist, who had responsibility for a wide range of paediatric and general surgery. He disliked Brasilia because 'There was nothing to do after 5 pm'. He preferred a liberal, American style of life!

At the new University of Brasilia, Raick took us to his academic laboratories, which were arranged in an arc nearly one kilometre long and dominating the campus. Each finger-like element of the arc was a two-floored laboratory with lecture theatres and large auditoria. The top floor was covered with floral gardens and shrubs. His laboratory was nearing completion: new equipment had arrived and he was setting up a well-organized biochemistry unit for cancer research and an electron-microscope laboratory.

As the day passed, Raick and I became good friends – many of our professional problems were mutual. Keen to continue discussion, he and his wife invited us to an evening meal at a chiascura, a meat restaurant, near the Presidential Palace, where we noticed armed guards. The restaurant lay beside the lake and we enjoyed fillet steaks, suco loranje (orange juice) and beer while watching herons wandering among trees that had huge, tendinous roots. The evening was comfortably warm, the humidity low.

A visit to Goiania, the capital city of Goias, had been agreed, but before we left, on 3rd August, Helen and I decided to visit the remarkable, half-underground, Brasilia Cathedral. Outside, the sun was very hot, the traffic heavy, with swarms of cars, making road crossings hazardous. We saw how many new buildings appeared superficially complete, although the infrastructure was scrappy, with red dust everywhere. Most blocks near our hotel contained banks and financial offices, but they were interspersed with coffee shops and bars where fruit juice gave welcome relief. Brasilia Airport was modern and spacious, with none of the noise and overcrowding encountered at Recife, Fortaleza and Salvador. An Internal Brazilian Airlines (VASP) clerk directed us and we were soon flying over vast areas of barren countryside and low, brown–grey, undulating hills interspersed with farms.

Goiania

At Goiania, we were met by a pleasant, slim, dark-haired Dr Vasco Cardosa, Head of the Pathology Department. Cardosa had a strong interest in liver disease and had worked with Sheila Sherlock in London. In the back of his car was a curious white helmet, part of his uniform as a Captain in the Brazilian army. He drove us through the arid, young agricultural town of a million people to the eight-storey Umurama Hotel, the skyscrapers recalling the cities of the South of France and Spain. Said to be the best in the city, the accommodation was not particularly clean, the heat intense. A noisy combination of guitar and electric organ filled the air in the half-empty dining room, where I reluctantly accepted some inedible fish, a bottle of Brazilian beer and a small cup of coffee, while Helen, who had developed a fever, stayed in her room and swallowed some asparagus soup.

Next day, as Helen rested, Dr Cardosa arrived early and drove me through the busy, cool streets to the Medical School. He explained that he spent two hours each day in army training, two hours in his private clinic and the remaining half-day in the hospital clinics. During the previous summer, he had been sent to Amazonia by the Brazilian army and was constantly afraid, partly because of disease – he contracted falciparum malaria – and partly because of the 'subversives', Colombians infiltrating Brazil.

The hospital, of 250–300 beds, was bustling and active. I was introduced to the consultant rheumatologist, and settled down for a few minutes with Dr Hitor Rosa, Associate Professor of Gastroenterology. He also had worked with Sheila Sherlock. In the senior staff room, I learned about the prevalence of oesophageal dilatation in Chagas' disease, its classification by grade, and the forms of palliative and radical surgery: there were more than 1000 cases on file at this hospital alone. In the adjacent room, where patients were arriving, slices of preserved liver lay before them in plastic bags! I was told that carcinoma of the liver, so common in China and South Africa, was not encountered in hepatic schistosomiasis here.

Many of the hospital rooms and small, six- or eight-bedded, wards, crammed with staff, nurses, patients and visitors, were very hot, although a cool air blew through the corridors. In one small ward, I saw a boy of 14 with an abdominal mass extending around the right hepatic flexure, down the right side of the abdomen and across to the left. The patient was awaiting an exploratory laparotomy, but it was already clear that he had Chagas' disease. I noticed a poorly nourished middle-aged man with South American blastomycosis and a little elderly man, malnourished and dehydrated with Chagas' oesophageal dilatation. He was about to have a gastrostomy as a first step towards oesophageal repair or resection. Not far away was a small, deformed, dark-skinned child who appeared to have had rickets but who was under treatment for leishmaniasis.

In a second ward, where the patients were wearing pyjamas but were not covered by sheets or blankets, I observed several with facial deformities. I wondered whether one patient with a flattened, scarred nose had rhinosporidiosis, but was told that he suffered from long-standing blastomycosis. In another bed was an elderly man with diabetes mellitus and a spontaneously amputated toe, which was lying exposed without dressings or coverings.

I met Professor Geraldo Pedra, Chief of the Orthopaedics Department, as his staff began to assemble. Speaking through an interpreter, I told them about our research. I realized of course that many diseases on which European and American research concentrated were of little interest to young medical staff in Brazil because they were so exotic (p.121). In a population where Chagas' disease was still prevalent, osteoarthritis seemed scarcely relevant!

In the cancer hospital, the wards were not crowded by Brazilian standards. The air-conditioned laboratories were well equipped with a new American Optical (AO) cryostat and microscope. But the attitude of younger staff struck me as casual: a young female Resident Medical Officer lounged casually on a sofa as her 'Chief' entered the room. My critical thoughts disappeared at lunch in a private club where clusters of canaries in the garden grounds contrasted with red-headed South American cardinals!

We went with Cardosa to his private clinic, a beautiful two-storey house decorated in a Portuguese style and staffed by three technicians, three secretaries and four pathologists. The laboratories were in open-air cloisters that ran round the garden. The bodies of stillborn infants lay in open tanks next to benches where technicians worked, their efficiency confirmed by the bound files of surgical reports in Cardosa's room. It transpired that he examined 10,000 biopsies a year and that his work included medico-legal autopsies. It was no surprise to find that his professional fees for private practice were high.

Soon afterwards, a Boeing 737 carried us to Brasilia en route to Belo Horizonte, a name signifying 'Beautiful Horizon'.

Belo Horizonte

The city, with a population of nearly 2.5 million, stretched into the distance, behind it the rugged brown–grey mountains of this mineral and iron ore region. The temperature was mild, the sunshine bright, but traffic noise and flashing lights meant little sleep. Next day, 5th August, Dr Gama had arranged for me to address the pathologists and rheumatologists from the Belo Horizonte Federal School of Medicine, and we drove past the new Medical School buildings at the 300-bed General Hospital. Professor Bogliolo, Head of Pathology, was away and we were introduced to his Associates, Dr Washington Lewes and Dr Pedro Raso, who gave me tissue blocks from cases of Chagas' and other parasitic diseases, the kind of gift in which pathologists delight! I met an enthusiastic young Dr Luis Carlos Del Ferreira; Dr Gama was trying to persuade him to learn how to reproduce arthritis experimentally. When I mentioned a visit to my laboratory, Gama was enthusiastic, although De Ferreira appeared more interested in Bill Ford's Manchester laboratory (p.239) of cellular immunology.

After my talk on 'The pathology of rheumatoid arthritis', I was disappointed by the pathology floor, where the laboratories were poorly equipped, the histological studies recalling those of Europe in the 1930s. However, the electron-microscope suite under the direction of Dr Tafori revealed interesting pictures of the tissues in Chagas' disease, and he generously offered me examples together with others of mice with the experimental condition.

Sabara and Minas Gerais

On the way to Sabara, in the State of Minas Gerais and 20 kilometres from Belo Horizonte, our guide was a charming female, clad in khaki culottes. From her, we learnt how the early explorers had made their way from the coast and settled in this attractive, fertile zone at a junction of two rivers. Gold was discovered by chance and between 1730 and 1750 there was a 'gold rush'. However, Sabara and Ouro Preto remained isolated, developing their own cultures with the aid of their immense wealth but not subject to the influence of the capitals in Salvador or (later) Rio. When roads were built and railways developed, Ouro Preto and Sabara lost something of their importance: gold sources had long been exhausted and diamonds were exceedingly rare.

Sabara had been built on many hills and had steep, winding streets with narrow stone pavements. In the square, we saw the Church founded by negro slaves but abandoned when slavery was abolished in 1888. We met the charming Director of the Museum of Gold, Dr Antonio Joachim de Almeida. His life's work had been to restore the buildings of the old mining town. Nearby, we saw de Almeida's reconstructed theatre, resembling Shakespeare's Globe, capable of accommodating 600 people, with dressing rooms, basement and a Royal Box, all arranged in wood with the simple lighting of the early eighteenth century. A short walk led us to the Museum of the Supervisor of Gold, where a magnificent small library recorded the history of Brazil and of mining. In each mining area, a single person weighed the gold from the mines and apportioned one-fifth to the State. The remaining four-fifths was changed into ingots and stamped with the mine crest.

The day had made an almost unique interlude to our programme. Late in leaving, our driver hurried along winding roads through the rocky hills, but we did not reach our hotel until 5.30 pm. As a result, a second lecture that I was due to give in Belo Horizonte was cancelled. Back in our hotel, I managed to absorb a fillet steak while Helen contented herself with yellow soup containing two poached eggs and bread.

Friday 6th August was a sightseeing day in Minas Gerais, taking us to the mining communities of a state half the size of Europe. In Dr Gama's Umpala car, we made our way through the chaotic traffic of Belo Horizonte at 8.30 am to the house of his sister-in-law. We could recognize the industrial centre because of the pall of smoke hanging over the polluted city. Mrs Gama displayed a deep interest in the history of this mining region, but I detected a slightly cynical view of the exploitation by England of Portugal! In the eighteenth century, long before independence, gold mines were used by treaty to finance the English Industrial Revolution. In return, England imported the wines and spirits of Portugal.

In Ouro Preto (Figure 17.5), churches were everywhere. There were often two pulpits: one for the devil's advocate, one for the advocate of Christ. The wealth of the area accounted for the costly European-style Baroque and Rococo architecture. Mineowners seemed able to reconcile the maltreatment of their West African slaves with the art they sponsored, among it the work of the greatest Brazilian sculptor, 'The Little Cripple' (Alejadinho-Antonio Francisco Lisboa). But the gold seams ran out and the development of diamond mines at Diamontina, about 300 kilometres from Belo Horizonte, added to the decline.

In the centre of the town was a statue of the dentist Joaquim Jose da Silva Xavier (Tiradentes), hanged as the leader of the Brazilian rebels when the Brazilian people rose up in 1823 against

Figure 17.5 *The countryside at Ouro Preto.*

the central Portuguese Government. The name Tiradentes (dentist) was given to a small city not far from here. Before lunch, we visited the mineral museum of the School of Mining and Engineering, where 25,000 minerals were on display: they included opals, beryls, agate, quartz and ores, derivatives of bismuth, magnesium, iron and copper (malachite green), and quartz formations more than 90 cm in size.

It was dark by the time we returned to Belo Horizonte. We stopped briefly to look at a garage advertising cars by exhibiting a cobra in a cage, the snake asleep inside a box. We reached our hotel at 6.30 pm, relieved to find that a dinner with the rheumatologists had been cancelled.

Dr Gama came early on Saturday morning, the 7th, to show us the flowers and wildlife of this dry, undulating countryside. In the widely scattered buildings of the Belo Horizonte University campus, we saw an art display and photographic exhibition of the works of Carl Orff, soon to be a visitor. One of Dr Gama's sons, whose wife was a ballet dancer who had performed at Sadler's Wells, had published a book of poetry. Nearby was a huge sports stadium, around it courts for tennis and volleyball, with people playing vigorously in spite of the heat. We came to the little Church of St Francis, designed by Niemeyer, its walls decorated with a painting of the saint with animals and birds. Nearby was a large, artificial lake widely used in spite of the hazard of schistosomiasis.

Many of the flowers in Belo Horizonte could be seen in Britain, but the trees were unusual, some from South Africa and Australia. Birds disliked eucalyptus, but by the lake there were many, including a large hummingbird-like creature. At the zoo, we found beautiful tigers, lions and leopards housed in confined, concrete pens. There was a great variety of vociferous parrots, some bright blue. Smaller green and orange birds led us to flamingos, herons and cranes, and finally to two young condors, each with a wingspan of almost two metres, talons as large as human fingers and enormous, beautiful, multicoloured heads.

At 12 noon, we journeyed back quietly to the hotel, before Dr Gama collected us again for lunch. To our delight, he appeared with a delicately moulded, purple–pink china antique dish containing a lightly boiled apple that his wife thought might please Helen. We went to an open-air, ranch-like building with shaded tables, an old waterwheel and meat cooked on spits, presented on sabre-like knives. After Dr Gama had said farewell, our journey to the airport was negotiated by a skilled taxi driver, who fought his way through a maelstrom of traffic.

Rio de Janeiro

We were met in Rio by two pipe-smoking friends from the British Council, David Blagbrough and a colleague, who drove us through this city of seven million people. The sun had set, but we could see, silhouetted behind the lake, the illuminated statue of Christ on the pinnacle of Corcovado (Figure 17.6). From the Hotel Debret, we glimpsed the Copacabana beach (Figure 17.7).

On Sunday 8th August, an early sunrise encouraged a walk to the seafront, where determined businessmen in shorts or bathing trunks were running or walking along the three-mile stretch of sand as the Atlantic waves thundered in. Beyond the beach were rocky shrub-covered slopes punctuated by favela-like slums, hundreds of indescribably poor wooden buildings supported on stilts and hanging precariously from the hillside.

On Tuesday 10th August, we set off early with Professor Bonomo to the Hopital dos Servidores do Estadu, the Federal Teaching Hospital. We were introduced to the Dean of Teaching, who was also the Chief of Dermatology, and the Chief of Internal Medicine; both had trained in the United States. Among the crowd were Luis Wertzman, whom we had met in Fortaleza, and his colleague de Paula, Professor of Pathology.[H] Although I had been asked to speak on osteoarthrosis, it was clear that my hosts would prefer a talk on rheumatoid arthritis and would welcome my views on the British

Figure 17.6 *Statue of Christ at Corcovado.*

Figure 17.7 *Copacabana beach at Rio.*

National Health Service. I didn't notice the extreme heat until I had finished: winter was ending, the humidity rising.

De Paula's son, a final-year student, drove us with his father and de Lacerda, titular Professor of Pathology at the State Medical School, to a restaurant, Antoninos, at Lagoa. As we entered, de Paula quietly pointed out the Minister of Health, whom we had seen the previous day in the Jockey Club. De Paula was the South American representative of the International Academy of Pathology. We set out to see his department, part of the extensive University Medical School built after the Second World War.

> On the walls of the rather neglected corridors was a collection of old watercolours of morbid anatomical specimens. Ten to twelve thousand biopsies were examined each year, but there was little sign of activity and few people were using the excellent German microscopes. The autopsy room, with four stainless steel tables, seemed neglected in spite of the evidence that 1000 autopsies were examined yearly. De Lacerda then took us to his private clinic, rented space in the large, modern, private hospital founded and maintained by Portuguese settlers who had access to the hospital through insurance schemes.

By contrast with the State department, the private hospital, three years old, was modern, with stainless steel lifts and a good diagnostic histopathology laboratory. The technical staff was shared between private laboratories and the State Hospital. The rented space and all the equipment and staff within the private laboratories were paid for by the seven consultants; de Paula and de Lacerda used the facility for their group private practice. They received 70 surgical specimens per day, each charged at a rate equivalent to £16.50, suggesting that the income was at least £250,000 a year, giving each consultant £20,000 per year from his part-time, private position. De Lacerda was also consultant pathologist to the Brazilian Navy, for which he received £7000 a year, and his post as titular Professor gave him another £12,000. At that time, the highest rate of income tax was 20%. The old building of the private hospital still stood beside the new, a relic of early Portuguese/Brazilian architecture; it had changed little since the eighteenth century. The difference, for patients, between the old hospital and the new was determined by the amounts that contributors were prepared to subscribe.

After saying farewell to Professor and Mrs Bonomo we set off for São Paulo, the plane a Lockheed Electra.

São Paulo

Committed to an intensive lecture programme on Wednesday 11th August, I was taken by Mr Chadwick to the Department of Pathology of the University Faculty of Medicine. Awaiting our arrival was Professor Thales de Britto, Chairman of Pathology, accompanied by Dr Horacio Friedman, a young pathologist. De Britto hoped Friedman would visit England. De Britto himself had worked at the Massachusetts General Hospital, Boston, and then in New York. Offered a post in Dallas, Texas, he preferred to return to São Paulo, where the Medical School was accounted the best in Brazil.

> In de Britto's spacious but modest rooms, I talked on 'Cartilage structure and function' for nearly two hours and then for a further hour on 'Elastic material and elastic diseases', after which Dr Friedman showed me a case of spontaneous limb atrophy, a rare disorder in which there is the emergence of a recessive characteristic leading to aplasia and atrophy of all four limbs.

In a tropical downpour, we went to lunch to an unpretentious restaurant, where for the next two hours, over excellent food and wine, the pathologists discussed cases of especial interest, one an example of Chagas' disease. I had to be careful with the batidas.[I] Later, in the evening, we set out for dinner with Mr and Mrs Stevens, who lived about half an hour's drive beyond the Coats and Paton's factory, the firm with which Richard Stevens, the son of the late Edwin and Joan Stevens of Edinburgh, had been associated for the past seven years.[J] Edwin was Helen's father's cousin. Richard had married Vicki Stevens – the two families had the same surname but were not related. We reached the Stevens's house, a modern building with a delightful swimming pool situated in several acres of wooded ground, at about 8 pm. I noticed three servants and a garage to hold as many as four cars; inside the house, I was delighted to meet a former Loretto schoolfellow, K. M. Rae.

Dinner consisted of delicious slices of Brazilian beef: Brazil was the second largest beef producer in the world. Gin and tonic before dinner, red wine with the meal, and luscious strawberries and cream followed. We were told that the many Japanese settled in Brazil had proved to be intensive producers of fruit and vegetables, working hard to market fruit and vegetables in a programme with which the native Brazilian agricultural worker seemed unable to compete. They had also concentrated on growing rice. Many of them had been in Brazil for two or even three generations, and a million or more, in the south of the country, maintained the traditions we had seen in Kyoto (Chapter 16). Although there were so many Japanese, the cars in Brazil were almost all Volkswagens built in Brazil, accompanied by a much smaller number of Italian Fiats.

> On the morning of Thursday 12th August, I returned to the hospital and lectured first on 'Inflammation' and then on 'Rheumatoid arthritis'. There was a large audience and much well-informed questioning. We discussed a case of Takayasu's syndrome and another of hypertension in a boy aged 12 who had renal tuberculosis and schistosomiasis.

Back in our hotel, we joined the Stevens for lunch. Some of the Brazilians were interested in continuing a discussion – we were among the few British pathologists to have visited São Paulo within living memory – and had telephoned to say that they would send three pathologists in place of three of the wives. De Britto and Carlos Corbett were there, together with Horatio Friedman, the book-officer of the British Council, a director of ICI (Brazil) and Dr John Forrest from University College London, also on a British Council tour.

The evening's discussion centred on medical training in Britain and America. The book-officer told me that the British Council would pay for copies of our British books to be sent to those we had visited in Brazil. I learnt that there was to be a Trade Delegation in 1977. This was an opportunity for the sale of British medical equipment, and Chadwick gave me the name of the official in London responsible for relevant export programmes. We made arrangements for Dr Friedman to come in July 1977 to the Department of Pathology in Manchester to work with me. His wife, a pathologist interested in bone disease, thought she would accompany him.

On Friday 13th August, a young Dr. Fernando arrived to take us shopping. She was interested in music and helped us to find three Brazilian records as well as prints of pictures of Ouro Preto. At the airport, Mr Chadwick confessed that he would be relieved when I and my specimens were safely back in Britain! Professor Raick had given me teaching specimens, including a Chagas' disease heart and part of a schistosomal liver; they were sealed in plastic bags and hidden in my suitcase, among my clothes!

And so, by BA703, via Rio, Recife and Madrid, back to London, Gatwick within 14 hours, only to find that the long hot summer had left the country scorched and brown, reminding us of the far-off Brazilian Ceará. Fortunately, the authorities at both airports confined their searches to our hand luggage!

V.

The rivers of Europe, Australia and the Middle East

CHAPTER 18

Back to Britain

Beside the Mersey

And I said to a man who stood at the gate of the year:
'Give me a light that I may tread safely into the unknown.'
And he replied: 'Go out into the darkness and put
your hand into the hand of God. That shall be to you
better than a light, and safer than a known way.'

Minnie Louise Haskins[1]

The time had come for a return from Belfast to mainland Britain. Responding to a call from Manchester, I was appointed to a new Chair of Histopathology at the Withington Hospital.

A new home

I took up my duties on 1st December 1976. We had to find a new home quickly. Michael Smyth, our London solicitor, had given invaluable support, but now we needed advice in Manchester. It was in this way that we came to know Hamid Husain[A] of Husain and Company, Withington. Our search succeeded when we came across 6 Oaker Avenue, West Didsbury (Figure 18.1) in a quiet turning off Barlow Moor Road, a highway on which a great volume of vehicles travelled eastwards from Didsbury to Chorlton-cum-Hardy, joining Princess Parkway, which led from the airport to the city centre.

Effectively a small town in its own right, West Didsbury was not far from Stockport and had an abundance of stores, among them an excellent bookshop. The small hotels and public houses were valuable places for family gatherings. Nearby, Burton Road had many less ostentatious stores that gave good value for money.

On the eve of our move, the weather was extremely hot and we spent an uncomfortable night in a small hotel before driving to our new, still empty house. Awaiting the arrival of the van bringing our furniture from Belfast, we encountered a small, black vehicle from which a mournful, Dickensian figure descended. He was the Sheriff's officer, sent to impound our possessions! The previous owner had been declared bankrupt and the authorities had decided

Chapter summary

- A new home
- The University Medical School
- The University Department
- My new department
- The National Health Service and diagnosis
- Teaching
- Research
- Visiting workers
- Conferences
- Examinations
- Committees and contacts
- Family life in Manchester
- Our grandmothers
- Philip
- The lithotriptor
- Health
- Retirement

Figure 18.1 *Oaker Avenue, looking towards Barlow Moor Road.*

to confiscate his worldly goods! We sent the Sheriff's representative to the correct address.

Number 6 Oaker Avenue was a substantial Edwardian mansion of three floors with four cellar rooms (Figure 18.2). The lounge extended for the whole depth of the house and French windows opened on to a modest garden, flanked to its right by a high stone wall and to its left by a long garage and fence. Double doors opened from the hall into the dining room. When Helen's mother, Emily, came to live with us early in 1979, a second handrail was added to the winding staircase, allowing her to climb safely to the first floor.

One next-door neighbour was Dorothy Ross. She struggled with her little Morris Minor car and from time to time Philip (p.249) helped when she found she couldn't engage the gears and was stranded in the middle of the city. From an early age, Dorothy had suffered from a chronic lung disease, the result of whooping cough, and I learnt later that she had developed amyloidosis, from which she died in 1995. She had known the artist L. S. Lowry, and it was not long before we were encouraged to buy some Lowry prints.[B] Across the road lived Rosalind and Colin Hoffman and next to them her parents, Dr and Mrs Hilson. Another neighbour was Mr Biron, an ex-serviceman and generous dispenser of liquid refreshment!

Figure 18.2 *Number 6 Oaker Avenue.*

Our daughter Rosalind and her husband Iain McQueen had settled in Glasgow, but would move to Cardiff. While still a student, my son Iain had decided that he needed a car of his own, and we bought a little Ford, on the rear window of which he mischievously placed a notice 'Short Vehicle'. Iain graduated in Medicine from the University of Birmingham in 1976. He had had the good fortune to meet Lynn Morgan (Figure 18.3), the daughter of a successful Leicester businessman and their wedding took place on 24th June 1978 in Oadby. Iain had accepted an appointment to the Manchester Eye Hospital.[2] For some months before he and Lynn found their own house, they lived with us as Iain pursued his work in ophthalmology.

Philip was by now well established in the School of Law at Birmingham University. When the time came for him to drive, we

Figure 18.3 *Iain Gardner and Lynn Morgan.*

found a secondhand white Wolseley for him and he soon displayed great driving skills. He and David, by now accustomed to Abbotsholme, a school of high repute in the Midlands, played tennis on the courts in Victoria Park and together we enjoyed golf at the nearby Northenden and Didsbury courses. During these years, there were family births and weddings. Rosalind's second son Alastair was born on 17th September 1978, while my brother Colin's son Perry was married on 6th April 1985, his daughter Philippa on 22nd May 1993.

The University Medical School

The Medical School of the University of Manchester[C] had benefited from a vast new £12.5 million Stopford Building, one of the largest in Europe, planned so that medical students who had studied preclinical sciences at St Andrews, where there was no teaching hospital, could move to Manchester to complete their clinical work. The Stopford Building was opened in 1973, the lengthy corridors painted unimaginatively in a drab ochre. Designed to accommodate medical, dental and nursing students, the edifice included the Departments of Anatomy, Physiology, Biochemistry, Pathology and Radiology, and by 1976 there were no fewer than 193 second-year and 268 third-year students. At first, all pathology teaching was centred there, provided by three professors (p.239).

A proportion of the students could learn hospital medicine and surgery in the Manchester Royal Infirmary, the MRI, the principal

Figure 18.4 *Entrance to the Withington Hospital.*

teaching hospital, but the remainder could only be taught by calling on the wards of the Hope Hospital, Salford, together with those of the Withington Hospital, Nell Lane, previously the Chorlton Union Workhouse (Figure 18.4), now a District General Hospital. The difficulty for staff as well as for students was that the Hope Hospital was four miles from the Stopford Building, Withington two miles to the south. It followed that the University was obliged to create two additional chairs in each subject. In this way, by 1976, five clinical chairs, those of Medicine, Surgery, Geriatric Medicine, Obstetrics and Gynaecology, and Psychiatry, came to be based at Withington. Similar arguments emerged with regard to the teaching of pathology and it was decided to add a corresponding chair in Pathology, the position to which I had been appointed.

The University Department

Within the Stopford Building, the direction of the Department of Pathology was in the hands of Peter O. Yates, Professor of Neuropathology. He had succeeded A. C. P. (Colin) Campbell, who had been Dean of the Medical School.[D] Yates was supported by Harold Fox, who held a personal chair in Gynaecological Pathology and by W. (Bill) L. Ford,[E] who had come to Manchester from Oxford to become Professor of Immunology. Yates, Fox and their many colleagues shared the clinical responsibility for the diagnostic laboratories of the MRI.

Figure 18.5 *The author at his microscope in Manchester.*

My first day's experience in Manchester was unusual! Finding my way to my office in the Stopford Building, I was approached by Dr M. Ingle Wright, whose husband was the well-known rheumatologist J. S. (John) Lawrence. Ingle came to my room and asked: 'Please help me with some photographs I need for a paper. I can't find anybody else!' We had never met before, but quickly settled at my microscope (Figure 18.5). Some time later, Peter Yates suggested that I join him as he prepared an atlas of computer tomographic (CT) images, derived from the Nobel-prize-winning work of Housman. However, by that time, some differences of opinion had arisen with regard to my wish to bring to my department an Egyptian who had worked with me in London. My other lectureships were less contentious. John McClure, who had worked with me in Belfast (p.192) before his move to Adelaide[F] (p.273), became my 'right-hand man' and Alastair Lessells[G] joined the Department as a Lecturer.

My new department

At Withington Hospital, the University had constructed a fine new building of six floors, including a spacious lecture theatre. The top floor was a large research laboratory, and there were offices for the Professors of Medicine (John Evanson), Surgery (Ron Sellwood) and Geriatric Medicine (John C. Brocklehurst). Max Elstein, Professor of Obstetrics and Gynaecology, centred his work in his clinical unit, and W. I. N. Kessel, Professor of Psychiatry, became Postgraduate Dean, with an office in the Stopford building.

> I corresponded with Neil Kessel on administrative matters and on one occasion received an unique rely. His letter said: 'Dear Dugald, Thank you for your letter which I have not received.'

In its original design, no allowance had been made for Pathology, and I was consigned to the ground floor of one of the old hospital blocks, the basement of which was to be a classroom. This arrangement had little disadvantage – my office was large enough for hundreds of books and papers; my experienced and dependable secretary, Mrs Irene Barlow, had space and privacy; and there were rooms for assistants and visitors. I selected the room opposite mine as a venue for research microscopes, including an integrating microdensitometer provided by the Nuffield Foundation.[H] The classroom demanded immediate attention. In Belfast (p.195), I had learnt the value of versatile space and I repeated my plan in Withington. A moveable screen, manufactured of soundproof material, was built, dividing the large room into two halves. The arrangement enabled two different classes to be held simultaneously, but allowed the entire room to be used when the whole class was present. Facilities for television teaching soon became available.

The National Health Service and diagnosis

The days of a senior clinical teacher in a medical school are punctuated by the insistent demands of undergraduate education, by the less frequent calls of postgraduate teaching, and by the need to attend, and often to chair, committees on a great variety of subjects, some relating to University matters, some to Faculty affairs, and many to those of the National Health Service, with whom each teacher has an honorary contract.

In addition to these tasks, I was committed to a full part in the diagnostic work of the Hospital, in which the laboratories, including those for histopathology, were part of the hospital building. This challenge, of a kind facing all clinical professors, was complicated by the imperative to raise money for the research on which the academic reputation of my new department would rest. Occasionally, the conflicting demands grew so great that one day a frustrated John McClure demanded: 'Why don't you do some real (hospital) work?' However, I was greatly helped by my consultant colleagues Martin Harris, Nagib Y. Haboubi and Dr (later Professor) Philip Haselton. Dr S. S. Banerjee, a Senior Registrar, moved subsequently to the Christie Hospital, where he became a consultant. In 1984, C. J. Kirkpatrick,[1] an outstanding graduate and international athlete who had completed his PhD with me in Belfast, came to join the laboratory. He was, however, reluctant to embark on the examinations for membership of the Royal College of Pathologists, the MRCPath, and moved to Germany, where he and his wife settled. Subsequently, Richard Fitzmaurice came to the Department as a trainee, migrating later to a pathology practice in St Anthony, Newfoundland[3].

Almost at once, a vacancy arose for a Chief Medical Laboratory Scientific Officer (CMLSO) to take charge of the day-to-day running of the hospital laboratory. After competitive interviews, Robert Jones was appointed, enthusiastic for the use of computer techniques in laboratory reporting. As an associate, he had Peter Sullivan, Senior MLSO.

Much of the biopsy work I undertook, like that of the Royal Victoria Hospital, Belfast, related to common European diseases, in particular to cancer. There were, of course, fewer autopsy cases of trauma of the kind I saw so often in Ulster during the 'Troubles'. However, an incidental part of my work was on behalf of HM Coroner. I had taken part in Coroner's autopsy practice during my time in Cambridge (p.111) and was reminded of this important part of the legal system, so different from that of Scotland. Coroners' autopsies demanded the occasional attendance at inquests, where each of us had to respond to searching questions in cases of unexplained death, suicide and 'cot death', cross-examinations that tested the precision of our work rigorously.

There were occasional cases of exceptional interest, and in March 1977 I was surprised to be asked by Dr Michael Mason on behalf of the Saudi Arabian Embassy to give an opinion on tissue taken from the hip joint of His Majesty King Khalid of Saudi Arabia – they had also requested a report from Professor H. A. Sissons. Some months later, a telephone call from the Embassy reminded me that I had not sent in a note of my fee. I had never indulged in private practice and naively asked for an amount sufficient to pay for a new textbook!

Teaching

I organized courses of lectures for our third- and fourth-year students and planned the weekly clinico-pathological conferences in a style I had developed in Belfast. At each meeting, I invited a physician or surgeon to describe a case of particular interest before I and my colleagues discussed the pathological implications.

Practical teaching centred on the rebuilt classroom, used both for small-group, 'tutorial' instruction and for larger classes. I encouraged the teaching of pathological ('morbid') anatomy in the hospital mortuary, following the practice that had been so successful in Ulster (p.195). In South Manchester, limited space determined that only small groups of students were able to attend, and there was no space for a television system of the kind we had pioneered in the North of Ireland. However, with a small group, it was easier to put questions to individual students. Seeking a diagnosis for a challenging specimen, I often quoted the words of Sherlock Holmes: 'When you have eliminated the impossible, whatever remains, however improbable, must be the truth.'

I continued postgraduate teaching, lecturing once or twice yearly in the Edinburgh Internal Medicine Course and occasionally in an instructional course in arthritis surgery at the Princess Margaret Rose Hospital, the Edinburgh orthopaedic centre.

Research

My intention was to continue the original work that we had undertaken in London and Belfast. My interest still centred on the rheumatic diseases, and new studies were begun of relevant cases drawn from the wide experience of the Withington Hospital.

I extended our investigations of the structure and disorders of the cartilage that formed the bearing surfaces both of normal and of abnormal synovial joints. When the need for electron microscopy re-emerged, the Stopford Building instrument proved inconvenient. However, I soon learnt that, in the University of Lancaster, Professor Potts and Ken Oates[j] were developing low-temperature electron microscopy (LTEM) (Figure 18.6). The collaboration that resulted led not only to much published work and to Ken's PhD,[4] but also to our lasting friendship. With Ken was a skilled assistant J. F. S. (Jim) Middleton.

The Arthritis and Rheumatism Council, the ARC, gave us much financial support. On one occasion, it was particularly interesting to recognise Helen Muir (p.175) among those who came on a 'site visit' to assess the validity of our application for a research grant (Figure 18.7). Outstanding among my co-workers was Nairn Wilson,[k] who had been with me in Belfast (p.198). I was equally fortunate in recruiting Pat O'Connor, who came with much experience in mechanical engineering. With Pat was another PhD graduate, Constance (Connie) Orford, one of the most perceptive of our group. Towards the end of her research grant, she took maternity leave and, to our dismay, did not return. Dr D. M. (Max) Lawton was an assiduous Research Fellow,[l] his particular area of interest the low-temperature scanning electron microscope.

Other very active investigators were Maria Warsky, a PhD student, and Jeremy Pidd, skilled in the electron microscopy of cartilage and bone. As he approached the time for the submission of his PhD thesis, he took the interesting decision to leave in order to join the police force. Dr Karen Butterworth, highly qualified in biochemistry, decided to practise surgery. Later, in March 1989, she applied for a temporary Lectureship and Prosectorship in Anatomy. Mark Mellor worked with Dr Haboubi, and in the summer of 1989 was awarded the MSc degree.

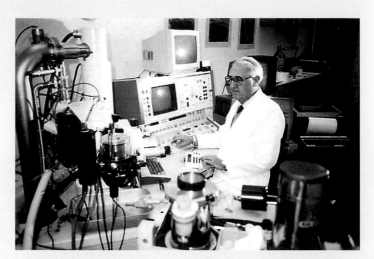

Figure 18.6 *Ken Oates with the low-temperature electron microscope.*

Figure 18.7 *The University Vice Chancellor, Mark Richmond, stands to the author's left during a site visit by the Arthritis and Rheumatism Council to our research laboratories at the Withington Hospital.*

The extensive Ciba Geigy laboratory at Stamford Lodge, Altrincham Road, Wilmslow, proved to be an invaluable source of ideas and resources (p.291) Note 21[A]. Tony Bradley was Head of the Section of Pathology. Paul Skelton Stroud, his Deputy, later became Head of Pathology for Ciba Geigy in Basel. In 1986, Dr Kris Jasani of the Pharmaceutical Division arranged for the laboratory to receive £500 each quarter in recognition of our contribution to their cartilage studies. With Ciba Geigy, we were able to pursue our analyses of animal responses to joint disorders, while, from time to time, I reported our work at their staff meetings. When controversies over the use of animals in research led to the dangerous exploits of 'animal rights' protesters, Ciba, now Novartis, built a defensive fence around their extensive properties before finally taking their work back to Switzerland.

Visiting workers

In March 1980, Dr Winfried Mohr came from Germany to spend one month with us. He was followed in 1982 by Roman Mazuryk of the Department of Pathology, Szczecin, Poland, who had been awarded a Fellowship by the Wellcome Foundation to spend a year in my Department.[5] A quiet and studious person, he was soon known as 'the silent Pole'. Several years later, Dr Mazuryk was a candidate for a higher degree, a necessary qualification for an Assistant Professor, but the Council of his Polish Institute decided that the quantity of his original contributions was not sufficient. However, the Polish Ministry of Health and Social Welfare awarded him one of their annual prizes. It was at this time that I enjoyed visits from Professor R. C. Nairn (p.280) ,who had left Aberdeen and settled in Melbourne, and from Leon Sokoloff of the State University of New York at Stony Brook, to whose encyclopaedic volumes I contributed.[6]

Conferences

An enticing web of conferences can easily entrap scientists! There were many gatherings in London, where, for example, the European Society of Pathology met in 1979. In 1981 we travelled to Australia (p.273), in 1982 to Kingston, Ontario (p.153) and in 1983 to Baghdad (p.291). In 1984, I was responsible for the organization of a Manchester symposium sponsored by the ARC on 'Bone, Joint and Connective Tissue Pathology',[M] and in October 1986, I took part in an international symposium on 'Degenerative Joint Disease' held at the Kennedy Institute. Our visits to Eastern Europe included a journey to Moscow (p.259) and to Poland (p.267). I had already been twice to Hungary and would go there again (p.256).

Examinations

I found professorial responsibilities to be similar to those in Belfast, with undergraduate examinations concentrated towards the end of the summer term. Through my association with Professor Austin Gresham (p.114), in 1976 I became an External Examiner for the Final MB of the University of Cambridge. At the instigation of Dermot Hourihane, in the same year I started examining in Pathology for the MB degree of Trinity College, Dublin[N] (p.197). I stayed with Dermot and his wife and learnt much of the ancient College itself, of the city where so much of the history of these isles had evolved, and of the *Book of Kells*.

> Examining in Dublin in the Royal College of Surgeons in Ireland on behalf of the Royal College of Surgeons of Edinburgh, the RCSEd, I recalled an experience of the late Andrew Shivas (p.155). On his first morning as examiner, Andrew told me that he had arrived promptly at the steps of the College, where the doors were not yet open. He rang the bell. A servitor appeared, rubbed his eyes and asked 'Can ye no sleep?' Later in the day, examining with a surgical colleague, Andrew remarked on a pile of unmarked scripts that lay upon their table. 'Had we not better assess these papers before lunch?' Andrew asked. 'No', said his colleague, 'That's not necessary. There's a simpler solution.' And he dropped the troublesome papers into a wastepaper basket.

My responsibilities as an examiner for the RCSEd (p.321) continued, so that on two occasions each year, usually in the spring and autumn, Helen and I were able to visit our old home city of Edinburgh for two or three days at a time. Occasionally, these visits might merge with normal holidays, allowing longer stays and visits to friends and family and to other parts of Scotland. Among the privileges of visiting the RCSEd was access to the Library, where I became acquainted with their talented Librarian, Marianne Smith, and with the literate but idiosyncratic Alison H. Stevenson. For a short period, I also played a small part in the examinations for the Membership of the Royal College of Physicians of Edinburgh.

It was at this time that I started to prepare a compact aide-memoir on pathology for young surgeons approaching the examination for Fellowship of the Royal Colleges of Surgeons. Initially in collaboration with my friend Sir James Fraser, President of the Edinburgh College until 1985, the surgical component of the writing passed to another friend, David E. F. Tweedle, a Manchester consultant. Published in 1986, the first edition of our book became *Pathology for the Primary FRCS*. It was reprinted in 1989 but a second edition in 1996 was retitled *Pathology For Surgeons in Training – An A to Z* and this title was retained, almost unchanged, for a third edition in 2002.

Figure 18.8 *The author as Adami Lecturer.*

In the course of the years, I acted as an (external) examiner for the degree of PhD (or DPhil) for the Universities of Birmingham, Sheffield, Durham, Edinburgh, Lancaster, Oxford and Calcutta, and for the degree of MD of the Universities of Cambridge, Glasgow and London and of the Queen's University of Belfast. On one occasion in Oxford, my co-examiner for the degree of BSc, now the MSc, was the distinguished diagnostician and teacher, A. H. T. Robb-Smith. His well known acerbic humour was in gentle evidence, but he was both fair and kindly to our candidates. A particular interest was added during the years 1971–88 when I was asked to advise on the qualifications of individuals being considered for personal chairs in the Universities of London, Edinburgh and Pennsylvania, and for a Readership in the University of Southampton and a promotional position in Khartoum.

My most rewarding time came when Professor Donald Heath (p.196) invited me to help with the examinations for Part I of the Final MB and Final BDS of the University of Liverpool. I benefited greatly from our friendship. His remarkably strong handshake and portly appearance belied the character of a disciplined teacher and investigator.[7,8] He shared my interest in photography and introduced me to parts of the city of Liverpool of which I was quite ignorant. Not far from his Department was the famous Liverpool School of Hygiene and Tropical Medicine, the origins of which recalled those of the London School (p.7). I continued as external examiner until 1990. Donald generously proposed to his University that I be invited to give the prestigious Adami Lecture.[O,9] For the occasion, on 10th November 1987, I was clad with a splendid gown (Figure 18.8), while, after the lecture, Helen and I enjoyed a formal University dinner.

Committees and contacts

The practical problem of attending Faculty and Academic committees in Manchester was considerable, since many met in the Stopford Building, two miles from Withington.

In addition, there were many extramural demands on my time. Thus, I was a member of the Medical Research Council (MRC), Physiological Systems Grants Committee A from 1976 to 1979; and of the Education and Scientific Research Committees of the ARC from 1967 to 1976 and of their Scientific Coordinating Committee from 1976 until 1983. In 1980, Eric Bywaters, the distinguished rheumatologist, persuaded me to become secretary of the Pathology Committee of the European League Against Rheumatism, EULAR (Chapter 13), of which he was the chairman. The result was a sequence of visits to Switzerland, Germany, Belgium, Poland and Hungary, and also friendship with many European colleagues. We particularly enjoyed a meeting in Geneva in Eric's company. He was travelling by himself. In 1984, he retired from EULAR and I succeeded him, retaining the chairmanship until 1990, when Peter Revell accepted the challenge with Winfried Mohr as secretary.

There were many other associations. I was a member of a number of editorial boards (p.180) and periodically undertook book reviews.[P] My membership of the Biological Research Advisory Board of the Chemical Defence Establishment of the Ministry of Defence, Porton (p.182) continued. Soon afterwards, on 20th July 1988, I received a kind letter from R. B. (Bob) Goudie, at that time General Secretary of the Pathological Society of Great Britain and Ireland, thanking me for the years during which I had been a member of the Society's Committee. I maintained a correspondence with Arnold Soren, Professor of Orthopaedic Surgery, New York University School of Medicine, and friendly discussions with Professor Ken Weinbren of the Royal Postgraduate Medical School, Hammersmith, which extended to our shared interests in Bellini and Smetana!

Family life in Manchester

For four years, our life flowed as peacefully as the waters of the nearby River Mersey. Iain and Philip came home during vacation times; David, living with us, confronted the challenge of the West Manchester College of Further Education, and Rosalind and Iain McQueen visited us when his professional work in neurology made this possible. In addition to family gatherings (Figures 18.9 and 18.10), there were social functions such as the Lord Mayor's Appeal for the Disabled, which included a dinner dance arranged by Councillor Hugh Lee at the Northenden Golf Club; visits to the Gateway theatre and to cinemas; concerts in the Free Trade Hall by the Hallé orchestra; and art exhibitions and museum displays.

But there were also accidents. One day, as David and I were in our rooms at the top of the house, we heard a strange noise, a thud, from downstairs. Hurrying down, we found Helen lying on the concrete garage runway, barely conscious, her head not far from a boulder. She had fallen while standing on a ladder, cleaning a window. Helped into the house, she sat in a chair while we telephoned for help. It became clear that she had broken her left arm. Taken

Figure 18.9 *Our sons (left to right) Philip, Iain and David, at a social gathering.*

Figure 18.10 *Rosalind (at left) holds her son David; my mother, Marjorie, cradles Jane, while Dr Iain McQueen gazes down on them.*

quickly to the Accident and Emergency Department of the Withington Hospital, the consultant orthopaedic surgeon, Mr H. Bertfield, told us that the fracture was too near the shoulder joint to be plated and that the slow and painful path to recovery was for the arm simply to hang in a sling. One consequence was that for 11 nights Helen could only sleep in an armchair. It was an extremely distressing experience, but gradual improvement encouraged her to attend physiotherapy classes. They were not a success – the exercises offered were impossibly painful – but, fortunately, a physiotherapist who lived nearby proved extremely helpful.

Our grandmothers

In 1979, changes in the Peters's household (pp.23,28) led my mother to come to Manchester, the city where her Aunt Car (p.5) had at one time lived. Very sadly, we had to tell her that we could not offer her accommodation in our home at Oaker Avenue. The reason was that, earlier in the year, Helen's mother, Emily Harrower, now aged 85, had come to live with us after the death of her sister Florence. We were fortunate therefore in finding rooms for Marjorie at Stott House, an Abbeyfield Home, no more than three minutes' walk from our house, and it was here that she welcomed visitors, particularly Colin and Denise when they came from Yorkshire to see us all.

In the last months of her life, Marjorie, by now physically incapacitated, moved into a rest home, Rydal House, Princes Road, Stockport, where she was well and comfortably cared for. She died on 22nd May 1987, in her 97th year, and her ashes were buried with those of my father in Minehead, Somerset. Helen's mother, Emily Harrower, died peacefully in a Manchester nursing home on 17th October 1987.

Philip

Philip (p.130) had shown a great aptitude for literature at school and a particular liking for T. S. Elliot. Musical, with a fine voice and a talented percussionist, his time coincided with the rise to fame of The Beatles. He was at the same time a natural athlete and enjoyed visiting Trafford Park, a beauty spot not far from our home. When he graduated from the University of Birmingham in 1978,[Q] we travelled to the ceremony (Figure 18.11). Gifted with a dry sense of humour, refined at St Paul's School, he clearly thought the graduation procedure slightly absurd, although his LL.B. degree enabled him to enter the legal profession, leading him first to a firm of local solicitors and then to the larger offices of Clifford Chance.

On the evening of 3rd December 1979, Philip was not well and took to his bed with a severe headache. Later in the evening, he was sick and drowsy. The following morning, 4th December, we went to his room, where we noticed that the windows were open, the rain blowing in, and found that he had died during the night. We had the immediate but deeply distressing task of telling David of the death of his brother. Sympathetic police officers came quickly and we phoned Iain, at work in the Eye Hospital, and Rosalind, in Glasgow. Iain was so upset that he shut himself away for the whole morning. A report from the Coroner's pathologist showed that Philip had developed a fulminating form of meningitis. The

Figure 18.11 *Philip graduating LL.B. Birmingham in 1978.*

Reverend Norman Leak, Minister of Grosvenor St Aidan's Church, conducted the funeral service with great sympathy and dignity. In the days that followed, much help and understanding was shown by our neighbours, Lena and Don Hilson, and by our friend Dorothy Ross.

In the months and years following Philip's death, a turmoil of thoughts led me to a new view of life and its meaning. I felt drawn towards Grosvenor St Aidan's church, with which, until then, I had had only occasional contacts. My mother attended the Sunday morning services regularly and was befriended by several of the established congregation. It was a simple matter to join her. I became a member of the choir and made good friends with other 'like minds'. Norman proved a good friend. Like his brother-in law, John Hick,[10] a controversial theologian in Birmingham, he did not hesitate to examine every side of a theological question. One Easter Sunday, he 'put the cat among the pigeons' by commenting that 'Easter is a pagan festival'. His remark did not go down well with some of the more conservative members of his congregation, but they provided a topic for our informal chats for months afterwards.

The lithotriptor

Not every aspect of our life at that time was so bleak. Rosalind's third son, Robert Andrew McQueen, was born in Cardiff on 4th October 1983. It was the year in which Norman Blacklock, Professor of Urological Surgery of Manchester University, achieved one of his ambitions: the construction at Withington of a unit that could treat the painful condition of urinary stone (calculus) without the need for invasive surgery, using the new technique of lithotripsy. The instrument, a lithotriptor, was a machine from which sound waves, focused on a urinary stone found by X-radiography, could be directed safely into the body of a patient, breaking up the stone. Professor Blacklock held the naval rank of Surgeon Captain. He was a Surgeon to Her Majesty the Queen and frequently accompanied the Royal family on voyages on HMS *Britannia*. When his new machine had been installed and tested in Manchester, he asked Her Majesty whether she would be prepared to declare the facility open. She agreed and, together with many of the staff, I was invited to attend the ceremony. Dressed formally, with my trousers suitably pressed, I stood in line with my colleagues (Figure 18.12) as the Queen exchanged kindly words with each of us.

Health

With the exception of my childhood illnesses and of those I experienced at school, I had been fortunate to have enjoyed good health. However, in 1981, not long before we were due to fly to Australia,

Figure 18.12 *Norman Blacklock introduces us to Her Majesty the Queen at Withington Hospital in 1983.*

I suffered the sudden prolapse of a disc in the lower left part of my spine. Pain tore down my leg, movement was almost impossible and the only relief I recall was to watch Manchester City playing Brighton and Hove Albion, my club, in the finals of the FA Cup. Our steadfast general practitioner, Clifford Kaye, prescribed analgesics and prolonged rest. He advised against flying. A younger partner, more realistic, said: 'Dr Kaye does not like air travel. But my advice to you is to take a chance. After all, you can rest on the plane.' And she was right. We accepted the challenge and, as Chapter 20 explains, all was well.

Early one morning in 1984, preparing notes for a lecture, I felt an uncomfortable, constricting sensation in my left chest and suspected the cause was coronary artery disease. Our doctor came quickly and I was taken to the Withington Hospital. Bed rest, the meticulous attention of caring nurses and of Dr Leonard, ensured that over the next few days I made a slow recovery. But then, out and about, I found that even slow walking caused a constricting sensation in my chest, angina of effort. In South Manchester, there were few facilities for coronary artery surgery, but my son-in-law,

Iain McQueen, recommended coming to Cardiff, where Professor Henderson had established a growing reputation.

It was not many days therefore before I found myself in a quiet room in the University Hospital of Wales at Heath Park. Bathed and washed, one day I was taken to a cardiac operating theatre, where the radiologist explained that he was about to inject an opaque dye into my femoral artery to locate any problems with my coronary arteries before attempting to correct them. A few minutes later, he said: 'I have found the site of the trouble. It is a plaque in the wall of the left coronary artery. I'll show it to you.' And he told me to look at the X-ray screens that hung above our heads. I muttered: 'Good. What now?' He replied: 'I'm inserting a catheter and displacing the block.' And that was that.

And so, after a few more days, I was allowed to return to my daughter's Cardiff home and then, a week later, to journey back to Manchester. I still have the X-rays and the catheter!

Retirement

By 1988, the possibility of returning to Edinburgh had arisen through circumstances explained in Chapters 22 and 23. After very careful thought, Helen and I agreed that it was the correct moment to ask the University for retirement. Anticipating our move, we began to search for accommodation in Edinburgh. When the time came to leave Manchester, my friends and colleagues arranged a generous farewell dinner. In the weeks that followed, I was told of a resolution adopted by the University Senate on 25th October 1988, and by the Council on 15th November, which stated that 'Senate wished to place on record its thanks and appreciation to Professor D. L. Gardner for his services to the University as Professor of Histopathology'. I had already been granted the title of Professor Emeritus and, in 1986, had been awarded the Manchester degree of MSc.

CHAPTER 19

A European scene

From the Tagus to the canals of Mons

The discussion of any subject is a right that you have
brought into the world with your heart and tongue.

Shelley[1]

Chapter summary
- PORTUGAL
- Lisbon and the Tagus
- HUNGARY
- Budapest and the Danube
- GERMANY
- Hamburg and the Elbe
- Wiesbaden and the Rhine
- DENMARK
- Århus (Aarhus) and the Kattegat
- RUSSIA
- Moscow and the Moscow River
- Leningrad and the Neva
- Kiev and the Dnieper
- POLAND
- Szczecin and the Oder
- Warsaw and the Vistula
- FRANCE
- Paris and the Seine
- BELGIUM
- Mons and the canals

Addressing the Irish people in 1812, Shelley continued:
'Resign your heart's blood before you part with this inestimable privilege of man.'

Shelley was right but discussion, debate and reasoned argument are
not confined to politics and, indeed, are lynch-pins of science. I
have been fortunate to have taken part in many conferences, society
meetings and committees in Europe and they are brought together
in this chapter. Because of the unusual nature of our experiences, I
place a particular emphasis on visits to Eastern European countries.

PORTUGAL

Lisbon and the Tagus

With the exception of a holiday in Germany in 1936 (p.19), my
military service (Chapter 9) in the same country and our honeymoon in Holland (p.88), neither Helen nor I had travelled on the
continent of Europe. Our decision to journey from London on
8th October 1967 to attend the European Congress of Rheumatology
in Portugal was therefore an exciting experience, only made possible
by the kind offer by our good friend Helen Miller (p.130) to care for
our home and four children while we were away.

The Cold War was still in progress, so Lisbon offered a first, limited but unusual opportunity for exchanging opinions with our East
European counterparts. The many British delegates included the
Chairman of the Management Committee of the Kennedy Institute,
W. S. C. Copeman (p.169). Will was a kind host, entertaining us
generously while overcoming his scorn for those who preferred ice
cream and lemonade to Stilton cheese and port at the end of a dinner! A full scientific programme allowed time for sightseeing, and
we visited Alcântara, Belém and the baroque–neoclassical Estrela

Basilica. It was during this meeting that Alan Dixon, a British rheumatologist, had a narrow escape when he swam in the Atlantic and
encountered the full force of the coastal waves.

Many years later, we visited Portugal again, on holiday (p.345).

HUNGARY

Budapest and the Danube

Stimulated by the visit to London of Professor Hari Jellinek (p.181),
Professor of Pathology in the Medical School of Budapest, I flew
to the Danube in May 1968 to present a paper[2] at the Hungarian
Rheumatology Society, travelling with the national airline, Malév
and staying at the Gelert Hotel. At the National Museum, Hari
reminded me that his country had been part of the Roman Empire,
while the Danube (Figure 19.1) remained a vital communication
between central Europe and the Black Sea. I consulted the history
of Byzantium[3] and learnt of the fall of Constantinople in 1453 and
the incursions by the Ottoman Turks as they swept across Europe.
Saved by the bravery of its townswomen, Eger, near the border with
Russia, was the furthest point reached by the Ottomans in their
attempts to assault Vienna.

Figure 19.1 *The Danube at Budapest.*

For centuries, Budapest had been in two parts: much of Buda, to the east, lay on a prominent hill overlooking the river. The heights offered a view of the famous Chain Bridge, designed by an Englishman, William Tierney Clark, who was also responsible for Hammersmith Bridge in London, and constructed under the supervision of an unrelated Scotsman, Adam Clark. On the highest point was the castle. Pest, to the west, separated from Buda by the Danube, was a heavily populated, urban plain.

Budapest still bore the scars of the brutal Russian attacks that followed the Hungarian uprising in 1956. Soon after my arrival, Hari said unexpectedly: 'This morning we are going to the Tourist Office to get the oil coupons for your car!' I said: 'But I travelled to Hungary by plane; my car is in London'. He explained: 'No matter! The coupons will provide enough oil for *my* car for the coming year!'. Later in the evening, I sat among the Russian officers who were attending a performance of Bela Bartok's *The Miraculous Mandarin*.

I had come to know one of the consultant rheumatologists, Dr Andreas Richter, in London. In Budapest, he evidently felt able to confide in me. I suspected, from an early conversation, that he hoped I might be able to help him fly to Switzerland, whence he believed he could move to a western country, perhaps Great Britain.

Dr Richter's English was not good, but he had the attractive habit of starting every sentence with the same preliminary phrase: 'Surely it is necessary that ….'. He asked me if I would like to see something of the countryside. Setting off in his little red Renault car, we journeyed to an estate, where, leaving the car, we walked to the centre of a large courtyard. He told me that he had something of importance to tell me. Looking around anxiously, assured that no one was listening, he whispered in my ear: 'The mixer has not come!' I had no idea what he was talking about and asked what he meant. Dr Richter explained that he had ordered a biochemical homogenizer, a piece of equipment resembling a kitchen blender. After a long delay, it had not arrived. He dared not complain, since the device had been agreed by the Academy of Sciences, a State organization regulated by the Communist party. To complain would imperil his position!

Like many State employees, Dr Richter worked for the State Hospital during the day. He then returned home, put on a white coat, and saw his private patients. This bipartisan approach was not mirrored by the rigid State approach to the elderly, who were not well cared for.

In the course of the next few days, we went by car to the headquarters of the Hungarian wine industry, at Eger. The town adjoins the northeast border with Russia and its proximity helps to explain the importance to Russia of Hungarian wines such as Tokay. The headquarters of the wine industry was in the Archbishop's palace; beneath it lay no less than four kilometres of cellars. After a full tour, we sat down in one of the cellars to a repast during which a fine range of wines was tasted.

In 1971, my new friends were hosts for the Hungarian Pathological Society. The meeting was to be held in Pecs in the south of the country. For my first night, I was given a room among the patients in a local hospital. The only inconvenience was the noise that began each morning at 5 am when the patients were being served breakfast. I moved to a hotel for the remaining days. There was sufficient comfort, but no hot water!

The Conference centred on advances in electron microscopy.[4] It had been possible to gather 20 speakers from 11 countries and I had been asked to chair a session on scanning electron microscopy. It was during this Congress that I had the privilege of being elected to Honorary Membership of the Hungarian Society of Pathologists and came to know Dr Miklos Bély from the Department of Morphology of the National Institute of Rheumatology. I recalled that during the time that Anna Kadar[A,5–8] (p.181) spent in London we had enjoyed a short visit by Dr T. Kerényi, one of her colleagues in Budapest. He was able to assist her in her studies of arterial elastic tissue and we later prepared two papers.[9,10] Following the meeting, Hari Jellinek came to London again. Western currency, and in particular the American dollar, was in short supply and Hari persuaded me to help by concealing a modest amount of foreign currency in London, to await his future needs.

On a third visit, Helen, David and I travelled to Budapest together (Figure 19.2). It was 30th June 1991. I had been invited to attend the European Congress of Rheumatology. Arriving in Budapest, Helen, David and I approached the Beke (Peace) Hotel on Lenin Street, as it was still called. The outside of the hotel was pockmarked with bullet holes, a grim reminder of the 1956 uprising. Accommodation was simple but comfortable, although the Hungarian idea of a poached egg resembled a form of soup and was very different from ours. For security reasons, as we left the hotel, we were given a 'guide', a young woman whose task it was to observe our movements and to report any suspicious activity. On one occasion, escaping her mentor, Helen lost her way and returned to the hotel with difficulty. Although the language was beyond us, German was widely understood and I had no difficulty in buying a box of matches ('ein Schachtel Streichholz') with which to light my pipe.

In the vast Metropole Hotel, we watched swimmers in the huge pool, where the warm water attracted many disabled people. The scene recalled the Health Spa centre at Lake Balaton, where, since Roman times, sick and handicapped individuals were lowered into the thermal waters, supported by collars made of leather and wood. It was an ancient practice and in the State Museum we saw examples of Roman collars identical with those in use today.

Our visit ended with a journey up the Danube to Vienna. The flowing river was calm but not blue; indeed, a murky grey colour gave a hint of the problem of industrial pollution. Approached by a stewardess on the boat, it was clear that Helen had developed

Figure 19.2 *Our group at the Citadel, Budapest. Dr Richter stands (at right).*

migraine. Landing at Vienna, she soon recovered. We had found a convenient family hotel by consulting our local library, reassured by the Austrian consulate in London. Clean, comfortable and only a short walk from the city centre and St Stephen's cathedral, it proved an excellent choice.

The following day, we visited the Schönbrun Palace and strolled through the palatial grounds. Later, we joined a bus tour and saw the great cemetery depicted in Graham Greene's *The Third Man*. The bus took us to the Vienna Woods and the hunting lodge where Crown Prince Rudolf of Austria, heir to the Austro-Hungarian crown, and his mistress, Baroness Mary Vetsera, were found dead on 30th January 1889. We travelled to the entrance of the vast underground lakes and caverns (Figure 19.3) in which a factory for the manufacture of Heinkel aircraft had been cleverly concealed during the Second World War. Within the caves, an extensive chain of waterways was accessible only by boat. Clambering in to a small craft, a guide conducted us through the mysterious, dark tunnels and chambers.

Flying back to London, I felt we had learnt more of Central Europe – but only a little.

Figure 19.3 *Underground caverns in the Vienna Woods.*

GERMANY

Hamburg and the Elbe

The International Academy of Pathology (IAP) met in Hamburg on 16th September 1974, and I was asked to talk on the pathology of the rheumatic diseases. The changes to the city where Helen and I had spent so much time in the early 1950s (p.97) were dramatic. Gone were the gigantic mounds of rubble that had lined the streets destroyed in the air raids of 1944. Instead, around the Barmbek Hospital, great numbers of new buildings had sprung up and desolate wastes had become fertile agricultural land.

Wiesbaden and the Rhine

In 1979, the European Congress of Rheumatology met in Wiesbaden. I found accommodation in a small inn, where the quality of the meals in the busy little dining room was surprisingly high. To wile away any hours not devoted to the Congress, I took with me *Darwin and the Beagle*,[11] but it was scarcely needed as the programme was a very full one.

DENMARK

Århus (Aarhus) and the Kattegat

Following the September 1977 London meeting of the European Society of Pathology, Professor Olaf Myre Jensen, of the Århus State

Hospital, the Amtssygehus, Denmark, invited me to organize a slide seminar,[B] bringing together nearly 200 Scandinavian pathologists. We had met in Hamburg. The weekend of 23rd–25th March 1979 was agreed, and the preparations began in Manchester. I could not find good examples in my own files of the 36 disorders I planned to demonstrate, and wrote to friends and colleagues in London, Edinburgh, Cambridge, Dublin, New York and Kingston (Ontario) for help. From each of the tissue blocks I received so generously, my technicians made the necessary microscopic sections and I sent them to Denmark for distribution to the participants in the Seminar.

On 22nd March, Helen and I flew to Copenhagen. The course organizer, Dr Claus Lund of Odense, took us by car to Jutland and on to Århus, where we quickly made many new friends. The conference, held at a centre called the Scanticon, extended throughout the weekend. The Scandinavian pathologists who had chosen to take part had sent their analyses to the course organizer, and I discussed each case in detail with the assembled participants. During a 'question and answer' session, I casually mentioned 'red herrings'. There was uproar! I was reminded that red herrings are a staple part of the Danish diet. The occasion was physically demanding, since, rather unwisely, I stood at the rostrum for the whole of the two-day presentations. I was asked why I had not followed the practice of an earlier speaker who had sat throughout his conference with a bottle of beer beside him!

Olaf and his wife Birgit, devoted to the sea and proud of their yacht, entertained us generously. They took us to the Moesgård Museum to see Grauballe Man, the remains of an individual sacrificed ritually during the Iron Age and remarkably well preserved because of the humid ground, which was rich in iron and tannins. Our return journey from Jutland to Copenhagen coincided with a bus strike – the ferry was crowded – but next day we enjoyed a tour of the city and visits to art galleries, theatres and halls as well as to the University hospital, the Københavns Universitets Retsmedicinske Institut, where Professor Torben Schiødt showed us his excellent electron microscope facilities. It was to be 24 years before we saw Copenhagen again (p.346).

RUSSIA

Moscow and the Moscow River

In 1983, the Iron Curtain had not yet been lifted, but we were not deterred from attending the European Congress of Rheumatology in Moscow (Figures 19.4 and 19.5) on 27th June. Our Manchester neighbours, the Sinclairs, had told their son-in-law, Peter Gwinnett, and his wife Karen, of our plans. Peter worked in Moscow for Barclay's Bank.

Figure 19.4 *Helen against a backcloth of a 'Wedding Cake' building.*

British Airways took us across Denmark, Bornholm and Riga to Moscow. During the flight, we were warned against photographing Russian territory and I was concerned about how the authorities would view my camera. I need not have worried: the Russians displayed little interest in amateur photographers.

At the large, modern but badly lit Moscow airport, a mirror reminded me of the sinister passport office in Russian-occupied Budapest (p.254). The examination of papers did not take as long as we expected, but the immigration officials demanded details of the currency we were carrying and of previous journeys to Eastern Europe. After an hour's wait, some British luggage appeared. Seasoned travellers suggested that the delay was because our cases were being X-rayed. The officials inspecting our baggage appeared preoccupied with our books: our chosen authors included Evelyn Waugh and Anthony Trollope. At once, there was a crisis! The security inspector clearly thought Trollope subversive! He called an associate and together they spent an hour searching for seditious passages and pornography before a silent man with a blue flag bearing the Congress symbol and a thin individual in a cap and long leather coat guided us through a crowd of East Germans. It was only after our return to Britain that I realized that the Russian security service must have known that I belonged to a scientific committee of the British Ministry of Defence (p.167). Even after the end of the Cold War, the KGB remained closely aware of foreigners (p.346).

Moscow airport was 36 kilometres outside the city, and we shared a taxi with Dr and Mrs Owen Davis from Chichester. The driver pointed out places of interest but we were dismayed as Dr Davis laughed when the driver explained that a red flag we were passing indicated President Andropov's residence. We wondered whether Davis would be arrested! At Intourist, passports and hotel vouchers were taken from us before we moved to the Hotel Rossia, a gigantic building accommodating 5000 visitors, divided by nationality into separate sections, each with their own entrance. On the ninth floor, Room 209 allowed us a view of the city, across a small church with an attractive array of gold and green domes. We chanced upon a small buffet on the floor below and discovered sweet but cheap black tea, brown bread, cheese and oranges, the only fruit.

Figure 19.5 *A view of the Moscow River.*

At the top of the staircase and lift that divided each floor sat forbidding ladies, watching us suspiciously. Our room had a little old bathroom in which the shower fitting was for decoration only. Two very small pieces of soap accompanied some hard toilet paper, while small towels completed the accessories! The malt whisky we had bought at Heathrow helped a reasonable night's sleep, the beds quite comfortable after we had pushed a large, square pillowcase into shape and fitted a thick acrylic blanket into a cotton envelope.

Next day, after a slight dispute about my signature, I managed to cash some traveller's cheques. We were delighted to find a souvenir shop where duty-free goods, including wooden carvings, filigree silver Russian dolls, lacquer vases and brightly painted china, were sold for foreign currency. It was at this moment that we enjoyed a first view of the many nearby cathedrals, the river and, not far away, rising into the sky, the red stonework of the Kremlin walls.

After several attempts ,we succeeded in contacting Peter and arranged to be at the Berioska shop early on Saturday 25th June. It was a cool day, but he and Karen invited us for a picnic lunch. They arrived in a black Volvo estate car and took us eight kilometres beyond the city to a country park near the Moscow River, with trees, stretches of rough grass and a sandy beach. Wooden sun 'beds' and square changing boxes were scattered about, but the most unusual feature was the blaring music coming from loudspeakers hanging from the trees. The music, continuing all day, took the form of songs and martial airs interspersed with snatches of what could have been Rossini. Peter encouraged us by saying: 'You'll get used to it!' One or two other British families appeared with their small children, but few Russians, although, on a fine Saturday, the park was said usually to be crowded. A cold tuna fish lunch followed, and then a visit to 'the facilities'. Karen reluctantly took some tissues from her handbag and we set out for a large hut hidden behind trees – there was no need to point the way since the toilets could be detected from a distance by the smell. Within the 'Ladies' there was a concrete slab with round holes cut into it. There were no partitions, no doors and, of course, no privacy. Some years later, images of the toilets at the concentration camps of Belsen and Auschwitz revealed the same design.

The Congress was to open the next day in the Soviet Centre next to the new, American-built Hotel Internationale, where the foreigners' supermarket was sited. At 4 pm, we returned to the city and bought some fruit. We were told that supplies for foreigners of meat, vegetables, soft drinks, wines, spirits and canned foods were erratic, so that much shopping was by mail order from Helsinki or Denmark. Peter and Karen helped us to select and register for post-Congress tours before we took a bus back to the Hotel Rossia, sampled the buffet and watched Moscow television, entranced by a Russian version of a Sherlock Holmes tale in which there were realistic views of the fog-bound River Thames and of English police-men.

On the following morning, we walked to the Congress Centre for a Chairman's meeting and met many familiar European faces. After a brief buffet lunch, we went by bus through the wet and chilly day to the Kremlin Congress Hall for the opening ceremony. Walking up the cobbled entranceway, we followed wide, sweeping stairways into the vast hall seating thousands of people, the front rows already occupied by employees of the Congress organizers. However, we found good seats, well placed to view the platform parties. The addresses began with three Russians making political propaganda about the nuclear arms race and how it was the duty of the medical profession to lead the way towards peace. After the speeches, uniformed women marched solemnly to the platform to present flowers, followed by a patient on crutches, vigorously applauded.

Returning to the vast auditorium after an interval, we found our seats 'stolen' by a group of Russian women who had sown pieces of paper to the cushions with needle and cotton. This, we learnt, was a Russian device for claiming priority. At the risk of causing an international crisis, and to the accompaniment of a loud wailing of abuse from a huge Russian woman, I pulled the papers off and seized our seats back just before an excellent performance of Stravinsky's *Rites of Spring*.

There followed a mad rush to the top of the building for an enormous buffet, a scene recalling the Imperial Russian meal described by C. S. Forester in *The Commodore*. Soon all the available chairs were occupied by the Russians, every table lined by jostling men and women, shoving and pushing shoulder to shoulder to reach the savory food, salads and breads. Bottles of wine and vodka arranged down the middle of the tables were soon emptied and replaced. Foreign guests had no choice but to join the scrum and elbow their way forward. Howard Bird joined us – by this time we had trapped a fresh orange and space for a plate. Small, hot cheese savouries were brought round on trays 'in the customary way'. Another mad scramble followed when ice cream appeared, and among the crowds we recognised George Nuki, Tiny Maini and Peter Darracott.

At the first scientific session, I could not avoid noticing the poor quality of the slides projected by Russian speakers. Meanwhile, Helen had gone to the eighth floor of the Hotel Internationale to 'size-up' the Ladies' Committee Room, where a warm welcome awaited her from three or four others. They were served tea and cakes by an attractive but large young interpreter, a teacher of English with a two-year-old child.

With time to spare, we were able to visit other parts of the city. Taxis stopped for us, but only when large banknotes were waved at them. Standing in Red Square, looking across at the imposing vista of the Kremlin, we watched a queue of people waiting to see Lenin's tomb. We started to cross the road, but Helen's way was barred by a gigantic, armed Russian soldier who blocked her progress. On the opposite side of the square was the drab frontage of GUM, the huge shopping centre frequented by Russian housewives seeking clothes and furnishings. Walking among the crowds, of whom many were 'well-endowed' women with red-dyed hair, Helen felt conspicuous because of her western clothes and slim figure. In Gorky Square, we paused at a bookshop and decided to experiment by buying some of Lenin's writings. The little book cost no more than 45 roubles and I was fascinated to be told that I could pay for it with a British banker's card. The Tretyakov Art Museum offered slides for sale and I bought a set. It was a summer day and the Lenin Hills were easily reached from the city centre, affording a fine view across much of Moscow. It was a popular place for weddings and we watched a party gathering (Figure 19.6).

Next day, a visit to Zagorsk showed us how an ancient monastery (Figure 19.7) could usefully combine religious duties with economic expediency. The monks could be seen going about their practices in one part of the establishment while the other half was in use as a site for commercial cine filming!

Figure 19.6 *A wedding party on the Lenin Hills.*

Leningrad and the Neva

Leaving Moscow on Sunday 3ʳᵈ July, we flew northwards to Leningrad (now St Petersburg). Among our group of orthopaedic surgeons and rheumatologists was W. A. (Willie) Souter of Edinburgh and his wife Cathie. A first sight of the Winter Palace (Figure 19.8), seen across the square, was breathtaking. Inside, within a single vast room, 80 of Rembrandt's paintings were displayed, guarded by an army of uniformed staff who exhibited a stern approach to anyone venturing near a work of art. Several miles from the city centre, the Summer Palace with its magnificent gardens reminded us of the breadth of Peter the Great's ambitions, while a glimpse of the cruiser *Aurora* (Figure 19.9) recalled the 1917 Revolution. We saw the vessel again in 2003.

Figure 19.7 *The monastery at Zagorsk.*

Figure 19.8 *The Winter Palace, Leningrad.*

Figure 19.9 *The cruiser Aurora at Leningrad.*

Kiev and the Dnieper

After a long flight to the south, we found the streets of Kiev to be lined with beautifully decorated stores filled with interesting goods, in sharp contrast to the drab shops of Moscow. But the long history of this ancient metropolis was characterized by contrasts between prosperity and disaster. A winding tunnel led down from the cathedral to the banks of the Dnieper River (Figure 19.10), and

Figure 19.10 *The river Dnieper at Kiev.*

we were reminded that the invading German armies of the Second World War desecrated the cathedral by stationing their horses in its precincts.

We were taken to a large hospital for an introduction to local medicine. It turned out to be not an orthopaedic or rheumatology clinic but a centre for cardiology. Patients, one or two unconscious, lay untended in beds without any sign that they were being resuscitated. Describing the equipment that I observed in a nearby room, I said later that it reminded me of the apparatus that might have been found in an animal house in the United Kingdom during the 1930s. I asked to be shown the main laboratory of the Clinic, but received no reply. Our hosts attached much more importance to the lunch that followed! Many delicious dishes were accompanied by a plethora of wines and spirits and by the inevitable speeches of welcome and salutation.

Next day, our guide suggested dinner at the Windmill Restaurant on the outskirts of the city. We were not the only guests – a large and noisy group of teenage girls was celebrating their examination results. As we sat down to dinner, almost all of them were on the nearby floor, gyrating through modern Russian dances with glee and laughter. As we ate, Kenneth Walton (p.180), one of our party, suggested that we should also be allowed to dance and that we should make our Western European presence felt by standing up and singing 'God Save the Queen'. Helen acted swiftly: kicking Kenneth gently under the table she said: 'We don't want an international crisis, however small! Let's sing *For Auld Land Syne*.' The idea worked like a charm. The school girls joined in enthusiastically – Robert Burns remains a hero in Russia – and soon all of us, British surgeons and physicians and Russian schoolgirls, were sharing the floor and exchanging jokes and dancing partners!

We returned to Moscow on Saturday 9th July and flew back to London the following day.

POLAND

Szczecin and the Oder

On 16th September 1984, Helen and I set out for Poland. The occasion was an invitation to visit Professor W. Parafiniuk of the Department of Pathomorphology at the Pomeranian Medical University in Szczecin and to talk to the Academy of Medicine of Szczecin. The visit was planned to coincide with a meeting of the European Congress of Rheumatology that was to take place in Warsaw. Helen carried a bottle of sherry that we had bought for our own use but found that we were not allowed to take it on the flight from Warsaw to Szczecin. Rather than throwing it away, she thrust it into the surprised hands of a passenger waiting to leave the country. Flying from Warsaw to Szczecin, we noticed that the tyres on the wheels of the old Russian aircraft were so worn that the inner tubes were often visible.

I misjudged my audience in the Academy of Medicine. They included many clinicians as well as pathologists and biologists, and it was clear that they were not happy with my descriptions of the many animal experiments that we had conducted in Manchester. However, the good nature of our hosts could not be faulted and they concealed any regrets at the topic of my lecture beneath a characteristic Eastern European courtesy. Later in the day, we dined with a large family and their friends in their early-twentieth-century stone-built terraced house. Sitting around the table, the subject of the Second World War and the German occupation could not be avoided. The host asked those who had lost relatives during this dreadful time to raise their hands. Every other person did so. The family was inordinately fond of dogs and had two enormous Alsatians. One had suffered paralysis after prophylactic inoculation against distemper. The animal was not 'put down' but was pulled everywhere on a sledge.

We visited a hospital, a modern structure built during the German occupation of the country. However, it was evident that infectious diseases such as tuberculosis were still common and that some laboratory tests necessary for modern medical practice were lacking. So scarce were medical resources that syringe needles had to be re-sharpened and used repeatedly. The country was still impoverished, and it was not uncommon for Western visitors to be importuned for items of clothing when travelling by bus or tramcar.

Warsaw and the Vistula

Moving to Warsaw, we were met by our friend Dr Theresa Wagner, Senior Lecturer and Consultant in the Department of Pathology of the Institute of Rheumatology, Warsaw. We also encountered Stefan Mackiewicz of the Department of Clinical Immunology, Poznań. The host for the forthcoming conference was Professor Eugeniusz Maldyk, the Director of the Institute, who made the arrangements for the accommodation of the many Eastern and Western European speakers who were attending. Theresa had no choice but to take us to the hotel that Maldyk had selected. As we approached the hotel, Theresa exclaimed in horror 'I have to apologize for this. I had no idea that this was where you were to stay'. The hotel was in an area closely resembling the most poverty-stricken parts of the East End of London. Entering the double doorway, we passed close to a foul-smelling lavatory. Upstairs, there was evidence of infestation of the bedrooms and there was no separate provision for male and female bathrooms. After breakfast, we decided to move to more civilized accommodation. This was not easy, since we had to recover our passports from a reluctant management without telling them why the documents were needed. But we were successful and escaped in a taxi to the Western-style Hilton, for which, of course, we had to pay!

My second visit to Poland was to take part in a meeting of the Pathology Committee of the European League Against Rheumatism (EULAR), which was held on 3rd May 1990. I stayed at a four-star hotel in the city centre, where I quickly learnt of the relative value of money in Eastern Europe. One day, I lost my comb and was able to buy a new one in the hotel shop for the equivalent of one far-thing, a quarter of an old penny!

The committee meetings over, we were shown parts of the coun-tryside. A small group of us left Warsaw in an East German Fiat car and drove out to Żelazowa Wola, Chopin's birthplace. On the way, I noticed farmers ploughing their fields with a horse drawing a single ploughshare. A large country house surrounded by gardens was to be the place for a recital of Chopin's piano music. I sat beside my Dutch friend Frits Eulderink as we listened to the limpid notes com-ing to us through the country air. But our joy at the pristine beauty of the scene was shaken when we looked down at the little river that ran at the bottom of the garden – the stream was black with oil and dirt, a horrid reminder of the appalling industrial conditions that still prevailed in many parts of this vigorous and hard-working country. Later, we listened enraptured to a recital of organ music in one of the few fine old churches that still stood in rural areas.

We wanted to repay the generous hospitality that we had enjoyed so much, and said to Theresa and her colleagues 'We would like to take you out to dinner this evening.' She replied: 'We do not eat in the evening.' In disbelief, we argued that this could not be so and repeated: 'Please come with us!' Reluctantly, Theresa, her husband and one or two others agreed to join the EULAR committee members. One of the first actions of the people of Warsaw, when the Second World War ended, was to rebuild the beautiful centre of their ancient city, and we were privileged to be taken to the famous Furry Dragon Restaurant, the Bazyliszek, in the mediaeval city square.

We enjoyed a splendid meal. Dr Refsum, my Norwegian associate, made the sensible suggestion that he pay the bill using his European credit card. It was only after the account was settled that we realized that 14 of us had enjoyed a dinner in the finest restaurant to be found in a European capital city for an amount equivalent to £36. Now we understood why the Poles had not wanted to put us to this (to them) enormous expense: £36 was the equivalent of a month's salary for a consultant of Dr Wagner's status.

Some years later, it proved possible to invite Dr Wagner to London. With her, we enjoyed a scientific gathering at the Barbican Centre. She then accompanied us to Edinburgh and we were able to introduce her to some parts of the Scottish Borders.

FRANCE

Paris and the Seine

On 10th December 1992, Helen and I joined a large group at the Hotel Montparnasse, Paris for the first Congress of the Osteoarthritis Research Society, the OARS. I gave a paper[12] and there was much lively discussion, which continued over a breakfast shared with Dr Alice Maroudas (p.299). Between scientific sessions at which Ken Brandt reviewed animal models of osteoarthritis, we enjoyed delicious French dishes at local restaurants and benefited from the Metro. For the first time, I realized that, unlike the underground trains of New York and London, the carriages ran on rubber tyres!

BELGIUM

Mons and the canals

I had come to know Dr Robert François in the course of my time on the Pathology Committee of EULAR. He was a consultant rheumatologist in the Belgian army and developed a longstanding and special interest in ankylosing spondylitis, an uncommon but severely disabling condition (p.128) that affected men much more often than women. After his time in the army, Robert had a private practice in Brussels. He was a member of the Belgian Society of Rheumatology and, with advancing seniority, had a clear ambition to become the president.

> Learning of my interest in the sacroiliac joints, parts commonly affected in ankylosing spondylitis, Robert suggested that we might collaborate. Beginning with my work in Adelaide in 1981 (p.280), I had accumulated a collection of pathological specimens of these joints. Robert proposed that we should seek to confirm or refute the concept, advanced by my late Manchester colleague John Ball, that the central lesion in this disease was inflammation of the ligaments that adjoin these joints. This was the condition he designated 'enthesitis'. Our studies,[13] made with the light microscope, took advantage of the many tissue sections that had been prepared for me by the skilled technicians in Edinburgh, in particular, by Robert Simpson.

Plans were afoot for the Belgian Congress of Rheumatology, to be held in Mons on 30th September 1998. As Chairman of the Congress, Robert asked me to present a paper with some of our results and also to act as Chairman of one of the sessions, an unusual responsibility for a foreign speaker. It was only later that I detected that there might have been an underlying motive for the latter suggestion: among scientists engrossed in every field of research, there are differences of opinion and interpretation that sometimes provoke hostility. Particularly in Belgium, where the French-speaking and the Flemish-speaking communities may hold very different views on a great range of topics, the expression of distinct opinions at public meetings may be embarrassing. Robert wished to avoid recrimination and excessive disagreement when he himself was in the chair and took the sensible course of selecting a 'neutral' chairperson.

The meeting was of great interest, the papers of high quality. Between the sessions, Helen and I had time to stroll up and down the sloping roads of this old town, redolent with tales of slaughter from the First World War. The Congress dinner that followed, with fine wine and many speeches, was unlike any we had ever experienced. Towards the end of the meal, live birds were released into the hall, flying across the heads of the startled diners!

After the meeting, we visited parts of Bruges, walking beside the canals and through the ancient, colourful streets. A small hotel in the centre of this beautiful old town allowed us to see libraries and art galleries. However, the outstanding event was the opportunity to visit some of the battlefields of the First World War. We joined a tour splendidly organized by a Belgian who used a small bus to carry 8–10 visitors. Among our fellow travellers were eager New Zealanders. Leaving Bruges, the bus travelled slowly through the countryside, stopping at small museums where relics of the

1915–17 campaigns were displayed. They included military uniforms, maps, water bottles, rifles, hand grenades and gas canisters. At Passchendaele, we were taken to the old trenches. Shell cases still lay around, timbers supported ancient trench walls, dugouts had survived and we could see the openings of tunnels. In Ypres itself, we viewed the rebuilt Town Hall, beyond the Menin Gate where the names of 50,000 dead are inscribed on the war memorial.

We returned to London from Brussels.

CHAPTER 20

Down under

The Gulf of St Vincent and the Murray River

Today I find from my observations of the sun ,…
that I am now camped in the centre of Australia.

John McDou'all Stuart[1]

Thoughts of the Southern Ocean had been in my mind when I considered moving to Brisbane or Melbourne in 1971. But 10 years later, these ideas became a reality when a startling letter came in February 1981 from Professor Vernon-Roberts.[A] Barrie Vernon-Roberts was Chairman of the Department of Pathology of the University of Adelaide, South Australia. He wrote to say that his University would welcome me as a Visiting Professor. He suggested that I might spend two months wholly in Adelaide, and a third visiting other Australian Medical Schools. His reason for proposing my name was our shared interest in the rheumatic disorders (p.121). It was little more than a year since Philip's death, and Barrie's letter came like a breath of fresh air. The Adelaide Medical School was associated in my mind with Florey's name,[B] and the idea of visiting his native city was exciting. Moreover, David was now free from his College: asked if he would like to come with us, the answer was an enthusiastic 'yes'!

Chapter summary
- Two new homes
- New friends
- The Royal wedding
- The Royal Adelaide Hospital
- Sightseeing
- A longer tour
- Further afield
- Victoria, New South Wales and Queensland

With the support of the University of Manchester and of the Health Authority, we set off on Sunday 19th July. A pause at Karachi gave a brief view of that crowded city. Singapore Airport was vast and cool, but outside the humidity was overwhelming. A taxi driver chose not to tell me that, by mistake, I had given him $20 instead of $2! The next day, we journeyed on to Sydney, where we met my cousin Jean Grieve's son, Jeremy, who was planning a vacation in Queensland. He invited David to join him on the 'golden beaches'.

From Melbourne, Helen and I flew on to Adelaide, where we were welcomed by my former associate, John McClure (p.240), now a Senior Lecturer in the University of South Australia. A first glimpse of Adelaide was revealing. The city of some 900,000 people was replete with shopping arcades and pedestrian precincts, the streets wide and clean (Figure 20.1)*. On the gateways to many buildings,

*The photographs I took during our first month in Adelaide were lost during the transport strike (p.274).

Figure 20.1 *University buildings in Adelaide.*

we saw brilliantly coloured birds, the delicate pink and grey galahs, as domesticated as the pigeons of London's Trafalgar Square. In the gardens and on the hills, early spring flowers of every form and colour were blossoming.

Two new homes

We were offered a charming little bungalow, a 'unit', in the Adelaide suburbs, for $60 a week. A bushy green cumquat tree in the front garden was laden with small, orange, tangerine-like fruit inviting Helen to make marmalade as she swotted her first Australian fly. All around were brightly coloured, feathery flowers, beside them a maroon buddleia. Invited to supper by Barrie's wife Jane, we met their son Evan, who was a medical student, their teenage daughters and Owen aged 4. Without central heating, our bungalow was cold, the bedclothes thin. Helen spread newspapers under the bottom sheet. We laughed at the idea that the pages were so warming because they were filled with Ian Botham's exploits as he dismissed the Australian batsmen during the current Test Match!

On 25th July, we heard that there was to be an immediate transport strike. As a precaution, we visited the well-stacked food shelves of Woolworths supermarket for supplies before returning to Barrie's house for lukewarm tea and coconut cake – the Vernon-Roberts were vegetarians. Jane's kindness – she arranged all our essential, early domestic supplies – did not conceal her highly critical views of the Australian way of life. We left to seek a Vienna sausage supper!

Our unit had been rented for one month. After four weeks, we therefore moved to St Mark's University College, near St Peter's Cathedral and north of the University, the Medical School a mile away. The Cathedral was the site of the archbishopric of South Australia – Adelaide was still staunchly Anglican – and one Sunday we heard the young Archbishop addressing his congregation on 'the role of women in the Church'. We met the College Master, Dr Edwards, a pleasant academic whose Scots wife had graduated at Dundee and St Andrews. Our new flat was sparsely furnished – there were few towels, no reading lamps and a one-bar fire although, happily, the tap water was hot. We joined College talks such as a review of Australian culture by Professor Dutton and enjoyed meeting students at their cafeteria-style dinners. But sometimes we escaped to Melbourne Street to find open sandwiches, salad and chocolate mousse cake at the Ginger Inn.

South Australia was a liberal society, the standards of conduct similar to those of Britain. But beneath this veneer lay a rich heritage brought largely from the United Kingdom but also from the countries of Central Europe, from where the revolutions of 1848 led many to emigrate to parts of Australia like the Barossa Valley. The standard of living seemed high, but as we travelled further we came across areas where poverty prevailed.

For newcomers, South Australian life appeared at first to have more in common with the United States than with Europe. Australian women worshipped the dollar and a pattern of clothes in which economy took precedence over style; men's dress was very informal except on professional occasions. We opened an ANZ bank account at a branch offering a drive-in facility. Helen took her cautious way to the shops, among them a Discount Buying Centre, a David Jones Store, and a health food shop where companies like Nivea and Palmolive had subsidiaries. At the elegant University Staff Club, I was given a membership card. Conveniently located, the Club proved invaluable as a meeting place and for meals that included huge, sizzling steaks and bananas fried in their skins, while the student cafeteria offered good meals for $10 a head.

On 18th August, it was time for the annual national budget and radio bulletins emphasized the problems in the Australian economy for pensioners, the unemployed and single parents while stressing the cost of medical cover and of education. With tongue in cheek, the radio bulletins encouraged listeners by claiming that the suicide rate among those aged 15–24 had doubled during the previous 10 years! The broadcasting scene was dominated by news of the continuing strikes. Air communication had ceased, although petrol rationing and steps to ensure essential food supplies and waste collections had been taken. Delays to the post meant that we could not know when our correspondence would reach Britain; even by 4th August, there was a backlog of three million uncollected letters. The South Australian radio, warning of union action, sounded a lighter note when, on 3rd August, they broadcast a 'family planning' week. There was a phone-in, interspersed with comments on the defeat of Australia in the second Test Match. On 8th August, after a long Parkinson ('Parky') programme on television, we watched Oscar Wilde's *Picture of Dorian Grey*. Two days later, we saw *Henry VIII*.

The South Australian Art Gallery offered a large collection of mediaeval and seventeenth- and eighteenth-century art works; it was complemented by the Modigliani Gallery in Fullerton Road, where an attractive wholesale collection of Persian rugs was being sold. The Festival Centre on the banks of the Torrens River was another fine building, while the City Library was supported by good booksellers and by a Government bookshop. We bought *Can You Draw a Kangaroo?* for the youngest Vernon-Roberts.

With the success of the Australian wine industry, the vineyards (wineries) were flourishing. Drive-in liquor stores were commonplace. For the first time, we encountered wine in two- and four-litre plastic boxes easily slipped into a refrigerator. Adelaide had many restaurants, and Dr Steve Malazzo invited us to meet a rheumatologist from Sydney together with the Michael Mason Research Fellow from London, Dr James. The variety of Australian foods never failed to amaze us, and, after an agricultural show, Helen and David came across a novel dish, a 'pie-floater' that resembled a Scotch pie in gravy and was bought from a street cart.

On 3rd August, tickets given to us by Dr Malazzo took us to a concert by groups including the Quartette Beethoven di Roma, at which we were enthralled by the Cesar Frank piano quintet. Adelaide had a number of modern cinemas, and on 5th August the Tourist Bureau showed *Kangaroo Island*, *Adelaide the Festival City*, *Murray Queen*, *The Yorke Peninsula* and *Bait*, a record of fishing off the New Zealand coast.

In the city, we found that, in the late afternoon, we were often the only people walking while streams of cars swung out of town at high speed. The bus service was a reliable way of reaching the city centre, the tickets costing 50 cents. For the same price, a touring ticket offered cheap journeys throughout Adelaide. The highways, not unexpectedly, were excellent, but secondary roads declined in quality in proportion to their distance from the city. Young people were allowed to drive at the age of 16 and the sale of high-powered cars was increasing. The accident rate was high, so we were saddened but not surprised to learn that Evan Vernon-Roberts had been severely injured during the previous year. We benefited from the air travel that had transformed communication between the large cities, as David found when he returned from the Gold Coast on 13th August.

Figure 20.2 *Cricket in Adelaide.*

Helen sometimes went into the city by herself or with David. From Glenelg Road, at nearby Parkside, a touring ticket took her to the seaside through the largely new area of Richmond Village, Torrensville, along Anzac Highway and past some much poorer areas and industrial sites. At the bathing beach were Catherine wheels and roundabouts, while nearby she saw extensive shopping areas and holiday flats, not always in good condition. Using the same ticket, Helen took the old brown tram back to Victoria Square, passing cars and taxis waiting at the crossing gates. On another evening, a visit to Ferguson Avenue showed us an attractive park and dell with bridges, paths and a barbecue area.

We had few opportunities for talking to the indigenous people but one day, near the railway station as rush-hour crowds gathered, we encountered two young dark-skinned girls drinking noisily from a beer bottle while two older men sat nearby. Later, on an outing down the Yorke Peninsula, we passed through an Aboriginal settlement. The cheerful waving people, children and dogs, basking in the hot sun, had gathered on the stony roads outside their simple houses and were astonished to see a University car (p.281). But we felt uneasy until we had left the settlement behind!

Cricket was very popular (Figure 20.2), competing with football on spring days. One afternoon we watched an Australian 'footy' match on the University Oval, a huge area[C] where a field umpire, two goal umpires and two boundary umpires, one a buxom, scantily clad female, controlled a mud-spattered game played over such great distances that three intervals were required between the four 'quarters', each of 25 minutes.

New friends

Visitors were welcomed openly and we were given great help by our hosts. At lunch with J. Lomax Smith one day, we met a friend of Dr Ey. Within five minutes, the Eys had invited us to lunch: Mrs Ey told us that she planned to cook a typical English dinner and wanted a good recipe for Yorkshire pudding! The Eys had a deceptively large, rambling old house with central heating, a heated swimming pool, a large wine cellar and a guest suite! On another occasion, when David had gone to the Royal Show with his gardening friend Geoffrey, Dr Malazzo entertained us to a 'small family supper', which turned out to be a full dinner party in the presence of the Lord Mayor-Elect and his wife, Dr and Mrs John Watson.[D]

On 2nd August, we drove a short distance to the Uniting Glenunga Church. We received an enthusiastic welcome and, to our embarrassment, were asked by the Minister to stand in order to receive a 'big hand'. Gracious! What a surprise. Before the service, two lady members of the choir sang catchy spirituals. The harmonium player kept things moving at a spanking pace reminding Helen of Taynuilt village church in the Scottish Highlands, where she played the harmonium while at school (p.73). By contrast with our only church visit was a brisk, rainy walk to the 'Bottle Drive In' to buy a four-litre box of chilled Alando rosé. On the next fine Sunday morning, a late start precluded any church parade, but for 30 cents we purchased a copy of the 140-page *Sunday Mail*. We wondered what Philip would have made of it all!

It was some days before we were able to visit Elma and Morris Walker.[E] He was the brother of Dr Hilson's wife, Lena, our neighbour in Manchester (p.236). An Edinburgh medical graduate, he was delighted to be able to talk of times past.

The Royal wedding

Shortly after our arrival in Australia, the wedding of Princess Diana and Prince Charles was due to take place in London. The great day dawned, 29th July 1981! Knowing of the strength of republican feeling in Australia, we expected that few local people would be interested. We were quite wrong. The newspapers gave full details of television programmes that would show the ceremony and the streets were deserted. We walked to the University Staff Club, and prepared for the wedding broadcast by enjoying curried rice soup, a huge steak with bananas fried in their skins and black coffee. Afterwards, we found only a few noisy members in the bar lounge not interested in the clear satellite images coming from London. As visitors, we felt able to ask the waitress whether the television sound might be turned up, and the broadcast was much improved when a lady came in who had worked at St Bartholomew's Hospital, London. She told us that she had met the Queen Mother at a garden party. By 9.30 pm, she and we were the only occupants of the lounge, the bar had closed and Diana and Charles were man and wife!

The Royal Adelaide Hospital

On 27th July, John McClure took us on a tour of the Royal Adelaide Hospital and the University Pathology Department, introducing us to Ted Richards, a quiet South African. We met many staff. Helen observed that several men shook my hand but not hers! Warned of this custom, she kept her hands hidden! Coffee from a vending machine was offered at 10 cents a cup, but cost more during working hours! There were differences from the laboratory practices to which I was accustomed in Britain because of the large volume of private work in Australia, although, unlike Brazil (p.219), good care was provided for all members of the public who needed it.

The diagnostic services in haematology, clinical chemistry, histopathology and electron microscopy, cytology, and microbiology were undertaken in the State Institute of Medical and Veterinary Science, the IMVS, which employed 800 people in a large building between the Medical School and the hospital. Barrie Vernon-Roberts occupied the Chair of Pathology in the University and held the title of Senior Director of the IVMS. He was Head of the Histopathology Department, responsible for 20,000 biopsies annually. Under his direction were 20 histopathologists, the title of specialist given to those with the qualification MRCPA (Member of the Royal College of Pathologists of Australasia). Their salaries ranged from $24,000–26,900 for Registrars to $44,000 for a Senior Director. I was reminded that the State of South Australia had its own Government and that medical employees in the IMVS were appointed by the State.

I set up my room with the aid of Sonia, Barrie's efficient and mature, Glasgow-spoken secretary. There began a large and varied series of laboratory and clinical meetings and visits. I attended hospital 'grand rounds' and many slide seminars. At an endocrine bone meeting, I was introduced to C. D. Thomas, P. Harding and M. Hooper, members of the Hospital staff. For one week, between 15th and 25th September, I was asked to chair daily early-morning discussions in each of which a member of Barrie's staff talked on a research topic. One example was the seminar given by Dr J. D. Lomax-Smith on renal and liver disease, another a contribution by Dr A. Nicholson on the morphology of terminal lung airways.

After each presentation, it was my task to comment on what had been said.

I learnt of the efficient reporting system used by the Royal Adelaide Hospital and of the sophisticated computers employed for the retrieval of clinical data. The mortuary suite of the Royal Adelaide Hospital compared favourably with the arrangements to which we were accustomed in South Manchester. The rooms opened almost directly from the main hospital corridor and the histological preparations were made by technicians working immediately next to the mortuary. Discussions on electron microscopy (Drs Mukerjee and Tarpen), the image analyser (Nick Fazzalari) and microbiology (Professor Barry Marmion[F]) were interspersed with library visits, mortuary demonstrations and slide seminars.

Much of the departmental research centred on spinal disorders, and Barrie's programmes were managed by his Deputy, Ted Cleary. Barrie, an authority on spinal disease, had developed a particular interest in the sacroiliac joints, a prime target for the crippling condition of ankylosing spondylitis. Nick Fazzalari, an expert in morphometry, was extending his measurements to case material obtained from the autopsy service, and I was drawn towards this work and began to collect specimens that led to research in Manchester (p.242), Lancaster (p.243) and Edinburgh (p.314). But there were other activities of great interest, and I met Dr Lomax Smith at the Queen Elizabeth Hospital to review his cases of renal disease, Dr Myers, Dr. James, and a former Edinburgh colleague, Professor Sherman.[2]

Our visit to Adelaide coincided with the annual meeting of the Australian Society for Experimental Pathology (the ASEP) and with that of the Royal College of Pathologists of Australasia (the RCPA). Both conferences were attended by a number of friends and colleagues, among them Feroze Ghadially (Saskatoon) (p.154), Neil Broom (Auckland) and Dennis Wright (Southampton). I was invited to be a 'keynote speaker' at each meeting.

On 24th August, I went off early to prepare for my talk to the ASEP. It was a day when I also enjoyed the privilege of meeting the University Vice Chancellor, an opportunity of thanking the University for their generosity in inviting us to Adelaide. At the ASEP meeting, which both Helen and David attended, Barrie gave a marvellous introductory eulogy, to which I did my best to respond[3] – Helen thought successfully

Two days later, on 26th August, it was the meeting of the RCPA. The lounge of the Grosvenor Hotel had been turned into a conference hall. I spoke on the pathology of rheumatoid arthritis.[4] Coffee and discussion were followed by a dinner–dance. The band played enthusiastically during noisy, uninhibited dancing of a kind we came to associate with Australia. Helen sat uncomfortably beside a brash forensic pathologist from Sydney. David, smartly dressed for the occasion, enjoyed a chat with Professor Richy Nairn[G] before leaving to watch the Test Match. Helen stayed to listen to Richy, who, with his wife, had been making helpful suggestions about our planned visit to Melbourne, but I retired home, exhausted.

A smaller meeting was that of the South Australian Rheumatology Association. We were driven to Flinders Medical School, 10 miles south of the city, by a young rheumatologist who overcame his 'anti-pom' attitude when he realized that we spoke similar languages! At Flinders, no more than a dozen people gathered in their splendid new lecture theatre. Sustained by boxes of red and white wine, cheese and 'crackers', we listened to two self-assured occupational therapists who gave us splints to handle while we immersed our hands in the viscous silicone oil that enabled cases of arthritis to exercise after surgery. Dr Vaughan Morgan, a plastic surgeon, drove us home. He spoke warmly of Glasgow, where he had worked for some years. He showed us the Hilton Hospital, which had fine facilities but only 57 students, competing academically with the Medical School of the University of Adelaide. Dr Morgan told us that he had been flying that afternoon – he and nine others owned a small plane, which took them skiing to the mountains around the Murray River.

During our absence, my loyal Manchester secretary, Irene Barlow, kept in close touch, providing news of local and national, political and administrative events. The time was approaching for the delayed celebrations of the Centenary of the University of Manchester Department of Pathology, and a letter reached me from Professor W. L. (Bill) Ford[H] telling me of plans for the occasion. On 17th July, only two days before our departure from Manchester, the Medical Research Council had written to say that their committees could not offer support for my proposed research on the 'Low-temperature scanning electron microscopy of human, dog and mouse osteoarthrosis'. Irene had the task of consoling my colleagues at home, but happily the Arthritis and Rheumatism Council, the ARC (p.169), was more generous and on 16th July wrote that they were pleased to offer £35,378 for our work. At precisely the same moment, the University of Manchester decided that they could not contribute to my antipodean travel costs!

Sightseeing

Recognizing that our time for sightseeing was limited, Barrie had arranged for us to have a University car at the weekends, a white General Motors Commodore with a coat of arms on its door. We began with a visit to Cleland Zoo Park, where David fed kangaroos and watched wallabies (Figure 20.3) while Helen cradled a koala bear. We saw the curious wombat, emus, cockatoos and many other colourful birds before driving up the 2000 feet of Mount Lofty to gain a panoramic view of Adelaide and the southern coast. Later, we joined Barrie to visit an old jam factory in Paynehan Road that had been turned into a museum of arts and crafts where pots were being made and glass blown. We returned to his house for tea and enjoyed Jane's griddle scones! All his family were there except his 14-year old daughter, still in Kyoto with her school choir.

Figure 20.3 *David feeding wallabies in the wildlife park.*

On Sunday 26th July, John McClure, with his little daughters, took us to his open-plan house in the Adelaide Hills for a chicken, rice and bramble pickle lunch. Afterwards, we drove past cherry and apple orchards to the folk museum and shops of the German village of Hahndorf. The blackened stumps of burnt gum trees, miraculously covered with green leaves, recalled the great fire of 18 months previously. A few days later, we joined John's Parents and Teachers Association dinner of home-made soup, Vienna schnitzel and *Apfelstrudel* in the village of Bridgewater. The meal was accompanied by Fritz, in lederhosen, playing his piano accordion and by a waitress, in Bavarian costume, rendering catchy tunes on cow bells.

The following weekend, we drove to Willunga through horse-raising, cattle-grazing, sheep-rearing country, passing forest reservations where evergreens contrasted with gum trees. The village was preparing for an Almond Blossom Festival. At Aldinga, we walked on the magnificent, deserted beach, gazed at the huge, breaking waves and realized we were looking towards the South Pole. I knew that, except for Kangaroo Island, there was no land mass between Adelaide and the Antarctic!

Our next visit was to the Torrens Gorge. The river was in spate and a narrow road cut through the winding and twisting valley. At Birdwood, we lunched in a hailstorm before visiting the National Museum with its collection of vintage cars and domestic appliances from bygone times. The displays included an ancient kitchen sink, sewing machines, fire irons, bellows, a washing board and a wringer. Returning via Inglewood, the Anstey Hill offered spectacular views of old Adelaide.

A longer tour

On the following Saturday we headed for the Barossa Valley along Portrush Road and Spencer Terrace, joining the main North Road to Elizabeth, a modern, dormitory town. We paused beside the Philip highway before going on to Gawlor, an old village, and a first sight of the famous wine-growing valleys, turning off to the Barossa Reservoir and the Whispering Wall for a picnic lunch. Tourist Route 4 took us to Das Alte Weinhaus, where we tasted their white Abendlese Rhein Riesling and bought three bottles at $3.30 each from the wife of the owner. It was a most attractive place, with a wattle-covered car park and sandy soil and fine views over nearby hills and valleys. Continuing sunshine encouraged us to follow signs pointing to the huge Sepelfeld Wine Yard, where the palm trees were identical with those of North Africa but the fruits did not ripen because of the climate. A conducted tour began with a short walk up a hill, from which a marvellous view of the whole yard and valley unfolded. Caroline, our guide, explained the pulping machines, pipes, distillers and the huge wooden maturing barrels where Solero sherry was produced. The tour finished in the tasting cellar, where Helen tried a dry sherry bought from the 'bottle shop' for $1.55. Continuing on the scenic route, we returned via the Greenhill and Portrush Roads.

Some days later, we took David to the Mount Lofty look-out to view Adelaide city, Port Adelaide, the coast and the South Sea. We returned to the Cleland National Park, where koala bears, holding each other in a row, were being given eucalyptus leaves. 'Milly', the curious wombat, was 'out': the keeper said that she was a nocturnal creature, wakened only for afternoon visitors! Among the wildlife were enormous birds, brolgas, quite unknown in Europe. They gathered in colonies and their size was so great that circles of clustered birds could be seen easily from a passing aircraft. Finally, we saw pelicans, spoonbills, ducks, parrots and cockatoos, before ending our visit in the snake house.[1]

On a sunny 29th August, we drove to Murray Bridge and a deserted peninsula with a dirt track road and much bird life, including pelicans, black swans, curlews, cormorants and a grey and pink cockatoo on a telegraph wire. With little signs of habitation, we travelled 44 kilometres through farmland, past cattle, sheep and some crops to Meningie, the scene reminiscent of a small western American town, with roads merging with dust tracks. We expected a Sheriff to appear at any moment from one of the colonial-type buildings! We set off again on 5th September to the McLaren Vale, fine rolling country with flatter, less commercialized vineyards than Barossa. We branched off at Happy Valley to find Wirra Wirra, a small vineyard where we bought three bottles of red Church Block for $9 before returning through Coramandel Valley, a winding road over the hills to Belair, from where we could see the Yorke Peninsula.

Further afield

For the last of our excursions in South Australia, I collected a Rent-a Car, a splendid three-litre automatic, air-conditioned vehicle on Thursday 9th September. We left the city via the main North Road via Gawler, Clare Valley and its picturesque villages and vineyards. At Willmington, Melrose, an attractive small village, boasted the oldest hotel in the Flinders. We arrived in intense heat at the out-post town of Quorn, travelling along wide roads that merged into sandy sidewalks, past small houses with verandas and wooden posts. The Australian Travel motel provided radio, television, a shower, a fridge and tea-making facilities. After a look around in the last of the daylight, Helen ate an excellent bar meal of schnitzel and chips while David and I contented ourselves with steaks. Once David had recovered from the shock of sharing our 'unit', we all slept very well, looking forward to venturing out into the Flinders proper.

Breakfasting on Saturday 11th September from the iced currant loaf that Helen had brought from the deli, we set off along the Hawker Road between scrubland and ranges of hills, past sites of historical interest. In many places, only a few stones remained of the walls of old homesteads. After a few successful years, early settlers had often been ruined by drought, ignoring warnings that they had migrated too far north. Everything looked green, but we were told that within weeks, as spring ended, all would be parched and yellow.

We entered the Flinders Range through the small town of Hawker. A sealed road took us to Wilpena Pound with its incongruous modern motel, shop and camping site. The miles of gravel tracks and watery creeks gave us some idea of the vastness of these ranges, unlike any mountains we had seen before. It was intensely hot, but, compass in hand, we walked through the wilderness, over small hills, through inclined valleys, scrambling up slopes of scrub to the centre of the Pound.

Returning to the car, we turned off at Arapoona before picnicking in Aroona Valley, an opportunity to look at the flowers and to watch for animal life. We went on through Brachina Gorge, where it proved to be slow-going along sandy tracks and a river bed. Several times we thought we had lost the road, but each time we safely negotiated yet another creek and Helen heaved a sigh of relief, accepting that the journey had been worth the risk because of the spectacular views. We came out onto the highway before turning back to Hawker.

Victoria, New South Wales and Queensland

On Wednesday 23rd September, we paid a sad farewell to our friends in Adelaide and took a flight to Melbourne (Figure 20.4). Here we again met Professor Richy Nairn. He encouraged me to talk to his department about our recent research. On the following day, he

Figure 20.4 *A street scene in Melbourne.*

entertained us to lunch at his club and arranged for us to visit the world famous Melbourne Zoo, where, for the first time, we saw living duck-billed platypuses[J] (Figure 20.5).

Five nights in Melbourne led on to Canberra (Figure 20.6) on 28th September, where the panorama of the University buildings made a remarkable contrast with the surrounding hills. Then, on 30th September, we hired a car to travel on to Brisbane to see our old friends, Cynthia and Chris Cummins.[K] They had settled on the Queensland Gold Coast in the seaside resort of Noosa Heads. After leaving England, Chris became a flying surgeon to Queensland and senior consult-

Figure 20.5 *A duck-billed platypus.*

ant surgeon in Toowoomba, with a base hospital at Townsville[6]. We found their house, the lawn running down to the edge of the sea where clusters of pelicans were feeding (Figure 20.7). A short distance away was an extraordinary but artistic building constructed solely from glass bottles that were laid in their hundreds, one upon

Figure 20.6 *Towards the University of Canberra.*

the other, to give multicoloured walls that glittered in the ocean sunshine.

With a few more days before we had to return to the United Kingdom, we decided to look at the Queensland coast, and flew from Brisbane to Cairns, nearly 1000 miles to the north and only 500 miles from the northernmost tip of eastern Australia. Hiring a tiny, open, jeep-like vehicle (Figure 20.8), we drove up the wind-swept coast (Figures 20.9 and 20.10). Stopping to look at the ocean waves, Helen considered a swim, only to be told by a local shopkeeper: 'People do swim here, but not on a day like this!' While she listened to this wise advice, I watched a tick crawling over the sand towards my bare foot. Each time I moved, the tick altered direction, attracted, I supposed by the warmth of my toes. I had no wish to be bitten and left the arthropod to its own devices.

Cairns had a large harbour packed with the yachts of wealthy pleasure-seekers and tourists, but also with commercial craft. It was from a ferry that we had our first full view of the Queensland coast, with its broad sands, mango swamps and great areas of

Figure 20.7 *At the water's edge in the Cummins' garden.*

trees extending towards the water's edge. A tiny dinghy with a transparent bottom allowed us to peer down into the inshore waters. Joining 10 others on a small aircraft, we flew up the coast, over the Barrier Reef and as far north as Lizard Island. On the return journey, we passed over a gigantic fish, its shadowy outline outlined against the sparkling tides. Driving back down the lonely coast on our way

Figure 20.8 *David and Helen on the road to Cairns.*

Figure 20.9 *A glimpse of the Queensland coast.*

Figure 20.10 *A view of the Queensland hills.*

Figure 20.11 *A part of old Sydney.*

SURGEONS COURT

This Court, on the site of Sydney's first hospital erected in 1788, is named in recognition of the surgeons who worked to maintain the health of the infant colony of New South Wales.

The Principal Surgeon, John White, with his assistants, William Balmain, Thomas Andel and Dennis Considen and their Junior, John Irving, battled to save the lives of the sick. Although medicines, drugs, surgeons' instruments and necessaries were brought out for the hospital by the First Fleet, there were no blankets or sheets. Furthermore, some of the drugs perished during the prolonged voyage and others were of inferior quality. However, Assistant Surgeon Dennis Considen discovered the native sarsaparilla to be a powerful antiscorbutic and an infusion of wild myrtle was used as an astringent in dysentery. The colony also suffered greatly from the lack of vegetables and a scurvy epidemic broke out in 1788 before the first crops could be harvested from the gardens at both sides of Sydney Cove and from the farm near Government House.

The surgeons battled sickness and disease throughout the early years of the hospital and achieved such successes as the smallpox vaccinations of 1804. In 1816, the hospital was demolished and the surgeons moved to the new Sydney Hospital in Macquarie Street.

In 1820, four houses were developed on this land and it is thought that demolished materials from the hospital were used in their construction.

William Davis was granted this land in 1836 by His Excellency, The Governor, Major-General Richard Bourke.

Between 1868 and 1869 Joseph Davis constructed two two-storey brick walled and shingle roofed shops in front of the original houses of William Davis.

Surgeons Court was opened up by the Sydney Cove Redevelopment Authority in 1979 to provide a forecourt to The State Archives entrance and to give access to Nurses Walk.

Figure 20.12 *Wall plaque at Surgeons Court, Sydney.*

to the airport, we saw vast fields of burning vegetation, the fields wreathed in smoke. It was the end of the sugar cane season.

On 7th October, we flew to Sydney, our last port of call, where three days allowed us to see the harbour, the opera house, the 'golden beach' and the eighteenth-century houses that marked the site of the old settlements in the city centre (Figures 20.11 and 20.12). The buildings resembled those of Henderson Row, close to the Edinburgh Academy, and were a fitting memorial to bygone days. An opportunity to visit the Ned Kelly Museum could not be missed. By an extraordinary coincidence, we met our former Edinburgh neighbours, Professor George and Mrs Jean Henry, who were visiting their son Christopher and were staying at the University Hotel, where we had rooms.

We left Australia on Saturday 10th October 1981. My last memory of this wonderful country is of the vast red deserts over which our plane flew for hours on end. By breakfast time the following day, we were in London.

CHAPTER 21

Iraq and Israel

From the Tigris to the Sea of Galilee

While he spoke we scoured along the dazzling plain,
now nearly bare of trees, and turning slowly softer
under foot. At first it had been grey shingle, packed
like gravel. Then the sand increased and the stones
grew rarer, till we could distinguish the colours of
the separate flakes, porphyry, green schist, basalt.

TE Lawrence[1]

*O*h, *to be in England now that April's there*! was in my mind
as I reached my office one spring morning in 1983. But
then I found a note on my desk that read: 'Can you go
to Baghdad on 2nd May and lecture for one hour?' I thought of
April Fool's Day

The slip of paper bore the name of Ian Birch, who had left my
Manchester laboratory some months previously to join Ciba-Geigy,
the gigantic Swiss pharmaceutical company[A] (p.244). I assumed the
note was a joke. It was not. He explained that Ciba Geigy, Horsham,
England, had received a telephone call from the parent company
in Basel, Switzerland. The call was for the Director, asking whether
three or four investigators could be found, at short notice, to join a
programme designed to enhance the export of Swiss drugs to Iraq.
The plan was to invite a number of workers taking part in research
on compounds manufactured by Ciba and other Swiss companies to
speak at a conference. One section of the meeting was to discuss the
rheumatic diseases, my special interest, and their treatment.

Chapter summary
- IRAQ
- The Conference
- A tour of Baghdad
- Beside the river
- Babylon
- ISRAEL
- Jerusalem
- Nof Ginossar

IRAQ

In the absence of the Ciba-Geigy Director, Ian sought his deputy,
but he also was not available. Ian therefore assumed the responsibility for finding another British speaker. Knowing of the work with
which he had been assisting in Manchester and the close association we had with colleagues at the Ciba laboratories at Wilmslow,
he forwarded my name to the conference organizer, Dr Thomas
Preiswerk. After a brief discussion with the University authorities,

I accepted the invitation and within a few days Helen and I found ourselves sitting in First Class accommodation, bound for Saddam Hussein's land. Flying by night, we knew, as did the authorities in Switzerland, that Iraq was at war with Iran, and I did not carry a camera. Although Iraq had air superiority, when we arrived at the five-star Baghdad Sheraton Hotel, we were reminded of the state of hostilities by a notice declaring 'In the event of an air raid, do not use the lift.'

In Manchester, one of my consultant colleagues, Nagib Haboubi, came from Iraq. His father had been a merchant whose trade included the purchase and further sale of Persian (Iranian) carpets and he and his wife had settled in Britain. When Nagib heard that we were to travel to his home country, he took discrete steps to inform his brother-in-law, Saad, of our proposed visit. The communication, bearing no address, was by confidential letter, since Saddam Hussein's secret service was active and agents constantly sought informers.

My first meeting with Saad, a charming and literate person who spoke excellent English, was in the entrance lounge of the Sheraton. I had arranged to have coffee with him on our first morning, before the conference began. In Arabic tradition, it was to be a conversation for 'men only'; in any event, the waiters, he said, were likely to be agents of the Intelligence Service and we should have to speak cautiously.

After a formal but warm greeting, Saad's first, astonishing, question was: 'How much wealth do you have?' I explained that in Britain, most consultant pathologists enjoyed a rather uniform salary dictated by the National Health Service, while those in University employment were paid similarly. I enquired: 'Why do you ask?' He replied: 'In Baghdad, if you are a pathologist, you are millionaire. Since you are a professor, I simply wondered how many millions you had.' His second question was equally revealing. He asked: 'How much land do you own?' I responded 'About 600 square metres in South Manchester.' I tried to hide my surprise when he added: 'You must come and have lunch tomorrow at one of my hotels. I have just purchased another 50 square miles of land in the south of the country.'

The conference began on Tuesday 3rd May. It should have been held in the hotel, but the threat of air attack had made it necessary to arrange for the gathering to be in a Health Centre, a modest building some distance from the city centre. The mornings were to be devoted to scientific presentations, the afternoons to sightseeing tours and visits. In the Manager's office, we were introduced to various Iraqi and Swiss doctors and to the Swiss Ambassador, who shook everybody's hands in a perfunctory manner. We seemed to be waiting for an official, but eventually took our seats in the brightly lit, air-conditioned hall. There were some 150 people present, with the front rows of seats largely occupied by the military, some quite senior, including a General. Although the course was intended for civilian practitioners, the majority of Iraqis present were in uniform. After two or three introductory speeches in Arabic, good presentations in English were given by representatives from Roche, Switzerland. Their lantern slides had been adversely affected by sunlight, but their talks were well received. Intervals followed for cans of grape juice and for the use of primitive and malodorous toilets.

The Conference

With regard to my contribution, I had been asked to accept the preferences of the local rheumatologists whom we had met earlier. In particular, it was felt that local practitioners would like to know of recent advances in the understanding of the causes of the common conditions of rheumatoid arthritis and osteoarthritis. Satisfied that my notes were in order, I had put on my dark, tropical suit and met Dr Terence Ryan, an Oxford dermatologist, and Dr Howard Bird, two of the other British speakers.

> There was inevitable delay in starting the meeting, but the talks kept to time. Ryan gave a clear lecture of special interest on aspects of vascular disease in aged skin. My contribution[2] went well, with a full, attentive audience, followed by good questions from the army representatives and the rheumatologists. Thomas Preiswerk operated the projector; he was clearly delighted, as was Dr Schmaid, Head of Ciba Geigy, Basel.

An interval for the toilets and for lunch was appreciated. The room had been very hot even with the windows opened and the fans in operation. I encountered a charming gynaecologist, Ms Ryan, present because of her osteoarthritic knees. She was bitterly disappointed that we had no time to visit and dine at her home, and had to content herself with an exchange of names and addresses.

> Dr Bird then gave an excellent account of drugs in the treatment of osteoarthritis. He was followed by a breathless Dr Williams, who had nearly missed his appointed time, having slept in. He failed to catch the conference bus and could find neither a taxi nor anyone to direct him to the Conference Centre. He had a bundle of slides about which he talked, but as he spoke we realized the difference between an illustrated chat and a formal lecture. His final joke was received in silence.

After a second break, we were invited back to the Manager's office for discussions with rheumatologists and an orthopaedic surgeon, who reminded us that many Iraqi doctors travelled to Britain for their postgraduate studies. I remembered how, after the Armistice of 1918, Britain had accepted responsibility for Mesopotamia, while France controlled Syria. It was therefore not surprising to be reminded that, for many years, Iraqi Universities had based their style of medical education on British systems, just as the Iraqi military followed British patterns of uniform and training. During our discussions, interesting local differences in the epidemiology of some rheumatic diseases emerged. Uric acid levels appeared higher than in the United Kingdom and were associated with a higher frequency of gout, a change possibly related to contrasting patterns of eating and drinking and with the rapid rise in the wealth of the country.

A Conference dinner was followed by an astonishing floor show, provided by a group of Filipino dancing girls, who seemed to be quite out of character with the religious ethics of this Muslim country. So enlivening was their music, so convincing their gyrations, that a new friend, Herr Roth, decided to join them on the dance floor. Helen told him that he was a 'naughty boy', an expression which seemed to amuse him highly and which he applied to himself several times over the coming days. As he danced, he called out 'I am a naughty boy!'

A tour of Baghdad

Following the morning session, there was some disagreement concerning a taxi to return us to the hotel. The matter was resolved by a Swiss economist, who commandeered a car that turned out not to be a taxi but a private vehicle driven by an office worker, who refused any payment. There was only time for a club sandwich, a vast, toasted affair of beef, chicken and salad. Dr Preizwerk joined us even later and had time to eat only half of Helen's meal. It was then a rush to catch a sightseeing coach – to avoid parking restrictions, the bus had already encircled the hotel three times.

Our guide was a young lady whose English was difficult to follow, but there was so much of interest to see that this was not important. The mixture of nationalities was no barrier to free, good-natured and friendly chat. We jumped out at the first mosque. Spiral steps allowed fine elevated views over the city. The shops and markets closed from 2 to 4 pm each day, but the streets were still swarming with a great variety of people, including schoolchildren dressed mainly in navy blue and white uniforms. Although it was acknowledged to be difficult to monitor families in rural areas, all children were expected to attend school from the age of 6 years and school education continued until as late as 20 years. The addition of a college education was an advantage to some, since it could delay conscription to the armed forces.

From the bus, we saw pavements crowded by a young dark-haired, dark-skinned population. Although I noticed that Saad and Jacob, Nagib's little nephew, had blue eyes, this was exceptional and I observed that the eyes of the majority of the people were very dark. There was a confusion of Arab dresses, Turkish costumes and Western-style T-shirts, but women wore black burkas, sometimes with their gowns covering Western-style clothes, while mothers carried babies or held young children by the hand. Views down the side streets recalled those of the Bible, or so we thought in the romantic mood inspired by this, our first visit to the Middle East. We were not surprised to see that few people moved about briskly, most adjusting their pace to the heat of the midday sun.

At the Baghdad Museum, the 'Madame Tussaud's' of Iraq, we observed life-size sculptures depicting old professions and customs – a water carrier, weavers, a bride-giving ceremony and circumcision. Some of those travelling with us, local visitors, could well have been behind the railings as exhibits! So long was spent wandering from room to room and down into the cool, stone cellars that, before the next scheduled pause, we found the road closed. We took to the narrow streets, strolling through the crowds to look at a fascinating range of wares that ranged from jewellery and clothes to shoes and bags. We saw the famous copper market, where, to the accompaniment of deafening noise, old men were teaching young boys to hammer out designs with the point of a nail. A tea carrier moved from one souq to another, dispensing small, narrow glasses from a curious metal pot. It was an essential service, we thought, on account of the heat, the tea given without payment. One of our Swiss companions came scurrying along the pavement with a bag of fresh fruit, which he said he couldn't resist.

The next stop was at the principal mosque, a focal point both for the local people and for tourists. The forecourt was filled with black-clad, squatting women purveying souvenirs and little, grubby children selling cards and ice lollies made of juice frozen in plastic bags. The women were offering evil-smelling water taken from pails and proffered in tins that looked like small, battered frying pans. It was obvious that the local people assumed that we were Christians – we were dressed in Western clothes. The laws were strict and we were allowed to look only at the mosque entrance. However, we were close enough to see the beautiful gold facings and mosaics that decorated the building. Prominent notices in English and Arabic forbade photography beyond a certain point. This did not deter Herr Roth, already known to the conference as a jolly Swiss extrovert, from asking a fez-wearing guard if he might take pictures. One officer replied 'Yes' but then noticed our little guide, clad in a short, very conspicuous purple dress. The guard shouted and several of his armed companions came rushing to his side. It was only with the aid of our Jordanian representative that an ugly situation was resolved. Meanwhile, during the angry arguments, the very foolish Herr Roth continued taking photographs.

Advised to leave all our personal possessions in the coach and hoping that the driver would not vanish with them, the tour ended at a new monument dedicated 'To the Unknown Soldier'. In their battles with the Iranians, the Iraqis had already suffered 160,000 casualties. The memorial was an enormous, modern, circular edifice created at an angle on a flat, marble base, approached up vast, shallow, brown and marble steps. The inevitable army guards scrutinized us carefully both outside and again within the building. In the huge, circular basement, uniforms from dead soldiers, each bearing a name and a citation, were displayed in glass cases. The sight of these poignant relics caused understandable distress to our Iraqi companions. Elsewhere, there were displays of weaponry. Our Jordanian companion spoke excellent English. Not surprisingly, he was very well informed and explained that the Iranians had every form of sophisticated missile. Other cases contained uniforms of historical interest, some hundreds of years old. But dominating all the exhibits, with their photographs of every aspect of present-day military life, and at the centre, were huge portraits of the Iraqi's beloved President, Field Marshall Saddam Hussein, 'hero of national liberation'. Few families in the country remained unaffected – many had similar photographs hanging in their front gardens - so it was not surprising to detect an air of unease and suspicion as local people watched visitors from the West peering at their honours.

Beside the river

After our tour of the war memorial, we returned to the Sheraton Hotel in time to meet Saad and postpone his generous offer of an evening visit to the markets. Standing outside the hotel waiting for him, it was hot, humid and smelly, and insects were beginning to emerge. Saad agreed to park his car and to come for a drink to the roof bar, where we enjoyed splendid views over the city as night began to fall. I suspect he was glad to return to his family, since his baby was ill. Following a Danish coffee-shop supper, we realized we were exhausted and, aided by glasses of iced Perrier, were quickly asleep. On Wednesday 4th May, the excellent room service brought a huge breakfast tray set out with orange juice, coffee, rolls and pastries, some kept for later use.

The discipline and formality of our public activities, the constant presence of guards, and the military dress of almost all those attending the conference contrasted strikingly with the informality and friendliness with which we were greeted when we visited Nagib's family. We sat in their garden, not far from the River Tigris, and used our fingers to savour portions of a great delicacy, a four-foot-long fish, possibly shabbout, caught from the vast river. It was a scene which could have come from any earlier century and, like our visit to Babylon, served to remind us of the antiquity of the country in which we were guests.

Babylon

After one of the conference sessions, Saad drove us southwards to visit the Hanging Gardens of Babylon. On the way to the ancient city, we encountered a military checkpoint every few miles. At one post, on the outskirts of Baghdad, the Iraqi soldiers spoke to Saad and asked who we were. Afterwards, he told me without a smile that they had been looking for army deserters. I did not fancy a firing squad or 20 years in an Iraqi prison, but at once realized that his answer reflected his own sense of humour.

Leaving Baghdad, we were soon in the open country, passing through deserted villages, along dusty roads, at first lined by date palms. There were sheep in evidence in the sparsely populated streets, and we saw sheep markets, a shepherd with a stick and a peasant woman with bags of grass, on a donkey. Donkey carts drove by and there were goats at the roadside. Dead animals lay beside the highway, but this did not prevent children playing outside their simple, windowless homes.

The ancient Hanging Gardens proved to be a deep, excavation extending down to form a sunken, stone-lined palace. There was very little vegetation. In the distance, we caught sight of a boy in Arab dress crossing the horizon on a donkey. It was a biblical image. That we were in the twentieth, not the first, century was quickly shown by another local figure selling Coca Cola from a tray. The heat was intense, so we bought a can and Helen drank some of the contents.

This time, the cars were better managed and we returned to the hotel in time to change for a lunch from the cold table. A sight-seeing coach and guide arrived to take us to the Iraq Museum, in Museum Square, Karkh. Thomas Preiswerk told us that one of the Swiss had studied archaeology and was better informed than our guide, but we felt it would be discourteous if the foreign visitors abandoned her. The Museum was full of chronologically arranged archaeological items extending back to 6000 BC. There were mummified bodies of all kinds covering the many different civilisations – Sumerian, Akkadian, Seleucid, Parthian, Sassanid and Abbassid. The large relics associated with Nebuchadnezzar reminded me of displays in the British Museum, the burial urns and the heads of special interest. Unfortunately, the Museum shop was closed when we emerged, hurried along by an anxious guard.

There was time for a drink before an evening reception at the Swiss Ambassadorial residence. The rendezvous was again in the Sheraton Hotel lobby, where, much to my surprise, Ms Ryan seemed much concerned about dress, particularly her own, which Helen thought very attractive. A small bus appeared to take us to the Embassy. However, a little Datsun car tried to overtake on the narrow, rough and dusty road and struck the offside edge of the bus. A pause followed while the two drivers argued about the metal strips dislodged from the side of the bus – we were only surprised that we had not been involved in an accident previously. The driving in Baghdad was wild and ill-disciplined and only the dry state of the roads helped to prevent more collisions.

The Swiss Ambassador was alert and more interested than when we first met him. The reception took place in his garden, the coarse grass so well watered that the heel of Helen's sandals sank into the soil. Almost immediately, we met the British Ambassador and his wife and talked with them until Helen felt it her duty to introduce him to one of the Swiss members of the party. We were not accustomed to meetings with diplomats, and, to us, His Excellency, Mr Moberly, might have stepped straight out of an Ealing comedy! I was not surprised to learn that he had taught budding diplomats. Underneath his 'stiff upper lip' there was, however, a shrewd, fluent-Arabic speaker. Once or twice, he turned his back on the assembly and gave me a few home truths. It was obvious that he held a lonely position where it was difficult to meet Iraqis freely and where the diplomats saw too much of their own, Embassy staff. His wife, we learned, was a paediatrician, although this was difficult to believe – she gave the impression that she would be more at home with the old aristocracy than in the wards of a children's hospital. She had been accepted recently at one of the Baghdad hospitals, to work on a part-time basis, and was obviously delighted to meet me. We found her an enigma, receiving much information but offering little in return.

Helen was relieved when the Swiss Ambassador suggested that we should sit on a garden seat because of the sinking heels! White-coated servants plied us with surprisingly disappointing, dry and uninteresting cocktail bites. The Ambassador's wife was in Switzerland with a young child, so he was on his own. I also learnt that he wanted to remain in Baghdad meantime, where he felt he could do a worthwhile job. Like Mr Moberly, he was a fluent Arabic speaker. The evening ended with a splendid dinner at the Sheraton Hotel. By this time, Helen was not feeling well and did not attend. I sat next to the Swiss Ambassador and watched some colourful floor displays. The time came to say goodnight and to thank our hosts for the trouble they had taken to entertain us and to show us something of the country.

Our journey home on Thursday 5th May was not without incident. Whether the cause was an item of food or perhaps the Coca Cola we had bought at Babylon, early in the morning Helen complained that she had diarrhoea and had vomited. We struggled downstairs and found that most of the European party had been affected in the same way. In fact, only I and the daughter of one of the other speakers had been spared. When we reached the airport, she and I were among the few able to reach the check-in desk, the greater number of our fellow travellers simply wondering whether they would be sufficiently well to travel. With small plastic bags provided by airlines for just such emergencies, the majority were able to keep their symptoms under control, but did not enjoy the flight and were relieved to reach London.

Thomas Preiswerk had flown home to Switzerland ahead of us. Aware of the sickly state of his guest speakers, he had taken great trouble to organize a car to drive us back to Manchester. At Heathrow, we were met by a white Mercedes and a skilled driver who whisked us all the way to Oaker Avenue. It turned out that he had enjoyed an earlier career as a professional footballer. An obsessive car-lover, he was deeply upset when a mischievous bird dropped an indiscreet deposit on the bonnet of his beautiful vehicle. The gift of a large bundle of sterling notes did little to relieve his anxiety, and he seemed glad to leave the North and return to London. It was characteristic of our host that, the following morning, Dr. Preiswerk telephoned from Basel to make sure we had recovered from the journey.

ISRAEL

My slight understanding of the Middle East was substantially extended when, in 1988, I was invited to take part in an international conference in Israel. The meeting, centred on 'Methods in Cartilage Research', was supported by the Bat-Sheva de Rothschild Foundation for the Advancement of Science in Israel and by 21 Israeli government ministries and European and American international scientific companies. It was to be held on 16th–26th March 1989, partly in Jerusalem, partly at the Nof Ginossar Kibbutz Guest house, near Tiberias on the shores of Lake Galilee, and finally at Herzliyya. One hundred and thirty-two people were expected. The conference was to be chaired jointly by Professor Alice Maroudas[B] of the Department of Biomedical Engineering, Technion-Israel Institute of Technology, Haifa, and by Dr Klaus Kuettner, Chairman of the Department of Biochemistry, Rush Medical College, Rush-Presbyterian-St Luke's Medical Centre, Chicago.

Helen and I flew from London to Tel Aviv. The security procedures at Heathrow were unusual. Our luggage and bags were searched in the customary way, but much more attention was given to our itinerary. I was asked: 'Who invited you to Israel? Why did they ask you, in particular? What is your profession, your special interest in the subject of the conference?' and so on. The concern of the Israeli security service was focused on identifying the purpose of the individual traveller rather than on any objects they might be carrying. They were particularly suspicious of the fact that we had paid our own fares, a most unusual occurrence.

Jerusalem

Landing at Tel Aviv in the evening, we were driven to Jerusalem, a distance of some 50 miles. Alice Maroudas welcomed us at the Hyatt Regency Hotel. Signing the register, I was dismayed to find that I had mislaid my wallet. Fortunately, the taxi driver was alert, honest and conscientious. As we searched the hotel foyer, he brought the wallet to Alice from the floor of his cab. We were greatly relieved and were able to enjoy six comfortable nights!

The meeting began on Friday 17th March with a gentle seminar on archaeology and a tour of sites of interest in old Jerusalem. It was an unforgettable experience. From the hotel, it was a short walk to local shops, a bus ride to the city centre. A student guide took a small group of us to the summit of the hills overlooking the 'Golden City'. Pausing beside the road, we were captivated by the view of the ancient capital, the temples, churches and houses spread out before us in an extraordinary panorama (Figure 21.1). Our guide asked if someone would volunteer to read an epic poem, chosen to enhance the occasion. He handed the script to me. Soon, we found ourselves within easy sight of the Omar Mosque, the Dome of the Rock. Surrounding the remains of the ancient foundations of Solomon's temple was the Wailing Wall. A large open space had been created to allow men in one part, women in another, to worship in what was effectively an open-air synagogue. In the centre of the city, we walked along the Via Dolorosa, the catacombs and cellars holding displays of the Dead Sea Scrolls. A visit to the Church of the Holy Sepulchre (Figure 21.2) explained some of the problems faced by the Christian communities and brought to mind the conflicts that initiated the Crimean War. Our guide told us that the monks of the different religious affiliations, their territories within the Church demarcated by painted white lines on the floor, could not agree who was to maintain the fabric of the Church, which was therefore cared for by the State of Israel!

From the hills, it was a short distance to the Yad Vashem Sanctuary, the memorial built on Remembrance Mount to the victims of the

Figure 21.1 *A panoramic view of Jerusalem.*

Holocaust. A 99-foot column erected in front of the building was inscribed with the word *Zkor* ('Remember'). Within, broad, winding corridors and underground chambers, hundreds of photographs and documents illustrated the persecutions of the years 1933–45 (Figure 21.3). A shrine in the form of a crypt, the Ohel Yizkor, bore on its walls the names of 21 concentration camps and a ceremonial flame was relit each morning.

To the south of the city lay the world-famous Hadassah Hospital and Medical School. There was no time to see the laboratories and wards, but we were permitted to enter the circular synagogue and to view the famous stained-glass windows created by Chagal. The windows illustrated the 12 Tribes of Israel. On our return to the United Kingdom, we made prints from transparencies that we purchased, and the Chagal windows are among treasured possessions on the walls of our home.

On the following day, we travelled by coach to Qumran, Masada (Figure 21.4), Ein Gedi and the Dead Sea (Figure 21.5). Under normal conditions, the time taken to travel to any of the historically interesting parts of the country was short; Israel was only 248 miles long, from 8 to 68 miles wide. However, military restrictions or the presence of convoys were liable to delay journeys. We were taken to the summit of the fortress of Masada by cable car and gained

Figure 21.2 *The Church of the Holy Sepulchre.*

Figure 21.3 *Inscriptions on the floor of the Holocaust Memorial.*

Figure 21.4 *At the summit of Masada. The Dead Sea forms part of the background.*

Figure 21.5 *Enthusiastic bathers in the Dead Sea.*

an impression of the isolation of the Israeli people who had been driven to suicide at this historic mountain refuge. The weather remained hot, and many of our party took the opportunity of floating in the waters of the Dead Sea.

Nof Ginossar

On Sunday 19th March, we left for Nof Ginossar. Our accommodation, where we remained for five nights, was in the kibbutz, on the shores of the Sea of Galilee (Figure 21.6).

The scientific meeting, divided into 13 parts, started at 2 pm with a two-hour session on 'The sampling, characterization and handling of live cartilaginous tissues'. With my former Manchester collaborators as coauthors, I spoke about the problems of articular cartilage sampling.[3] After an evening dinner, a second session centred on 'Methods for the extraction, separation and analysis of the constituents of the cartilage matrix'. An early start on the morning of Monday 20th March led to the third part of the meeting, beginning with a review session on 'Qualitative and quantitative structure (morphology) of cartilage'. My contribution was devoted to our studies of low-temperature scanning electron microscopy.[4] A following session on 'Immunology of cartilage components' was at 11 am, the subsequent one ('Cartilage tissue composition and organization') at 7.30 in the evening.

Figure 21.6 *A view of the Sea of Galilee.*

The conference had been planned with great care. Full allowance had been made for those who knew little of the geography and history of Israel. Monday afternoon was therefore devoted to a tour to Nazareth (Figure 21.7) and Mount Tabor. Meanwhile, Helen joined a tour of the northern part of the country, which included a view of the Golan Heights.

On Tuesday 21st March, the meeting reviewed 'Cartilage organ and cell culture' and 'The turnover of living and isolated cartilage'.

In the afternoon, a visit to Tiberias allowed us time for relaxation and discussion.

On 22nd March, two further topics followed: 'Cartilage solute exchange' and 'Mechanical and electrical properties of cartilage'.

Again, there was an absorbing interlude, with a guided tour of the Kibbutz.

Figure 21.7 *An approach to Nazareth.*

This was followed by Helen Muir (p.175), who gave an invited lecture on 'Historical development of methods in cartilage research'.

In the evening, a talk about Israel was followed by a performance on Biblical harps and a display of classical Israeli dancing. Knowing of her devotion to ballet, it was not surprising to see that Dr Muir was tempted to join the dancers!

On 23rd March, the scientific topics were 'Modifiers of cartilage metabolism', 'Recombinant nucleic acid methodology in the study of cartilage metabolism' and 'The renewal and repair of adult articular cartilage'. The final parts of this wonderfully interesting, productive and highly organized conference were devoted to 'New approaches in monitoring in vivo cartilage metabolism and/or degenerative processes' and to a broad discussion on 'Ideas for future studies of cartilage'.

The scientific sessions were interspersed with a walking tour, and it was interesting to see that a number of the older participants suffered from disorders of the articular cartilages that they had been discussing!

For our last two nights, we returned to Jerusalem (Figure 21.8) and stayed at the Sharon Hotel before our journey home. As the time for our departure approached, Helen awoke with a severe migraine and wondered whether she would be able to fly. Alice, imperturbable as usual, coined a phrase that has stayed with us ever since. She said: 'Don't vurry!'

Figure 21.8 *Helen with Peter Revell in Jerusalem.*

VI.
Home again

CHAPTER 22

The fixed period

In sight of Queensferry

Far from the madding crowd's ignoble strife
Their sober wishes never learned to stray;
Along the cool sequestered vale of life
They kept the noiseless tenor of their way.

Thomas Gray[1]

William Osler had firm views on how long medical school staff could be of value.[2] Describing 'the comparative uselessness of men above forty years of age', he wrote: 'the effective, moving, vitalizing work of the world is done between the ages of twenty five and forty.' Addressing Johns Hopkins University as he was about to leave, he quoted *The Fixed Period*, the novel in which Trollope discussed the practical advantages of a scheme by which men aged sixty should retire for a year of contemplation before a 'practical departure by chloroform'.

Chapter summary
- Another new home
- A new laboratory
- Research
- Collaboration
- Academic activities
- Meetings
- The passage of time

When Osler wrote in 1905, the population of England was 37 million, the life expectancy for males 45 years and that for females 48 years. A century later, the population had risen to 51.5 million and the life expectancies to 77.7 years and 81.9 years, respectively. Thirty additional years, I thought, should surely modify Osler's opinions, and it was my instinct to remain active for as long as possible.

The solution came with a proposal to create a Senior Research Fellowship in the Pathology Department of the University of Edinburgh, forming an Osteoarticular Unit that would enhance the resources available to Orthopaedic Surgery and Rheumatology. The costs were to be financed by the Arthritis Research Council, the ARC, now Arthritis Research UK, who had already agreed in principal. I had discussed the idea with the Head of the Department, Alastair Currie, and with his successor, Colin Bird, who submitted formal proposals to the Council. The ARC ratified the request in December 1987 and I was offered the position, with Honorary Consultant status, for a three-year period from 1st June 1988. I had no hesitation in accepting: the University of Edinburgh was a natural focus for my research and I retained close working relationships both with the Royal College of Physicians of Edinburgh, the RCPEd, and with the Royal College of Surgeons of Edinburgh, the RCSEd.

Another new home

The opportunity of returning to Edinburgh in 1988 was attractive to Helen and to our family. Helen's sister, Florence, remained in Buckland Village, near Aylesbury, but her brother and his wife, Enid, still lived in Bo'ness, on the banks of the Firth of Forth. Our daughter, Rosalind, was comfortably settled in Cardiff, where her husband, Iain McQueen, was a consultant neurologist at the University, Heath Hospital. Our elder son, Iain, was established as a consultant ophthalmologist at the Derby Royal Infirmary, while our younger son, David, was studying at the University of Sussex, where he graduated in American Politics in 2001 (Figure 22.1).

Figure 22.1 *David Gardner, at his graduation from the University of Sussex, 2001.*

Once again, we sought a home in Edinburgh, large enough to welcome occasional visitors. We were fortunate to light upon a flat in a new building, Fountainhall Court (Figure 22.2), near the Mayfield Church and in walking distance of the University Medical School at Teviot Place.

The 'Development' as it was called, within easy reach of the excellent Edinburgh bus service, had been built on the site of an old garage and comprised three adjoining four-storey blocks each of eight flats. They were well served by lifts. A parking area in front of the building and a modest garden behind the two southerly blocks offered the amenities we sought, and their location within walking distance of convenient shops was a final point in their favour. On our first visit to the site, we met a friendly resident who generously invited us to see her home. After viewing her rooms and the spacious neighbourhood, we had no hesitation in deciding to pay the £60,000 required by Bett Brothers, the builders.[A]

Edinburgh offered many social attractions. We had become familiar with the Edinburgh International Festival from its earliest days in 1947 (p.73) and were closely aware of the Festival Fringe. Music remained a principal interest, and we soon resumed attending the

Figure 22.2 *Fountainhall Court, Edinburgh with the Mayfield Church in the background.*

Scottish Opera. *La Traviata* and the *Marriage of Figaro* were favourites, but later, in 2006, we could not resist Wagner's entire *Ring Cycle*.

In the coming months, our love of the Scottish Borders and in particular for Peebles (Chapter 11), took us back to this ancient town increasingly often. It was only 20 miles from the home in St Boswells of my cousin, Jean Grieve, her son Tony and his family. We had spent many happy times in Peebles during earlier years (p.130), and in 1989 decided to seek a holiday home there. Our eyes lighted upon a bungalow-style house, 'Millwood', 10 Kingsmeadows Gardens, part of the old Kingsmeadows Estate, where Kingsmeadows House now belonged to the Standard Life Insurance Company. The house (Figure 22.3), with a half-acre garden, had five bedrooms and a delightful living room (Figure 22.4) with a timbered, 'chapel-style' ceiling and a Baxi coal fire. There were frequent views of the sky both at dawn and as the sun set (Figure 22.5).

Figure 22.3 *10 Kingsmeadows Gardens, Peebles.*

Figure 22.4 *David (left) and Iain Gardner, in our living room, Peebles.*

Figure 22.5 *A glimpse of the night sky at Peebles.*

To the south, across a small road, lay the grounds of Priorsford Primary School, already one of the largest in the Scottish Borders. To the north was a large area of woodland owned by the Town Council. Our neighbour on the east aspect of the house was a very elderly, retired farmer, Mr Mitchell. On an early visit, he asked me to help him start his Volvo car. I noticed that the milometer showed that the vehicle, several years old, had been driven for only 800 miles. As he set off uncertainly down the road, I wondered whether I would ever see him again! On the other side lived George Johnston, a retired merchant navy officer, and his wife Ruth, a busy secretary working in the offices of the Edinburgh Royal Infirmary.

On 30th May 1989, my 65th birthday, celebrated with a large family lunch at the Old Howgate Inn on the road to Peebles, catalysed old friendships, and we resumed social gatherings with John and Jenny Richmond (p.124), Angus Stuart (p.160) and many others. In Peebles, I was astonished to encounter Bill Symmers, whom I had first met in Birmingham in 1953 (p.116). Bill told me that he had come to know the Royal Burgh during his time in the Royal Navy. In the course of the Second World War, Peebles Hydro, the famous hotel overlooking the river Tweed, had been a convalescent centre where he helped to care for the sick and wounded. Later, when he and his wife visited Peebles, their love for the Borders led to the purchase of an old schoolhouse. However, she died not long before he was due to retire, so he came to live in Peebles by himself, surrounded by his immense library. By 1990, Bill was not well; I visited him from time to time, listening to his tales of travel and people and satisfying his liking for chocolate! He died in 2000.

Early in 1992, we were visited by Susie Pike (Figure 13.6), Helen's niece. She had become critically ill with ovarian cancer and, in the knowledge that she might never see Scotland again, her husband, Sean Travers-Healy, asked if they might visit us. We welcomed them to Edinburgh and, a little later, took them to Peebles for what turned out to be Susie's last visit. She died on 19th April, aged 42.

Over the coming years, we made periodic visits to our son Iain and his wife Lynn in Derby, travelling by British Midland Airways, 'BMI Baby' as it came to be called. Our journeys to Cardiff to see Rosalind and Iain were sometimes for Christmas, usually by car or by trains that ran from Edinburgh to Preston before joining the route to Wales. There were also less frequent journeys to York and thence to Pocklington, where my brother Colin and his wife Denise lived in the tiny village of Nunburnholme. Their daughter, Philippa, continued her social work while her husband, Peter Betteridge, pursued a responsible position in the automobile industry.

A new laboratory

The years from 1988 to 1991 offered the invigorating opportunity of combining the research I had developed in Manchester with the freedom from the burden of academic administration and teaching associated with most senior university appointments. I understood my 'terms of reference' to mean the continued investigation of the nature and causes of the connective tissue diseases.[3–5] The focus was to be on the microscopic structure and composition of articular cartilage. My experience in London, Belfast and Manchester had taught me many of the problems faced when a new research laboratory is established. The first challenge is to secure good accommodation, the second to find good staff. A third task is to obtain the necessary equipment and then to learn how to use it.

Colin Bird gave me the necessary space in his department in the 1960s building at the corner of George Square (p.160) and an office adjoining the electron microscope laboratory. It was conveniently near a darkroom, a laboratory dealing with cytogenetics and another where research was being undertaken with a HOME microscope.[B] In advance of my return to his Edinburgh Department, Professor Bird had invited Donald Salter[C] to specialize in osteoarticular pathology, and he became a close collaborator and friend.

I was fortunate in the choice of technical staff. The Chief Medical Scientific Officer (MLSO), Jimmy Waugh (p.126), had retired and had been succeeded by Kenny Rae and by Bob Donaldson. With their support, Colin Bird had suggested that Bob Simpson, skilled in the preparation of bone and joint specimens, should be my senior technician. Bob, hard-working and conscientious, was soon joined by a young Scott McArthur, whose unfulfilled ambition was to complete a thesis for an MPhil degree. David C. Findlay came in September 1991 for a short period and Catrina Kivlin worked with us during 1992–93 before moving to the Edinburgh Institute for Animal Health. I had the help of Joyce Wood after she left the RCSEd (p.328) and the assistance of the late Mrs Wyatt. Later, Alan Smith, whose father had been a College Officer of the RCSEd, successfully undertook the challenge of cutting histological sections of sacroiliac joints, and Donald Salter's technician, Lynsey Fairbairn, gave skilled support.

Within the £188,000 allocated for my project, £58,523 provided a Zeiss Axiophot microscope, a Polycut microtome, a Faxitron X-ray cabinet and a Sight-Systems Image Analyser. Over the years, I had established a vigorous interchange of ideas with Ciba-Geigy (Novartis) (p.291), and I remained in close touch with W. A. Bradley, Head of Preclinical Safety, and with Dr Paul Skelton-Stroud, at Stamford Lodge, Wilmslow. Dr Kris Jasani in Horsham, Sussex was their International Cartilage Project Leader, but Paul was my immediate collaborator. In February 1993, Tony Bradley granted me £1000 for laser scanning microscopy and subsequently added £2000, together with £3000 for a video camera. A grant of £34,699 from the Scottish Home and Health Department to the Department for a Zeiss laser scanning confocal microscope proved to be of crucial significance. The instrument cost £49,570 and the difference was met by the Faculty of Medicine. By the time the instrument arrived early in 1989, my former colleague, David Woodward, had become part of the Zeiss sales team, and he and Pat Gunter were closely involved in the installation of the new instrument. Together with the Axiophot microscope, the scanning instrument provided a basis for new and sophisticated studies not only of sections of preserved (fixed) tissue, but also of fresh, hydrated tissue blocks, which we studied by transmitted-light, phase-contrast, epifluorescence and confocal epifluorescence techniques.

Research

In addition to our interest in arthritis, much time in Manchester had been devoted to developing methods for the microscopic study of the bone, cartilage and synovium of normal synovial joints. In earlier work, we had demonstrated the irregularities of normal cartilage-bearing surfaces, and we resumed the measurement of these features.

With the continued help of Dr Oates in Lancaster, we obtained further evidence of the detail of articular structures,[6–8] However, with the new technique of laser scanning confocal optical microscopy (CSOM), we were able to extend our results greatly,[9–11] and through the generosity of Colin Bird and his successor David Harrison, I was encouraged to continue this work for some years after my Fellowship ended,[12–14] sometimes with the help of Edinburgh PhD students,[15,16] occasionally with the talented assistance of visiting workers.[17,18] From time to time, our investigations extended to unrelated topics, and one day A. T. Saadi and I were surprised to find that we had discovered how to locate bacteria on the surfaces of cells viewed in three dimensions.[19]

The investigation of joint mechanics that we had begun in London and extended in Belfast was greatly helped by the support of Professor J. A. (Joe) McGeough and his students[20,21] in the Edinburgh University Department of Mechanical Engineering. Nevertheless, my main concern was with the cells and extracellular matrix of cartilage itself,[22–25] interests that did not always reach publication.[26] Added to this field of work was our new interest, shared with David Hulmes, in the hyaluronate of synovial fluid.[27–29] We turned to a pharmaceutical company, Fermentech, for supplies of this polysaccharide and, with the further help of Ken Oates, made low-temperature scanning electron micrographs of cartilage surfaces to which hyaluronate had been applied.

As the years passed, I was able to extend my interest in the paired sacroiliac joints. I had brought normal joint material from Australia (Chapter 20) and began to collect further specimens in Edinburgh, work that took me to the modern hospital autopsy suite in Lauriston Place, constructed while the building of the new Edinburgh Royal Infirmary at Little France was in progress (the first patients were admitted in 2002). A great deal of time was spent in the systematic measurements of the sacral and iliac cartilages, and by the time this work was concluded, it had become clear that the two opposing cartilages, apparently subject to closely similar vertical and tangential loading stresses, were of strikingly different composition and proportions.[30,31]

It was during this time that I received an unexpected but enthusiastic approach from Dr Robert François. He was a well respected Belgian rheumatologist, soon to be President of the Belgian Society of Rheumatology (p.270). Robert had an intense interest in the sacroiliac joints because of their almost invariable involvement in ankylosing spondylitis, the subject on which Bruce Cruickshank had written his PhD thesis (p.128). Working together, in an intensive study of the many cases I had collected, we established that there was a great variety of sacroiliac abnormalities in ankylosing spondylitis and that the joint disorder in this disease could not be adequately explained simply on the basis of inflammatory changes in the synovial, entheseal joints.[32,33]

In addition to these topics, there was an unusual opportunity, created through our collaboration with Novartis, for the investigation of experimental arthritis in primates.[34] There were also moments when technical developments attracted special attention[35–37] and, behind this entire operation, the demand for reviews of the field in which I was engaged.[38–40]

I had no hospital duties, but my contract allowed me access to tissue specimens from patients for research purposes. I was encouraged to make a contribution to the work of the Scottish Bone Tumour Registry.

In one instance, a 7-year child was found to have an haemangioma of developmental origin. In another, I recognized a chondrosarcoma in the elbow of a 15-year-old girl, operated upon to correct a physical disability. With Richard Fitzmaurice, who had remained in Manchester after we moved to Edinburgh, I reported an unusual case of thymoma.[41] Our studies of synovial metastases continued in the hands of an honours BSc student, M. J. W. Strachan.[42,D]

Collaboration

In science, opportunities for meeting people are most precious and often lead to long-lasting contacts and the exchange of information, experiences and views. As part of the Registrar Training Programme for orthopaedic surgeons and in collaboration with Professor Sean Hughes, I took part in the teaching programmes organized by Ms M. M. McQueen, Senior Lecturer in the Clinical Research Unit of the Princess Margaret Rose Orthopaedic Hospital, Edinburgh, and by Mr W. (Willie) A. Souter, known internationally for his pioneer elbow operation, the Souter Strathclyde arthroplasty. In 1989, Gordon Duff of the Rheumatic Diseases Unit told me that he hoped to pursue confocal microscopy, but his plan was not fulfilled since in 1990 he moved to a Chair in Sheffield. C. M. Court-Brown planned to study the biomechanical properties of geriatric bone, and among others with whom I collaborated briefly was the distinguished authority on bone disorders, Juliet Compston. I joined forces with W. J. (Bill) Gillespie,[E] who succeeded Sean Hughes in the Edinburgh Chair of Orthopaedic Surgery in 1993.

One of Joe McGeough's graduate students was Bruce Leslie, who joined our work on the mechanics of synovial joints. In September 1988, G. Howard Moody[F] asked for help in his field of dental pathology: he had started to measure lead concentrations in teeth. Another valued friend and colleague was Professor Verna Wright of Leeds, who sadly died in 1998. Close collaboration also evolved with Professor George Nuki of the Rheumatic Diseases Unit, now at the Western General Hospital, while I pursued thoughtful discussions with Robin Stockwell, who had a personal Chair in Anatomy and had worked with J. E. Scott. In the Department of Physiology, our work brought us close to the interests of Andrew Hall and Peter Bush.

One of our plans was to extend our understanding of the three-dimensional structure of cartilage by comparing CSOM and magnetic resonance imaging (MRI) images. I therefore made contact with Professor Laurie Hall of the Herschel Smith Laboratory for Medicinal Chemistry in Cambridge. His

University laboratory, equipped with the most modern hardware for MRI, was sited in a new building at the Forvie site on Robinson Way. During one of my visits, Hall reviewed the application of his methods to articular structures and I talked to the Strangeways Research Laboratory Tea Club on 'How rough are the bearing surfaces of synovial joints?'

In April 1989, Dr Ilkka Kiviranta of the Department of Surgery of the University Central Hospital of Kuopio, Finland, kindly sent me a copy of his valuable doctoral thesis. We had discussed his work while sailing on the Sea of Galilee a few weeks previously (p.299). Within three months of arriving in Edinburgh, I had been approached by a considerable number of other individuals anxious to take part in our research programme, while some, including Dr Shirley Ayad of Manchester, continued to be valuable sources of information regarding specific topics, in her case the autofluorescence of collagen.

In December 1988, Dr Winfried Mohr of the Pathology Committee of the European League Against Rheumatism, EULAR, asked whether I could assist a medical student from the University of Ülm to study in Edinburgh for six months. In the following year, Professor Frits Eulderink, from the same Committee, enquired whether we could help a young Dutch graduate, Dr Elisabeth Christine Wijnvoord, who wished to gain experience in Britain. A visit by Dr Ostergaard in 1997 led to his collaboration with Donald Salter, and in May 1989 Dr R. I. Davis from the Royal Victoria Hoapital, Belfast, confirmed that he planned to visit us.

Academic activities

In 1989, I was invited to assume the responsibility for the Museum of the RCSEd (Chapter 23). Meanwhile, I continued to take part in the postgraduate lecture programme in Internal Medicine, although my research fellowship did not include any formal responsibility for undergraduate or postgraduate teaching. However, in October 1989, David Hulmes asked me to help with a course for honours students in biochemistry, in which his teaching centred on the composition and properties of the extracellular matrix. There were frequent meetings with many of the Department of Pathology colleagues I had come to know in earlier years, in particular with Mary MacDonald and Ian Smith (p.161). Through my new responsibilities in the RCSEd, I often encountered Neil MacLean: he had retired from his consultant appointment at the Western General Hospital. My new associates included David Lamb, Andrew Krajewski and Juan Piris.

I continued as an examiner in Pathology for the Medical and Dental Faculties of the University of Liverpool, and in April 1989 Professor Donald Heath wrote to me about two candidates. They had been trapped in the crowd at the time of the Hillsborough Stadium football disaster and were close to some of those crushed to death by the crowd. Donald asked that their terrible experience should be taken into account in assessing their examination performances, and we agreed that this would be fair and just.

One of the responsibilities of senior scientists and clinicians is to give informed support for job applications. An example was the request in September 1995 for a Certificate of Completion of Training for Richard John Fitzmaurice by the Royal College of Physicians and Surgeons of Canada. During the years 1987–92, I also acted as referee for a variety of scientific journals[G] and wrote a number of book reviews of which the volume by Bartl and Frisch[43] was one example. In addition, there were periodic visits to publishers in London in preparation for a successor to my *Pathology of the Connective Tissue Diseases*.[3] The larger, new book was to be entitled *Pathological Basis of the Connective Tissue Diseases*. I asked John Anderson of the Manchester Department of Biochemistry for help and my colleague, John McClure (p.240) gave advice on disorders such as amyloidosis and metabolic bone disease. In February 1989, John C. Brocklehurst wrote from Manchester to enquire whether, in collaboration with Dr Pat O'Connor (p.243), I would contribute a chapter to the fourth edition of his *Textbook of Medicine and Gerontology*.

Meetings

During my retirement research fellowship and for some years after its formal end, I was able to attend a variety of conferences and symposia. Helen accompanied me on most of these occasions, opportunities for travel to countries as diverse as Japan (Chapter 16), Brazil (Chapter 17), Russia (Chapter 19), Australia (Chapter 20) and Iraq and Israel (Chapter 21), in addition to the times we had spent in the United States (Chapter 12).

In some cases, I revisited centres to which I had been previously, as was the case with the meeting in Warsaw early in May 1990 (Chapter 19) of the Pathology Committee of EULAR[H] during my time as Chairman. Attendance at this Committee was often sparse, with no more than 10 or 11 representatives of the 33 eligible countries attending. Scandinavian, Dutch, German and British representation was usually strong, whereas few came from France or Spain. I was elected an Honorary Member of EULAR in 1991.

It was inevitable that in the course of my laboratory work I should continue to attend meetings of the Pathological Society and of the British Society of Rheumatology and to speak at a variety of scientific meetings and seminars.[I]

The passage of time

We made visits to Cardiff, to Derby and to Brighton to see our family and to Pocklingon where my brother Colin lived. It was with great sadness that I learned in 2002 that he had become seriously ill with prostate cancer. Despite the best possible treatment, he died in 2003. A funeral service in Yorkshire was attended by relations and friends from all parts of the United Kingdom, and it was Colin's wish that his ashes should be scattered across the countryside he had loved so dearly.

Helen's brother Gordon (Figure 22.6) and his wife Enid moved from Bo'ness to Edinburgh in 2001. Our family was growing quickly. Iain

Figure 22.6 *(from left to right) Enid Harrower; her sister Louise Brown; Fergus Harrower; Gordon Harrower.*

and Lynn had no children but Rosalind was now proud of her three sons and her daughter. As grandparents, we had the delight of watching from a distance the development of the youngsters and of helping with their education. Rosalind's eldest son, David McQueen, at first a student of classics at Oxford, chose to follow his interest in music and became a professional French horn player. In April 1999 he married Silva Vučković, an outstanding soprano from Serbia, and they have two charming daughters, Anya and Sophia (Figure 22.7), both blessed with musical talent. Jane McQueen gained a first class honours degree in microbiology from the University of Edinburgh in 1998 and worked for BUPA and other companies, combining her knowledge of science with skills in computing. She married Richard Shotton (Figure 22.8) on 21st February 2004 and they have a son, Thomas (Figure 22.9) and a daughter, Anna (Figure 22.10). Even at school Alastair, Rosalind's

Figure 22.7 *David McQueen and his family.*

Figure 22.8 *Richard and Jane Shotton.*

Figure 22.9 *Thomas Shotton.*

Figure 22.10 *Anna Shotton.*

second son (Figure 22.11), had begun to use his literary ability while Robert, Rosalind's youngest son, computer literate from an early age, joined NOKIA the Finnish, international computer organization and established his own company in Cambridge.

Figure 22.11 *(left to right) Robert, Alastair and David McQueen at the wedding of their sister Jane, 2004.*

CHAPTER 23

Jewel in a Crown

A surgical museum

I could scarcely sleep for excitement the
night after seeing the periodic table.

Oliver Sacks[1]

One evening in 1988, our Manchester telephone rang unexpectedly. A voice said 'It's Ian Kirkland. I believe you're coming back to Edinburgh. Would you like to help the Royal College of Surgeons?'[A,2,3] Ian, the College Museum[B,4] Conservator, explained that he was not well and might have to retire.[C,D] I replied: 'That's interesting. I'll certainly think about it but I'll be taking on a half-time Fellowship and won't have much free time.' Then, in the following March, after we had settled in Edinburgh, Malcolm Macnicol, College Treasurer, wrote that there were 'moves to restructure the pathological specimens in the College Museum' and that my name had 'come up as someone who might be interested'.

I considered these suggestions very carefully. There were reasons for *not* becoming involved with museology, the science of museum curatorship. I knew only too well that museums, like libraries, were 'soft options' when money was short. Throughout the world, museums confronted financial difficulties, forcing them to compete for money by lowering academic standards in research and education,[5] while exploiting shops, cafes and 'Open Days'. There was also an uncertain relationship between academic departments and the College. Anatomy and pathological anatomy, central to the Surgeons' collections, were 'old hat' in universities, where teaching in medical schools was increasingly computer-based. But in the College, as I knew from my own experience, examiners clung to approaches to which they had been accustomed 20, 30 or more years previously. The contrast with the revolutionary changes taking place in the practice of surgery itself was striking.

On the other hand, there were compelling reasons *in favour* of protecting and developing the Museum. I realized that I was biased – my father had been a Fellow of the College, I had long been an examiner and my son Iain was an ophthalmic surgeon. Moreover,

---

Chapter summary
- **Change was in the air**
- **Museum Volunteers**
- **Museum personnel**
- **The impact of examinations**
- **The collections**
- **Progress**
- **New displays**
- **Exhibitions**
- **Scientific research**
- **Historical research**
- **Oral biographies**
- **A conclusion**

the importance of the Museum as a venue for postgraduate teaching and examination was beyond dispute – its influence extended throughout the world, while the Museum, and with it the Library, remained centres where the records of Scottish surgery[6] were held in perpetuity, encouraging historians, writers, poets, artists and scientists to travel to its doors. Since there seemed every possibility that modern technology could revolutionize the accessibility of the collections, I welcomed the opportunity of drawing the Museum into the new age of computing, substituting modern methods of display and explanation for those still in use in the years following the Second World War.

And so I agreed to become the Honorary Conservator.

Change was in the air

At the end of the twentieth century, William Playfair's Anatomy Museum was still the centre of his 1832 edifice although there had been extensive developments of buildings owned by the College in Hill Square and Hill Place (Figures 23.1 and 23.2). In the Museum, I found that exciting developments had already begun in 1984,

Figure 23.1 *Hill Square, with the public entrace to the Museum (third white door from left), the King Khaled Symposium hall (at extreme right) and the 1967 Lister Memorial building (at rear), behind the Pfizer building.*

Figure 23.2 *The Playfair Hall, repainted in 2003.*

when the Sir Jules Thorn Charitable Trust gave the College a generous grant, a benefaction that came through the friendship between the late Professor Eldred Walls[E] and the Thorn family. An imaginative new exhibition had been constructed in the hall that had been the 1908 Cathcart Museum (Figure 23.3). By 1989, the lower floor of that part of this small hall had been converted into a display entitled '500 years of Scottish surgery'. With the assistance of Alan Simpson of the National Museum of Scotland and Ian MacLaren, a member of the College Council, together with the drive and foresight of the College President, Tom McNair, 24 fine cases had been constructed, illustrating the Incorporation of Barber Surgeons in 1505, the impact on seventeenth-century Edinburgh surgeons of the clinical teaching in Leiden, the foundation of the Edinburgh Medical School, the emergence of Anatomy, the story of grave robbing (Figure 23.4), anaesthesia, and, finally, a display of the lives of nineteenth- and twentieth-century Edinburgh surgeons, in particular of Joseph Lister.

The emergence of the Jules Thorn Exhibition led inexorably to a dramatic change in the way the College, anxious for money, came to view the public. Until the construction of the new Hall (Figure

Figure 23.3 *The Cathcart Hall as it was in 1908.*

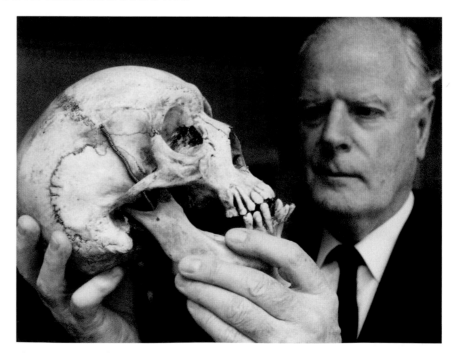

Figure 23.4 *The author holds the skull of Brogan, a young boy at the time of the Burke and Hare murders. The skull is recognizable because of the deformity of the teeth.*

23.5), only examination candidates and Fellows[F] of the College and their guests were allowed into the Museum. Exceptions were made when the Royal Patron – the Duke of Edinburgh – Royal guests and other distinguished visitors were entertained. The public were admitted only when the City of Edinburgh held a 'Doors Open' Day, recalling the annual opening of the Museum to the citizens of Edinburgh on Queen Victoria's birthday.

The Council realized that there was little point in having their fine new exhibition unless it was publicized, and I was asked to invite the police and representatives of the City of Edinburgh to inspect the Hall, seeking permission for a public entertainment licence. Despite the absence of a lift – there was a staircase and a chair lift at the side entrance to Playfair's Anatomy Hall – the facilities, including those for disabled persons, were judged adequate.

The exhibition was opened cautiously in 1990, when visitors were accepted on two weekday afternoons between 2 and 4 pm, without charge. However, word soon got about, and schools, university departments, companies, colleges, banks and societies learned of the exhibition and began to take advantage of it. Local people leapt at the opportunity of seeing a medical sanctuary

Figure 23.5 *A view of the Sir Jules Thorn Hall.*

long hidden from their eyes, and visitors began to come from all parts of this country and abroad. Many were from the medical and nursing professions, but most were laypersons of every possible background. For me, this led to a surge in interest as I encountered authors, historians, artists, broadcasters and scientists and conducted them around the collections. To begin with, there were few groups of medical students, but we soon attracted parties from Scottish schools and Colleges, including Heriots, Watsons, Strathallan, Glenalmond and Loretto. I learned a good deal about each school from the dress, behaviour and punctuality of the visiting groups, but I was careful not to reveal my thoughts to the teachers who brought the girls and boys! The school occasions were in striking contrast to visits by the German Society for the History of Medicine, the Harveian Society, the Society of Authors and the Institute of Anatomical Sciences and to those by organizations such as Queen Margaret College, Edinburgh, educating 'health care professionals'.

One day, the first visitor was from Tibet! On another occasion, a senior charge nurse who had come from the Massachusetts General Hospital, Boston, told me that surgeons in her famous institution had recently completed the transplantation to a young girl of an entire half pelvis. On another afternoon, a very tall, elegantly dressed figure caught my attention, his flowing, white hair resting on his shoulders. He was a Professor of the History of Medicine from Moscow! His presence contrasted with the slight appearance of Professor McDonald from Guelph, Ontario. She commented: 'I am editing a *Life of Florence Nightingale* in sixteen volumes and have completed nine.' When Sultan Azlan Shah, the Yang Di Pertuan Agong IX of Malaysia, visited the College in 1994, one of

Figure 23.6 *The Sultan of Malaysia examines the effigy of Joseph Lord Lister during a visit to the Jules Thorn exhibition.*

his interests centred on the life-size model of Joseph Lister (Figure 23.6). Later, representatives of the Sultan of Brunei presented us with inlaid wooden boxes containing their country's coinage.

Not all our visitors were as eminent or so well intentioned!

When a mischievous schoolboy pressed the rather too conspicuous alarm button, sirens and bells rang throughout the College and a conference in the new Symposium Hall was abruptly halted, the participants dispersed in Hill Square. On another occasion, a man drew me to one side and said: 'I have plenty of money and a large house in Edinburgh. I want to set up a private Anatomy Museum of my own.' Aware that anatomy museums could only be created with the agreement of HM Inspector of Anatomy, and then only in authentic medical schools, I asked: 'How can we help?' Our visitor relied: 'I simply wanted to ask whether you had any spare eviscerated bodies.' It was shortly before Gunther von Hagens burst upon the public scene, exploiting for commercial profit the invaluable technique of plastination.

Very soon, the Jules Thorn Hall came to have a companion room. John Menzies Campbell,[G] a Glasgow dental practitioner, gave his remarkable collection of dental surgical artefacts and artwork to the College in 1964 on condition it was displayed 'in perpetuity'. Despite this proviso, the world-famous material had remained in an upper room at 9 Hill Square, where it could not easily be viewed by the public. In 1992, it was decided to place the prestigious collection in a museum of its own, providing an international focus for the history of dentistry, a task challenging the skills of the Dental Conservator, Paul Geissler.[H]

Figure 23.7 *The new Dental Museum.*

With the advice of Les Mitchell of the Edinburgh College of Art and of Alistair Milligan, the floor between the two levels of the 1908 Barclay Hall was restored. The new Dental Museum (Figure 23.7) was created in the lower half, with fine cases for displays and television monitors within the walls. The upper half, designated the Mekie Room, was to be for meetings and committees.[1]

Museum Volunteers

Opening the Jules Thorn Hall and the Menzies Campbell collections to the public created a demand for additional security and for the guidance of visitors. We appointed a Security Officer, David Wilson, a retired businessman and computer enthusiast, and I was delighted to find that retired surgeons, friends and colleagues were pleased to assist with the kind of practical work, such as the description of anatomical specimens and cataloguing, that every large museum demands. Some were among the growing group of practising surgeons who created new displays (p.331). The volunteers began to have a life of their own and, as a small reward for their help, we arranged twice-yearly lunchtime gatherings to which informal talks were given by, among others, Professor Tony Busuttil, forensic pathologist; Dr Geissler; Mr Jim Foster, the newly appointed College Chief Executive; our friend Stella Mason, from the English College of Surgeons; John Burnett, from the National Museum of Scotland; and Alan Mackail, a retired chemist.

Museum personnel

I realized I would have to work closely with the President of the College[J] and his Office Bearers (Figure 23.8), but anticipated support from the Museum, Library and Archives Committees, in particular from Tony Gunn, the Honorary Librarian and Alistair Masson, the Honorary Archivist, both of whose views on conservation corresponded closely with my own.

Figure 23.8 *Professor P. D. Boulter as Acting President at the College Meeting on 11th October 1990 when the author was admitted to the Fellowship.*

The administration of the College was in the hands of skilled personnel. Margaret Bean, the College Secretary, directed the College employees; both she and the Bursar, Leslie Allan, were equally supportive, but I realized that my efforts would be impossible without the help of the Museum staff. The day-to-day work centred on the secretary, Violet Tansey, who had served the College for 47 years. From the time of Professor Mekie's retirement – she had been his 'right-hand person' – she had been obliged to deal not only with correspondence and with enquiries from all parts of the world but also with almost every aspect of Museum work, ranging from the collections and catalogues to the welcoming of visitors and guests. Violet was joined in 1994 by Sheena Jones, but finally retired in 1995. The Museum technician, James Bathgate, had worked with me in the Medical School. He was succeeded in 1994 by Joyce Wood. I soon benefited from the great skills of the Museum photographer, Max McKenzie. He had been appointed in 1974 and given a studio, a darkroom and a processing room. Max contributed to almost every aspect of the College's programmes until his appointment ended abruptly in 1999.

The impact of examinations

The vivas that were part of the examinations for the Fellowship were held in the bays of the Playfair Anatomy Museum. Even if planning was precise, these tests tended to interrupt both our conservation work and tours conducted by volunteers. I continued to take part in the examinations until 1994, always partnered by a surgical Fellow. They were fascinating opportunities for meeting eminent consultants, including Sir Michael Woodruff (p.157) and Sir John Bruce, as well as others such as John Cook, who told me about his experiences in Africa, where he had collaborated with Dennis Burkitt. The morning sessions were followed by convivial lunches preceded by a substantial round of drinks. Until recent years, the liberal provision of wine that accompanied the meals sometimes led examiners to fall asleep during a viva! But the occasions could be entertaining!

Called courteously to a table by the Senior College Officer, the late Mr James Walker, a former RAF Warrant Officer, we tried to put candidates at their ease. To one nervous but smartly dressed young man, I said: 'That's an interesting tie you're wearing. Tell us about it.' He replied: 'Well, sir, that's the tie given to each of us who have had a pint of beer at every one of the 79 pubs owned by Watney's Breweries in London.' I saw the eyebrows of my fellow examiner, Mr McCormack, a thoracic surgeon, rise in astonishment. To bring the oral examination back to a calmer note, and thinking of antisepsis, I enquired: 'Tell us about the important role of alcohol in surgery.' Without hesitating, the candidate responded: 'Indeed, many surgeons become alcoholics.'

The collections

Busy with the Jules Thorn Hall, I had to become familiar with every corner of Playfair's neoclassical building and the adjoining College properties. A good physique was called for! I started with a long climb from the front entrance at Nicolson Street, up the 'bell' tower at the south corner, a place where a flag was hoisted on special occasions. Another climb at 4 Hill Square took me past flats now leased to postgraduate students and their families, to the Conservator's office, which I particularly liked because of the view it offered of Hill Square. I found a preparation room on the third floor and, above it, a further flat, which had been the venue for the secretarial work of Mrs Turner, who had done so much to help Eric Mekie and Neil McLean[K] (p.161) in preparing *An Atlas of Surgical Pathology*.[7] The Museum store was in basement cellars at 12 Hill Square.

My first glimpse of the Playfair Hall itself, the principal part of the Museum, was enthralling. My eyes were caught by Charles Bell's paintings (Figure 23.9),

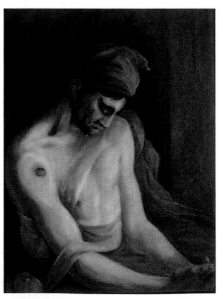

Figure 23.9 *The painting by Charles Bell of a wounded survivor of the Battle of Corunna (1809).*

Figure 23.10 *The McDowell saucer.*

produced after the battle of Corunna in 1809, when he went from London to the south coast of England to care for the wounded brought back by the Navy from north-west Spain.[8] In 1996, when Eldred Walls and I arranged an exhibition of Bell's life and work,[9] I was able to get copies of Bell's later Waterloo paintings from the Wellcome Library, and for some years they also hung on the Museum walls. Less conspicuous artefacts were sometimes equally fascinating. One example was the little porcelain dish (Figure 23.10), part of a set taken back to his home in Kentucky in 1795 by a young Ephraim McDowell after he had finished his medical education in Edinburgh. McDowell achieved international recognition when, in 1809, with neither anaesthesia nor antisepsis, he successfully removed a huge ovarian tumour from a coloured lady.

The collections included more than 15,000 anatomical and pathological specimens, among them the 2000 items sold to the College by Charles Bell in 1824 for £3000. The shelves of the Playfair Hall bore rows of specimens in glass jars. At the corner of each bay, a mahogany box contained transcripts of the case notes relating to the patients from whom an organ had come. In the cupboards, bays and store were 3000 surgical instruments. They included a case made in Berlin and carried on the 6000-ton motor vessel *Die Grille*, the yacht given to Adolf Hitler by 'a grateful German people', together with many works of art, photographs, drawings, books, manuscripts, lantern slides, and cine and video films. On the walls of the adjacent Conference Hall was the copy of the Keir portrait of King James IV of Scotland, together with paintings of former College Presidents and distinguished Fellows. However, many of the College's works of art, including the paintings made by Medina between 1700 and 1705, hung in the corridors.

Progress

It was time to modify, develop and enhance the Museum halls and rooms.[10] The timber floor of the Playfair Anatomy Museum and that of the adjacent Hall was frail, leading to a suggestion that it might be protected by a covering made from the material used to construct aircraft wings. The roof wiring was replaced, while the obsolete installations of the 1908 Barclay Hall vanished when the new Dental Museum (p.326) was designed. I arranged for blinds to be installed in the Anatomy Museum and decided that the display cabinets and shelves of the main floor should be reconstructed. I knew that any new plan had to be approved by Scottish Heritage.

My intention was that the cabinets should be made mobile and fitted with removable shelving. Pilot models were therefore installed and the individual shelves restored. The results were encouraging. Each new unit would accommodate computer-based displays, but, when two or more units were moved, would allow separate work areas to be created. The Museum Committee tested the first 'mobile room' by meeting within it, and approved the concept, but then learnt that the College was at present unable to meet the cost of converting the remaining 12 display cabinets in the same style.

Joyce Wood and I began to reorganize the Museum laboratory, but our labours were delayed when she was called by the College to undertake alternative, essential work. The store demanded urgent attention, and I arranged for the floor to be cemented, the wiring and lighting modernized, exhaust fans to be fitted and radiators installed. Bruynzeel-style shelving then increased storage capacity fivefold, and I was delighted when the arrangements were approved by the Scottish Museums Council. In 2005, new stores were planned for a Quincentennial Hall (Figure 23.11).

Figure 23.11 *The 2005 Quincentennial Hall (at left); the addition, extended in 1884, to Playfair's 1832 building (at right) with the Lister building (in background).*

To allow access to the museum contents by visitors from around the world, it was clearly essential to construct a new catalogue in the form of a computer database.[L] We appointed Angus Whyte, a much respected PhD student of Strathclyde University, who continued with this work until 1995. With David Wilson's help, a first step was to review all the museum specimens, selecting those in irreversible decay for disposal and relabelling those to be retained in accordance with their new catalogue entries. The work was intensely time-consuming and to deal with those in the gallery of the Playfair Anatomy Museum took three years. Nevertheless, it was an opportunity to photograph each item. Meanwhile, Mr Gillan of the Edinburgh Gallery of Modern Art undertook the restoration of the Charles Bell paintings and Christine Bullock completed a similar task with the Menzies Campbell artwork.

The Museum continued to welcome donations of specimens, books, artwork and every kind of relevant artefact.[M] Lady Woodruff had donated a large proportion of Sir Michael's collection of medals and other items to the College, and I designed a display of his life's work.

New displays

My next step was to prepare new displays. I was aware not only that Museum specimens were used for postgraduate education and during Fellowship examinations, but also that the collections were scrutinized by consultant surgeons from all parts of the world. Any new exhibit had to be precise in terms of contemporary surgery while offering an accurate account of the relevant history and sufficiently simple to be understood by laypersons. I decided to add computer workstations to the new Playfair Hall displays, allowing visitors to read about the explanatory text while simultaneously enabling examiners to use the stored images as part of their questioning.

To construct the new displays,[N] I was fortunate to enlist the help of a small army of practising surgeons, each able to advise on a special field of surgery and surgical history. Tony Bleetman was outstandingly helpful, and later Robyn Webber gave much of her time to preparing a display on urinary calculus (stone). By 1999, 29 displays had been created, some in the Playfair Hall gallery, the majority on the main floor. The need for the skilled assistance of designers and artists was obvious. I sought the advice of Duncan Macmillan, Curator of the University Talbot Rice Gallery. During Peter Edmond's chairmanship of the Museum Committee, the Council allotted £250,000 enabling me to appoint a Graphics Artist, Michelle Patterson. She moved to the Art College in 1996 and was succeeded by George Ajayi, but before long support was no longer available.

The passage between the Playfair Hall and the Jules Thorn Hall was also reconstructed, the hundreds of items that lay on the crowded shelves removed to store. A team of 12 volunteers then created a new display entitled 'Edinburgh surgeons and war', with emphasis on the Napoleonic and Crimean campaigns and on the First and Second World Wars. I chose the display cabinets at the east end of the Playfair Hall to explain 'The laboratory in surgical practice'. With the completion of my work on the life of Henry Wade, a display of his 'Life and times' was placed on the stairway leading from the west end of the Anatomy Museum to the gallery.

Exhibitions

The idea of periodically mounting special exhibitions for the public was promoted in 1993 by Michael Esson, who became our 'Artist in Residence'. His drawings, inspired by the legendary John Hunter, formed a display at 9 Hill Square. On his departure for Australia, Michael presented the College with a portfolio of his works. I followed his example, and over the next few years, usually at the time of the Edinburgh Festival, we presented *The Art of Sir Roy Calne* (1994), *Breast Cancer Care* (1995), *Charles Bell: Surgeon, Physiologist, Artist and Author* (1996), *The Chloroform Sesquicentenary* (1997), *The Art of the Dentist* (1998), *50 Years of Surgery 1948–1998: The Origin of the British National Health Service* (1998), *Henry Wade 1876–1955* (1999)[11] and *Surgery Comes Clean: The Life and Work of Joseph Lister* (2002). To prepare the National Health Service exhibition, I was fortunate to have the help of 22 consultant surgeons. The exhibition, in the Sir Jules Thorn Hall gallery, was opened by the Minister of Health of the Scottish Parliament, Sam Galbraith[O] on 6th July 1998, fifty years and one day after the Health Service was inaugurated.

Scientific research

The Museum was a centre for scientific and historical research, particularly in disorders of growth and of the skeleton. Within the collections were the numerous skulls accumulated by David Greig, elected Conservator of the Museum in 1920, as well as many examples of conjoined twins and of spinal disease. In turn, each of these collections became the object of scientific enquiry, sometimes by Fellows in Edinburgh, sometimes by visiting scientists from Oxford and other Universities, and occasionally by workers from overseas.

My own investigations began when I found a human skeleton in the attic store at 9 Hill Square that, I suspected, might provide an answer to the mystery of why Arthur Conan Doyle had introduced an Andaman Islander into his famous tale *The Sign of the Four*. The disinterred skeleton had been presented to the Museum in 1879 by Dr E. S. Brander of the Indian Medical Service and had remained untouched for 120 years. With the expert help of colleagues in Oxford and Canberra, Australia, we were able to prove that the mysterious skeleton was indeed Andamanese (Figure 23.12).[12] The investigation occupied some years, but provided an example of how museums, with advantage, can exploit the techniques of cytogenetics.

On another occasion, the College was given the diseased shoulder of an elderly man who had developed a slowly growing tumour of cartilage, a chondrosarcoma. By the time it had been removed surgically, the neoplasm was more than 14 inches, 35 centimetres, in diameter, too large to be accommodated in the X-ray machines of the Royal Infirmary of Edinburgh. The patient's story led me to a report on a patient with severe disabilities whose case had been investigated

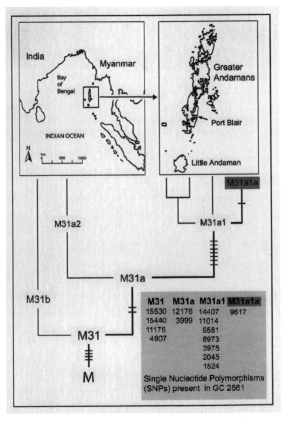

Figure 23.12 *A diagram showing the inheritance of the small skeleton that the author found in the College. The mutations present in the DNA of the RCSEd skeleton indicate membership of M31a1, found only in the Andaman Islands. (Reproduced by courtesy of the Journal of Medical Biography.)*

by orthopaedic surgeons, and, in passing, to Walter Scott's tale of *The Black Dwarf*, the dwarf of Mucklestane Moor.

In response to my enquiries, consultant endocrinologists from St Bartholomew's Hospital, London, sent us copies of the radiographs of the skull and hands of a giant who had come to this country for treatment of his anterior pituitary tumour. After the giant's death, the hospital forwarded microscopic sections of his adenoma. The display enabled us to construct an exhibit on 'Gigantism' and attracted much interest, in part because the giant's hands were twice the size of those of any visitor. While these studies were continuing, in response to a request from workers in Boston, Massachusetts, who were studying the mechanisms of congenital cardiac deformity, the specimen described in Chapter 10, an unique example of left inferior vena cava, was loaned to them. My microscopic slides from our cases of Thorotrast-induced cancer (Chapter 13) remained a focus of intense interest, partly because of their association with the surgical work of the eminent neurosurgeon Norman Dott, partly because of the possibility that other museum specimens might shed light on disorders such as bone cancers that might have resulted from the global spread of radioactive elements from events such as the 1986 nuclear disaster at Chernobyl.

Historical research

One of the interests of the Museum to me was the collection of microscopes, and I was privileged to be asked to give a College Christmas Lecture on 13th December 1993 on 'The magic of the microscope'. Preparing for this popular school outing, with an anticipated audience of 200 young people, I came across the tiny, modern instruments carried in the field by those pursuing the malaria parasite, a subject to which my father had given much time during the First World War (p.2). I had become familiar with modern methods such as those of laser scanning confocal microscopy during my research, and this talk to a young, enthusiastic audience allowed me the chance of contrasting the old and the new.

In April 1994, an invitation to speak to the West Linton Historical Society on 'William Fergusson: his life and times' took me into the life and times of a remarkable man who had overcome the disadvantage, as a student, of having assisted Robert Knox during the time of the grave robbers William Burke and William Hare.[p] To prepare this talk, Helen and I visited Fergusson's grave and found it in a ruinous state, the huge headstone covered with thick ivy. I persuaded the Tweeddale Council to undertake restorative work, which was not without drama – during their labours, the stone fell upon and injured a workman.

An increasing familiarity with the College collections and their history led me to the remarkable life and work of Henry Wade. Born in 1876, Wade served as a young surgeon during the South African campaigns of 1899–1902. He became a Fellow of the Royal

College of Surgeons of Edinburgh in 1903 and in the same year was elected Conservator of the College Museum. During the next few years, he undertook scientific, laboratory work of the highest quality and came close to anticipating the Nobel prize-winning work of Peyton Rous in which young Rous showed for the first time that a virus could cause cancer. My account of Wade's life was published in 2005.[11]

An invitation to speak to the Section of History of the Royal Society of Medicine on 24th April 1997 about 'Charles Bell and the faces of the wounded' drew me to the life and work of this remarkable man, a study to which I returned some years later in contributions to the Edinburgh Science Festival. Bell's surgical responsibilities during the Napoleonic campaigns of 1809 and 1815 played a part in the addresses I gave to the College Section of Accident and Emergency Surgery on 'Emergency surgery in war', to the University Department of Pathology on 12th March 1997 on 'War wounds: 1815 and 1915 – the contrasting experiences of Charles Bell and Henry Wade', and to the Probus Club of Stamford Bridge on 6th May 1997 on 'Surgery in the nineteenth century'.

Oral biographies

Complementing my own work and continuing to enlarge the College historical records, I was able to persuade a number of eminent senior College Fellows to record their reminiscences, among them Mr Noel Gray, Sir Michael Woodruff and Professor John Gillingham, CBE. On a more routine basis and conscious of the need to place our activities on record, I prepared Annual Reports for the Museum Committee, while, during my years as Honorary Conservator, I published three books[11,13,14] and a number of papers.[Q,15–18]

A conclusion

By 1999, I realized that College policy towards their historic Museum was changing, a reflection of the views of the Council. It was time to move on! I remained deeply grateful to the College for enabling me to extend my interest in medical and surgical history and for giving me an interest that I could continue late in life. Through the good offices of Professor John Gillingham, I was designated Conservator Emeritus.

CHAPTER 24

Looking back – the end of my path

The colour of life

To travel hopefully is a better thing than to
arrive, and the true success is to labour

Robert Louis Stevenson[1]

In this last chapter, I recall the circumstances in which I
became a pathologist. I then turn to my own memories, and
to recollections of my family and our friends. I describe the
holiday travels we made and, finally, express my thoughts on the
significance of our experiences and of the meaning of our lives.

I came to pathology, the study of the nature and causes of disease, by chance. The sequence of events that led to my profession
began because of the educational channels chosen for me by my
father. Greatly influenced by those I encountered as I made my way
through medical schools and hospitals in England and Scotland,
I decided to become a physician. But then, good fortune led to a
research appointment centred on laboratory skills, practised in a
university department of pathology. It was a short step to an established position in this subject.

The lessons I have learnt are not new. The pattern of our lives
is only in part determined by conscious choice, and the fact that I
met and was helped by such a variety of people in so many countries, was fortuitous. During the 70 years in which I was involved in
pathology, I was lucky enough to encounter and work beside very
many outstanding medical and non-medical laboratory scientists, of
a range of nationalities. It was also by chance that, over the years,
I observed or became aware of a remarkable range of fundamental
and technical discoveries.

> **Chapter summary**
> - The colour of memory
> - The colour of people
> - The colour of reading
> - The shades of writing
> - Paper and canvas
> - Theatrical scenes
> - Colour in print
> - Sporting colours
> - Family and friends
> - Reunion
> - On vacation
> - A celebration
> - Life's meaning
> - En fin

During my student days in Cambridge, my colleagues and I were close to
the new, quickly advancing knowledge of the blood groups, including the
discovery of the Rhesus factors. It was during these same, wartime years that
we saw the dramatic impact made by the new antibiotic, penicillin. As a
House Surgeon in the Royal Infirmary of Edinburgh, I read by chance of the

first use of corticosteroids in the treatment not only of endocrine deficiencies but also of common inflammatory disorders, which came to include rheumatoid arthritis. As young clinical pathologists, we learnt of the pioneering work of Frederick Sanger, who, in 1951, determined the structure of the insulin molecule. During my time in the United States, I was fortunate to meet the scientists at the Cleveland Clinic whose research led from the artificial kidney to the introduction of the autoanalyser, the computer-controlled instrument that took clinical chemistry from the classical methods of manual, 'glass-tube' chemical measurement to a technology that revolutionized the speed of hospital diagnosis. Some years later, I saw the automatic cell-counting devices that allowed the numbers of blood and other cells to be made quickly and precisely. Later again, encounters with scientists in Lancaster and Cambridge led me to an understanding of low-temperature electron microscopy and electron-probe X-ray microanalysis.

If discoveries continue to be made at the same pace as those I mention, what will the laboratory sciences, and in particular pathology, be like in the twenty-second century? It may be safely assumed that there will be revolutionary technical advances as striking as those that brought us the telegraph, telephones, radio (wireless), petrol-driven cars, prophylactic immunization and blood transfusion during the decades immediately before and after the end of the twentieth century. Magnetic resonance and other forms of imaging already permit a form of autopsy without the use of knives. Whichever advance comes first, I suggest that hospital pathology and its contribution to surgery will soon be altered beyond recognition when new 'microscopes' make it possible to identify the cells of diseased tissues and organs, and therefore to establish diagnoses, by methods that do not necessitate cutting into the body. With advances of this kind, we may anticipate radical alterations in pathological science and our approach to hospital care and admission.

Looking even further ahead, is it possible that all the major causes of human mortality – infectious and parasitic disease, cancer, malnutrition, trauma, heart and vascular disease – may be sufficiently controlled by the twenty-second century that the expectation of life, for both men and women, may increase to 120 or more years? Will pathology and pathological science no longer be necessary?

But will there still be life on Earth? Or will natural changes in climate, brought about by the accumulation of atmospheric carbon dioxide or through an accident of human behaviour such as nuclear war, bring the human race to an end?

The colour of memory

Memory is subjective and selective. We remember touch, taste and smell, but people, places and activities are recalled principally as signals that reach the brain from our ears and eyes.

And here I pay tribute to Roy Plomley, who demonstrated so well how individuals bring to mind the music they associate with the happiest or the most poignant moments of their lives. In his radio programme, *Desert Island Discs*, Plomley invited a range of speakers to picture their responses to music, were they to be castaways.[A]

I remember how a 78 rpm, clockwork-motor gramophone and a wireless with thermionic valves brought tranquillity and happiness to troubled times. I can still chant *I have a Song to Sing O!* from the *Mikado* of the 1930s. *Sheep May Safely Graze* brings to mind our times in Louth in the 1950s, just as the rousing tones of Eric Coates's *Dambusters March* are vivid reminders of the anxieties of the Second World War. But our greatest delight has always been opera, partly because of the work itself, partly because of the excitement of being among a captivated audience gripped by Mozart, Wagner, Verdi, Puccini or Bartók. *Der Ring des Nibelungen* and *La Forza del Destino* instantly bring back the sights and sounds of the Edinburgh International Festival; *Elektra* is an immediate reminder of Oldenburg; and, in a flash, *The Miraculous Mandarin* takes me back to an evening in Budapest, sitting among a cluster of Russian officers. Films such as *Amadeus,* rich in music, are as captivating as a televised performance of the Vienna Philharmonic Orchestra playing the *Radetzky March* and the *Blue Danube,* but cannot compare with the unique sensations of a live performance.

Thinking of Roy Plomley, I wonder how I might occupy myself on a desert island. Rather than choosing eight records of the *sounds* I loved best, I believe I might select recordings of my favourite *images*. Light, and particularly colour, unites all human life and pictures offer a wonderful way of recalling experiences, personalities, thoughts and literature, so that an arresting painting or photograph can be even more thought-provoking than a Chopin prelude or a Verdi aria!

> There is one important proviso. Those of us who have worked with microscopes are acutely aware that there are important differences between what we see when light is passed *through* a tissue slice, as it is with the transmitted-light microscope, and the views we obtain when light is shone *upon* such an object, as it is with a dissecting microscope. In our use of computer screens, we see pictures conveyed by *transmitted light*, whereas, in reading books, light shines upon the page and is *incident*. Is it possible that the brain interprets information conveyed in the former mode differently from images arising from the latter? Can it be that what we read from a printed page may convey a different meaning from the same message seen on a transilluminated screen?

The colour of people

At one end of the spectrum of human memory, we recognize the chosen few who have been so close to us that their personalities appear to extend beyond the visible spectrum, into *infrared* wavelengths. I picture my father, my mother and my brother Colin in their holiday clothes, Helen in her nurses' uniform, our children in the colours they wore to school. Other relatives, by contrast, I remember less happily as pale brown or even, sadly, as dull blue or violet! Some kind friends and colleagues appear in my imagination as roseate; others, mean or less generous, as faint purple or pale lilac. I can imagine images of notable criminals such as Hawley Harvey Crippen or infamous figures such as Adolf Hitler by picturing them devoid of visible light, beyond the range of sensation of the human retina and sensed only in *ultraviolet* wavelengths, invisible to the human eye or disappearing into darkness!

The colour of reading

My earlier chapters have told of the medical and scientific texts with which I was preoccupied. Beyond those already quoted, one of the finest remains *Diseases of Occupations*,[2] in which Hunter's text records the signs, symptoms and pathological processes resulting from employment and the extraordinary variety of ways in which, over the centuries, men have risked life and limb to feed their families. The power of Hunter's records is so great that, even with illustrations reproduced only in black and white, their impact assumes the warmest possible hue.

I am endlessly fascinated by learning of the struggles of the greatest physicians, surgeons, scientists and nurses and, through the printed word, have been able to picture each of them. William Osler,[3] Joseph Lister,[4] Charles Darwin,[5] Marie Curie[6] and Florence Nightingale[7] stand out, together with those like Thomas[8] and the Medawars[9] who wrote of the philosophy of Medicine and Science, pioneers whose views can be overshadowed, however, momentarily, by the inspiring but sometimes provocative works of Hawking[10] and of Dawkins.[11]

Dipping into Van Loon[12] and Schweitzer[13] was as close as I came to reading the story of my favourite composer, J. S. Bach. I picture Schweitzer himself, in his later days, struggling in the deep colours and primitive conditions of his French Congolese hospital. For quite different reasons, the revised version of Kobbé's *Complete Opera Book*[14] became a favourite in part because we discovered that the Earl of Harewood's marriage took place on the same day as our own!

Travel and adventure were different matters! Although I was never a mountaineer, the presence in our family home of several volumes recording the Everest expeditions of the 1920s were enthralling and I was drawn particularly to the exploits of Frank Smythe[15] and to those of Colin Thubron,[16] with either of whom I would have happily journeyed. It was perhaps for similar reasons that my favourite authors included Mann[17] and Forster,[18] and may explain why I found such delight in Dostoyevsky,[19] Hemingway,[20] MacLean,[21] Masters,[22] Pasternak[23] and Solzhenitsyn.[24]

In those of us born within a few years of the end of the First World War, the 'Great War', and at school during the Second, it was only to be expected that the records of campaigns and battles, recent and old, should remain with us for the rest of our lives. From the sunlit South Downs, I watched Spitfires taking part in the Battle of Britain, so it was not surprising that my early fascination with Winston Churchill's earlier tales[25] should quickly extend to the records of war published by Taylor,[26] Montgomery[27] and Keegan[28] and to graphic but fictional tales of war such as those of Tolstoy.[29]

Fortunate to come from a family where books were enjoyed, and benefiting from my Scottish and English inheritance, it was only to be expected, as my earlier chapters have shown, that Walter Scott, Robert Louis Stevenson, Jane Austen, Alexander Dumas and Anthony Trollope were often near my bedside, with Forster and Galsworthy not far away. In spare moments I enjoyed detective stories and placed Agatha Christie[30] on a pedestal, not because of her style but on account of the ingenuity of her plots. Conan Doyle[31] continued to come a close second, with Simenon[32] and Le Carré[33] jointly third.

But after all these works comes my favourite *The Story of San Michele*, Axel Munthe's masterpiece.[34] A multilingual Swedish psychiatrist, in a single volume Munthe captured the vivid colours of his life on Capri, his medical times in Paris where he studied under Charcot and encountered Pasteur's searches for a vaccine against rabies, and his moving experiences during an epidemic of cholera in Naples.

The shades of writing

As the years passed, I had little choice but to continue writing in the stark and arid hues demanded by medical and scientific journals and texts. However, as my time as Conservator of the Museum of the Royal College of Surgeons of Edinburgh, the RCSEd, drew to an end (Chapter 23), my fascination with the life of Henry Wade enticed me to biography,[35] a style in which I was free to employ warmer colours than in my scientific papers.

One reason for my interest in the life and work of this great man arose in part from his origins in Falkirk, West Lothian, not far from Helen's birthplace, Bo'ness, and from Bathgate, where my father grew up. Another was his purchase of Pilmuir House, East Lothian, within a few miles of Musselburgh, where I had been at school. There was also his outstanding work in cancer research during the early years when he was Conservator of the RCSEd Museum. The fact that he had been a recognized hero in the First World War after serving as a young surgeon in the South African campaigns of 1899–1902 added to the fascination of his complex life. I was pleased when the Royal Society of Medicine not only published my work in 2005 but awarded me an author's Certificate of Merit.

Paper and canvas

From the times of Prehistoric Man, colour has been integral to Art. The real delight of painting first came my way when Helen and I found ourselves in Haarlem on our honeymoon in 1949 (p.88). I enjoy painting and drawing, but have always confessed to being, by instinct, a photographer, perhaps because of the chance that gave me a camera when I was very young (Chapter 3). In London, the Turner Exhibition took me to the National Gallery in 1972, and a search for the works of Lowry[36] led us to the Whitworth Gallery in Manchester some years later. An exhibition of the work of Helen's artistic uncle, Ashley Havinden, was the occasion for a family visit in 2003 to the Dean Gallery, Edinburgh. We also met the distinguished impresario Richard Demarco and as recently as 2010 listened to his impassioned call for the Edinburgh Festival to be a true celebration of Art and Music, not of comedy and jazz.

Theatrical scenes

In earlier chapters, I tell of the fascination with which my mother viewed the theatre, particularly during her early life in London. I acted on stage at school and extended my taste for drama in my student days. Helen shared this interest and in London and in Manchester we enjoyed plays by Samuel Beckett, Noel Coward and Harold Pinter, as well as occasional Shakespearean productions. As a boy, the film *Snow White and the Seven Dwarfs* made a deep impression not only for its wit and fun but also for its early use of colour. *Henry V* and *Hamlet* were introductions to Lawrence Olivier's marvellous acting. It was early in the war years of 1939–45 that my mother and I saw *For Whom the Bell Tolls*, but Ingrid Bergmann made a further impact with *Casablanca*. My mother claimed to have seen *The Sound of Music* 12 times! *A Passage to India*, *Room with a View*, *Dr Zhivago*, *Lawrence of Arabia*, *The Wilmslow Boy* and *True Grit* are among those I still enjoy, and we have good reasons for loving the 1999 video *Joseph and the Amazing Technicolor Dreamcoat* (p.171).

Colour in print

Tissue pathology, histopathology and stamp collecting, philately, have much in common. Very many of the microscopic images viewed by pathologists in the course of their diagnostic duties come from sections stained with coloured dyes or from cells and tissues to which antibodies, labelled with coloured molecules, are attached. Following the discovery of the first synthetic dye, mauveine (aniline purple), by Perkins in 1856, postage stamps began to be printed with such agents (Figures 24.1–24.3), and it was during this time that tissue pathology started to benefit increasingly from the use of similar compounds. The vivid colours of synthetic organic dyes made a dramatic impact on both fields.

Figure 24.1 *The line-engraved one-penny black stamp of 1840.*

Figure 24.2 *The surface-printed, Die II, one-penny lilac stamp of 1881.*

Figure 24.3 *The five-shilling, bright carmine stamp of 1902.*

Sporting colours

Encouraged to play games throughout my schooldays, I learnt that even the most skilled or most dedicated sportsperson encounters a conflict of time should they choose to play competitive games while pursuing a profession. I played rugby football at school and, briefly, at university, but neither this game nor association football, soccer, was practicable later. I was never awarded a 'Blue'. Table tennis was part of my home life from our earliest days, but tennis, a game encouraged in Helen's family home by the grass court that was part of her garden at Bo'ness, was not so frequent. Golf was an invariable part of holiday times, and many of my older friends find solace in this game, which brings companions together on the many Scots courses and in the splendid clubhouses where, as the eminent neurosurgeon John Gillingham once remarked, 'all the significant political affairs of the City, and even of the Country, are decided'. To my regret, after suffering three prolapsed intervertebral discs, I was compelled to accept that to climb the steep slope of the Peebles golf course or even to approach the putting green at Kailzie was no longer practicable, and I gave my treasured Bobby Locke golf clubs to my son, Iain.

Family and friends

It was always clear that the competitive life of an academic pathologist would call for a degree of dedication that was bound to influence family life. For years, I found myself in the laboratory not only on many evenings but also on Saturday and even Sunday mornings. But no matter where we were, few of the successes of my adult life would have been possible without my happy and contented home and without the unfailing support of my wife and family. During our 62 years together Helen and I have enjoyed the inestimable delights of a daughter, Rosalind, and then of three sons, Iain, Philip and David. After Rosalind's marriage to Iain McQueen, the greatest blessing of these years was the birth, first of their children, David, Jane, Alastair and Robert, and then of our great-grandchildren (Chapter 22). The pleasure that came from our son Iain's success in medicine and his outstanding career as a consultant ophthalmologist was no less than that of meeting Lynn Morgan, whom he married in 1976. The tragic and sudden loss of our son Philip in 1979 (p.249) left a scar that can never fade. Cut short at the beginning of a promising career as a lawyer, his athleticism, literary talents and inquiring mind in every aspect of a young life remain almost too difficult to mention. Philip's younger brother David was faced with a challenge at least equal to those that Helen and I had to accept. David had grown up not so much in Philip's shadow but in his brotherly care, sharing the delights of sport and music and struggling consequently to overcome a particular sensation of loss.

Beyond our own immediate lives with their constraints and demands, we have enjoyed a great number of visits by relatives and friends, especially from my mother, my brother Colin and his wife Denise; from my cousin Jean Grieve; from close friends like Bill and Joan Hunt (p.134) and Margaret Daniel (p.101); and from medical and scientific colleagues from many parts of the world.[B] As part of the social scene, we received invitations not only to take part in events organized by the Medical Schools and Colleges with which I worked but also to a wide variety of occasions, of which the visit to the Royal College of Surgeons by Albert II, Sovereign Prince of Monaco, in 1997 was one; the reception in Edinburgh given in 2004 by HRH Prince Turki Al Faisal, United Kingdom Ambassador to the Kingdom of Saudi Arabia, another.

Reunion

With these recollections in mind, it was of very great interest to join the reunion of my fellow students of 1945–48 and to discover whether any of my friends had entered laboratory medicine. Few had become pathologists – many were general practitioners – and there was much discussion on how our chosen specialities had prospered. The year 1998 marked the 50th anniversary of our 1948 graduation (p.75) and this reunion we believed to be our last, partly because we had lived for so many years away from Edinburgh, but also because we were not as enthusiastic about large parties as some of our colleagues: I had not been to any of the previous 10-yearly gatherings. My friend Douglas Bell, formerly Secretary to the Scottish Medical and Dental Defence Union, the SMDDU, shouldered the burden of organizing the occasion, in which entertainment at the New Club and a dinner at the Royal College of Physicians of Edinburgh were happy events. It was inevitable that many of my fellow students were no longer present – none of us was less than 70 years of age – and I did not see Jock Keenan, Harry Coll or Colin Hay, while James Fraser had died in 1997. Others, including Robert Duthie, managed to attend in spite of serious illness, and Pat Brown had travelled again from Australia to be present.

In 2008, Douglas Bell was once more the moving force for a 60th-year reunion, helped by J. K. (Jake) Davidson. This time the dinner was in the RCSEd, and John Marks, who had at one point been Chairman of the British Medical Association, described in entertaining terms his experiences in medical politics.[37]

On vacation

As I explained, we benefited greatly from opportunities to attend Society meetings and Conferences in the United States and Canada (Chapter 12), in the Far East (Chapter 16), in Brazil (Chapter 17), in many parts of Europe (Chapter 19), in Australia (Chapter 20) and in the Middle East (Chapter 21). But there were always holidays both in Scotland and in England and we were frequently able to visit not only the Scottish Borders, the Highlands and West Lothian but also Somerset and many parts of Northumbria.

The freedom granted by retirement added the attractive possibility of journeys to parts of Europe and the Mediterranean that we had not seen before. The full records of our travels rest in my archives,[C] and here it is sufficient to mention briefly a selected few of the unusual places we visited during our travels and to offer a fuller account only of the adventure that celebrated our 50th Wedding Anniversary.

In 1990, we joined the MTS *Orpheus* on a voyage to Italy, North Africa and Spain, visiting Pompeii and Alicante. In Tangier, it was the Day of the Passover and so many lambs were being sacrificed that a large part of the sea near the harbour was coloured a dull red. From Casablanca and Marrakech, Cadiz and Seville, where we visited the Alcazar, the ship sailed to Lisbon and Oporto before a further voyage to Santiago de Compostela. At the Cathedral, we watched the spectacular Botafumeiro ceremony, in which a huge container of incense was swung in an ever-increasing arc across the transept of the cathedral, over the heads of the spellbound worshippers and visitors.

Following the tragic death from ovarian cancer of Florence Pike's daughter, Susie (p.312), we took Florence to Luxembourg in September 1992, en route to Alsace and Triers. Florence was an authority on wine, and we met some of her associates and visited a range of cellars. Beneath the Josef Friederich Gymnasium, an ancient school close to the vineyards, we saw the cellars through which the Romans carried vats of wine to vessels waiting on the waters of the Mosel. Returning home, Florence acknowledged that, for a few days, she had been able to overcome her grief. In August 1993, she came with us when we visited Padua and Verona, where we enjoyed a performance of *La Traviata* before driving to the battlements of the walled town of Soave, and then to the shores of Lago di Garda. From our hotel near Alba, in Piedmont we savoured a superb view across the hills of the Langhe and dinner at the nearby mediaeval Castello before visiting three of the principal wine producers. We returned home from Turin. A further holiday in Italy, in October 1995, took us all to Tuscany.

In June 1997, again accompanied by Florence, we sailed from Aberdeen to Orkney and the Shetlands. In Orkney, the Italian Chapel is a small but highly ornate Roman Catholic building on Lamb Holm. It was constructed by Italian prisoners during the Second World War. The captives were housed on the previously uninhabited island while they constructed the Churchill Barriers to the east of Scapa Flow. The coach drivers, speaking with articulate ease in their lovely dialects, gave gripping accounts of the history of the islands and of the Stone Age settlements that are seen both as forts and as huge, 5000-year-old monolithic rocks that enhance the landscape.

In September 1997, Helen and I journeyed to the Aegean on the MTS *Minerva,* sailing from Izmir on 10th September to a succession of Greek Islands. Skopelos came first, followed by tours of Thasos, Delos, Tinos, Syros in the Cyclades, Patmos, Leros and Samos. At Tinos, the Greek Orthodox Church of our Lady attracted great numbers of pilgrims, many of whom we watched crawling up the steep stone steps on their hands and knees, seeking the healing powers attributed to the icon discovered in 1822 at the time of the War of Greek Independence. A few hours at Symi led us to Rhodes and thence to Crete, where we saw the vast British and German Second World War cemeteries before an introduction to Minoan civilization during a morning at Knossos and an afternoon at Heraklion.

A voyage from London in August 1998 took us across Schleswig-Holstein to Latvia, Estonia and St Petersburg, which we had last seen in 1983. Our introduction to Riga and Tallinn and a further view of the Winter and Summer Palaces in St Petersburg (Leningrad) were of outstanding interest.

Florence Pike's 80th birthday fell on 6th December 2000, and on 14th November she came with us to visit the vineyards of Spain. In Barcelona, we ascended the magnificent cathedral designed by Gaudi. A voyage to Crete, Benghazi, Tunis and Carthage followed in May 2001, and in July 2003 we undertook a return visit to the Baltic, starting in Hamburg and travelling via Lübeck to Latvia, Estonia, St Petersburg, Copenhagen and Stockholm. A sight of the *Vasa* (Figure 24.4), the extraordinary warship built but capsized in Stockholm in 1628, remains my most vivid memory of this voyage. The vessel was salvaged in 1961 and a gigantic museum constructed around it.

We made our most recent venture to the Mediterranean in September 2004, sailing from Dover to St Peter Port in the Channel Islands, then to Bilbao and on to La Corunna, a fishing village in Charles Bell's time (p.329) but now a substantial coastal port. A visit to the wine cellars of Oporto was followed by the sight of the Gulbenkian Museum at Lisbon before we journeyed to Cadiz, Corsica, Naples and Sorrento.

Figure 24.4 *The Vasa, the huge Swedish warship that foundered shortly after its launch in 1628. The vessel was salvaged in 1961 and since 1987 has lain in the Vasa Museum in Stockholm.*

A celebration

In September 1999, we celebrated 50 years of marriage by flying to Istanbul to join the *Minerva* for a voyage to the Black Sea. At Suleiman the Great's picturesque Blue Mosque, the mosaics were concealed by echelons of bright lights. In the Basilica cisterns, made known to cinemagoers through the theatrical exploits of James Bond, we walked gingerly through the cavernous spaces on raised wooden platforms. The enormous cathedral of Hagia Sophia seemed to epitomize the fall of Constantinople in 1453, the walls now covered with Islamic plaques.

A voyage of nearly 500 nautical miles took us to Trabzon. One night, the ship was becalmed for two hours because of engine trouble. It was an opportunity to learn of the strange waters of the Black Sea and of the five great rivers that flow into it. Near the surface, the water is fresh, but, beneath, the deep waters are rich in poisonous hydrogen sulphide. At Trabzon, the sight of giant lorries carrying steel plates and cables and of a huge number of scattered, modern apartment blocks, gave a wholly misleading impression of the marvellous hillsides to which a bus soon carried us. The road was the beginning of the route through the Pontine Mountains to Erzurum. Transferring to a smaller vehicle, we reached the end of a mountainous trail and found ourselves climbing a precipitous mountainside until we were on the narrow terraces of the Sumela Monastery (Figures 24.5 and 24.6), built on a precipitous cliff face and notorious for having been the resting place of the icon known as the Black Virgin.

Figure 24.5 *The Sumela Monastery near Trabzon.*

Figure 24.6 *Visitors leaving the Sumela Monastery.*

We reached Sochi on 12th September. A visit to a tea plantation and a display of dancing by girls in traditional costume did not conceal the uncomfortable fact that the border with Georgia was closed – the country was at war with Abkhazia. Two hundred and fifty further sea miles took us to Yalta, with an immediate reminder of the 1945 meeting between Churchill, Roosevelt and Stalin in the beautiful, white Livadia Palace (Figure 24.7). The contrast with the seaside could not have been greater! Thousands of holidaymakers and tourists, with little planes taking off from and landing on the water; tea and coffee gardens; and water skiing, recalled Brighton beach (Figure 24.8).

By the next morning, we were at Sevastopol and the Malakoff Fort, fiercely defended by the Russians in the summer of 1855. The Sevastopol Panorama turned out to be one of the most memorable exhibitions we had ever seen. The walls of this huge circular building displayed a spectacular sequence of scenes from the Crimean War, while, reaching outwards, models of cannons, muskets and wounded soldiers created the closest imaginable replica of the original battlefields.

Figure 24.7 *The Livadia Palace at Yalta.*

The opportunity to stand at Balaclava, 17 kilometres from Sevastopol and a journey of many hours for horse-drawn artillery in 1854, offered a chance to see the spot where Raglan issued his infamous orders. And then on to Odessa (Figure 24.9), linked in my mind with the investigations of macrophages by Eli Metchnikoff but better known for the 192 Potemkin Steps that stretch upwards from the water's edge to the town. Two hundred miles further on, we visited Constanta, Varna and Nesebar. The sight of the flat coastline recalled the plight of the catastrophic British Army as it reached the Black Sea in 1854. At Çanakkale, a ferry carried us across to the Gallipoli Peninsula, where the isolated beauty of the steep shores remains in shocking contrast to recollections of the appalling slaughter of the First World War. From the heights, we could see the cemetery marking the landings of the Lancastrians in 1915, and a walk along the shores (Figure 24.10), at the site of the Australian onslaught, added to the insight we had gained from the 1981 film commemorating the disastrous campaign.

Figure 24.8 *Helen standing at the Visitors' Beach, Yalta, beside a gigantic penguin.*

Figure 24.9 *The Potemkin Steps at Odessa.*

Figure 24.10 *The Australian Beach at Gallipoli.*

The graphic items contained in the Turkish war museum were reminders that the suffering had not been by one country only.

Life's meaning

For many medical and surgical men and women, preoccupied with clinical tasks and the care of patients, retirement comes as a considerable physical and mental challenge. Some retired colleagues[D] occupy themselves with library tasks, acting as members of editorial boards to journals and continuing the editing of their successful textbooks. But I recalled William Osler's wise advice: 'Always have *slightly* too much to do!' and took a conscious decision not to decline into hibernation.

It is a mistake to assume that we can maintain physical health indefinitely. In 1998, I had experienced the prolapse of another but higher right-sided intervertebral disc, and in 2004 a third prolapse affected a high left-sided disc. The attacks were much more troublesome than the first in 1981 and resulted in muscle weakness, which was not helped when, one day, I caught my left foot on the edge of a pavement and tore my gastrocnemius muscle. It was suggested that some of my physical problems were attributable to osteoarthritis of my left hip joint and in 2009 I accepted the wise advice of the distinguished orthopaedic surgeon, Colin Howie, to have the joint replaced. The operation was a success and in reply to the kindly enquiries of family, friends and neighbours, I began to say that the large piece of metal in my left side had given me a magnetic personality!

Osler's words affected Helen at least as much as me. In a busy life, for many years I had been away from home for much of each day, leaving her to tend to innumerable domestic tasks and, latterly, giving her the time and freedom to meet her friends and to join the classes of the Edinburgh School of Extramural Studies. Confronted with the reality of a 24-hour day to be filled usefully and actively, I realized that there was a risk of taking the easy way out, of succumbing to the lure of the armchair and television. There was also the threat of losing contact with family, with friends and with former colleagues at home and in other parts of the country. I was reminded how valuable time was when, through the generous support of Professor David Harrison, my Honorary Fellowship in the College of Medicine and Veterinary Medicine was extended until 2012.[E]

En fin

At a moment when a new species of human relative, Denisovan Man, has been discovered in Siberia, I cannot escape the questions 'What is Life?' and the corollary 'What is Man?' Each time such a discovery is made – and many more can be anticipated – new light is thrown on the origins of the human race, the antiquity of Man extended, the diversity of mankind widened.

I have never consciously avoided these issues, but equally have never wholly escaped them by plunging into the world of religion. At school in Edinburgh (p.41), I had been confirmed within the Episcopal Church of Scotland. However, for many years, neither Helen nor I had played an active part in the life of any established religious organization. In Louth, we joined the choir for performances of Bach's cantatas. In Germany (p.97), the Army chaplains did not approach us; although we attended a performance of Bach's *St Matthew Passion*, this was a concert performance and we did not go to any local church or cathedral. In Manchester, we had little immediate inclination to attend the local church in Didsbury and seldom visited the renowned cathedral, although, in 1979, after Philip's death, I joined Grosvenor St Aidan's United Reformed Church (p.249). In Edinburgh, we lived within easy access of St Columba's Church, Blackhall, where, for some months, our children attended the Sunday School. However, I did not feel drawn towards the rather formal, even rigid, pattern of worship, although, later, I enjoyed the thoughtful sermons preached at the Parish Church in Peebles by the Reverend David MacFarlane.

I face the same difficulties confronted by so many of us. The first is to reconcile writings such as those of the Bible, the Hebrew Bible (the Tanakh and the Talmud) and the Koran, suggesting that life on Earth is relatively recent, with the scientific evidence demonstrating that the Earth, a planet of the Sun, is at least 4.5×10^9 years old and that human life, traced back through the hominids to the pre-hominids, has evolved from simpler forms of life over many millions of years. The second problem is to judge whether there is another being, a God of infinite wisdom and power who 'made the Earth'. A third challenge is to know whether to accept the concept that God rules a 'Heaven' to which all but 'sinners' may expect to be welcomed after the end of their lives on Earth. These are questions that began to form in my mind when I first became intrigued by astronomy. Later, approaching Stephen Hawking's writings[10] tentatively, I recalled James Jeans's books that were always at hand when I was a university student and compelling fiction like *The Black Cloud*.[38] I have never been in doubt that the boundaries of our universe extend to at least hundreds of millions of light years and that there are other universes, with boundaries reaching to infinity. The question remains: What *is* infinity? It has always seemed possible to me that within or beyond these universes is something or somebody whose nature and form it is not within our capacity to comprehend. Lurking in the background, therefore, is the instinct all of us possess, some expressing it more openly than others, that there is a force, a being to which or to whom we turn instinctively in times of deep mental or physical stress. This remote power or person, residing within or external to the known Universe, is God. It must be accepted that the human mind finds it difficult to survive without the idea of this intangible and ethereal 'other world'. The challenge I confront is one shared with many scientists, and indeed with a large proportion of the world's population. As I write, I notice, however, that Geza Vermes's *Jesus the Jew*[39] rests on my bookshelf beside *The Piltdown Forgery*,[40] reminding us that the deliberate misrepresentation of evidence has been used to distort scientific argument.

Notwithstanding these reservations, I have attempted to follow the writings of scholars including John Henry Newman and of philosophers ranging from Jean Jacques Rousseau (p.98) and Bertrand Russell to Brian McGee. In the same way, I have always enjoyed and benefited from the friendship of those who have committed themselves to religious belief more strongly than I have, in particular theologians I have known well. Charlie Moule (p.52) and Norman Leak (p.249) have been foremost among these good people.

Endnotes

Chapter 1

A. Thomas was born in the Gorbals, Glasgow, on 23rd November 1839. He died in Paisley in April 1900; John, born in the Gorbals on 25th May 1842, died in London in April 1897; Matthew, born in the Gorbals on 3rd January 1845, died on 17th September 1859; Archibald, born in the Gorbals on 18th May 1847, died at Wemyss Bay on 12th June 1925; Margaret, born at Laurieston on 17th February 1850, died on 29th March 1853; Dugald was born at Laurieston on 29 June 1852.

B. There was a close relationship between the Gardners and the Garroways. In 1883, Thomas Alexander Garroway married Catherine Muir, sister of Jean Muir, who would become Mrs Dugald Gardner. The Garroways had three children: Edward (Eddie), who entered the Merchant Navy but contracted rheumatic fever and died at the age of 21 years; Annie, who trained as a nurse and married Alexander (Sandy) Stockan; and Catherine Isabella (Ella), born on 15th May 1924.

   A family of cousins were the Rankins, of whom some moved to South Africa while others settled in Argentina. Nancy Rankin (pp.19 and 33) remained in this country.

C. Reverend John Lindsay was minister to what was then the Bathgate United Presbyterian Church. He became the Chairman of the local Education Authority. The Bathgate High School was named the Lindsay High School. On his retirement, John Lindsay lived in Midmar Gardens, Edinburgh, where his kindly wife, a lady of formidable presence and, to young children, commanding stature, presided over a fine Edwardian house with grace and generosity. My particular recollection is the tempting bowl of fruit she kept at the head of her staircase!

D. St John's United Free Church, Bathgate celebrated its centenary in 1912

E. A copy of the 60,000-word record is held by the Library of the Wellcome Centre for the History of Medicine. The diary begins on Christmas Day 1916 and extends to 15th February 1918.

F. A copy is in the keeping of the Royal College of Surgeons of Edinburgh.

G. Alfred Harry Young was born in Warrington in 1852. He became Surgeon to the Manchester Hospital for Consumption and Diseases of the Chest and then Surgeon to the Salford Royal Hospital, now the Hope Hospital, in 1883. In 1885, Young was appointed to the Chair of Anatomy at Owen's College, where he became Dean of the Faculty of Medicine. For a period, he acted as University Pro-Vice Chancellor. He died in Didsbury on 23rd February 1912, survived by his wife and by a daughter.

H. Herbert Welchman never lost his interest in fruit, and at Christmas time, during the 1930s, he was in the habit of sending his daughter Marjorie a long wooden box containing six jars of Tiptree jam. He became the proud possessor of a 20-horsepower Humber tourer, which he overturned accidentally in 1922 when he reached the dramatic speed of 50 mph: he was on his way to remonstrate with his army son Roger, whose mess bills, his father thought, were too large. Such accidents were frequent when motor vehicles first came into the hands of pioneers, and Herbert Welchman followed in the footsteps of Dr Arthur Conan Doyle, who narrowly escaped death in 1904 when driving his 12-horsepower Wolseley within the grounds of his own house.

I. Herbert Guy died in Winchester in 1940, Cicely in 1953. Marjorie (Welchman) Gardner had the following step-brothers and sisters:

- Ernest Guy, born in 1901, became a Lieutenant Commander RN and died in Madagascar in 1942

- Frances Audrey, born in 1902, in 1927 married a naval officer who became Admiral Sir William Andrewes KBE, CB, DSO. The Andrewes family is distantly related to Dr William Heberden, physician to King George III. Audrey died on 14 November 2006, at the age of 104.

- Philip Raymond, born in 1903, was a rather unsuccessful business entrepreneur. He did not marry, and died in 1962.

- Cicely Joan, born in 1905, married Nicholas Hurst in 1937. Awarded the MC on the Somme, he added a bar to his MC in 1921 during a campaign on the North West frontier of India when he was a Colonel of the 9th Gurkha Rifles, Indian Army.

- John Roger DSO, born in 1908, became a Colonel in the Welsh Regiment. As second-in command, he sailed from North Africa and landed at Salerno with the Yorks and Lancs during the Second World War. Subsequently he commanded the Sherwood Foresters, leading them in Italy. He spent time in Greece, and, when Germany capitulated, was stationed in Austria. In 1937, he married Valerie P. Riley of Minehead. He died in 1989.

- Norah Millicent, born in 1915, married Major Roger P. Williams in 1939, who we met in Germany (p.97). She died in 2004.

J. Marjorie was an ardent theatre and light-opera-goer, in London and in Brighton. She made careful notes of her theatrical and musical preferences. Among the D'Oyly Carte operas that she saw were *Iolanthe*, *Patience*, *The Pirates of Penzance*, *The Mikado*, *The Gondoliers*, *The Yeomen of the Guard*, *Trial by Jury*, *Ruddigore*, and *Princess Ida*.

Chapter 2

A. Among my father's friends was Dr John Gordon Thomson (1878–1937) who worked at the London School of Tropical Medicine from 1914 to 1929.

B. George Morgan LSA (Lond), MRCS (England), LRCP (London) was a gold medalist of Charing Cross Hospital Medical School. He went to Brighton in 1885 as a house surgeon to the Royal Alexandra Hospital for Children, where he was eventually appointed full surgeon in 1895, the year in which he became a Fellow of the Royal College of Surgeons of Edinburgh. His use of the title 'Dr' was a matter of convenience for a general practitioner: as a surgeon in England, he would have been addressed as 'Mr'. He died in Brighton in 1943.

C. As a young boy, Colin's ready smile won the hearts of our parents' many friends. Warm-natured, open and gifted, he benefited from a generous and outward-looking nature. In spite of a strong physique, he did not enjoy games. Instead, his talents lay in the theatre, music and literature. In 1944, he was called to the Navy, serving on a corvette. Colin's ambition was to be a farmer and he worked as an apprentice on a farm near Minehead. His next move was to attend the Royal Agricultural College at Cirencester to acquire the National Diploma in Agriculture. Then, in 1952, he met and married Denise Marley. Their children, John Peregrine Thomas and Philippa, were born on 10th January and 26th December 1953, respectively. Colin was appointed Manager of the BOCM Show Farm at Epping and joined the Farmer's Club, of which he later became a President. In 1968, he was given the responsibility for the sale of animal feeding stuffs to the entire North of England. Moving to Anlaby, Yorkshire, his challenges widened to a Unilever company retailing more than 15,000 agricultural products. He retired in 1987 to Nunburnholme, York and died in 2003.

D. *Little Lord Fauntleroy* was the first of the children's novels written by Francis Hodgson Burnett, an author of Anglo-American origin. The book came out as a serial in *St Nicholas Magazine* in 1885 and as a book published by Scribner's in 1886.

E. Derived from *Prontosil rubrum*, the agent discovered by Domagk, sulphanilamide, was the first commercially available drug capable of inactivating the streptococci of erysipelas, scarlet fever or maternal sepsis. With its use, the mortality of puerperal infection fell dramatically.

F. Penicillin was discovered by Alexander Fleming in 1929. Three days after the outbreak of war in 1939, Howard Florey (p.273), aware of the biochemical studies of Ernst Chain, applied to the Medical Research Council for a grant to support work on microbial antagonism. Enough penicillin had been produced in Florey's laboratory to allow clinical trials to start in 1941, but by the time I was a student in Cambridge (p.49), the drug was still so scarce that it was being extracted from the urine of wounded soldiers to allow it to be re-used.

G. In 1931, my father's sister Annie (p.7) became Matron of Bangour Mental Hospital, Broxburn, where she worked from 1914 until her retirement to Brighton in 1943. Retirement brought enforced and unaccustomed leisure and she died not many months later.

H. My father supported Nancy financially, and she was able, from time to time, to visit Brighton. Nancy lived modestly in Ardmillan Terrace, Edinburgh. She never complained of her poverty. When my wife Helen and I visited her in 1953, we found that her little flat was still illuminated by gaslight. Next to her kitchen was a recess no larger than a cupboard where, in a traditional Scottish manner, a bunk bed took the place of kitchen shelves.

I. In 1969, my father's trustees, the Bank of Scotland, accepted that Colin and I might purchase an annuity for our mother. We were each granted a one-half share of the trust capital, while she lived on a modest income from the annuity. My mother's cousins, Phyllis and Evelyn Milne, and my father's first wife, Muriel Milne (p.2), had inherited a little money from the late Thomas Guy Welchman. After Muriel's death, the residue had passed to Phyllis and Evelyn. Phyllis died in 1959 and, in another development, in 1978 Evelyn agreed to receive a single final payment.

Chapter 3

A. Douglas Arthur Crow was Ear, Nose and Throat surgeon to the Royal Sussex County Hospital and Consultant Otolaryngologist to the Brighton Infirmary. Like my father, Mr Crow had graduated from the University of Edinburgh and had been a Temporary Captain in the Royal Army Medical Corps. Crow was a man of unusual artistic and architectural sensitivity who had designed and built a beautiful modern house outside Brighton. When war was declared in 1939, he took his own life.

B. At the age of 17, two years younger than my brother Colin, Derek survived an attack of poliomyelitis while working in Ireland. The virus caused partial paralysis of one leg. He was treated at Stanmore Orthopaedic Hospital. Later, he studied law and became a partner in Woolley, Bevis and Diplock of Hove. He died in 2009.

C. A florin was a two-shilling piece, equivalent to 10 pence in decimal currency.

Chapter 4

A. Loretto House School, as it was at first called, was founded by the Reverend Thomas Langhorne in 1827, the year in which Thomas Arnold was appointed Headmaster of Rugby School. Reverend Langhorne retired in 1851 and was succeeded by three of his sons, the eldest, also Thomas, becoming titular Headmaster.

B. In 1854, Jules Verne, on his way back to France, reached London from Edinburgh in a 15-hour, non-stop journey for the price of two shillings.

C. Almond, Headmaster of Loretto from 1862 to 1903, was responsible for making the school a viable and admired twentieth-century institution and for establishing its philosophy.

D. An alternative, modern, version to which my attention has kindly been drawn by William Durran[7] might read: 'You've ended up with Sparta, see what you can make of it!'

E. I met Miss Jackson again in 1947 when I found that she had come to hold a similar position in the Edinburgh Missionary Society Cowgate Dispensary, where I lived for some months as a medical student (p.62).

F.   Burdened by a heavy frame, C. H. Stuart Duncan (Loretto 1910–14 and 1919–47) earned a mildly vulgar soubriquet. He was a serious and cultivated musician who undertook his duties with care and enthusiasm, mastering the production of oratorios such as *Messiah* with the same skill that he displayed when he accompanied chapel services and played organ voluntaries.

G.   When Reverend R. A. Goodwin left Loretto in 1940, to move to the south of England, it was to establish a public house. This was no surprise to the chapel wardens, who had observed that at the end of each Sunday morning service, Reverend Goodwin would consume all that was left of the communion wine, not an unusual custom; indeed, it was required of priests that all wine consecrated for a service should be drunk or destroyed.

H.   'Hutch', an outstanding teacher and sportsman, played for the Grange (Edinburgh) cricket club.

I.   As a teenager, I had collected scale models of naval vessels. A replica of HMS *Hood* had been one of my prized possessions. The warship held a special place in the affections of the public, carrying the Royal Family, politicians and dignitaries to every part of the world.

Chapter 5

A.   Clare is the second oldest of the 31 Cambridge colleges. Founded in 1326, the College was endowed a few years later by Lady Elizabeth de Clare (Lady de Burgh), granddaughter of King Edward I of England. In 1942, the life of the College centred on the seventeenth-century quadrangular building close to King's College chapel. Within this older part of the College were the Master's Lodge, the library, the dining hall and kitchens, and many Fellows' rooms.

B.   Bryan (later Sir Bryan) Thwaites combined his musical skills – he played the organ and sang in the Madrigal choir – with rowing. He became the first reserve for the Boat Race crew and vanished early each morning for their demanding training. His mathematical talents were employed by the Government during the Second World War and later he became Professor of Mathematics at Southampton University, Principal of Westfield College, London, and Chairman of the Wessex Regional Hospital Authority. We met again when he briefly joined the Board of Management of the Mathilda and Terence Kennedy Institute of Rheumatology (p.174).

C.   Ian Stoddart spent a long life as a general medical practitioner in Winchester and, fortuitously, cared for some of my mother's family who lived near him, at St Cross.

D.   David Cornelius Morley was the kind of friend who always seemed to stimulate activity, whether in the classroom of the Part II Pathology class or outdoors. His energetic personality led him into Tropical Medicine and he became Professor of Tropical Child Health at the Institute of Child Health, London. For his many original contributions he was awarded the CBE. He died on 2nd July 2009.

E.   Charlie was born in China on 3rd December 1908, his father a missionary, his great uncle a scholarly Bishop of Durham, his grandfather the first Principal of Ridley Hall, Cambridge. In 1951, Charlie's interpretation and exegesis of the New Testament culminated in his appointment to the Lady Margaret Chair of Divinity, the oldest Chair of the University of Cambridge and once held by Erasmus. Charlie played a leading role in the translation of the New Testament for the New English Bible.

F.   The word 'Tripos' was originally given to the final honours examination in Mathematics, and was in two parts: it derived from the name for the three-legged stool on which candidates sat. Later, the term 'Tripos' was extended to final examinations in other subjects. The Natural Sciences included those fields relevant to students of Medicine.

G.   The notebooks are now held by the Library of the Royal College of Surgeons of Edinburgh.

H.   Charles Sherrington shared the Nobel Prize with Adrian in 1932.

I.   One half of my Biochemistry Notebook 2 (1942) is devoted to theory, the complementary half to practical biochemistry classes

J.   Gowland Hopkins, who died in 1947, shared the Nobel Prize with Christiaan Eijkman in 1929.

K.   On his appointment as Clinical Pathologist to the Sussex County Hospital in the 1930s, Janes' annual salary was £300.

L.   Whitby's son Lionel Gordon Whitby became Professor of Clinical Chemistry and Dean of the Edinburgh Faculty of Medicine. We met during the planning of a teaching programme.

M.   Dean's Cambridge Department, first established in 1883, was a spacious building in Tennis Court Road. In 1922, he was appointed, under old regulations, to the Chair of Pathology of the University of Cambridge. The terms of his appointment meant that he was the last holder of a Cambridge Chair who had no retirement age, a fact that always caused him much amusement.

N.   In 1945, Alexander Fleming, Ernst Boris Chain and Howard Florey were awarded the Nobel Prize 'For the discovery of penicillin and its therapeutic effects for the cure of different infectious maladies'.

O.   Miss E. M. Bennett and R. D. Cundall, D. S. Kerr, J. W. MacLeod, H. Middleton, J. E. Phillips, R. T. Sears, R. S. Smith, E. F. Soothill and myself. Each of us qualified in Medicine during 1948 or 1949.

P.   Some years later, Dr Spooner left Cambridge and moved to a Chair of Microbiology at the London School of Hygiene and Tropical Medicine.

Q.   McCance was a leading exponent of physical fitness. He cycled 16 miles to work each day, ate no lunch and expected his younger colleagues to follow a similar regime.

R.   The University of Cambridge was the proud inheritor of a renowned School of Medicine the origins of which could be traced back to the fifteenth century. However, the subjects taught were *preclinical*; they included Anatomy, Physiology, Biochemistry, Microbiology and Pharmacology. By 1945, the disciplines had extended to include Radiotherapy, Clinical Chemistry and Haematology. Informal teaching in the *clinical* subjects of Medicine, Surgery, Gynaecology and Obstetrics was given by individual teachers to small student groups, but these disciplines, the backbone of the classical medical schools in London, Dublin, Scotland and Wales, had not yet been recognized formally.

Chapter 6

A. Michael Mills followed me in 1949 as Resident House Physician to Dr Fergus Hewat. After National Service with the Fleet Air Arm, Michael settled in general practice at Kingstanding, Birmingham. He died on 9th May 2010.

B. The Livingstone Dispensary was an integral part of the building of the Edinburgh Medical Missionary Society, inaugurated in 1841.[3] A first Medical Mission Dispensary had been opened in 1853 for the sick poor of the Irish community. By 1858, larger premises were needed and a whisky shop at 39 Cowgate was leased: it became The Edinburgh Medical Missionary Dispensary and Training Institution. The site included accommodation intended for students whose aims were to become medical missionaries, the pre-Reformation chapel and an almshouse.

C. By 1946, the only remaining part of the Livingstone Dispensary was the Magdalene Chapel. The Chapel had been sold in 1857 to the Protestant Institute of Scotland together with the land on which the Mission Dispensary and Training Institution came to stand. After the death of the explorer David Livingstone in 1853, a decision was taken to replace the dingy quarters of the old Mission Dispensary and Training Institution with a new structure opened in 1878 and named after him. Later, the Dispensary was absorbed into the National Health Service.

D. Dr John Brown, the son of an Edinburgh minister of the Church of Scotland, was the medical adviser to the eminent surgeon James Syme and subsequently to Joseph Lister and his wife Agnes, Syme's daughter. Dr Brown was a prolific and exceptionally fine essayist.

E. As a student, Colin Paterson Hay, from Stranraer, had returned to Medicine after a period in the Royal Air Force. After training positions in Cumbernauld and Leicester, he became a general practitioner in Doncaster and served as a clinical assistant in otolaryngology to the Doncaster Royal Infirmary until his retirement in 1988.

F. Among them was Douglas Bell, who entered general practice before becoming Medical Director for the Health and Safety Executive of Scotland and a member of the Council of the Medical and Dental Defence Union of Scotland. His friend James (Jake) K. Davidson came to be a consultant radiologist at the Glasgow Western. He was involved with the Clyde Tunnel workers in the late 1960s and was an authority on bone necrosis in compressed air workers and a leading member of the Decompression Sickness Panel. Another close colleague was John Richmond (p.124), who had been at school in England, worked closely with Sir Stanley Davidson and achieved distinction as a President of the Royal College of Physicians of Edinburgh.

G. James had come from Oxford, where he had flourished not only in physiology but also in golf – he was a golf 'Blue'. His father, Sir John

Fraser, had been Regius Professor of Surgery of the University of Edinburgh and Principal of the University of Edinburgh, but died in 1947. Like his father, James qualified in Surgery and became Professor of Surgery in Southampton. In later years, he was Postgraduate Dean of the School of Medicine and Surgery of the Edinburgh Royal Colleges.

H. Harry Coll was a little older than the rest of us and came to Edinburgh from South Africa. House Surgeon to Professor Robert Kellar (p.67), he settled in Llandaff, Cardiff as consultant paediatrician to the Merthyr and Aberdare Hospital group.

I. James (later Sir James) Rognvald Learmonth, Regius Professor of Surgery of the University of Aberdeen and from 1935 Surgeon to His Majesty the King in Scotland, succeeded Sir David Wilkie as Professor of Systematic Surgery in Edinburgh in 1939. In 1949, King George VI developed thromboangiitis obliterans and Sir James, accompanied by Dr Gillies, anaesthetist, and by his own theatre staff, performed the operation of sympathectomy on the King, at Buckingham Palace on 12th March.

J. Bram married a Scots girl and settled in this country, but died not many years later, in Aberdeenshire.

K. Alexander Murray Drennan succeeded to the University of Edinburgh Chair of Pathology in 1931 after leaving the Queen's University of Belfast (p.191). He retired in 1954, aged 70, but lived to be 100.

L. R. F. Ogilvie was an Elder of St George's West, Shandwick Place, one of the most prominent Edinburgh churches. He drove a black Austin Westminster car with the same steady, slow care with which he played difficult golf. His well-known text *Pathological Histology*, first published in 1943, was one of the first textbooks on this subject in this country to have every photomicrograph reproduced in colour.

M. T. C. Dodds was coauthor with me, at first with the late Professor Bruce Cruickshank, of *Human Histology*.[9] However, for me, the part he played in making possible the colour illustrations for my 1958 MD thesis and for his contributions to many of my scientific papers were of greater importance. In 1970, the late James (Jim) Paul, Dodds's longstanding and skilled assistant, wrote of his former master, listing the many books to which he had contributed (Chapter 11).

N. My Notebook 9, recording lectures given in 1947, is held in the library of the Royal College of Surgeons of Edinburgh.

O. Clinical tutors had two roles. In their hospital work, they were the equivalent of Registrars. In teaching, they were responsible for the systematic education of undergraduate students and assisted in coaching postgraduates.

P. Fergus Hewat was a veteran of the First World War. He represented an older tradition of medicine, dressed immaculately in black jacket, pinstripe trousers, high, winged collar, and waistcoat. He lived in Chester Street, drove himself to the hospital in a beautifully maintained, second-hand 1936 Roll Royce cabriolet, played golf with skill and was a kindly and generous physician whose references written on my behalf undoubtedly helped me to obtain later employment. Dr Hewat had been President of the Royal College of Physicians of Edinburgh from 1943 to 1945. He died in 1957, aged 73 years.

Q. Until the beginnings of the National Health Service, consultants to the voluntary, teaching hospitals gave their services for no financial reward, but depended on private practice for their income.

R. The old building was named after its 1906 red stone architecture.

Chapter 7

A. William Beveridge laid his Report[4] before the wartime British Parliament in 1942. It centred on his belief that the five great needs of our society – squalor, ignorance, want, idleness and disease – should be corrected. In 1946, Aneurin Bevan, then Minister of Health, introduced his National Insurance Act, and in 1948 the National Health Service was initiated.

B. Our qualifications had to be recognized by the General Medical Council. My degrees were MB (Bachelor of Medicine) and ChB (Bachelor of Surgery). I was a BA (Bachelor of Arts) of the University of Cambridge and became MA in 1950.

C. Professor Sir Edward Appleton succeeded Sir John Fraser, who had died in 1947, but he did not take up his position officially until 1949. As an undergraduate, I had heard Appleton speak in Cambridge (p.49) at a meeting of the University Astronomical Society. The world-famous physicist had agreed to explain his interpretation of the cosmos. I understood only his first sentence – his arguments were unintelligible to a medical student!

D. When I was one year old, my father had prudently taken out insurance policies on my life and on that of my brother. The annual premium was £21. The policies accumulated annual bonuses, and 50 years later my policy was worth £15,000. It was a lesson I passed to our sons and daughter.

E. Before the Second World War, a resident House Physician or House Surgeon was given 'board and lodging' in the hospital, but neither a salary nor an honorarium. Clinical Tutors were paid £35 per annum.

F. My contemporaries included Seamus Burke, a Resident Anaesthetist and an 'elder statesman'; J. K. ('Jake') Davidson (p.345); Lindsay Davidson, who became a Professor of Medicine in Africa, but died in 2011; Lindsay Wilkie, who settled in Australia; John Gould, who attained qualifications in Medicine and in Dentistry and became Dean of the Faculty of Dental Surgery of the Royal College of Surgeons of Edinburgh; and Sir James Fraser (p.65), who succeeded to the Presidency of the Royal College in 1982.

G. In 1948, before the days of sterile plastic bags, blood collected from donors was stored in glass jars.

H. The possibility of replacing a diseased kidney by transplantation did not become realistic until after 1966, when Michael Woodruff (p.157) undertook the first operation in this country.

I. Robert Mahler entered the field of clinical chemistry and moved to Guy's Hospital, London. He gained the Chair in this subject in Cardiff before returning to London. He became Editor of the *Journal of the Royal College of Physicians of London*.

J. W. Quarry Wood had been one of my father's examiners in 1924 (p.7). He was an enthusiastic fisherman. One day, travelling to a hospital in the Scottish Borders, he was seen to leave his car and wade into the nearby River Tweed, hoping for a salmon. But he had forgotten to remove his bowler hat! At his retirement dinner, he was presented with an inscribed silver tray, in the centre of which the 'river scene' had been carefully engraved.

K. David Tulloch had come from military service to take up medicine. Later, after graduation, he established a successful general practice in Great King Street, Edinburgh. One of his interests was in old cars: wearing a bowler hat, he could be seen driving a beautiful 3½ litre open Bentley through the city streets. I encountered him again some years later (p.158).

Chapter 8

A. The Infirmary Residency mess had a quaint, semi-serious organization of its own. There was a Mess Chairman, a Treasurer and a Secretary.

B. Ashley Eldred Havinden (1903–73), married to Helen's aunt Margaret Kirk Sangster, was a distinguished modern artist who achieved fame in the world of advertising. An exhibition of his life's work was held in the Scottish National Gallery of Modern Art in October 2003.

C. The ancient city of Haarlem was the birthplace of Franz Hals, one of our favourite artists, and the Museum contained his *Officers of the Guild of Arquebusiers*.

D. In Edinburgh, London and Dublin, the Royal Colleges of Physicians offered Membership by examination, as did the Royal College of Physicians and Surgeons of Glasgow. The Membership examinations of the United Kingdom are now combined to offer an MRCP (UK).

E. John Pike, DFC and bar, a schoolmaster before the Second World War, had been an outstanding bomber pilot in the Royal Air Force. He married Florence Harrower in 1945. After the War ended, he became Bursar to Westminster School, London, and then moved to a similar position at Ashridge College, Berkhamstead.

F. Charles Albert Lillicrap became Mayor of Lincoln in 1956. He died suddenly in 1969.

G. John Halliday Croom, a fine clinician and a kind and skilled teacher, was the son of Sir John Halliday Croom, who had been Professor of Midwifery of the University of Edinburgh from 1905 until his retirement in 1921.

H. It was with great sadness that some months later we heard of her premature death from cancer. Tommy Morgan died in early 2009.

I. Notebook I: varied material; Notebook II: signs of disease such as Cheyne–Stokes respiration and jaundice; Notebook Δ: fevers and infectious diseases; Notebook S: atrial fibrillation, renal failure, gastric hyperacidity and endocrine disorders; Notebook X: surgery of lung abscess and pulmonary tuberculosis, bronchial stenosis; Notebook Z: abstracts of journal articles. My last MRCPEd Notebook, inscribed 'Helen Harrower, Hygiene (Linklater)', ranges from parathyroid disease to scabies and impetigo.

Chapter 9

A. In 'diversionary answering', the trick is to thank a questioner warmly and then to move subtly to an unrelated topic. It is a method widely employed by politicians dealing with television interrogators.

B. My brother-in-law, John Pike, DFC (Chapter 8, Note E) had been appointed to the staff of Ashridge College following his time as bursar to Westminster School, London.

C. Hamburg, a city of two million souls, was the capital of the Hanseatic League, a city familiar to readers of Thomas Mann's *The Magic Mountain*.[10] Hamburg shipyards had constructed many great liners and during the war, had built the infamous battleship, the *Bismarck*. The Universities, schools and hospitals were known internationally, the suburbs affluent. There was an excellent golf course, designed in the 1930s by an Englishman, and a large zoo. However, by 1950, Hamburg had not recovered from the 1943 'blanket' bombing and subsequent firestorm. Throughout Germany, almost one-quarter of all housing had been destroyed and in Hamburg the proportion was much greater. By 1950, although much had been done to restore buildings and roads, the destruction that remained was almost as great as the devastation that followed the 1945 atomic bombing of Hiroshima and Nagasaki. Vast areas were desolate and for four or five miles, roads from the city centre to the suburbs were still lined with piles of rubble, 50 or 60 feet high.

D. The widely spaced, three-storied hospital blocks had many large windows. A vast central heating system based on a huge boiler house sent hot water to the wards where double or triple glazing guarded patients from the winter. The ground floor of a redbrick administrative block contained the offices of the Commanding Officer and the Registrar, together with a library of useful contemporary medical works. The block also contained accommodation for the QAs.

E. Large numbers of houses were requisitioned from the German population. We never discovered to whom our property had belonged.

F. One of the most short-sighted decisions of a post-Second World War British Government was their failure to take over the Volkswagen factory sited in the British Zone of Occupation. Had Britain assumed control of this factory, there is little doubt that within three or four years we would have owned a significant part of the European car manufacturing potential. As it was, the Government and the people lived to regret a weak decision, watching Volkswagen rise to dominance in Western and Eastern Germany, in South America and in other parts of the world.

G. Sadly, Bill's hereditary deafness, already a handicap, contributed to his premature retirement in 1972. He died in 1980 aged only 55.

H. After the War, the Army was confronted by the loss of many long-serving RAMC officers who had been demobilized or retired, who had returned to civilian life, or who had moved to other occupations. There remained a smaller number determined to continue their career. Many had served in Europe or the Far East. Some had been prisoners. These officers were faced with the challenge of working with young graduates fresh from hospital training in the United Kingdom and with no understanding of the physical and mental stress to which their seniors had been subjected.

I.   After the Second World War, the Duchy of Oldenburg had merged with Lower Saxony. The city of Oldenburg lay in the lowlands of the North Sea. It was a charming town of 100,000 inhabitants situated in the flat country near the Dutch border and the Ems–Weser Canal. Oldenburg was a centre of food processing and light manufacturing industries, within easy reach of Bremen.

J.   Michael Brudenell became a consultant at King's College Hospital and attended Princess Margaret.

K.   After leaving the Army, George who had been serving a four-year 'Short Service' commission, joined Lederle, a pharmaceutical firm in the United States. He and Ruth moved to North America, where they settled in Suffern, New York State.

Chapter 10

A.   Pathology, as my Preface emphasizes, a broad term extending to the science or study of disease (SOED), is often confused in the public mind with Forensic Pathology.

B.   NAAFI – the Navy, Army and Air Force Institute, the trading organization of the British armed forces.

C.   The use of laboratory science to help in the diagnosis and treatment of disease developed slowly, so that by 1878 only one London hospital had the facilities to conduct scientific enquiries into the nature of a disease.[5] In 1939, the country had no more than 85 pathologists, in contrast with 500 physicians and 1100 surgeons. After the Second World War and with the establishment of the NHS, the numbers grew quickly, and by 1960 there were 725 pathologists compared with 2280 physicians and 2040 surgeons.

D.   A. M. B., as we called him, was a man of immense knowledge, talent and learning. He had come from the London Hospital, where he had been a contender for the Chair of Pathology when it was filled by Dorothy Russell. Such was his popularity and the respect in which he was held that, after his relatively early death, past and present Junior Assistant Clinical Pathologists combined to make a generous presentation to Mrs Winifred Barrett.

E.   Gleeson White was an ex-serviceman who had returned to civilian practice. Because of the standard reply he tended to give to those asking his advice, he was often nicknamed 'sub it and see!', a reply indicating that a bacteriological specimen should be subcultured.

F.   N. R. Laurie (1906–60), a quiet, unassuming man of whom we saw relatively little, had an involuntary habit of raising his eyes to look upwards as he spoke. Some years later, as he developed and then died from a cancer of the adrenal glands, we wondered whether the ocular tic had been a preliminary sign of the malignancy.

G.   John Marks was a consultant to the Cambridge Maternity Hospital, from which many requests came for studies of blood. There was close collaboration between the Hospital's Haematology Laboratory and the University department, where Race and Taylor had conducted pioneer work into the nature of the Rhesus (Rh) factor, first described by Sanger.

H. Dr Anthony George Ackerley became Consultant Pathologist to the Leicester Hospital Group. He died in 1997. Dr Frederick Ephraim Dische was Consultant Pathologist to Dulwich Hospital, London. Dr David Derek Gellman qualified as a physician and moved to the United States in 1956 and then to Winnipeg, Canada. He died in Vancouver in 2003. Dr Hugh Middleton became a Medical Registrar in 1952, but died suddenly in 1956. Dr Christopher Sotheby Pitcher was later to be Consultant Haematologist to Stoke Mandeville Hospital, Aylesbury. Dr Richard Wellesley Spencer practised as Consultant Chemical Pathologist to the Cornwall and Isle of Scilly District Health Authority.

I. My lifelong friend Geoffrey Austin Gresham worked closely with A. M. Barrett and became Professor of Morbid Anatomy and Histology at the University of Cambridge, Honorary Consultant Pathologist to Addenbrooke's Hospital, Cambridge, and Home Office Pathologist to East Anglia. He died on 23rd July 2009.

J. Dr John Horsman Rack worked in Cambridge until 1967, when he became Consultant Pathologist to the Norfolk and Norwich Hospital Authority. I discovered in the course of a visit to him in Manchester in 1956 that he was an aficionado of Schubert's songs. He died in 1995.

K. The collection of bone marrow was in theory a simple and safe procedure that called for the injection of a little local anaesthetic into the skin of the chest wall and the insertion into the underlying bone of a very short, sharp wide-bore needle with a 'guard' preventing the needle from penetrating more than one centimetre.

L. Some years later, our paper became the object of international controversy when a group of clinical anatomists wrote from Boston, Massachusetts, to ask whether they might examine the heart themselves. With due care, the organ was carefully packed and sent across the Atlantic. It was safely returned and now rests in the museum of the Royal College of Surgeons of Edinburgh. The Americans then wrote to ask whether we would revise the descriptions we had made at the autopsy since our report of a left inferior vena cava was not compatible with their theory of cardiac development. I explained that to alter an anatomical record prepared under the direction of Dr A. M. Barrett would be unethical and wrong.

M. The Pathological Society of Great Britain and Ireland, the 'Path Soc', played an important part in our young lives as aspiring pathologists in training. The reason was simple: the Society was a forum in which our work, presented as simple, short talks or as 'demonstrations' displayed on boards to be viewed and read, could be heard and seen by all Society members. They included not only those in training and others who were consultants within the NHS or in a University Department, but also the most influential members of the profession, in whose hands rested decisions on promotion and appointment. Presentations to the Society were therefore an important part of the competition for positions in every part of the country. Among those I first encountered at that time were W. St C. Symmers (p.175) and Bernard Lennox. I also met a future friend and colleague, Kenneth Walton (p.180).

Chapter 11

A. The College of Pathologists (Chapter 10), granted a Royal Charter in 1970, was not founded until 1962, so Membership only came to concern me later.

B. A Senior House Officer received £852 per annum, with £150 per annum deducted for board and lodging.

C. After the Second World War ended, Professor Stanley (later Sir Stanley) Davidson concluded that the rheumatic diseases were dangerously neglected. J. J. R. Duthie accepted one of the Senior Lectureships created to address this deficiency and was given the responsibility for developing Rheumatology at the Northern General Hospital, where he was made Physician in Charge and Director of Research. In 1964, the growing prestige of his scientific investigations led to his promotion to Reader and, in 1968, the Arthritis and Rheumatism Council provided sufficient support to allow the University of Edinburgh to elect him to a personal Chair in Medicine (Rheumatology), a position from which he retired in 1977.

D. Rowland Alexander died suddenly in 1971 at an early age.

E. George Lightbody Montgomery rose to the rank of Brigadier during the Second World War. He came to Edinburgh from the Chair of Pathology at the Glasgow Royal Infirmary. Not long after his arrival in the University of Edinburgh, he succeeded to the office of Dean of the Faculty of Medicine.

F. Bruce Cruickshank accepted a Senior Lectureship in Pathology in Glasgow in 1956. Not long afterwards, he was appointed to the Chair of Pathology in the Medical School of Salisbury, Rhodesia (Zimbabwe), subsequently becoming Professor of Pathology at Sunnybrook Hospital, Toronto. After retirement, he settled in Ontario and finally in California.

G. Aged 14, TC Dodds began work as an Edinburgh technician in 1921. At that time, an external, wooden stair reached up to the pathology and microbiology laboratories (p.125). One day, he passed Professor Ritchie, who said: 'Get out of my way, boy.' Characteristically, Dodds replied 'Get out of <u>my</u> way! Dodds illustrated *Human Histology* (Churchill Livingstone). With him, I completed the 1964 and 1968 editions in collaboration with Bruce Cruickshank, the third, without Bruce, in 1976. Dodds was awarded the Rodman Medal, the Lancet Trophy and posthumously, the Combined Royal Colleges Medal.

H. Douglas Henry Collins was Professor of Pathology of the University of Sheffield and the author of a standard text on articular and spinal diseases. A kindly personality, he was a music lover and played the cello. He died suddenly in 1964 aged 57.

I. Caragheenin, a polysaccharide prepared from seaweed, caused mild inflammation when injected into animal tissues. It could be sterilized and was a convenient agent for provoking experimental arthritis. To examine the cells that were part of the inflammatory response, I chose to place a cylinder of the material in the peritoneal cavity of a rat. It happened one day that no suitable glass tube was available and I chanced upon cigarette papers. The reaction was astonishing! Cigarette paper, it transpired, was acutely inflammatory! I conveyed this to the tobacco manufacturers, suggesting that they might like to provide money to allow this discovery to be pursued further, but received no reply from them.

J. I came to know and respect Dr Agnes MacGregor, Senior Consultant Pathologist to the Royal Edinburgh Hospital for Sick Children, when we were co-examiners for the Fellowship of the Royal College of Surgeons of Edinburgh, the RCSEd (p.328).

K. Clement Bryce Gunn entered Heriot's Hospital (Heriot's School) in 1869, aged eight. Matriculating as an Edinburgh University student in 1876, one of his fellow students was Arthur Conan Doyle, of whose intellectual prowess Gunn had a low opinion. Clement Gunn's recollections of Joseph Bell the surgeon, the prototype for Sherlock Holmes, were very different and he wrote of Bell with admiration.

L. Centred on what had been a Georgian house, the history of which can be traced back to King David II in 1296 and now owned by Angela, Lady Buchan-Hepburn, the nearby grounds include an ornithology centre, a putting green and a fishing pond. In the huts, enthusiastic birdwatchers can use television to follow the migration and nesting of ospreys.

M. Wilfrid (Bill) Estridge Hunt, born in 1917, was educated at Wellington College, Berkshire before moving to Trinity College, Oxford in 1935 to study Medicine. From the London Hospital Medical College, Whitechapel, Bill qualified BM (Oxford) in 1942 and was commissioned into the Royal Army Medical Corps, but was prevented from joining the D-Day landings in 1944 because of a knee injury. Leaving Queen Charlotte's Maternity Hospital, London, he moved to St Mary's Hospital, and in 1954 was appointed Lecturer in Pathology in the University of Edinburgh, where he remained until 1966. He died in 2001.

N. Angus E. Stuart possessed a highly original mind and the enthusiasm for quickly advancing areas of medical research, particularly those related to the immune system and the cells responsible for the defences of the body against disease. Angus had graduated from Glasgow in 1948 and, after a house appointment and service with the RAMC, held hospital posts in pathology in Melbourne and Tasmania. In 1954, he returned to Britain and, after positions in the Universities of Glasgow and Dundee, was appointed Lecturer in Pathology at the University of Edinburgh in 1955. A travelling Fellowship to the Institut Pasteur and Broussais Hospital in the University of Paris followed in 1958. In 1960, he became a Senior Research Fellow at the University of Edinburgh, and a Senior Lecturer in 1966. He was promoted to Reader in 1967, before moving to the Chair of Pathology at the University of Newcastle upon Tyne in 1978.

Chapter 12

A. Harry Goldblatt was one of the most influential of twentieth-century experimental pathologists, described as 'the cleverest scientist not awarded a Nobel Prize'. In 1934, his work led to the properties of renin being clarified, paving the way for the demonstration of angiotensin and angiotensinogen.

B. The autoanalyser was an instrument in which the cells of a blood sample were separated from the fluid (plasma) by dialysis, allowing the automated measurement of the chemical constituents of the fluid. The principle was soon adopted in hospital laboratories.

C. Willem Johan Kolff had constructed the world's first effective artificial kidney during his wartime research in the Netherlands. He moved to the Cleveland Clinic in 1950, before becoming Director of the Institute of Biomedical Engineering at the University of Utah in 1967.

D. Western Reserve University became Case Western Reserve University (CWRU) after merging with the Case Institute of Technology.

E. Strongly influenced by Harry Goldblatt, Howard Karsner and Enrique Ecker, Alan Moritz was appointed as Pathologist-in-Charge of the University Hospitals of Cleveland in 1931. In 1937, he moved to Boston to the first American chair of legal medicine, the George Burgess McGrath Professorship at Harvard, before returning to Cleveland in 1949.

F. Cleveland was an industrial city of some two million people.

G. Jeff graduated from WRU and specialized in Rehabilitation Medicine. He moved from Syracuse to Chicago, then to Pittsburgh and to Philadelphia. He and Barbara visited London in 1989 and Edinburgh in 1998. He died from pancreatic cancer in March 2005.

H. Dr Byrom visited the Kennedy Institute during the late 1960s. When he retired, he gave me the beautiful Zeiss operating microscope that the Medical Research Council had provided for his experimental surgery.

I. After leaving college with a first degree, it was customary in 1959 for American medical students to attend four years of medical school classes before graduating MD. However, a select number added three years of research to their studies so that they qualified MD, PhD. As a final year MD/PhD student, Neil had a grant of $30,000 for a summer project. Using this grant, he had recruited seven student helpers.

J. My Notebook Φ is entitled *Experiments on Blood Vessels Made in the Laboratory of Dr EH Bloch, Physiology Department Cleveland Western Reserve University, Cleveland, Ohio, Head: Dr George Sayers Ohio during March–April 1959 and July–August 1959.*

K. My new colleagues included Drs Reegan, Lowell W. Lapham, Bolande, Ross, Arquilla, Krieg, Leonard, Abbott, Schoenberg, Clemmons, Chapnick, Haines, Moore, Kahn and Hammond. Among the younger trainees, I made many friends. Art Krieg became particularly close.

L. My notebooks give details of the graduate teaching sessions on pathology and histopathology and details of the Cleveland methods of teaching, classes, training of residents and supervision of research. The teachers included Moritz (Chairman), Reagan (gynaecological pathology), Bolande, Koletsky, Ebert, Ivemark, Moore, McCorkal, Peterjohn and Lapham (neuropathology). On 27th September 1958, Alastair Currie was a visiting speaker.

M. Attending the American Association of Pathologists (Notebook D) cost me $32.70.

N. Speakers at the lymphocyte course were Gross, Bloom, Sundberg, Ackerman, Low, Hamilton, Bollman, Harris, Dougherty, Schrek, Jones, Schwartz, Custer and Brewster.

O. Donald Bunce wrote to me in May 1989 to tell me he had developed a metastatic carcinoma.

P. In 1971, Dr King invited me to the Pathobiology Conference in Aspen, Colorado, but I could not attend.

Q. Feroze Ghadially, a man of extreme originality and talent, was a Parsee. He explained to me how, arriving in London with no job, he became a violinist with the London Symphony Orchestra. He was also a sculptor and had exhibited his work nationally.

Chapter 13

A. My salary was £2400 per annum.

B. Andrew Shivas had been in the Merchant Navy. He was a versatile histopathologist, and also a skilled musician, said to have been able to play every instrument in the orchestra. Andrew preceded Ian Skinner Kirkland as Conservator of the Museum of the Royal College of Surgeons of Edinburgh (p.321).

C. A Cambridge and St Thomas's graduate, Nigel Harcourt-Webster and I shared many interests. He moved to St George's Hospital Medical School, London in 1966, then as consultant histopathologist to St Stephens Hospital in 1970. He died in 1998, aged 68.

D. As I describe in Chapter 6, the name 'Earngarth' appears in Gibbon's *Decline and Fall of the Roman Empire*.

E. Tom Dodds became Director of the Department of Medical Illustration in 1962.

F. During his time as a Japanese prisoner of war, Michael Francis Addison Woodruff used his skills to make a grinding machine allowing grasses to be turned into a life-saving food for the starving inmates. An interest in skin grafting led him to concentrate on the concept of transplanting tissues and organs to replace those destroyed by disease. He was appointed Professor of Surgical Science in Edinburgh in 1957. It came as no surprise when he decided to risk his surgical future by attempting the first British renal transplant. Michael Woodruff achieved international recognition, was elected a Fellow of the Royal Society of London in 1967 and knighted in 1969. Yet behind a façade of confident, worldly success I learnt much of the inner powers of this scholarly, deeply religious Wesleyan Methodist friend and colleague when, during his retirement, we talked together shortly before he published his memoirs.[3]

G. John (later Sir John) Crofton was President of the Royal College of Physicians of Edinburgh from 1973 until 1976. He died in 2009.

H. East Fortune, a village in East Lothian two miles northwest of East Linton, was known for an airfield constructed in 1915 to help protect Britain from attack by German Zeppelin airships. In 1919, the British R34 made the first airship Atlantic crossing from this field to

Mineola, New York. In 1922, the hospital was opened as a tuberculosis sanatorium. When the Second World War erupted, the airfield came into service with the RAF and the patients were taken to Bangour Hospital. The hospital re-opened after the war, but as tuberculosis declined, the hospital was chosen in 1956 to house the mentally handicapped. It closed in 1997.

I. Christine Laing completed her PhD thesis in 1964 and left Edinburgh, moving to North America, where she was recruited in 1974 by Dr Weeks in Vancouver.

J. The injection of Thorotrast was a new approach to finding defects in the arteries of the brain. Interest centred on the fact that thorium was opaque to X-rays – Thorotrast within arteries could be seen quite clearly, allowing pathological lesions in the blood vessels to be recognized. The problem, overlooked when Thorotrast angiography began, was that the element thorium is radioactive as well as radio-opaque. It has a half-life of 10^{10} years.

K. As mentioned in Chapter 11 (Note N), Angus Erskine Stuart made innovative studies of the thyroid gland and of the reticulo-endothelial system.[17] He had many other interests and served as Honorary Secretary of the Edinburgh Pathological Club, an organization founded in 1886 by Sir John Batty Tuke, and in 2009 published a *Memoir of Medicine*, interviews with distinguished Edinburgh physicians and surgeons, recorded by Angus himself and by David Simpson, Andrew Shivas and Stewart Fletcher. Following the death of Professor G. L. Montgomery in 1993, Angus completed a *Festschrift* commemorating Montgomery's life and work in an invaluable record of his time in the Edinburgh Chair.

L. A. Whitely Branwood was by training and practice a physician. He had been Clinical Tutor to Professor Murray Lyon and achieved undergraduate respect for the quality of his much sought-after tutorials in Medicine. He joined George Montgomery in research into the nature and distribution of coronary artery disease. He loved cars, although poor eyesight led him into occasional difficulties, so that, on one occasion, he drove his pale green Bugatti straight through some Edinburgh road works. Leaving Edinburgh, he became Professor of Pathology at the Cornell Medical College, New York. He died in 2004.

M. Neil McLean, quietly spoken and honest to a fault, was universally liked and admired for the way in which he had overcome a wartime injury that severely damaged his hearing. He was widely regarded as a skilled and experienced diagnostic pathologist, but by dint of hard work also completed sophisticated research in heritable disorders and cytogenetics. Later, he undertook extensive work for the Royal College of Surgeons of Edinburgh.

N. Douglas Bain succeeded Agnes MacGregor as Pathologist to the Royal Edinburgh Hospital for Sick Children. He revolutionized the laboratory by introducing techniques for the study of cytogenetics.

O. It was during these years that I first met and came to know Kathryn MacLaren, one of the most gifted histopathologists of our time.

P. Mary MacDonald was held in respect not only for her quiet and warm personality and skills in the developing science of electron microscopy, but also because her husband, James Robson, a physician of distinction and authority on renal disease, had helped Michael Woodruff to identify a suitable patient to receive the first British kidney transplant.

Q. Iain Smith succeeded Douglas Bain as pathologist to the Royal Edinburgh Hospital for Sick Children.

R. My seminars included a talk to the Pathological Society on 'Focal renal glomerular necrosis' (1958), to the Aberdeen Medical School on 'Evolution of vascular necrosis in experimental hypertension' (1960), to the Royal Infirmary of Edinburgh on 'Aspects of arteriolar behaviour in experimental hypertension' (1961), to the Atherosclerosis Discussion Group on 'A new concept of malignant hypertension' (1962), and to the British Society for Research into Ageing on 'Osteomalacia – a common disease in elderly women' and on 'Quantitative histochemistry of the heart in experimental hypertension' (1963). With Christine Laing and Julia Sowerby, I spoke to the Royal Society of Medicine in 1965 on 'Histochemical and microchemical studies of myocardial function', and in April 1966 I gave my Honeyman Gillespie Lecture on *The pathology of rheumatoid arthritis* to the Royal Infirmary of Edinburgh, as well as addressing the Scottish Thoracic Society on Pathology of the lungs in the connective tissue diseases.

Chapter 14

A. The Copemans, an influential family tracing their inheritance back to Dutch settlers in the seventeenth century, enjoyed connections with almost every branch of London medical and scientific society. W. (Will) S. C. Copeman, author of *A History of Gout* and editor of a well-known *Textbook of Rheumatology,* was the son of the late Sir Walter Monckton Copeman, a former President of the Royal College of Physicians of London. Will was a kindly, Edwardian figure. He was driven around London in a large, black Rolls Royce bearing his coat of arms. Like Winston Churchill, Will Copeman claimed never to have travelled on the Underground. One of his patients was the King of Tunis. Another was the present writer, who had the misfortune one day to injure his right knee on the edge of a piece of household furniture.

B. Since 2010, Arthritis Research UK, formerly the Arthritis and Rheumatism Council, has been the principle national organization supporting research into the causes and cures for rheumatism. The Empire Rheumatism Council, the ERC, as it was called, was founded in 1936.

C. The 1960s equivalent of *PubMed* and other computer-based bibliographical indices.

D. Mathilda Marks died in 1964.

E. L. E. Glynn was consultant pathologist to the Canadian Red Cross Memorial Hospital at Maidenhead. An authority on immunology and the rheumatic diseases, he was scientific advisor to the ARC. He died in 2005, aged 95.

F. The seven-storey block towered into the sky opposite the Convent School in Bute Gardens.

G.   Members of the Management Committee included Mrs Neville Blond; General Sir Robert Drew; R. J. Fenney; Frank Hart, House Governor of Charing Cross Hospital; Dr Frank Dudley Hart; Terence Kennedy (President); the Right Honourable Lord Kindersley, Chairman of Rolls Royce; W. Gordon Lilley; Gordon McLachlan of the Nuffield Provincial Hospitals Trust; and Dr Seymour J. R. Reynolds, Dean of the Charing Cross Hospital Medical School. The Honourable Sir Marcus Sieff, Chairman of Marks & Spencer, had been invited to become a member but declined until 1969, when, it is said, he was satisfied that the Institute had become a 'going concern'. My friend Sir Bryan Thwaites (p.50), Principal of Westfield College, London, was a member until he became Chairman of Northwick Park Hospital.

H.   Lord Reith visited the Institute early in 1968 and was greatly interested in the electron microscope. We became engaged in a long talk about the precision of the engineering, electron theory, the atom and cosmology.

I.   I first met William (Bill) St Clair Symmers at the Pathological Society in 1953, the year in which he became Professor of Pathology at Charing Cross Hospital Medical School. Born in 1917, his father had been Professor of Pathology of the Queen's University of Belfast (p.185) and Dean of the Medical School. Graduating in Medicine in 1939, Bill served in the Royal Navy in the Second World War. He joined Payling Wright in preparing *General Pathology* and eventually assumed the entire responsibility for this enormous compendium. His fascination with rare diseases led to books entitled *Curiosa* (1974) and *Exotica* (1984).

  Bill was known for his anecdotes. During his student days, he had studied at the Aschoff Institute. One day, walking through the Bavarian woods, whistling a melody from one of the works of Richard Strauss, a voice called out: 'If you choose to whistle my tunes, please make your notes more accurate!' The voice was that of Strauss himself. That evening Bill found himself in the company of Adolf Hitler.

J.   Dr Ravinder Nath Maini's early interest in the responses of lymphocytes in inflammatory arthritis paved the way for his later innovative research on the immunosuppressive role of antibodies to agents such as tumour necrosis factor alpha (TNF-α) in the treatment of rheumatoid arthritis.

K.   Dr Dudley Dumonde had been Senior Lecturer in Immunology at the Wright-Fleming Institute of St Mary's Hospital Medical School.

L.   Dr Helen Muir, the granddaughter of Sir Edward Muir, Principal of the University of Edinburgh, was a scientist of distinction who had studied at Oxford under the guidance of Professor Robinson on the synthesis of penicillin, the subject of her doctoral thesis.

M.   Drs Lucille Bitensky and Joseph Chayen had been working in the laboratories of the Royal College of Surgeons of England, at Lincoln Inn Fields.

N.   Hajime Inoue arrived with his young Japanese wife and their two small children. In error, they were directed to unsuitable accommodation in Earl's Court. When Helen heard of this, she invited them to stay with us. It was an interesting introduction to the Japanese way of life! Each morning, all our guests rose early and went together to the bathroom, where Hajime instructed them how to use the facilities before they left the house for a walk. Mrs Inoue insisted on helping with the washing-up. But the Japanese demand standards of cleanliness beyond those of the British. Singing Tchaikovsky songs, she kept the hot water running continuously as she dealt with the dishes, so that, by the evening, the supply was exhausted.

O.   In October 1970, Dr MacGillivray returned to Ontario, specialized in Rheumatology and was elected FRCP(C).

P.   The occasion of Princess Margaret Rose's death on 9th February 2002 brought back many memories. She had been a particularly attractive and popular young person and had supported many charities, and a number of organizations had been named after her, among them the Edinburgh Orthopaedic Hospital. The hospital, known as the Edinburgh Hospital for Crippled Children was opened in 1932 but renamed The Princess Margaret Rose Hospital for Crippled Children in 1934. In 1937, the word 'crippled' was abandoned, and in 1957, in recognition that more and more adult patients were being treated, the hospital acquired its final name, The Princess Margaret Rose Orthopaedic Hospital. By a strange coincidence, it closed on 31st December 2001.

Q.   At various times, I was a member of the Editorial Boards of the *Journal of Pathology and Bacteriology*, *Annals of the Rheumatic Diseases*, *Investigative and Cell Pathology* and *Annals of Immunology*, and enjoyed a vigorous correspondence with C. L. Oakley FRS, Editor of the *Journal of Pathology*. For a short time, I acted as a Consultant Editor to *Ultrastructural Pathology* and to the *European Journal of Experimental Musculoskeletal Research* and was briefly an Editorial Adviser to the *Biochemical Journal*.

R.   They included the Heberden, the Pathological Society of Great Britain and Ireland, the British Society of Immunology, the British Society of Rheumatology, the Association of Clinical Pathologists, the Bone and Tooth Society, the Osteoarthritis Research Society, the International Academy of Pathology, the European Society of Pathology, the Royal Society of Medicine, and the Scottish Society for the History of Medicine. I was sometimes called on to address groups that were neither scientific nor medical. Among them was the Brighton and Hove branch of the National Council of Women, to whom I spoke in June 1967.

S.   William Henry Walton was Professor of Experimental Pathology in Birmingham. He published many papers in the fields of arterial disease and immunology and was Director of the Rheumatism Research Wing. He died in 2008, aged 88.

Chapter 15

A.   The reasons for concern were not far to seek. Differences in political and religious views between England and Ireland could be traced back for centuries. In 1967, the Ulster Volunteer Force, the UVF, was formed in response to an apparent revival of the Irish Republican Army, the IRA, and in 1968 protests by the Northern Ireland Civil Rights Association descended into violence. The British Army was brought in to keep the peace, but a militant group, the Provisional IRA, took up arms. On 12th August 1969, tensions erupted in Londonderry. On

30th January 1972, 26 civil rights protesters in 'Derry' were shot by the British Army on the infamous 'Bloody Sunday' and 14 died. On 'Bloody Friday', 21st July, the Provisional IRA detonated car bombs in and around Belfast. Nine people were killed, 130 injured. The Troubles continued throughout our time in Belfast

B.   Over many years there had been a close association between Queen's and universities and colleges in England, Scotland and Wales. The Queen's University owed its origin to Prince Albert, Queen Victoria's Consort. In 1845, he had been responsible for the establishment of the Queen's University of Ireland, embodying the Queen's Colleges of Cork, Galway and Belfast. It was a time when Trinity College, Dublin was an Anglican institution. The Belfast Queen's College opened in 1849. In 1879, the Royal University of Ireland replaced the Queen's University and in 1908 the Royal University was dissolved, to be replaced by the National University of Ireland and the Queen's University of Belfast.

C.   Seeking to encourage me, Sir Eric gave me a charming book.[2]

D.   From 1962, Robert T. Spence had been Secretary to the Belfast Hospitals Management Committee. He became Group Secretary and held this position until 1974.

E.   Professor Archer returned from Chicago to become the first (Blackmore) University Professor of Ophthalmology. He told me that one reason he and his wife had left the United States was because of the extent of violent crime in Illinois.

F.   Mr Morgan was appointed Headmaster of Stewart's Melville School, Edinburgh in 1978.

G.   Thomas K. Marshal, State Pathologist since 1958, became University Professor of Forensic Medicine in 1973.

H.   The Musgrave Chair of Pathology passed from J. Lorain Smith in 1904 to W. St C. Symmers and then in 1929 to A. Murray Drennan. He was succeeded by J. S. Young in 1931 and in 1937 by a young John Henry Biggart (JHB) a lecturer in neuropathology in Edinburgh. JHB assumed an increasingly influential position in Belfast during the Second World War, held in respect both by students who regarded him as 'God' and by his fellow consultants who viewed him as the 'King of the North of Ireland'. I was told that as Dean of the Faculty of Medicine (1943–71) he might sometimes assume sole responsibility for admitting medical students. Called into his office on the ground floor of the Institute of Pathology, an applicant might be asked: 'What games do you play?' If the reply was: 'I play in the first 15 at Inst' (the Royal Belfast Academical Institution), JHB might say: 'Very good. You're accepted'.

I.   Florence McKeown was a highly experienced diagnostician and teacher. She had been John Henry Biggart's trusted lieutenant and became an authority on diseases of old age, a subject on which her book[11] was widely praised. She had held a Personal Chair in Morbid Anatomy from 1967 until succeeding to the Musgrave Chair, which she retained until 1983.

J.   Ingrid Allen progressed to a Chair of Neuropathology in 1979, retiring from this position in 1997. She achieved international recognition for her research on infections of the nervous system and multiple sclerosis.

A former Deputy Lieutenant of Belfast, she became Dame Ingrid and, since 2008, her portrait has hung in the Canada Room of the Great Hall of the University.

K. When Bill Hunt (Chapter 11) came for six months to work in the Institute as a locum pathologist, he was greatly liked by the Belfast staff. He was helped by Frank O'Brien and was a gifted teacher with a great sympathy for students with learning difficulties. His colleagues admired his intrepid spirit when, at some risk to himself (his elder brother, General Hunt, was Chief of the Imperial General Staff) he wandered along the Falls Road claiming that his aim was to photograph members of the IRA!

L. Among others I knew who had been Japanese prisoners were Michael Woodruff (p.157) and Bernard Lennox.

M. Desmond and I discussed new methods for standardizing the naming of disease, in particular the use of the United States SNOP and SNOMed nomenclature.

N. At the Battle of the Boyne (1690), the Catholic forces of the former King, James II, were soundly defeated by the army of William III, who had succeeded to the throne in 1688.

O. Donald Albert Heath, George Holt Professor of Pathology at Liverpool University from 1968 to 1993, died on 10th February 1997. An authority on lung disease, he and his associates Harris, Williams and Smith were the authors of outstanding books.[12–14] Donald was an intrepid explorer of mountainous regions and a leading authority on the diseases of populations living at high altitudes. He travelled widely in the Himalayas and Andes and displayed the same characteristics in Belfast. Inquiring by nature, on one visit he said he would be particularly interested in visiting the restaurant favoured by Dr Ian Paisley!

P. Charles James Kirkpatrick joined me in Manchester before moving to a distinguished career in Germany (Chapter 18).

Q. Nairn Wilson also renewed his work with me in Manchester (Chapter 18), where he was beginning his own outstandingly successful studies in the Department of Restorative Dentistry.

Chapter 16

A. Professor V. R. Ott and I had corresponded in 1970 when I sent him the Kennedy Institute Annual Report for 1968 and a copy of my *Pathology of Rheumatoid Arthritis* (1972). He was Direktor der Klinik und Institut für Physikalische Medizin und Balneologie der Universität Giessen, Bad Nauheim.

B. The cost of attending the 1973 Conference was £600. The Academic Council of the Queen's University of Belfast provided £18.75.

C. Some city names may have changed since our visit to China. Pinyin is now the official system used to transcribe Chinese characters in order to teach Mandarin Chinese in mainland China and other parts. A romanization system was developed in the People's Republic of China in 1958. The International Organization for Standardization adopted pinyin in 1982.

Chapter 17

A. Bonomo was Director of the Rheumatology Centre of the Faculty of Medicine of the Federal University of Rio.

B. Fortaleza, with a metropolitan population of more than three million, was the capital city of the State of Ceará, 1000 miles north of the new capital of Brazil, Brazilia.

C. John Harold Talbott became a good friend. He had been Editor of the *Journal of the American Medical Association*. We corresponded with him later and met him in London.

D. Schistosomiasis often originates from snails living in contaminated water. The snails shed larvae, which penetrate the skin of exposed persons before being carried to the liver or urinary bladder, where chronic inflammation and tissue damage are provoked. The pattern of disease found in the Middle East differs from that encountered in South America and the West Indies. Worldwide, the infestation may affect as many as 200 million people, but new treatments have led to a reduction in the prevalence of the disease.

E. Chagas' disease is caused by a parasitic protozoan *Trypanosoma cruzi* carried by blood-sucking triatomine bugs, which live, for example, in the woodwork of poor rural huts. In South America, 90 million people were at risk in the 1990s, with 16 or more million thought to be infected. Improved hygiene and modern treatments have reduced these numbers.

F. Amoebae are protozoa that inhabit the human intestine in the form of cysts. The disease is contracted from food contaminated by faeces.

G. Malaria and leprosy were encountered quite frequently in cities like Rio. Tuberculosis was also rife and might complicate visceral leishmaniasis.

H. De Paula was coauthor with Wertzman of a book on the systemic connective tissue diseases.

I. Batida was Brazilian rum; resembling water, it was recommended at many Brazilian Government functions.

J. The Stevens acted as consultants to construction and industrial works. Their son, Martin, spent two years in Amazonia supervising the erection of small hospitals and medical aid posts built of steel and aluminium in Birmingham, England and brought to Brazil by ship. He was afraid that the Brazilian agencies responsible for providing the 24 million cruzeiros necessary for the work had failed to allow enough money for staffing. In any case, both medical and nursing personnel were difficult to obtain for the Amazonian region except by giving excessive salaries, so that a nurse might expect as much as £20,000 a year. Although the climate was very hot and humid, life in Amazonia was by no means always unpleasant. However, there were hazards, and on one occasion Martin's plane had made a forced landing after running out of fuel and it took him two days to get to the nearest town.

Chapter 18

A. Hamid was a staunch Rotarian and presided over the 38th Charter Dinner of the Wythenshawe Rotary Club in November 1985. He had liberal financial views and advised me to 'write a novel rather than one of those medical books'.

B. My Lancaster colleague Ken Oates (p.243) had worked with Professor Irene Manton in Leeds. She was a devoted collector of Lowry's paintings, which covered every wall of her house.

C. The University of Manchester, the first of the great civic universities, had been established in 1851 as the John Owens College. Medical teaching had begun when the 12 houses comprising the Manchester Royal Infirmary, the MRI, were opened in 1752. During my years in Manchester, the Vice Chancellors, who determined University policy, welcomed and regulated our grant applications and influenced our work, were Sir Arthur Lewellyn Armitage (1970–78) and Sir Mark Henry Richmond (1981–90).

D. In my time, the Dean was J. R. Moore of the Dental School. By nature authoritarian, Joe was proud of his earlier association with the Paratroops and remained a dedicated walker.

E. Professor Ford was killed in a car accident in Australia on 19th November 1984. An obituary notice in the *Scandinavian Journal of Immunology* described him as 'one of the leading immunologists of his generation'.

F. John McClure joined Barrie Vernon Roberts in Adelaide (Chapter 20) in 1978. He returned to the United Kingdom in 1983 and became a Senior Lecturer and Honorary Consultant Pathologist in Manchester. In 1987, he succeeded to the Procter Chair of Pathology, devoting much time to the British Red Cross Society, of which he became Chairman and of which he is the honorary Vice President. For his services to the Society, he was awarded the OBE.

G. Alastair left Manchester to become a Consultant Pathologist to the Western General Hospital, Edinburgh.

H. The Nuffield Foundation was not the only source of support. My laboratories were inspected by the ARC in 1983 when the Council was assessing an application I made for a further research grant.

I. James Kirkpatrick moved to a Chair of Pathology at the Rheinisch-Westfälische Technische Hochschule, the RWTH, at Aachen, West Germany. In May 1993, he succeeded Professor Wolfgang Thoenes in the Chair of Pathology at the Johannes Gutenburg University of Mainz and has been President of the German Biomaterials Society

J. Among his other many talents, Kenneth Oates included music: he played the tympani in the Northern Orchestra. His wife Margaret was herself a professional musician.

K. Nairn Wilson (Chapter 15) is Dean and Head of King's College, London Dental Institute at Guys', King's College and St Thomas' Hospitals. He has been President of the General Dental Council, Pro-Vice Chancellor of the University of Manchester, Chair of the Specialty Advisory Board in Restorative Dentistry of the Royal College of Surgeons of Edinburgh RCSEd (1992–94) and Dean of the College Faculty of Dental Surgery (1995–98).

L. In May 1988, Max Lawton's work on X-ray microanalysis of the mouse knee meniscus was presented at the 9th European Congress of

Electron Microscopy, and in June 1988, his paper 'Biocompatibility of hydroxyapatite ceramic: response of chondrocytes in a test system using low temperature scanning electron microscopy' was accepted by the *Journal of Dentistry*.

M. The speakers included Professors M. I. V. Jayson, René Lagier and R. N. ('Tiny') Maini. They were supported by Drs Judith Adams, Paul Byers, Mary Catto, K. Cumming, H. Ellis, A. J. Freemont, A. Malcolm, John McClure, A. J. Palfrey, Peter Revell, Jacqueline Weiss and C. G. Woods.

N. Trinity College had been founded as an Anglican establishment in 1592 during the reign of Queen Elizabeth I.

O. John George Adami was of Italian origin. A Demonstrator in Pathology at Cambridge in 1887, he moved to McGill University, Montréal in 1892. He was the author of one of the most respected pathology textbooks, a copy of which rested on the shelves of my teacher in Cambridge, A. M. Barrett. After returning to this country, Adami became Vice Chancellor of the University of Liverpool in 1919.

P. In one example, acting for the *Journal of Pathology*, I reviewed a volume by K. Kuhn and T. Krieg, *Connective Tissue: Biological and Clinical Aspects* (Volume 10 of *Rheumatology, an Annual Review*), published in London and New York by Karger in 1986. I had also been a member of the editorial boards of the *Annals of the Rheumatic Diseases*, the *Journal of Anatomy* and *Ultrastructural Pathology*.

Q. Philip's original plan had been to enter Sidney Sussex College, Cambridge, but he failed to gain acceptance. I often wondered whether an application from his original *alma mater*, St Paul's School, London, would have been more helpful than one from Campbell College, Belfast.

Chapter 19

A. Dr Anna Kadar (p. 178) rose to a senior position in the world of Eastern European pathology and became a member of the council of the International Academy of Pathology, the organization that had been the International Academy of Medical Museums when it was founded in 1905.

B. In preparation for the seminar, each participant received the records and microscopic slides of patients suffering from tuberculous arthritis, polymyositis, osteonecrosis and 30 other conditions.

Chapter 20

A. I had met Dr Barrie Vernon-Roberts in London. In July 1976, P. F. Vowles, Academic Registrar to the University of London, invited me to join a board including the University Vice Chancellor to consider conferring the title of Professor of Bone and Joint Pathology on Barrie, a Senior Lecturer at the London Hospital Medical College. He had been awarded the Margaret Holdroyde Prize by the Heberden Society in 1972 and was a member of the Editorial Board of the *Annals of the Rheumatic Diseases*.

B. The Medical School was renowned as the academic home of Howard Florey, who had been born in Adelaide. In 1945, together with Ernst Chain and Alexander Fleming, he was awarded the Nobel Prize for the discovery, development and use of penicillin.

C. The ground was 135–185 metres long, 110–155 metres wide.

D. Dr Watson, a Fellow of the Royal College of Physicians of Edinburgh, was a consultant to the Queen Elizabeth Hospital

E. We kept in touch with Elma long after Morris's death and in January 2007, while in Scotland, were astonished to receive from her a huge case of Australian wine.

F. Professor Marmion had been a coauthor in a study of experimental arthritis.[5] He had left Edinburgh not long before our visit to Adelaide, lived in the Adelaide Hills and welcomed us to his lovely house.

G. Professor Nairn had left Aberdeen and London for the Southern Hemisphere. He visited Manchester in 1982.

H. Bill was killed in a motor accident (Note 18[E]). He was being driven by an expatriate who had been one of his own PhD students.

I. Shortly before our visit, an entirely new variety of 'gastric-brooding' frog had been discovered in Queensland. Like some forms of fish, this maternal frog was found to carry its tadpoles in it stomach. As the young grew larger, the mother would sink further into the water in which she was swimming. Eventually, at term, the tadpoles would be spat out.

J. Colonies where platypuses live are 'platypuseries'.

K. After wartime service in India, Chris was among the flood of ex-service medical officers returning to Britain to seek a civilian appointment. I met him when he joined the County Infirmary, Louth as a surgical registrar in 1950 (p.90). When we returned from Germany, he was working at Papworth, a centre for cardiovascular surgery. With typical tenacity, Chris passed the Edinburgh FRCS examinations. Impoverished, but determined to pursue his chosen career, he moved to Australia as a locum in general practice, then as a surgeon in the Flying Doctor Service of the Department of Home and Health Affairs, based at Longreach, Queensland and covering an area seven times greater than the United Kingdom.[6] Chris and Cynthia lived at Pelican House, Tewantin. After Chris's death, Cynthia settled in Toowoomba.

Chapter 21

A. In 1996, Ciba-Geigy merged with Sandoz to become Novartis.

B. Alice Maroudas and her mother escaped the horrors of the Holocaust in their native Poland and, after the Second World War, settled in South Africa before moving to Great Britain. I had had the privilege of working with Alice in London, at Imperial College (p.179). It was through her good offices that I was given access to a scanning electron microscope, the tool used for our early studies of the fine structure of articular cartilage-bearing surfaces.

Chapter 22

A.   The slightly cumbersome address of our flat was Flat 4, Block 5, Fountainhall Court, Fountainhall Road, Edinburgh EH9 2NL.

B.   Hardware for the HOME (highly optimized microscope environment) microscope was manufactured by Zeiss of Oberkochen, software by the French firm Alcatel.

C.   Donald Salter, a Lecturer in Pathology in the Edinburgh University Department of Pathology, visited me in Manchester and I quickly came to know and respect his ability and dedication. He became a Senior Lecturer/Honorary Consultant in 1990 and a University Reader in 2002, before his promotion to the Chair of Osteoarticular Pathology. In 1999, he acted as Secretary of the Scottish Affairs Committee of the Royal College of Pathologists and in 2009 was appointed a Member of the Experimental Medicine and Translational Research Committee of the Chief Scientist's Office.

D.   M. J. W. Strachan became a consultant endocrinologist in Edinburgh.

E.   W. J. (Bill) Gillespie held the Chair of Orthopaedic Surgery at Christchurch School of Medicine of the University of Otago in 1981. In 1989, he moved to a similar position at the University of Newcastle, New South Wales, but returned to Edinburgh in 1993 to be George Harrison Professor of Orthopaedic Surgery, a Chair that had been held with distinction by Walter Mercer, J. P. James and E. S. P. Hughes. Dean of the Dunedin School of Medicine at the University of Otago, New Zealand since 1998, Bill Gillespie was chosen to be the first Dean of the new Hull/York Medical School in March 2002 and was succeeded in 2007 by A. H. R. W. Simpson.

F.   Under the direction of Professor John C. Southam, Howard Moody had been responsible for much of the teaching in the Department of Dental Surgery and for diagnosing and reporting the surgical samples. He had benefited from Voluntary Service Overseas and planned to extend his studies to the field of bone loss in dental disease.

G.   Journals I assisted included the following: *Annals of the Rheumatic Diseases*; *British Journal of Rheumatology*; *Clinical Science*; *Connective Tissue Research*; *European Journal of Experimental Musculoskeletal Research*; *Histochemical Journal*; *Histopathology*; *Journal of Anatomy*; *Journal of Bone and Joint Surgery*; *Journal of Microscopy*; *Journal of Rheumatology*; *Microscopy and Microanalysis*; *Paraplegia*; and *Scanning Microscopy International*.

H.   At that time, the Pathology Committee comprised Maldyk, Bely, Mohr, Kaklamanis, Tanka, Eulderink-Rusakova, Revell, Malcolm, François, Wagner, Ekinci, Papazoglou, Gardner, Geiler, Refsum, Aufdermaur, Govoni, Grabaek, Govoni, Dreher, Ripoli Gomez, Lagier and Myhre Jensen.

I.   A list of my lectures and papers is held in the RCSEd.

Chapter 23

A.   There are 18 British Colleges. The Irish College retains its title of The Royal College of Surgeons in Ireland. The story of the Edinburgh

Surgical College extends back to July 1505, when the Edinburgh Barber Surgeons petitioned the Town Council, asking for a 'Charter of Incorporation'. In 1697, the first Surgeons' Hall was constructed in High School Yards, but the demand for space increased and William Playfair designed the new Surgeons' Hall, opened in 1832.

B. The formation of a Museum can be traced back to the seventeenth century, when the collections were held in the first Surgeons' Hall. In 1805, the collections became the responsibility of the newly appointed College Professor of Surgery, John Thomson. In 1825, the new position of Conservator attracted a salary of £150. Robert Knox, whose involvement with the Burke and Hare scandal later diverted him from a life of academic brilliance, accepted the post in 1826.

C. Ian Kirkland was a distinguished paediatric surgeon whose judgement I trusted; he was also an enthusiastic fisherman and sportsman. To his record as a 'scratch' golfer he could add his youthful trial as 'standoff half' for the Scottish international rugby team. The College's *Ian Kirkland Angling Trophy* is contested annually on the waters of Scottish rivers and lochs.

D. Ian's predecessor from 1974 to 1984 was Dr Andrew Shivas (p.155), a Senior Lecturer in Sir Alistair Currie's University Department of Pathology. Andrew worked closely in the College of Surgeons with the internationally respected pathologist Edith Dawson, but was instructed by Professor Currie to save specimens of interest in the University, not in the College. In this way, the College was deprived of important items such as those relating to cardiac and transplant surgery.

E. Professor Eldred Walls had been Professor of Anatomy at the Middlesex Hospital Medical School, London, where I met him in 1967. He was an eminent anatomist, Dean of the Medical School and respected author.

F. The Fellowship, a token of fitness to practise as a consultant surgeon, could be obtained in three ways: first, by examination, the normal approach attempted by surgeons in training in this or other countries; second, on a personal basis (*ad eundem*), to reward some senior person; and, third, on very exceptional occasions, on an Honorary basis to persons of great distinction, of whom Joseph Lister was one example.

G. Dr Menzies Campbell presented his unique collection of dental specimens and works of art to the College in 1965. He gave his library to the Royal College of Surgeons of England.

H. Paul Geissler, DDS, FDS, RCSEd, was Senior Lecturer and Consultant in Restorative Dentistry of the University of Edinburgh, and President of the Royal Odonto-Chirurgical Society of Scotland and of the British Society for the Study of Prosthetic Dentistry.

I. Eric Cameron Mekie, Conservator from 1955 to 1974, was an Edinburgh graduate who published a *Handbook of Surgery* in 1937. He became Professor of Surgery in Singapore, before retiring back to Edinburgh after the Second World War. Professor Eric Mekie's contribution to the Museum was of enormous importance, but his failing eyesight brought his work to an end.

J. My first President was the charming Geoffrey Chisholm (1988–91), but I came to know his successor, P. D. (Paddy) Boulter (1991–94), even better. Paddy strongly supported my efforts to modernize the Museum. I also benefited from my friendship with a former President, the distinguished neurosurgeon John Gillingham, one of whose family had attended the Edinburgh Academy at the same time as our son Iain.

K.   Dr Neil McLean (Note 13[H]), Consultant Pathologist to the Western General Hospital, Edinburgh, devoted much of his time after retirement to the preparation of the College's *Atlas of Surgical Pathology*,[7] abandoned for financial reasons after only two volumes had been completed.

L.   No catalogue had been made since the extensive work of Eric Mekie. But, first, we rehoused the important old GC catalogues in fireproof cabinets, where the Wilson, Bell and MacGillivray records were already accommodated together with the rebound SB books, initiated by Henry Wade when he became Conservator in 1903.[11] Facsimile copies of some of the old catalogues were made for display.

M.   From my own collections, I was able to pass to the museum the integrating microdensitometer and interferometer I had used in Manchester (p.240), a Zeiss operating microscope, a Leitz research microscope, a video camera and computer system, large numbers of microscopic slides, and many lantern slides and books. After our visit to Japan in 1994, I gave the Museum powdered pearl bought in a jeweller's shop in Nagoya, where it was sold as a remedy for 'rheumatism'. My colleague Dr Oates (p.243) gave us a scorpion to add to the display on the origins of Greek medicine. When a BBC team came to film an episode for their series *The Great Detectives*, I added the recently issued British postage stamps to the display on Sherlock Holmes.

N.   The new displays ranged from 'Adrenal medulla and cortex', 'Aneurysm' and 'Arthritis', to 'Pituitary gigantism', 'Parasitic disease', 'Peptic ulcer', 'Thyroid disease' and 'Urinary calculi'.

O.   Mr Galbraith was accompanied by the College President, Arnold Maran.

P.   Moving to King's College London and specializing in the surgery of the palate, Fergusson's surgical practice flourished and he became President of the Royal College of Surgeons of England and Surgeon to Her Majesty Queen Victoria.

Q.   I benefited from the expert help of Dr Michael Barfoot, Lothian Health Authority Archivist, with the records of the Royal Infirmary of Edinburgh, and was assisted greatly by Dr Gail Davies, whose doctoral studies encompassed the story of Dr Ford Robertson, whose research I investigated during my studies of Henry Wade.

Chapter 24

A.   In the BBC radio series Desert Island Discs, first broadcast in 1942, a 'castaway' is consigned in theory to a desert island but allowed to select eight pieces of music, one as a favourite, and encouraged to speak about the recollections that each piece inspires.

B.   Among them were Ted Gillman (p.165), who visited us in Edinburgh after his move from South Africa, Theresa Wagner (p.268) from Poland, Anna Kadar from Hungary, Leon Sokoloff from the United States, and others from Germany and Scandinavia. Hajime Inoue joined us in

London from Okayama, and his younger colleagues, Takashi Hayashi and Keiichiro Nishida, were visiting orthopaedic surgeons.

C. I made extensive notes on many of our travels and kept a record of the talks given by speakers who accompanied our cruises. My notes are with my personal archives in the Library of the RCSEd.

D. Andrew Gunn, Honorary Librarian, and Alastair Masson, Honorary Archivist, gave much of their time in retirement to the RCSEd.

E. Returning from Manchester to Edinburgh in 1988, I had been lucky to be able to take up a part-time Research Fellowship in the Department of Pathology of the University of Edinburgh (Chapter 22). Coincidentally, I became Conservator of the Museum of the RCSEd (Chapter 23).

References

Preface

1. Hall, PA, Wright, NA, editors. *Understanding Disease: A Centenary Celebration of the Pathological Society*. Chichester: Wiley, 2006.
2. Gittings, Robert. *The nature of Biography*, London: Heinemann, 1978.
3. Krebs, H. *Reminiscences and Reflections*. Oxford; Clarendon Press, 1981.
4. Goethe, Wolfgang von. *Von Bedeutung des Individuellen in vollst (letzter hand)*. Stuttgart, Tubingen: Cotta, 1942; 59: 215.

Chapter 1

1. Plato (429–347 BC). *Epistles*, IX.
2. Röntgen WC. Über eine neue Art Strahlen. *Sber Phys-med Ges Würz* 1895: 132–41.
3. Gardner T. Some clinical features of acute lobar pneumonia, with special reference to 200 consecutive cases. MD Thesis, University of Edinburgh, 1910.
4. Gardner T. Some observations on the malaria parasites under the influence of various doses of quinine administered orally: enumerative methods employed. In: Ross R, ed. *Observations on Malaria by Medical Officers of the Army and Others*. London: His Majesty's Stationery Office, 1919: 299–318.
5. Welchman J. *Welchman Chronicles*. Goosey: John David Welchman, 2010.
6. Blackmore RD. *Lorna Doone. A Romance of Exmoor,* 6th edn, 1873 (first published by Samson Low, Son & Marston, 1869).
7. Dobson GMB. *Exploring the Atmosphere*. Oxford: Clarendon Press, 1963.
8. Taylor AJP. *The First World War: An Illustrated History*. Harmondsworth: Penguin, 1972.
9. Keegan J. *The First World War*. London: Pimlico, 1999.
10. Trollope A. *Barchester Towers*. London: Everyman's Library, 1992 (first published 1857).

Chapter 2

1. Carroll L. *Alice's Adventures in Wonderland*. London: Macmillan, 1865.
2. Beveridge WH. *Social Insurance and Allied Services*. London: His Majesty's Stationery Office, 1942 ('The Beveridge Report').

3. Stevenson RL. *Kidnapped*. In: *Young Folks*. London: Cassell,1886.

4. Speer A. *Inside the Third Reich*. New York: Macmillan, 1970.

5. Wilson RMcN. *The Beloved Physician: Sir James Mackenzie*. London: John Murray, 1930.

Chapter 3

1. Shakespeare W. *As You Like It*, Act 2, Scene 7. Cambridge: Cambridge University Press, 1926 (First Folio 1623).

2. Sandblom P. *Creativity and Disease. How Illness Affects Literature, Art and Music*. New York: Marion Boyars, 1992.

3. L'Etang H. *Ailing Leaders in Power 1914–1994*, London: Royal Society of Medicine Press, 1995.

Chapter 4

1. Churchill RS. *Winston S Churchill*. Volume I: *Youth 1874–1896*. London: AmP Publishers Group, 1966.

2. Stewart F. *Loretto One-Fifty. The Story of Loretto School from 1827 to 1977*. Edinburgh: William Blackwood, 1981.

3. Taylor FS. *Inorganic and Theoretical Chemistry*, London: Heinemann, 1939.

4. Sacks O. *Uncle Tungsten. Memories of a Chemical Boyhood*. London: Picador, 2001.

5. Jeans J. *The Universe Around Us*, Cambridge: Cambridge University Press, 1938.

6. Churchill WS. *Marlborough: His Life and Times*, London: George G Harrap, 1934.

7. Durran WH, ed. *The Loretto Register*, 6th edn. Musselburgh: Loretto School, 2000.

Chapter 5

1. Dickinson EE. *Complete Poems*, No. 185, 1891.

2. Tuker MAR. *Cambridge*. London: Adam and Charles Black, 1907.

3. Weatherall WM. *Gentlemen, Scientists and Doctors. Medicine at Cambridge 1800–1940*. Cambridge: The Boydell Press/Cambridge University Library, 2000.

4. Gray H. *Anatomy, Descriptive and Applied*, 25th edn (ed TB Johnston). London: Longmans, Green, 1932.

5. Austen J. *Emma, A Novel in Three Volumes*. London: John Murray, 1816.

6. Jeans J. *The New Background of Science*. Cambridge: Cambridge University Press, 1934.

7. Jeans J. *The Universe Around Us*. Cambridge: Cambridge University Press, 1938.

8. Churchill WS. *Marlborough: His Life and Times*. London: George G Harrap, 1934.

9. Freud S. *Introductory Lectures on Psycho-analysis*. London: George Allen & Unwin, 1940.

10. James W. *The Variety of Religious Experience: A Study in Human Nature*. 1902.

11. *The Holy Bible Containing the Old and New Testaments*. London: Society for Promoting Christian Knowledge, 1939.

12. *Human Histology*. Edinburgh: Churchill Livingstone: 1st edn (with B Cruickshank and TC Dodds), 1964; 2nd edn (with B Cruickshank and TC Dodds), 1968; 3rd edn (with TC Dodds),1976.

13. Sherrington C. *Integrative Action of the Nervous System*. New Haven, CT: Yale University Press, 1947 (The Silliman Lectures of Yale University 1904, first published 1906).

14. Willmer E. *Tissue Culture. The Growth and Differentiation of Normal Tissues in Artificial Media*, 3rd edn. London: Methuen, 1958.

15. Krebs H. *Reminiscences and Reflections*. Oxford: Clarendon Press, 1981.

16. Bernal J. *The Origin of Life*. London: Weidenfeld and Nicolson, 1969.

17. Muir R. *Textbook of Pathology*, 14th edn. London: Hodder Arnold, 2008 (first published London: Edward Arnold, 1924).

Chapter 6

1. Nightingale F. *Cassandra*, Part 1. Part of an unpublished work, *Suggestions for Thought to Searchers after Religious Truth*, 1852 (revised and privately printed, 1859).

2. Chambers R. *Traditions of Edinburgh*, Edinburgh: W&C Tait, 1824. Edinburgh, Chambers, 1980; paperback edition 1996.

3. Wilkinson J. *The Coogate Doctors. The History of the Edinburgh Medical Missionary Society, 1841 to 1991*. Edinburgh: The Edinburgh Medical Missionary Society, 1991.

4. Brown J. *Horae Subsecivae*, new edition. London: Adam and Charles Black, 1897 (first published 1860).

5. Davidson S. *Principles and Practice of Medicine*. Edinburgh: E and S Livingstone, 1952 (21st edn, New York: Elsevier, 2010).

6. Johnstone RW. *A Textbook of Midwifery, for Students and Practitioners*. London: Adam and Charles Black, 1913.

7. Gibbon E. *The History of the Decline and Fall of the Roman Empire*. London: Allen Lane, 1994 (first published in six volumes between 1776 and 1788).

8. Scott W. *Ivanhoe*. Harmondsworth: Penguin Books, 1984 (first published in Edinburgh by Constable and in London by Hurst Robinson, 1820).

9. Cruickshank B, Gardner DL, Dodds TC. *Human Histology*. Edinburgh: Churchill Livingstone, 1964 (2nd edition, 1968; 3rd edn, 1976).

Chapter 7

1. Osler W. *Aequanimitas, With Other Addresses to Medical Students, Nurses and Practitioners of Medicine*. London: HK Lewis, 1906.

2. Mann T. *The Magic Mountain*. London: Secker & Warburg, 1924.

3. Dickson Carr J. *The Life of Sir Arthur Conan Doyle*. London: John Murray, 1949.

4. Beveridge WH. *Social Insurance and Allied Services*. London: His Majesty's Stationery Office, 1942 (the Beveridge Report).

Chapter 8

1. Muller W. *Die Winterreise* (1823–24), music by Franz Schubert (1827).

2. Brownlie AR. *The Treasured Years*. Kilmarnock: ICS Books, 2006.

3. Lewis T. *Pain*. New York: Macmillan, 1942.

Chapter 9

1. Ecclesiastes 3: 1–8. *New English Bible: The Old Testament*. Oxford: Oxford University Press/Cambridge: Cambridge University Press, 1970.

2. Rousseau JJ. *The Confessions of Jean-Jacques Rousseau*, Harmondsworth: Penguin, 1953.

3. Risse GB. *Mending Bodies, Saving Souls. A History of Hospitals*. Oxford: Oxford University Press, 1999: 422–48.

4. Calvert M. *Prisoners of Hope*. London: Jonathan Cape, 1952.

5. Childers RE. *The Riddle of the Sands*. Ware: Wordsworth Classics, 1993 (originally published 1903).

6. Gardner DL. The infected hand. *J R Army Med Corps* 1951; **97**: 359–63.

7. Gardner DL. Streptococcal tonsillitis: an explosive epidemic. *J R Army Med Corps* 1952; **98**: 326–34.

8. Gardner DL. The treatment of group A streptococcal tonsillitis. *J R Army Med Corps* 1953; **99**: 1235–7.

9. Greene G. *The Third Man*. Originally written by Graham Greene as a film script, it later became a novella (London: Penguin, 1999).

10. Mann T. *The Magic Mountain (Der Zauberberg)*. New York: Fischer Verlag, 1924.

Chapter 10

1. Shaw GB. *The Doctor's Dilemma: A Tragedy* (1906).

2. Gardner DL, Cole L. Long survival with inferior vena cava draining into the left atrium. *Br Heart J* 1955; **17**: 93–7.

3. Gardner DL. Aureomycin-resistant staphylococcal enterocolitis. Report of two fatal cases. *Lancet* 1953; **ii**: 1236–8.

4. Du Maurier D. *Rebecca*. London: Victor Gollancz, 1938.

5. Foster WD. *Pathology as a Profession and the Early History of the Royal College of Pathologists*. London: Royal College of Pathologists, 1981.

Chapter 11

1. Traherne T. *Meditations on the Six Days of Creation*, 1717, VI.

2. Eco U. *The Name of the Rose*. London: Martin Secker & Warburg, 1980.

3. Paul J. A photographer of distinction: Thomas Cairns Dodds. *Med Biol Illus* 1970; **20**: 243–4.

4. Collins D. *The Pathology of Articular and Spinal Diseases*. London: Edward Arnold, 1949.

5. Gardner DL. *The Pathology of Rheumatoid Arthritis*, London: Edward Arnold, 1972.

6. Gardner DL, Duthie JJR, Macleod J, Allan WSA. Pulmonary hypertension in rheumatoid arthritis: report of a case with intimal sclerosis of the pulmonary and digital arteries. *Scot Med J* 1957; **2**: 183–8.

7. Richmond J, Gardner DL, Roy LMH, Duthie JJR. The nature of anaemia in rheumatoid arthritis. III. Changes in the bone marrow and their relation to other features of the disease. *Ann Rheum Dis* 1956; **15**: 217–26.

8. Richmond J, Roy LMH, Alexander WRM, Gardner DL, Duthie JJR. Nature of anaemia in rheumatoid arthritis. IV. Effects of the intravenous administration of saccharated oxide of iron. *Ann Rheum Dis* 1958; **17**: 406–15.

9. Gardner DL, Roy LMH. Tissue iron and the reticuloendothelial system in rheumatoid arthritis. *Ann Rheum Dis* 1961; **20**: 258–64.

10. Gardner DL. Severe toxic reaction to hydralazine. *Lancet* 1957; **i**: 46.

11. Gardner DL. The response of the dog to oral L-hydrazinophthalazine (hydralazine). *Br J Exp Pathol* 1957; **38**: 227–35.

12. Gardner DL. Lesions in the hypertensive rat kidney produced by hydralazine. *Nature* 1958; **181**: 915.

13. Gardner DL. The effect of hydralazine (L-hydrazinophthalazine) on the kidneys of rats treated with cortexone. *Br J Exp Pathol* 1958; **39**: 552–6.

14. Buchan J. *The Thirty-Nine Steps*. Edinburgh: William Blackwood, 1915.

15. Buchan J. *Greenmantle*. London: Hodder & Stoughton, 1916.

16. Scott W. *Guy Mannering; or The Astrologer*. London: Longman, Hurst, Rees, Orme & Brown/Edinburgh: Archibald Constable, 1815.

17. Scott W. *The Surgeon's Daughter* (final tale in *Chronicles of the Canongate*). Edinburgh: Cadell/London: Simpkin and Marshall, 1827.

18. Gunn CB. *Leaves from the Life of a Country Doctor*. Edinburgh: The Moray Press, 1935; reprinted Edinburgh: Birlinn, 2002.

19. Gardner DL. Observations on the pathology of rheumatoid arthritis. PhD thesis, University of Edinburgh, 1957.

20. Gardner DL. The influence of hypotensive drugs on renal structure in experimental hypertension. MD thesis, University of Edinburgh, 1958.

Chapter 12

1. Stevenson RL. *Virginibus Puerisqe*. London: Kegan Paul, 1881.

2. Sobel D. *Galileo's Daughter. A Drama of Science, Faith and Love.* London: Fourth Estate, 1999.

3. Hooke R. *Micrographia: Or Some Physiological Descriptions of Minute Bodies Made by Magnifying Glasses. With Observations and Inquiries Thereupon.* London: J Martyn & J Allestry, 1665.

4. Gardner DL, Kreig AR, Chapnick R. Fatal systemic fungus disease in rheumatoid arthritis with cardiac and pulmonary mycotic and rheumatoid granulomata. *Arch Interamer Rheumatol* 1962; **5**: 561–86.

5. Gardner DL, Laing C. The prevention of hypertensive vascular disease. Paper presented to the Boston Meeting of the American Association of Pathologists, 1959.

6. Gardner DL. Prevention of hypertensive vascular disease in rats given intermittent hydralazine. *Am J Pathol* 1959; **35**: 672.

7. Gardner DL. Pathogenesis of arteriolar disease in experimental hypertension. Lecture to the Medical School of Western Reserve University, Cleveland, Ohio, September 1965.

8. Gardner DL. Vascular diseases in experimental hypertension. Paper presented to the American Heart Association, 15 October 1965.

9. Bunce DFM. *Atlas of Arterial Histology.* St Louis, MO: Warren H Green, 1974.

10. Gardner DL. Generalized osteoarthritis. Paper given at Conference on Clinical Patterns and Pathological Features in Osteoarthritis, Kingston, Ontario, October 1982.

Chapter 13

1. Johnson S. Preface to a *Dictionary of the English Language*, 1755.

2. Woodruff MFA, Robson JS, Ross JA, Nolan B, Lambie AT. Transplantation of a kidney from an identical twin. *Lancet* 1961; i: 1245–9.

3. Woodruff MFA. *Nothing Venture Nothing Win.* Edinburgh: Scottish Academic Press, 1996.

4. MacKay JMK, Sim AK, McCormick JN, Marmion BP, McCraw AP, Duthie JJR, Gardner DL. Aetiology of rheumatoid arthritis: an attempt to transmit an infective agent from patients with rheumatoid arthritis to baboons. *Ann Rheum Dis* 1983; 42: 443–7.

5. Gardner DL. Hazards of surgery in rheumatoid arthritis. Paper presented at the Edinburgh Royal Infirmary, 1960.

6. Gardner DL. Anaesthetic and postoperative hazards of rheumatoid arthritis. Association of Clinical Pathologists, Glasgow, April 1961.

7. Gardner DL, Macpherson AI, Maloney AF, Richmond J. Leucoencephalopathy after portocaval anastomosis in a patient with hepatic cirrhosis. *J Neurol Neursurg Psychiatry* 1964; 27: 530–5.

8. Gardner DL. The pathogenesis of experimental hypertensive vascular disease. Address to the London Hospital, 1960.

9. Gardner DL. Pathogenesis of malignant hypertension. Address to the Edinburgh Pathological Club, 1962.

10. Pearse AGE. *Histochemistry. Theoretical and Applied*. London: J and A Churchill, 1953.

11. Gardner DL, Faed MJW, MacGregor AB. Isolated visceral arterioles in culture. *J Pathol Bacteriol* 1964; 87: 131–6.

12. Gardner DL, Ogilvie RF. The late results of the injection of Thorotrast: two cases of neoplastic disease following contrast angiography. *J Pathol Bacteriol* 1959; 78: 133–44.

13. Gardner DL. The role of the Open University in the teaching of medicine. Address to the Royal Society of Medicine, 1960.

14. Gardner DL. *Pathology of the Connective Tissue Diseases*. London: Edward Arnold, 1965.

15. Gardner DL. *The Pathology of Rheumatoid Arthritis*, London: Edward Arnold, 1972.

16. Gillman T. On some aspects of collagen formation in localized repair and in diffuse fibrotic reactions to injury. In: Gould BS, ed. *Treatise on Collagen*. Volume 2: Biology of Collagen, Part B. New York: Academic Press, 1968: 331–407.

17. Stuart AE. *The Reticuloendothelial System*. Edinburgh: E & S Livingstone, 1970.

Chapter 14

1. Szent-Györgyi A von. In: Good IJ, ed. *The Scientist Speculates*. New York: Basic Books, 1962

2. Gardner DL. *Pathology of the Connective Tissue Diseases*. London: Edward Arnold, 1965.

3. Gardner DL, Chalmers J, Conacher WDH, Scott PJ. Osteomalacia – a common disease in elderly women. *J Bone Joint Surg* 1967; **59-B**: 403–23.

4. El-Maghraby MAHA, Gardner DL. A comparative study in young male animals of 10 species of the distribution of alkaline phosphatase activity in small arteries. *Histochemie* 1968; **16**: 227–35.

5. Gardner DL, El-Maghraby MAHA. Synthetic orcein as a stain for chick embryo cartilage matrix. *Stain Technology* 1969; **44**: 127–9.

6. Maghraby MAHA, Gardner DL. Development of connective tissue components of small arteries in the chick embryo. *J Pathol* 1972; **108**: 281–91.

7. Gardner DL, Hall TA. Electron-probe analysis of sites of silver deposition in avian bone stained by the v. Kossa technique. *J Pathol* 1969; **98**: 105–9.

8. Albright J, Kunstel M. *Bombshell: The Secret Story of America's Unknown Atomic Spy Conspiracy*. New York: Times Books, 1997.

9. Gardner DL, McGillivray DC. Articular cartilage is not smooth. An investigation by immersion incident-light microscopy. *J Pathol* 1970; **101**: ix–x.

10. McGillivray DC, Gardner DL. In vivo studies of surfaces of cartilage. *Proceedings of the 4th Canadian Conference on Research in the Rheumatic Diseases*, 1972: 289–91.

11. Gardner DL, Woodward DH. Scanning electron microscopy of articular surfaces. *Lancet* 1968; **ii**: 1246.

12. Gardner DL, Woodward DH. Scanning electron microscopy and replica studies of articular surfaces of guinea-pig synovial joints. *Ann Rheum Dis* 1969; **28**: 379–91.

13. Gardner DL, McGillivray DC. Living articular cartilage is not smooth. *Ann Rheum Diss* 1971; **30**: 3–9.

14. Gardner DL, McGillivray DC. Surface structure of articular cartilage. *Ann Rheum Dis* 1971; **30**: 10–14.

15. Gardner DL. The Heberden Oration. The influence of microscopic technology on knowledge of cartilage surface structure. *Ann Rheum Dis* 1972; **31**: 235–58.

16. Gardner DL, Gryfe A, Woodward DH. Comparative study by scanning electron microscopy of synovial surfaces of four mammalian species. *Experientia* 1969; **25**: 1301–3.

17. Gardner DL, Gryfe A, Woodward DH. Scanning electron microscopy of normal and inflamed synovial tissue from rheumatoid patients. *Lancet* 1969; **ii**: 156–7.

18. Gardner DL. *The Pathology of Rheumatoid Arthritis*. London: Edward Arnold, 1972.

19. Gardner DL, Thomson D. Thrombotic microangiopathy in rheumatoid arthritis. *Scot Med J* 1969; **14**: 190–3.

20. Gardner DL. Modern views on the nature of rheumatoid arthritis. *Orthopaedics (Oxford)* 1971; **4**: 1–24.

21. Gardner DL. Epidemiological studies of rheumatoid arthritis. *Br Med J* 1967; **ii**: 651–2.

22. Gardner DL. A cure for rheumatoid arthritis? *R Soc Health J* 1969; **89**: 51–2.

23. Gardner DL. Rheumatism. Progress certain but effective control some years off. *Medical News Tribune* 1971; **3**: 8–9.

24. Gardner DL. Facilities for treatment are least good in those parts of the country where rheumatic diseases are commonest. *Medical News Tribune* 1971; **3**: 10–11.

25. Gardner DL. What is rheumatism research? *Arthritis and Rheumatism Council Magazine* 1968; **10**: 9–12.

26. Gardner DL, Soria-Herrera C, Morley J. Experimental turpentine arthritis. Measurement of treated and untreated inflammatory responses by the accumulation of ^{131}I-albumin. *J Pathol* 1971; **104**: iii.

27. Gardner DL, Gryfe A, Sanders PM. The mast cell in early rat adjuvant arthritis. *Ann Rheum Dis* 1971; **30**: 24–30.

28. Gardner DL, Quagliata F, Sanders PM. Inhibition of rat adjuvant arthritis by a new immunosuppressive agent, rubidomycin. *Experientia* 1968; **24**: 1028–9.

29. Gardner DL, Quagliata F, Sanders PM. Suppression of adjuvant arthritis by a new cytotoxic compound, rubidomycin. *Ann Rheum Dis* 1969; **28**: 163–71.

30. Gardner DL, Pearse AD. Preparation of unfixed undemineralised bone sections: the Bright bone cryostat. *J Clin Pathol* 1972; **25**: 26–9.

31. Gardner, DL Histopathology and the future. *J Clin Pathol* 1970; **23**: 119–23.

Chapter 15

1. Shakespeare W. *Hamlet* Act I, Scene v.

2. Evans EE. *Mourne Country: Landscape and Life in South Down*, 2nd (revised) edn. Dundalk: Dundalgan Press (W Tempest), 1967.

3. Clarke R. *The Royal Victoria Hospital Belfast: A History 1797–1997*. Belfast: The Blackstaff Press, 1997.

4. Toner PG. *Pathology at the Royal: The First Hundred Years 1890–1990*. Belfast: The Royal Group of Hospitals, 1990.

5. Pantridge F. *An Unquiet Life. Memoirs of a Physician and Cardiologist*. Belfast: The Heart Fund, The Royal Victoria Hospital Belfast, 1989.

6. Baillie M. *A Series of Engravings, accompanied with Explanations which are intended to illustrate the Morbid Anatomy of some of the most important Parts of the Human Body; divided into ten fasciculi*. London: G and W Nicol, Booksellers to His Majesty, 1812.

7. Gardner DL. *The Pathology of Rheumatoid Arthritis*. London: Edward Arnold, 1972.

8. Armstrong CG, Bahrani AS, Gardner DL. In vitro measurement of articular cartilage deformation in the intact human hip joint under load. *J Bone Joint Surg* 1979; **61-A**: 744–5.

9. Mackay JMK, Sim AKS, McCormick JN, Marmion BP, McCraw AP, Duthie JJR, Gardner DL. Aetiology of rheumatoid arthritis. An attempt to transmit an infective agent from patients with rheumatoid arthritis to baboons. *Ann Rheum Dis* 1983; **42**: 443–7.

10. Gardner, DL. The pathogenesis of rheumatoid arthritis. In: Walker GF, ed. *Ninth Symposium on Advanced Medicine, Royal College of Physicians of London*. London: Pitman Medical, 1973: 19–47.

11. McKeown F. *Pathology of the Aged*. London: Butterworth, 1965.

12. Heath D, Williams DR. *Man at High Altitude*, Edinburgh: Churchill Livingstone, 1977.

13. Heath D, Smith P. *The Pathology of the Carotid Body and Sinus*. London: Edward Arnold, 1985.

14. Harris P, Heath D. *The Human Pulmonary Circulation. Its Form and Function in Health and Disease*, 3rd edn. Edinburgh: Churchill Livingstone, 1986.

Chapter 16

1. Bird I. *Unbeaten Tracks in Japan: An Account of Travels on Horseback in the Interior*. London: John Murray, 1911 (first published 1881).

2. Elliott RJ, Gardner DL, Gilmore RStC, Longmore, RB. The measurement of cartilage collagen as hydroxyproline. In: Dixon AStJ et al, eds. *Abstracts of the 13th International Congress of Rheumatology. Excerpta Medica* 1973; **299**: 29.

3. Gardner DL, Longmore RB, Gilmore RStC, Elliott RJ. Age-related changes in articular cartilage determined by interferometry. In: Dixon AStJ et al, eds. *Abstracts of the 13th International Congress of Rheumatology. Excerpta Medica* 1973; **299**: 132.

4. Gardner DL. Pathophysiological studies of articular disease (1), 13th International Congress of Rheumatology, 1973 (unpublished).

5. Gardner DL. Pathophysiological studies of articular disease (2). The measurement of undulations seen on the surface of non-loaded human articular cartilage, 13th International Congress of Rheumatology, 1973 (unpublished).

6. Gardner DL. Contribution of microscopy to the understanding of osteoarthritis. Address given at the celebration of the 40th Anniversary of the Foundation of the Department of Orthopaedic Surgery of the University of Okayama Medical School, 11 June 1994.

Chapter 17

1. Kipling R. *Just-So Stories*. London: Macmillan, 1902.

2. Chagas C. Nova tripanozomiaze humana, Estudos sobre a morfolojia e o ciclo evolutivo do *Schizotrypanum cruzi n. gen., n. sp.*, ajente etiolojico de nova entidade morbida do homem. [New human trypanosomiasis: studies of the morphology and life-cycle of *Schizotrypanum cruzi*, aetiological agent of a new morbid entity of man.] *Mem Inst Oswaldo Cruz* 1909; **1**: 159–218.

3. Solzhenitsyn A. *Cancer Ward*. Harmondsworth: Penguin, 1971.

Chapter 18

1. Haskins ML. *The Desert*, 1908.

2. Fenton PJ, Gardner ID. Simultaneous bilateral intraocular surgery. *Trans Ophthalmol Soc UK* 1982; **102**: 298.

3. Fitzmaurice RJ, Gardner DL. Apparent immunity of synovial tissue to metastasis. *Proceedings of the Pathological Society*, 6–8 January 1993.

4. Oates K. The development of methods for the analysis of structure and composition of biological tissues using low temperature electron microscopy. PhD Thesis, University of Lancaster, 1984.

5. Gardner DL, Mazuryk R, O'Connor P, Orford CR. Anatomical changes and pathogenesis of OA in man, with particular reference to the hip and knee joints. In: Lott DJ, Jasani MK, Birdwood PFB, eds. *Studies in Osteoarthrosis: Pathogenesis, Intervention, Assessment*. Chichester: Wiley, 1987: 21–48.

6. Gardner DL. General pathology of the peripheral joints. In: Sokoloff L, ed. *The Joints and Synovial Fluid*. New York: Academic Press, 1980: 315–425.

7. Harris P, Heath, D. *The Human Pulmonary Circulation: Its Form and Function in Health and Disease*. Edinburgh: Churchill Livingstone, 1986.

8. Heath D, Williams D. *Man at High Altitude*. Edinburgh: Churchill Livingstone, 1977.

9. Gardner DL. Pathology and the nine ages of rheumatism (the Adami Lecture). *J Pathol* 1993; **169**: 1–8.

10. Hick J, ed. *The Myth of God Incarnate*. London: SCM Press, 1977.

Chapter 19

1. Shelley PB. *An Address to the Irish People*, 1812.

2. Gardner DL. Pathogenesis of rheumatoid arthritis based on a study of 146 necropsies. *Proceedings of the Hungarian Rheumatology Society*, 1968.

3. Norwich JJ. *A Short History of Byzantium*. London: Penguin, 1997.

4. Gardner DL. Scanning and transmission electron and reflected light-microscope studies of articular cartilage surfaces in health and in experimental arthritis. *Proceedings of the Hungarian Pathological Society*, 1971.

5. Kadar A, Bush V, Gardner DL. Direct elastase treatment of ultrathin sections embedded in water-soluble Durcupan. *J Pathol* 1971; **103**: 64–7.

6. Kadar A, Gardner DL, Bush V. The relation between the fine structure of smooth-muscle cells and elastogenesis in the chick-embryo aorta. *J Pathol* 1971; **104**: 253–60.

7. Kadar A, Gardner DL, Bush V. Susceptibility of the chick-embryo aorta to elastase: an electron-microscope study. *J Pathol* 1971; **104**: 261–6.

8. Kadar A, Gardner DL, Bush V. Glycosaminoglycans in developing chick-embryo aorta revealed by ruthenium red: an electron-microscope study. *J Pathol* 1972; **108**: 275–80.

9. Kadar A, Gardner DL. The effect of elastase digestion on normal and copper-deficient chick embryo aortas in young chickens. *Proceedings of the European Pathological Society*, 1973.

10. Kerényi T, Bush W, Gardner, DL, Kadar A. The ultrastructure of partially digested elastic tissue. *Proceedings of the European Pathological Society*, 1973.

11. Moorhead A. *Darwin and the Beagle*. London: Hamish Hamilton, 1969.

12. Gardner DL. Cell density of cartilage measured by confocal microscopy (CSOM). *Proceedings of the Osteoarthritis Research Society*, 1992.

13. François R, Gardner DL, Degrave E, Bywaters EGL. Histopathologic evidence that sacroiliitis in ankylosing spondylitis is not merely enthesitis. *Arthritis Rheum* 2000; **43**: 2011–24.

Chapter 20

1. Stuart JM. *Journal entry, April 22ⁿᵈ 1860, at Small Gum Creek.*

2. Sherman DJC, Delamore IW, Gardner DL. Gastric function and structure in iron deficiency. *Lancet* 1966; **ii**: 845–8.

3. Gardner DL. The contribution of electron microscopy to the understanding of connective tissue diseases. *Australian Society for Experimental Pathology*, August 1981 (unpublished).

4. Gardner DL. Recent advances in the pathology of rheumatoid arthritis. *Royal Australasian College of Pathologists*, Adelaide, August 1981 (unpublished).

5. Mackay JMK, Sim AKS, McCormack JN, Marmion BP, McCraw AP, Duthie JJR, Gardner DL. Aetiology of rheumatoid arthritis. An attempt to transmit an infective agent from patients with rheumatoid arthritis to baboons. *Ann Rheum Dis* 1983; **42**: 442–7.

6. Cummins CFA. The Flying Surgeon Service. *Med J Aust* 1960; **2**: 341–4.

Chapter 21

1. Lawrence TE. *Seven Pillars of Wisdom: A Triumph*. First published for general circulation 1935: 83. Wordsworth Edition, with an Introduction by Angus Calder, 1997.

2. Gardner DL. New understanding of the nature of osteoarthritis and of rheumatoid arthritis. *Swiss Conference, Baghdad*, 1983 (unpublished).

3. Gardner DL. Articular cartilage samples. In: Maroudas A, Kuettner K, eds. *Methods in Cartilage Research*. London: Academic Press, 1990: 4–6.

4. Gardner DL, Oates K, Lawton DM, Pidd JG, Middleton JFS. Methods for the study of cartilage by low temperature scanning electron microscopy and related techniques. In: Maroudas A, Kuettner K, eds. *Methods in Cartilage Research*. London: Academic Press, 1990: 63–7.

Chapter 22

1. Gray T. *Elegy Written in a Country Churchyard* 1751: lines 73–76.

2. Osler W. *Aequanimitas, With Other Addresses to Medical Students, Nurses and Practitioners of Medicine*. London: HK Lewis, 1906.

3. Gardner DL. *Pathology of the Connective Tissue Diseases*. London: Edward Arnold, 1965

4. Gardner DL. *The Pathology of Rheumatoid Arthritis*. London: Edward Arnold, 1972.

5. Gardner DL. *Pathological Basis of the Connective Tissue Diseases*. London: Edward Arnold/Philadelphia: Lea & Febiger, 1992.

6. Gardner DL, Elliot D, Simpson R. Rapid bone morphometry with blocks, not sections. Application of confocal scanning microscopy to the diagnosis of metabolic bone disease. *J Pathol* 1990; **160**: 166A.

7. Gardner DL, Oates K, Lawton DM, Pidd JG, Middleton JFS. Methods for the study of cartilage by low temperature scanning electron microscopy and related techniques. In: Maroudas A, Kuettner K, eds. *Methods in Cartilage Research*. London: Academic Press, 1990: 63–7.

8. Lawton DM, Lameletie MD, Gardner DL. Low temperature scanning electron microscopy of the superficial envelope of canine chondrocytes in culture. *Cell Biol Int Rep* 1991; **15**: 47–54.

9. Gardner DL, Elliot D, McArthur SD. Confocal scanning fluorescence microscopy for the identification of mineralization fronts within bone blocks. *J Pathol* 1990; **160**: 175A.

10. Gardner DL, Simpson R, Salter DM, Cunningham DS. Scanning optical microscopy in diagnostic bone histopathology. *J Pathol* 1991; **163**: 181A.

11. Gardner DL. Scanning optical microscopy and the diagnosis of osteoarticular disease. *Microsc Microanal* 1991;**15**: 33–7.

12. Gardner DL, Wyatt B, Strachan RK, Cunningham DS. Cell density of cartilage measured by confocal microscopy (CSOM). *Osteoarthritis Cartilage* 1993; **1**: 13.

13. Gardner DL, Oates K. The impact of confocal scanning optical microscopy on pathological practice. *Br J Hosp Med* 1993; **49**: 160–71.

14. Gardner DL. Fibrillation of osteoarthritic cartilage in the context of drug trials: the use of confocal scanning microscopy. *EULAR Bulletin* 1993; **2**: 62.

15. Leslie BW, Gardner DL, Cunningham DS, McGeough JA. Radial collagen fibres of human knee joint meniscus measured by confocal scanning optical microscopy. *J Pathol* 1997; **181**(Suppl 1997): 47A.

16. Adams CI, Bush P, Gardner DL, Walker C, Hall AC. Confocal scanning microscopy of live meniscal chondrocytes: 3-dimensional representation. *Proceedings of the 11th Congress of the European League Against Rheumatism*, 1999.

17. Nishida K, Gardner DL, Cunningham DS. Cartilage roughness measured by confocal scanning optical microscopy (CSOM) after safranin O staining. *J Pathol* 1997; **181**(Suppl 1997): 47A.

18. Nishida K, Gardner DL, Inoue H. Roughness of hydrated articular cartilage surfaces measured by confocal scanning optical microscopy. In: *Proceedings of SIROT 99*. London: Freund, 1999: 315–20.

19. Saadi AT, Gardner DL, Cunningham DS, Weir DM, Blackwell CC, Weir D. Detection of bacterial binding to epithelial cells by confocal scanning optical microscopy. Bacterial counting. *J Pathol* 1993; **170** (Suppl): 182.

20. Moran RS, Gardner DL, Keating JF, McGeough JA. Finite element analysis of the compressive behaviour of the human knee joint meniscus. *Proceedings of 11th Congress of EULAR*, 1999.

21. Leslie BM, Gardner, DL, McGeough JA, Moran RS. Anisotropic response of the human knee joint meniscus to unconfined compression. *Proc Inst Mech Eng [H]* 2000; **214**: 631–5.

22. Salter DM, Hughes DE, Simpson R, Gardner DL. Integrin expression by articular cartilage chondrocytes. *J Pathol* 1991; **163**: 181A.

23. Salter DM, Hughes DE, Simpson R, Gardner DL. Integrin expression by human articular chondrocytes. *Br J Rheumatol* 1992; **31**: 231–4.

24. Reid IA, Gardner DL. Three-dimensional distribution of nuclei of articular cartilage. *J Pathol* 1992; **169**: 160A.

25. Leslie BM, Gardner, DL, Cunningham, DS, McGeough, JA. Radial fibre proportions in human knee joint menisci. *Acta Anat* 1998; **163**: 212–17.

26. Gardner DL, Strachan RK, Wyatt BC, Marsden M, Hulmes DJS, Harvey RE, McInnes N. Meniscectomy selectively alters cellularity of superficial zone tibial cartilage. Unpublished manuscript.

27. Gardner DL, Oates K, Simpson R. Interaction of hyaluronic acid with osteoarthrotic cartilage surfaces: a low temperature scanning electron microscopic study. *J Pathol* 1989; **158**: 358A.

28. Strachan RK, Smith P, Gardner DL. Hyaluronate in rheumatology and orthopaedics: Is there a role? *Ann Rheum Dis* 1990; **49**: 949–52.

29. Gardner DL, Strachan RK, Hulmes DJS, Marsden ME, Cunningham DS, Wyatt BC, Harvey RE. Influence of hyaluronate on cell density and proteoglycans of articular cartilage in experimental osteoarthritis: confocal scanning and biochemical studies *J Pathol* 1993; **170** (Suppl): 309.

30. McLauchlan GJ, Gardner DL. Sacral and iliac cartilage and bone: thickness, proportions and cell numbers. *Proceedings of 11th Congress of EULAR*, 1999.

31. McLauchlan GJ, Gardner DL. Sacral and iliac cartilage thickness and cellularity. Relationship to subchondral bone thickness and density. *Rheumatology* 2002; **41**: 375–80.

32. François RF, Gardner DL, Bywaters EGL. The sacroiliac joint in ankylosing spondylitis. *Rheumatology Europe* 1995; **24**: 87.

33. François R, Gardner DL, Degréve E, Bywaters EGL. Histopathologic evidence that sacroiliitis in ankylosing spondylitis is not merely enthesitis. *Arthritis Rheum* 2000; **43**: 2011–24.

34. Gardner DL, Skelton-Stroud PN, Fitzmaurice RJ. Akute Muramyl-Dipeptide-induzierte Arthritis beim Pavian Papio cynocephalus. *Z Rheumatol* 1991; **50**: 86–92.

35. Gardner DL. Articular cartilage samples. In: Maroudas A, Kuettner K, eds. *Methods in Cartilage Research*. London: Academic Press, 1990: 4–6.

36. Gardner DL, McArthur SD, Cunningham DS. A new quantitative scanning optical method for the identification of covert osteoarthrosis. *J Pathol* 1991; **163**: 171A.

37. McArthur SD, Gardner DL. Articular cartilage fibrillation and permeability to dye, Light Green SF. A method for the detection of pre-microscopic disease? *J Bone Joint Surg* 1992; **74-B**: 668–72.

38. Gardner DL. Pathology and the nine ages of rheumatism. Advances in knowledge of the connective tissue diseases. *J Pathol* 1993; **169**: 1–8.

39. Gardner DL. Problems and paradigms in joint pathology. *J Anat* 1994; **184**: 465–76.

40. Gardner DL, Salter DM, Oates K. Advances in the microscopy of osteoarthritis. *Microsc Res Tech* 1997; **37**: 245–70.

41. Fitzmaurice RJ, Gardner DL. Thymoma with bone marrow eosinophilia. *J R Soc Med* 1990; **83**: 270–1.

42. Strachan MJW, Gardner DL. Apparent immunity of synovial joints to metastasis: response of tumour cells to supernates from synovial cell cultures. *J Pathol* 1989; **158**: 355A.

43. Gardner D. Review of 'Biopsy of Bone in Internal Medicine. An Atlas and Source Book. Bartl R, Frisch B. Dordrecht, Boston, London: Kluwer Academic Publishers.' *Rheumatology* 1994; **33**: 302–3.

Chapter 23

1. Sacks O. *Uncle Tungsten. Memories of a Chemical Boyhood*. London: Picador, 2001.

2. Cresswell CH. *The Royal College of Surgeons of Edinburgh. Historical Notes from 1505 to 1905*. Edinburgh: Oliver & Boyd, 1926.

3. Dingwall HM. *A Famous and Flourishing Society. The History of the Royal College of Surgeons of Edinburgh, 1505–2005*. Edinburgh: Edinburgh University Press, 2005.

4. Tansey V, Mekie DEC. *The Museum of the Royal College of Surgeons of Edinburgh*. The Royal College of Surgeons of Edinburgh, 1980.

5. Delingpole J. Ouch! Is this the direction our museums have to go? *The Times*, Saturday 18 March 2006.

6. Guthrie D. *A History of Medicine*. London: Thomas Nelson, 1945.

7. Mekie DEC, Fraser J. *A Colour Atlas of Demonstrations in Surgical Pathology*, volume 1. London: Wolfe Medical, 1983.

8. Gordon-Taylor G, Walls EW. *Charles Bell: His Life and Times*. Edinburgh: E & S Livingstone, 1958.

9. Walls EW, Gardner DL. *Charles Bell 1774–1842: Surgeon, Physiologist, Artist and Author*. Edinburgh: Royal College of Surgeons of Edinburgh, 1996.

10. Gardner DL. *Is There a Future for Medical Museums*? International Academy of Pathology, 2006.

11. Gardner DL. *Surgeon, Scientist, Soldier: The Life and Times of Henry Wade 1876–1955*. London: Royal Society of Medicine Press, 2005.

12. Gardner DL, Macnicol MF, Endicott P, Rayner DRT, Geissler P. A little-known aspect of Arthur Conan Doyle (1859–1930). The call of India and a debt to Walter Scott (1771–1832). *J Med Biogr* 2009; **17**: 2–7.

13. Gardner DL. *Pathological Basis of the Connective Tissue Diseases*. London: Edward Arnold/Philadelphia: Lea & Febiger, 1992.

14. Gardner DL. *Pathology for Surgeons in Training* (with DEF Tweedle). London: Edward Arnold, 1996 (reprinted 1998); 3rd edn, 2002.

15. Gardner DL. Die 'Infirmaries' in Edinburgh: Ihre Geschichte und Gründung. *Historia Hospitalium* 1996; **19**: 7–19

16. Gardner, DL. Robert Knox and Joseph Lister: pioneers of vascular physiology. *J R Coll Physicians Edinb* 2003; **33** (Suppl 12): 42–5.

17. Gardner DL. Henry Wade 1876–1955 and cancer research: early years in the life of a pioneer of urological surgery. *J Med Biogr* 2003; **11**: 81–6.

18. Gardner DL. Early twentieth century surgical urology: the 1909–1939 experience of Henry Wade. *Surgeon* 2003; **1**: 166–76.

Chapter 24

1. Stevenson RL. *Virginibus Puerisque*. London: C Kegan Paul, 1881.

2. Hunter D. *The Diseases of Occupations*, 5th edn. London: Hodder & Stoughton, 1975.

3. Osler W. *Aequanimitas, With Other Addresses to Medical Students, Nurses and Practitioners of Medicine*. London: HK Lewis, 1906.

4. Godlee RJ. *Joseph Lister*, 3rd edn. Oxford: Clarendon, 1924 (1st edn, 1917).

5. Darwin C. *The Origin of Species*. London: John Murray, 1859.

6. Reid R. *Marie Curie*. London: Granada, 1974.

7. Woodham-Smith C. *Florence Nightingale*. Harmondsworth: Penguin, 1951.

8. Thomas L. *The Youngest Science*. Oxford: Oxford University Press, 1985.

9. Medawar PB, Medawar JS. *The Life Science*. London: Granada, 1977.

10. Hawking SW. *A Brief History of Time: From the Big Bang to Black Holes*. London: Bantam, 1991.

11. Dawkins R. *The Greatest Show on Earth*. London: Bantam, 2009.

12. van Loon HW. *The Life and Times of Johann Sebastian Bach*. London: George G Harrap, 1945.

13. Schweitzer A. *J. S. Bach*, enlarged German edition. Leipzig: Breitkopf & Härtel, 1908 (English translation by Ernest Newman, London, 1911).

14. Kobbé G. *The Complete Opera Book*. Edited and revised by the Earl of Harewood. London: The Bodley Head, 1987.

15. Smythe FS. *Mountaineering Holiday*. London: Hodder & Stoughton, 1941.

16. Thubron C. *Among the Russians*. London: Heinemann, 1983.

17. Mann T. *The Magic Mountain*. Frankfurt: S Fischer, 1924 (English translation by JE Woods, 1995).

18. Forster EM. *A Passage to India*. London: Edward Arnold, 1924.

19. Dostoyevsky F. *Crime and Punishment*. London: JM Dent, 1911.

20. Hemingway E. *For Whom the Bell Tolls*. New York: Scribner, 1940/ Harmondsworth: Penguin, 1941.

21. MacLean A. *Where Eagles Dare*. London: Fontana, 1974.

22. Masters J. *Bhowani Junction*. Harmondsworth: Penguin, 1960.

23. Pasternak B. *Doctor Zhivago*. Milan: Feltrinelli, 1957/London: Fontana, 1958.

24. Solzhenitsyn A. *The Gulag Archipelago*. Paris: Editions du Seuil, 1973/ Glasgow: Collins/Fontana, 1973.

25. Churchill WS. *Frontiers and Wars* [His four early books covering his life as soldier and war correspondent edited into one volume]. London: Eyre & Spottiswoode, 1962.

26. Taylor AJP. *The Struggle for Mastery in Europe*. London: Oxford University Press, 1954.

27. Montgomery of Alamein. *A History of Warfare*. London: Collins, 1968.

28. Keegan J. *The First World War*. London: Pimlico, 1999.

29. Tolstoy L. *War and Peace*. London: Macmillan, 1942 (originally published 1869).

30. Curran J. *Agatha Christie's Secret Notebooks: Fifty Years of Mysteries in the Making*. London: HarperCollins, 2009.

31. Doyle AC. *The Sign of the Four*. Edited with an Introduction by Christopher Roden. Oxford: Oxford University Press, 1993 (originally published 1890).

32. Simenon G. *Maigret Goes to School*. London: Hamish Hamilton, 1957/ Harmondsworth: Penguin, 1992.

33. Le Carre J. *The Spy Who Came in From the Cold*. London: Pan, 1974 (originally published 1963).

34. Munthe A. *The Story of San Michele*. London: John Murray, 1929.

35. Gardner DL. *Surgeon, Soldier, Scientist. The Life and Times of Henry Wade 1876–1955*. London: Royal Society of Medicine Press, 2005.

36. *The Paintings of L. S. Lowry*. London: Jupiter Books, 1975.

37. Marks J. *The NHS: Beginning, Middle and End?* Oxford: Radcliffe, 2008.

38. Hoyle F. *The Black Cloud*. London: Heinemann, 1957.

39. Vermes G. *Jesus the Jew. A Historian's Reading of the Gospels*. London: SCM Press, 2001.

40. Weiner JS. *The Piltdown Forgery*. London: Oxford University Press, 1955.

Index

Reader's Notes
Page numbers in italic denote figures.

CG = Colin Gardner (brother); DG = Dugald Gardner (author); DILMcQ = David Iain Lindsay McQueen (grandson); EMS = Edinburgh Medical School; INFMcQ = Iain Norman Fanshawe McQueen (son-in-law); MG = Marjorie Gardner (mother); RCSEd = Royal College of Surgeons of Edinburgh; RG = Rosalind Gardner; TG = Thomas Gardner (father).

The entries for the author and his wife, Helen, are in subject format. The Mac... and Mc... names are conflated.

A
Aalsmeer 89
Aarhus (Århus) 258–9
Abbotsholme School, Derby 187, 238
Aboriginal settlement 277
Abscess, mastoid 25
Academy of Medicine, Poland 267
acupuncture 215
Adair, Dr Gilbert 55
Adami Lecture 246, *246*
Adamson, W. A. D. FRCSEd 69, *70*, 84
Addenbrooke's Hospital 59, 111
    laboratories 114
    morbid anatomy 114, 115
Adelaide 273–84
adenoma 334
Adrian, Professor E. D., FRS 55
Air Training Corps (ATC) 45
Aitken, Lewis and Heather 156
Ajayi, George 332
Al Faisal, Prince Turki 344
Alan Stubbs and Partners 172
Alba 345
Albert II, Prince of Monaco 344
Alcazar, Tangier 345
Aldinga, Australia 282
aldosterone 137
Alejadinho Antonio Francisco Lisboa, sculptor 227

Alexander, Dr Rowland 124
Allan, Leslie 328
Allan, Dr W. S. A. 161
Allen, Professor Ingrid 191, *197*
Almond, Dr Hely Hutchinson 34
Altmann, F. P. 175
American Association of Anatomists 180
American Heart Association meeting 150
Americium[95] 160
amoebiasis 222
amphetamine 95
Amsterdam Gate, Haarlem *89*
anaemia, in rheumatoid arthritis 129
anaesthetics
    chloroform 25
    nitrous oxide 26
    pentothal 105
anatomy 53–5
Anatomy Museum, Royal College
    of Surgeons Edinburgh *323*, 330
Andamanese skeleton 333
Anderson, Dr 182
Anderson, Dr W. White 87
Anderson, Professor John (Jock) Allan Dalrymple 38, *204*

Andrews, J. D. 34
angiotensin 146
animal model for arthritis 128
animal rights protests 244
ankylosing spondylitis 128, 270, 314
Annandale, Professor Thomas 2
anomalous inferior vena cava *116*, 116–17
anterior pituitary tumour 333
antibiotics
    'broad spectrum' 117
    chloramphenicol 117
    chlortetracycline 102
    penicillin 15, 82, 106
    streptomycin 94
    sulphonamides 15, 82, 106
    resistance 117
Appachalians *148*
Appleton, Sir Edward FRS 75
Archer, Professor Desmond 187
Archers, The 99
Armistice Day 30
Armstrong, Dr Cecil 153, 198
Aroona Valley, Australia 284
arsphenamine 82
arthritis
    experimental 314
    research 128

Arthritis and Rheumatism
    Council, ARC 169, 174,
    176, 177, 180
  Education and Scientific
    Research Committee 247
  Scientific Coordinating
    Committee 180, 247
arthroplasty 315
Aschoff, Ludwig 127
Ashby, Sir Eric FRS 185
Association of American
    Pathologists 146–8
astronomy 352
Athenaeum, election to 180
Atlas of Surgical Pathology 329
atomic bomb 178
aureomycin 117
Aurora 264, *265*
Australia 273–89, 281–9
Australian Society for
    Experimental Pathology
    280
Australian Travel motel 284
Austria 107–108
autoanalyser 83, 115, 137, 338
autopsies 83, 94, 129, 156–8,
    188, 223, 231, 241, 338
Ayad, Dr Shirley 316
Azlan Shah, Sultan 326, 326

B
baboon studies 159, 198
Babylon 296–8
Bacon, Dr Paul 175
Baghdad 292, 294–6
Baillie, Mathew 196
Balaclava 349
balance 126
  decimicro 160
Balaton, Lake 256
Baldwin, Ernest 56
Ball, Dr John 270
Baltic 346
Bamburgh 164–5
Banerjee, Dr S. S. 241
Bangkok 209, *210–11*
banking, in 1930s 15–6
Barber Surgeons Incorporation
    321, 381
Barcelona 346
Barclay Hall 326–7, 330
Barlow, Irene 240, 281

Barmbek Military Hospital *98*,
    98–104, 258
Barnett, Dr 147
Baron, Mr 28, 29
Barossa Valley, Australia 283
Barrett, Dr Arthur Max *58*, 58,
    114, 115, 116
Barrett, Dr Stanley 161
Barrie, Dr Herbert 171
Basilica, Istanbul 347
Bathgate, James 126–7, 328
Bat-Sheva de Rothschild
    Foundation for the
    Advancement of Science
    299
Bean, Margaret 328
Beaumont Research
    Laboratories, Mt Sinai
    Hospital 137
Beijing 214
Beke Hotel, Budapest 256
Belfast
  hospitals 187–9
  Queen's University of 185
Belgian Congress of
    Rheumatology 270
Belgian Society of
    Rheumatology 314
Belgium 269–71
Bell, Sir Charles FRS 329, *329*,
    331, 332, 335
Bell, Dr Douglas 344, 345
Belo Horizonte 226, 228–9
Belsen 58–9, 105–6
Bély, Dr Miklos 256
Beneke, Professor 200
Bennett, Brigadier J. 102
Bennett, Cecil 193
Bernard, Claude 57
Bertfield, H. FRCSEd 248
Berti, Major 103
Bessborough Hotel, Saskatoon
    154
Best, George (driver) 15, 16, 59
Bettridge, Peter and Philippa
    (née Gardner) 238, 312
Beveridge Report 14
Bicknell, Alan 112, 119
Biggart, Sir John Henry 157,
    182–3, 191, *193*, 194
  Dennis (son of Sir JH) 192
Biggart House 185

biochemistry 55–6, 316
Biological Research Advisory
    Board 167, 200
biopsy 156–7, 188, 241, 279
Birch, Ian 291
Bird, Professor Colin 307, 312,
    313, 314
Bird, Dr Howard 263, 293
Birdwood, Australia 282
Birmingham Medical School
    171
Biron, Mr 236
Bismarck, battleship 47
Bitensky, Lucille 175
Black, Dr James 161
Black, Sister *70*, 84
Black Forest 21–2
black market in Germany
    109–10
Black Sea 347
Blacklock, Professor Norman
    250, *251*
'blackshirts' 21–2
Blackwood, Dr William 66
Blagbrough, David 229
Blaschko, Hermann ('Hugh') 55
blastomycosis 225
Bleetman, Tony FRCSEd 332
Bloch, Dr E. H. 144
blood counts 115
blood platelet counts 116
blood transfusion 117–18
Blood Transfusion Service 83
Blue Mosque, Istanbul 347
Boa Viagem Hotel, Brazil 219
Bone and Tooth Society 200
bone marrow sampling 115
Bo'ness 135, 149
  dockyard 72
Bonomo, Professor Israel 219,
    229
book reviewing 317
books
  DG's interests 26–7, 32, 74,
    130–1, 150, 258, 260,
    340–1, 352
Booth, F. E. *40*
Boston 146–8
Botafumeiro ceremony 345
Boulter, Professor P. D. FRCSEd
    328
Boy Scouts organization 29

Boyd, Dr George 162
Boyd, Professor J. D. 54–5
Boyd, T. J. *40*
Brachina Gorge, Australia 284
Bradley, W. A. (Tony) 244, 313
Brander, Dr E. S. 333
Brandt, Dr Ken 175, 269
Branwood, Dr Whitley 150, 161
Brasilia 222–4
Brazil 219–33, *220–1*
Bridges, Mrs Freda 17
Briggs, W. A. 175
Brightelmstone (Brighton) 10
Brighton
    defence in WWII 12, 46
    early life in 9–12
    school holidays at 46
    university vacations in 59
Brighton and Hove Golf Club
    18
Brighton and Hove Natural
    History Museum 30
Brighton, Hove and Sussex
    Grammar School *27*, 27–32
British Army of the Rhine
    (BAOR) 97–8
British Medical Association
    (BMA)
    DG invited to join 75
    father as local secretary to 16
British Military Hospitals
    98–104
British Restaurants 50
Brocklehurst, Professor John C.
    240, 317
Broom, Dr Neil 280
Brown, Dr 70
    Brown, Enid *see* Harrower, Enid
Brown, Henry Colin 38, *40*
Brown, Major Peter 100, 104
Browning, General 'Boy' 120
'brownshirts' 20
Bruce, Sir John FRCSEd 329
Brudenell, Michael FRCS 105,
    110
Bruges 270–1
Brunei, Sultan of 326
Budapest 254–6
Buffalo 150
Bullock, Christine 331
Bunce, Dr Donald F. M. 151,
    151, 181

Bunraku 206
'Burchetts', Sussex 156
Burke, Dr. W. 78, *85*
Burke, William 334
Burkitt, Dr Denis Parsons FRS 328
Burn, Mr 133
Burnett, John 327
Bush, Peter 315
Busuttil, Professor Tony 327
Butcher, R. G. 175
Butterworth, Dr Karen 243
Byers, Dr Paul 200
Byrom, Dr F. B. 159
Bywaters, Professor E. G. L.
    (Eric) 163, 181, 247

C
Cadet Force 37
Cairns, Australia 286
Callam, Dr W. D. A. 69
Calvert, Major Michael 102
Cambridge 111
Cambridge University 47,
    49–60, 111–20
    Natural Sciences Tripos 53,
    57–8
Cameron, Major General 107
Cameron, Professor Sir Roy 160,
    167
Cameron, Stuart 193
Campbell, Ian FRCSEd 84
Campbell, Professor A. C. P. 239
Campbell College, Belfast 187,
    199
Canada 148–9, 152, 153–4
Canberra 285
    University *286*
cancer
    radioactive isotopes as causes
    159
    blood tests in patients 116
caragheenin provokes
    inflammation 128
cardiac deformity, congenital
    116, 333–4
cardiology 121
cardiology centre in Kiev 266
Cardosa, Dr Vasco 224
Carmichael, Dr Katherine 67
cartilage
    collagen measurement 204
    extracellular matrix 314, 316

research methods 299, 303–5
    surfaces 179, 198
    three-dimensional structure
    314–6
Castellani, Dr (Sir) Aldo *8*
Castelnau guest house, London
    169
Cathcart Hall *324*
Cathcart Museum 323
Catholic Mater Hospital 189
cell-counting device, automatic
    338
Chadwick, Mr 231
Chagal windows 301
Chagas' disease 222, *222*, 224–6
Chalmers, John FRCSEd 177
Charing Cross Hospital Medical
    School
    Kennedy Institute of
    Rheumatology,
    Directorship 169, 172
Charles, HRH Prince: marries
    Diana 278–9
Chayen, Joseph 175
Chemical Defence
    Establishment, Biological
    Research Advisory Board
    247
China 214–17
Chisholm, Sister 79, *80*, 81
chloramphenicol 117
chlortetracycline 102, 117
chondrosarcoma 315, 333
Christ statue, Brazil 229, *230*
Chrystal Macmillan building
    160
Churchill, Winston 38, 44
Ciba Geigy 244, 291, 313, 314
cinemas 32, 342
City Hospital, Lisburn 189
Clare Bridge, Cambridge 51
Clare College, Cambridge 49,
    50–59, *50*, 120, *120*
    Memorial Court 49, *50*
Clark, Adam 255
Clark, William Tierney 255
Cleary, Dr Ted 280
Cleland, Dr A. 35
Cleland Zoo Park, Adelaide
    281, 283
Clements, A. B. 29
Cleveland, Ohio 140–6, 150, 338

Cleveland Orchestra 141
clinical care at RIE 80–5
Clinical Chemistry at
    Addenbrooke's Hospital
    114, 115
clinical skills 67–70
clinical surgery test 74
clinical trials 106
clinicopathological conferences
    146
Clive of India 34
Clostridium difficile 117
Cole, Dr Leslie 116
Coleraine *192*
Colhoun, Dr 196
Coll, Dr Harry 65, *70*, 345
Collee, Professor John Gerald
    162
College Fire Squad, Clare
    College 51–2
Collins, Professor Douglas
    128
Collis HJG 169
colour vision 17, 55, 338, 343
Colquhoun, Angus 46
Compston, Dr Juliet 315
computer tomography atlas
    240
Conan Doyle, Arthur 333
concentration camps 105–6
Congress of Rheumatology
    meetings
    Lisbon 181
    Tokyo 203
Constitution, USS 147, *147*
Cook, John FRCSEd 329
Cooke, T. D. V. 153
Copacabana Beach 229, *230*
Copeman, Dr W. (Will) S. C.
    169, 172–7, *176*, 180, 181,
    182, 253–4
Copenhagen 259
Corbett, Carlos 233
Corcovado *230*
cormorant fishing 217
Cornell University Medical
    School 150
coronary artery disease 251–2
coroner's autopsy 115, 241
'cot death' 115
Coulson, Dr Walter 161
County Down *187*

Court-Brown, Dr C. M. 315
Cowan, Mr 37
'Craigdhu', Bo'ness 156
Craigleith View 155–6
Crane, Dr W. J. (Bill) 167
Cranham Cottage, Minehead
    23
cricket *277*, 278
crimes in Germany 110
Critchley, Dr MacDonald 102
Crofton, Sir John 157
Crookham army training centre
    97–8
Croom, Dr J. Halliday 95
Crossland, Professor Sir Bernard
    198
Crow, D.A. FRCSEd 25
Croydon Airport *30*, 30
Cruickshank, Professor Bruce
    126, 128, 314
Crusaders 30
Crystal Palace fire 18
Cuddy, The 130
Cummins, Christopher FRCSEd
    90–1, 285
    Cynthia 285
Currie, Professor (Sir) Alastair
    196, 307

D
da Silva Xavier, Joaquim Jose
    227–8
Dale, Dr M. F. 175
Daniel, Lieutenant (Sister)
    Margaret *101*, 101–2, 125,
    132, 138, 158, 180
Danube *254*, 254–7
Dark, Richard 38
Darling, Grace 164
Darracott, Dr Peter 263
daunorubicin 177, 179
Davey, Margaret Elizabeth *see*
    Rickard, Margaret Elizabeth
    (DG's maternal great-great-
    grandmother)
Davidson, Dr J. K. (Jake) *85*, 345
Davidson, Dr James 66
Davidson, Professor Sir L.
    Stanley P. 60, 67, 125
Davies, Dr D. V. 54
Davis, Dr and Mrs Owen 260
Davis, Dr R. I. 316

Dawyck Gardens 131
de Almeida, Dr Antonio
    Joachim 227
de Britto, Professor Thales
    231–233
de Lacerda, Professor 230
de Moubray, G. L. L. *40*
de Paula, Professor 229, 230
Dead Sea *302*, 303, *303*
Dean, Professor Henry Roy 56,
    56–7, 58, 114
Del Ferreira, Dr Luis Carlos 226
Delbarre, Dr F. 219
Demarco, Richard 342
Denmark 258–9
Dental Museum, RCSEd,
    Edinburgh *327*, 326–7, 330
dental student examinations
    163
Denver, Colorado 152
Derby Royal Infirmary 93–4,
    308
Devereux, Vera 6
diagnostic tests 83
Dickinson, Eric 32
Die Drei Zigeuner hotel,
    Lermoos 107–8
digitalis 82
Directors of Studies 162
Dische, Dr Frederick Ephraim
    and Silvia 138
Diseases of Occupations 340
Disney Land 149
Dixon, Dr Alan 254
Dixon, chauffeur 119
Dixon, Reginald ('Reg') 16
Dnieper River, Russia 265–6,
    266
Dobson
    Alice 6, 74
    Dr (Alice's father) 6
    Dr G. M B, F.R.S. 6
Dodds, Thomas Cairns 66, 127,
    127, 157, 160
Domestic Science School,
    Edinburgh 73
Donaldson, Bob 313
Dott, Norman FRCSEd 159, 334
Dragoon Guards 102
Drennan, Professor A. Murray
    66, 126
drug addiction 85

drug development 82
Dublin 190
Duff, Sir Gordon W. 315
Dumonde, Dr Dudley 175, 177
Duncan, C. H. Stuart 39
Dunster *19*
Duthie, Professor John James
    Reid (Ian) 124, 125, 158,
    169, 180, 198, 203, *204*
Dutton, Professor (Adelaide) 275
dwarfism 334
dyes, coloured 342

E
ear infection 25
Eden, Anthony 44
Edinburgh 19
    International Festival 308–9
Edinburgh, Duke of 325
Edinburgh Royal Infirmary
    School of Nursing 171
Edinburgh University
    Medical School, (EMS)
        foundation 323
        hospital practice at 68
        see also Medical School
            new building 160, *160*
        Pathology Department
            124, 125–8
Edmond, Peter FRCSEd 332
Edward Lewis Foundation 175
Edwards, Dr (Adelaide) 275
Eger 255
Elizabeth II, HM Queen, opens
    Withington Hospital new
    unit 250, *251*
Elliot, Dr Roy 198, 204
El-Maghraby, Dr M.A. H. A.
    176, 177–8, 207
Elmes, Professor Peter 195
'Elmpark', Earngarth Road,
    Bo'ness *72*, 72, 112, 135, 156
Empire Exhibition, Glasgow 19
Else, housekeeper 111
Elstein, Professor Max 240
emergency medicine 78
Esson, Michael 332
Eulderink, Professor Frits 268,
    316
European Congress of
    Rheumatology 253, 256,
    258, 259, 267

European League Against
    Rheumatism(EULAR) 163
    Honorary Membership 317
    Pathology Committee 163,
        181, 247, 268
Evans, Professor (BRAB) 167,
    182
Evans, Robin 219
Evanson, Professor John 240
Everest 118
Eves, Doreen and Derek 189
examining students 162–3, 181,
    196–7, 245–6, 316–7, 329
Expo 70, Kyoto 203, *205*
Ey, Dr 278

F
Faed, Dr Michael 159
Fahmy, Dr Chalmers 70
Fairbairn, Lynsey 313
Falconer, C. D. (Dale) *70*, 84
Falshaw, Norah 6
Fassbender, Professor 209
Fazzalari, Nick 280
Feldberg, Wilhelm Siegmund
    FRS 55
Feldman, Joan 178
Fell, Dame Honor Bridget FRS
    198
Fellowship of RCSEd,
    examining students for
    163, 197, 328
Fenske, Herr 99
Fergusson, William 334
Fermentech 314
Fernando, Dr 233
Field Dressing Stations 104
Final MB Examinations at EMS
    73–4
Findlay, David C. 313
Fitzgerald, Dr Patrick 152
Fitzmaurice, Dr Richard 241,
    315, 317
Fleming, Captain 102, 103
Flinders Medical School 281
Flinders Range, Australia 284
Florence, Italy 109
Florey, Professor Sir Howard
    FRS 57, 163, 166, 273
Floyer, Dr M. A. 159
Flying Scotsman 33
Fonteyn, Margot 110

food rationing 107
Forbes, William 66
Ford, Professor W. (Bill) L. 239,
    281
forensic pathologists vii
Forrest, Professor Alistair
    Douglas 38–9
Forrest, Dr John 233
Fortaleza 220–2, *221*
    Medical School 222
Fortaleza Conference 219
Forth Bridge *43*
Foster, Jim 327
Fox, Professor Harold 239
France 269
François, Dr Robert 269–70,
    314
Frank, J. R. FRCSEd *70*
Fraser, Professor Kenny 194
Fraser, Professor Sir James
    FRCSEd 65, *78*, *85*, 245,
    345
Freeman, Michael FRCS 208
Fresno 149
Friedman, Dr Horacio 232,
    233
Froggatt, Sir Peter Leslie 194
'Front, The', Brighton 11
Frost, Muffet (HG's cousin) and
    Lionel 150, 152, 153
Fujiyama, Mount *214*
Furry Dragon Restaurant,
    Warsaw 269

G
Gabuzda, Dr George J. 146
Gaddum, Professor John Henry
    FRS 67
Gairloch *119*
Galbraith, Sam 333
Gallipoli Peninsula 349, *350*
Gama, Dr 226–9
Gardner
    Annie (aunt) 1, *7*, 19
    Colin Guy Muir (brother) 20,
        28, *29*, *36*
    as Best Man 87–8
    birth 10–1
    death 318
    DG visits to 312
    schools 26, 36
    wedding 108

Gardner – *contd*
David (son) *164, 165, 166,*
191, 310
birth 155
graduation, Sussex
University *308,* 308
in Manchester *248*
moves to Belfast 186
schools 170, 187
sports 238
visits Australia 273 *et seq*
visits China 212, 214, 215
visits Hungary 256
West Manchester College
247
Denise (wife of CG) 108,
249
Dugald (author) *36, 105, 191,*
193, 197, 207, 309
career
Adami Lecturer,
University of
Liverpool *246,* 246
in army 97–110, 119–20
Catholic Mater Hospital,
Consultant at 189
Director of Kennedy
Institute, London
169
Director of Institute of
Pathology, Belfast
188, 191–3, *197*
Director of Studies,
Faculty of Medicine,
Edinburgh 162
Honorary Consultant to
SE Regional Hospital
Board 155
as Hospital Consultant
156–8
Junior Assistant Clinical
Pathologist,
Addenbrooke's
Hospital 111
as Edinburgh medical
student 61–74
as Cambridge medial
student 49–60
memberships 180,
199–200, 246–7,
256, 317
moves to Belfast 185–7

Nuffield Fellow,
Cleveland, Ohio
137–146
organizes ARC
symposium 244
Pathology Department
of Edinburgh
University
lectureship 134–5
new staff room *161*
research 126–30
senior lectureship 155
senior research
Fellowship 307–8
Professor of
Histopathology
at Withington
Hospital, Manchester
235–52, *239, 243*
Professor Emeritus,
Manchester
University 252
Public communications
116–17, 199–200,
212–13, 259, 267,
293, 303, 334–5
Publication of books 163,
245, 317, 341
Resident House
Physician at RIE
76–83, *78*
Resident House Surgeon
at RIE 84–85, *85*
reunion with fellow
students 344–5
Secretary of Pathology
Committee, EULAR
181
Senior House Officer
at Louth County
Infirmary 91–5
Visiting Professor,
University of South
Australia, Adelaide
273–89
Education and qualifications
prizes 38
school in England 25–32
school in Scotland 32–47
at University of
Cambridge 49–60,
337–8

BA 60
MA 60
ScD 252
at University of
Edinburgh 61–74
PhD 135
MB, ChB 73–4
MD 135
at University of
Manchester
MSc 252
family and friends 1–8, 38–9
DG as grandparent
318Dugald (DG's
grandfather) 1
Frank (DG's great-uncle)
5–6, 27, 32
life in Manchester
247–8
support 343–4
visits to 312
[for children and
grandchildren] see
also under Gardner;
McQueen
illnesses 25–6, 59, 105,
250–2, 350–1
interests
acting 37
art 342
cars 91–2, *91,* 99–100,
108, 123, 141,
148–9, 172, 190,
281, 284, *287*
cinema 32
colour vision 17, 55,
338–43
films 32, 342
music 17, 29, 39, 52–3,
73, 93, 103–4, 141,
255, 276, 308–9,
339, 340, 351
philosophy of life 352
photography 31
religion 41–2, 351–2
smoking 36
social 65, 118, 171,
189–90, 247, 276
stamp collecting 17, 342,
343
theatre 227, 342
woodwork 30–1

life events
    50th wedding
        anniversary 345, 347
    acquires TV 155
    birth 9, *9*
    dental care 35–6, 105
    early years in Brighton
        9–12
    engagement to HG 73, *74*
    honeymoon 88–90
    joins Cubs 29–30
    marriage 87–90
    retirement 252, 341–53
    wartime activities 44–7,
        49–51
research
    arthritis 128–9, 158–160,
        177–80, 197–8
        collagen measurement
            204
        extracellular matrix
            314
        methods 299, 303–4
        surfaces 179, 198
        three-dimensional
            structure 315–16
    at Cambridge 116–17
    cartilage disorders 243
    in Cleveland, Ohio 141–8
    connective tissue disease
        163, 312
    grants 149–50, 198, 243,
        244, 281, 313
    hypertension research
        129, 143–6, 150,
        159, 177
    in London 169–183
    at Lancaster 243
    in Pathology
        Department,
        University of
        Edinburgh 128–30,
        313–6
    research for PhD 127–8
    in Rheumatic Diseases
        Unit, Northern
        General Hospital,
        Edinburgh 121 *et seq*
    rheumatoid arthritis
        158–60
    synovial microscopy
        313–14

    at Withington Hospital,
        Manchester 242–4
sport interests
    cricket 278
    cycling 41
    fives 40
    golf 40, 65, 134, 199,
        217, 238, 343
    hockey 40
    physical exercises 32
    rugby 39–41, *40*, 53, 103,
        120, 199, 343
    running 40
    skiing 104
    table tennis 343
    tennis 40, 53, 71–2, 238,
        343
travels and holidays 118
    after retirement 345–50
Helen (wife) (née Harrower)
    14, *105*, *113*, *165*, *166*,
    191, *192*, *257*, *260*
interests 93
    music 73
    religion 351
    theatre 342
life events
    caring for grandchildren
        200
    at DG's graduation 75
    engagement to DG 73, *74*
    falls in Manchester
        247–8
    gives birth to
        David 155
        Iain 110
        Philip 130
        Rosalind 104–5
    illnesses 209, 224, 256–7,
        298
    joining DG in Hamburg
        99
    marriage to DG 87–90
    meets DG 71–2
    nursing 79
    retirement 345–50, 351
    supporting DG 343–4
moves and travels
    at opening of Nuffield
        Rheumatic Diseases
        Unit *124*
    Belfast 186, *191*, *192*

    Cambridge *113*
    Peebles 132
Iain Dugald (son) *8*, *113*, *123*,
    164, *166*, *310*
    Birmingham Medical
        School 171, 219
    birth 110
    birthday celebrations 130,
        138, 149
    on board *Hanseatic 139*
    Derby Royal Infirmary 308
    DG's visits to 312
    graduation 200, *201*
    helps in research
        laboratories 159
    on holiday *130*
    illnesses 141–2, 156, 171
    marries Lynn Morgan 237,
        237
    medical career 171
    moves to Cambridge 112
    schools 122–3, 141, 155,
        169
    sport interests 171
    surgical career in
        ophthalmology 187
    visits Belfast 199
    visits Manchester 247, *248*
    winter in USA *142*
Jean (DG's grandmother)
    (née Muir) 1
Jean (DG's great-
    grandmother) (née
    Livingstone) 1
Lynn (née Morgan) (wife of
    IDG) 237
    DG's visits to 312. 344
Marjorie (DG's mother) *9*, *20*,
    28, *36*, *122*, *248*
    80th birthday 172
    becomes Chairman of
        Brighton and Hove
        branch of the ARC 172
    birth 5
    death 249
    DG's memories of 340
    illness 22
    love of music 16–17
    meeting DG's father 3
    moves 23, 156, 248–9
    theatre 342
    visits 107, 118, 148, 156,

Gardner – *contd*
  Perry (CG's son) 238
  Philip (DG's son) *123*, *164*,
      165, *166*, *191*
    Birmingham University
        171
    birth 130
    car 237–8
    death 249–50
    illnesses 171–2
    law career 171, 249, *249*
    moves to Belfast 186
    music interests 170–1, 190
    schools 155, 169–70, 187,
        199
    sport interests 171, 190–1
    thoughts on 344
    in USA 138, 149
    visits Manchester 247, *248*
    winter in USA *142*
  Philippa (CG's daughter)
      see Bettridge, Peter and
      Phillipa
  Rosalind (DG's daughter)
      113, *123*, *164*, *165*
    birth 104–5, *105*
    on *Hanseatic 139*
    DG's visits to 312
    driving 170
    engagement to Iain
        Norman Fanshawe
        McQueen 186
    gives birth to
      Alastair 238
      David 200
      Jane 200
      Robert 250
    in Glasgow 219
    on holiday *130*
    illnesses 144, 171
    marriage to Dr. McQueen
        187
    moves to Cardiff 237, 308
    music interests 170–1
    nursing career 171
    schools 122–3, 141, 155, 169
    winter in USA *142*
  Thomas (DG's father) 1, *3*, 8,
      8, *20*
    army service 76–7
    attitude to NHS 76
    birth 1

    books 17–18
    career advice to DG 38
    cars 16, 18, *20*
    character 14–15
    death 23, 64
    as doctor 2, 13–16
    FRCSEd 7–8, *8*
    illness 22–3
    local secretary to BMA 16
    London School of Hygiene
        and Tropical Medicine
        7, 8
    Lorna Doone 4
    memories of 340
    Ross malaria Commission
        3
    school 1–2
    stamp collecting 17
    work 1–2
    WWI years 2–3, *3*
  Thomas (DG's great-
      grandfather) 1
  Thomas (DG's great-uncle) 1
Geissler, Dr Paul 326, 327
General Medical Council, rules
    76
George IV, HM King 10
George VI, HM King, death
    107–8
George Square, Edinburgh 160
German language 109
Germany 258
    in 1936 19–22
    post-WWII 97–107
Gettysburg 148, *149*
Ghadially, Professor Feroze N.
    154, 280
Gibson, Mr and Mrs 62, 182
Gieben, Dr Bram 74
gigantism 334
Gilbert and Sullivan operas 29
Gilchrist, Ronald 37, *40*
Gillespie, Ronald 46
Gillespie, Professor W. J. (Bill)
    315
Gillett, Roy 176
Gillan, Mr 331
Gillies, Dr Robert (Bob) 63,
    194
Gillingham, Professor John
    FRCSEd 335, 343
Gillman, Dr Ted 165, 169

Gilmore, Ruth 198, 208
Gloucester, Duke and Duchess
    of 174, *175*
Glover, Don and Sue 140–1
Glynn, Dr L. E. 172, 175, 208
Goiania 224–6
gold mines, Brazil 227
Goldblatt, Dr Harry 137, 145,
    145, 150
Goldsmith, Mr 18
golf 40, 65, 134, 199, 217, 238,
    343
Goodwin, Rev. R. A. 42
Gorevic, Peter D. 176
Gorky Square, Moscow 263
Goudie, Professor R. A. B. (Bob)
    247
Gould, Dr John *85*
gout 294
Grahame, Rodney 175
Grandchildren *see under*
    McQueen
Gray, Beryl 110
Gray, Miss 35
Gray, Noel FRCSEd 335
Great Wall of China 215
Green, Dr H. L. H. 54
Greenlees, Dr J. R. C. 34, 38,
    42–4, 46, 47
Greig, David FRCSEd 333
Gresham, Professor Austin 114,
    245
Greyfriars Church, Edinburgh
    187
  Greyfriars Bobby 63, *64*
Grieve
  Jean (cousin) *28* and Jim 75,
      164, 309
  Jeremy 273
  Tony 309
Gross, Dr J. 147
Grosvenor St Aidan's Church,
    Manchester 250
Grueter, Madeline 208
Gryfe, Dr Art 176
Guilin 217
Gunn, Dr Clement Bryce 132
Gunn, Tony FRCSEd 328
Gunter, Pat 313
Guy Fawkes's night 123
Gwinnett, Peter and Karen 259,
    261–2

H

Haarlem 88–90, 342
Haboubi, Dr Nagib Y. 241, 243, 292, 296
Hacking, David 51
Hadassah Hospital and Medical School, Jerusalem 301
Hadrian's Roman Wall 165
haemangioma 315
haematology 83, 114, 115
Hagia Sophia, Istanbul 347
Hahndorf, Australia 282
Hailsham, Lord 170
Hall, Dr Andrew 315
Hall, Dr T. A. (Ted) 178–9
Hamburg 98–104, 107
Hamilton, Dr 148
Hamilton, Ontario 153
Hammermakers Incorporation, Edinburgh 62, *63*
Hammersmith, Mayor of 176
Hammond, Pamela 212
Hanging Gardens of Babylon 296–7
Hannington's store, Brighton 13
Hanover 110
Hanseatic, HSS 138
Harcourt-Webster, Dr Nigel 156, 162
Harding, Dr P. 279
Hardingham, Professor Tim 175
Hare, Mrs 64
Hare, William 334
harmonium playing 73
Harris, Dr G. W. FRS 54
Harris, Professor H. A. 53
Harris, Harvey 156
Harris, Dr Martin 241
Harris, Nettie 26
Harris, Phillip FRCSEd 156
Harrison, Professor David 314, 351
Harrower
   David B. (Davie) (HG's father) 87, *88*, 118, *123*, 138, 156
   Emily (HG's mother) *88*, *122*, *123*
      death 249
      and grandchildren 149

helping with DG's wedding 87
   moves 156, 236, 248–9
   visits 118, 199
   Enid (HG's sister-in-law) 135, 156, 308, 318, *318*
   Fergus *318*
   Florence Pike (HG's sister) 91, 118, *166*
   Florence Sangster (HG's aunt) 112, 119, 156, 249
   Gordon (HG's brother) 108, 135, 156, 308, 318, *318*
   Helen *see* Gardner, Helen (wife)
   Louise Brown *318*
Haselton, Professor) Philip 241
Haslam, Peter 114
Havinden, Ashley and Margaret 88, 342
Hawking, Stephen 352
Hay, Colin 64, 65, 67, 73, 345
Heart, congenital abnormalities 116, *116*
Heath, Professor Donald 196, 199, 246, 316–17
Heberden Society 129
   Oration, 1971 179
Hedderwick, Major G. 45
Helen's Bay, Belfast 186, 189
Helicobacter pylori 22
Henderson, James 46
Henderson, Professor A. 251–2
Herrera, Dr Carlos Soria 176
Hewat, Dr Fergus 68, 70–1, 76–7, 79, 80, *80*, 81, 86, 90
Hick, John 250
Hickman, Barbara 174
'High Biggin' 6
Hilson, Lena and Don 236, 250
Hilton Hospital, South Australia 281
histochemistry 159
Histon, Cambridge 112–3, 118
histopathology 180, 279
hockey 40
Hoffman, Rosalind and Colin 236
Holland, Henry 10
Holland, honeymoon in 88–90
Holocaust memorial, Jerusalem 300–1, *302*

Holy Island 164
Holy Sepulchre Church, Jerusalem 300, *301*
Home Guard 44–5
Homeric, SS 149
Homer-Smith, Dr 148
Hong Kong 217
Hood, battlecruiser 47
Hooper, Dr M. 279
Hope Hospital, Salford 239
Hopkins, Sir Frederick Gowland FRS 55–6
Horder, Sir Thomas 26, 59
Hourihane, Professor Dermot *197*, 197, 245
Howard, Dr 223
Howarth, T. E. B. 169
Howell, Dr David 219, *220*
Howie, Colin FRCSEd 351
Hughes, Professor Sean 315
Hulmes, Dr David 314, 316
Human Histology 127
Hummel statue *101*
Hungarian Pathological Society 256
Hungarian Rheumatology Society 254–5
Hungarian Society of Anatomy and Pathology, Honorary Member 199
Hungary 254–7, *254*, *257*
Hunt, Dr Wilfred Estridge 134, 161, 191–2, *192*
   Joan 134
Husain, Hamid 235
Hussein, Field Marshall Saddam 296
Hutchinson, S. T. 45
hyaluronate, of synovial fluid 314
Hyashi, Dr Takashi 212
Hyatt Regency Hotel, Jerusalem 299
hydralazine
   hypertension and 159
   and SLE 129, 143
hypertension research 137, 143–6, 159, 177

I

immunology 200
influenza, death from 1, 3

Inoue, Professor Hajime
  ('Jimmy') 176, 179, 204,
  205, 206–7, 208, 211, 212,
  213
Institute of Pathology, Belfast
  188, 191–3
interference microscopy 159
internal medicine at EMS 68,
  79–83
International Academy of
  Pathology 258
International College of
  Angiology 180
Internationale Hotel, Moscow
  262
Iraq 291–9
Irvine, Professor W.T. (Bill)
  FRCSEd 101
Irvine, Douglas 175
Israel 299–306
Istanbul 347
Italy 109, 345, 346

J
Jackman, Thersie 6, 23, 156
Jackson, Miss 35, 63
Jacobs, David 170
Jacobson, Dr W. U. 55
James, Dr 276, 280
Janes, Dr 56
Japan 203–9, 211–14
Japanese language 211–12
Jasani, Dr Kris 244, 313
Jeans, Sir James 38, 50, 352
Jellinek, Professor Hari (Harry)
  181, 254, 255, 256
Jensen, Professor Olaf Myre
  258–9
Jerusalem 299–303, *300*
Johnston, George 311
Johnston, Rev. William Bryce
  87
Johnstone, Professor R. W. 67
Jones, Robert 241
Jones, Sheena 328
Josef Freidrich Gymnasium 345
Jules Thorn Exhibition 323,
  325, 329
Junior Assistant Clinical
  Pathologist, Addenbrooke's
  Hospital 114
Junior Training Corps (JTC) 44

K
Kadar, Anna 178, 181, 256
Kahn, Joseph R. 137, 146
Kailzie Gardens 134
Karachi 273
Kaye, Dr Clifford 251
Keenan, Dr Jock 69–70, 345
Kellar, Professor R. J. 67
Kennedy, John, Nigel and
  Priscilla (Scilla) (née
  Stoner) 17
Kennedy, Terence Frank 172,
  176
Kennedy, Terence Leslie F.R.C.S
  194
Kennedy Institute of
  Rheumatology 172–7, *173*
  Royal patron 176–7, *176*
Kentner, Louis 52–3
Kerényi, Dr T. 256
Kerr, Norman 133
Kessel, Professor W. I. N. 240
Kidd, Anthony Charles 39
kidney, artificial 137
  transplantation 157
Kiev 265–7, *266*
kimono factory 207
Kindersley, Lord 176
King, Dr Donald West 152
King's Cross station 33
Kingsmuir Hotel, Peebles 132–3
Kingston, Ontario 152, 153
Kinney, Dr Thomas D. *145*,
  149–50
Kirkland, Iain FRCSEd 134, 321
Kirkpatrick, Professor C. J. 198,
  241
Kiviranta, Dr Ilkka 316
Kivlin, Catrina 313
Kiyomizu Centre 207
Knopf, Mr and Mrs 140
Knox, Robert 334
Kobe 208
Kodama, Professor 180–1
Koletsky, Dr Simon 137, 143,
  144, 150
Kolff, Dr Willem 137
Krajewski, Dr Andrew 316
Krebs, Dr Hans 55, 56
Kremlin Congress Hall,
  Moscow 262–3
Kuettner, Dr Klaus 299

Kyoto 203–7, *205–7*

L
La Corunna 346
Laing, A. C. *40*
Laing, Christine 159
Lakeside Hospital, Cleveland
  141–2, 143, *143*
Lamb, Dr David 316
'Lanes, The', Brighton 11
Lankester, Dr Leslie 172
Laurie, Dr N. R. 114
'Laverock Bank' hotel 19
Lawrence, Dr J. S. (John) 240
Lawton, Dr D. M. (Max) 243
lead levels in teeth 315
Leak, Rev. Norman 249–50,
  352
Leake, Dr Chauncey D. 146
Learmonth, Professor Sir
  James FRCSEd 65, 67, 69,
  129
Leeuvenhoek Cancer Research
  Laboratories 89
Leiden 90
leishmaniasis 225
Lendrum, Professor A. C. 159,
  182
Lenin Hills, Moscow 263, *264*
Leningrad 264
Leonard, Dr 251
Lepow, Dr Irving ('Lee') 144,
  150
leprosy 222
Lermoos 107
Leslie, Bruce 315
Lessells, Dr Alastair 240
Lester, Ralph 28
leukoencephalitis, viral 159
Lewes, Dr Washington 226
Lewis Electron Microscope
  Laboratory 176
Lillicrap, Dr Charles 93–4
limb atrophy, spontaneous
  232
Lincolnshire 92, 93
Lindisfarne 164
Lindsay, Reverend John (DG's
  godfather) 2
Linklater, Mr 53–4
Lister, Joseph (Lord) *322*, 326,
  326,

Memorial Lecture 163
lithotripsy 250, *251*
Little, W. J. C. *40*
Littlejohn, Professor Sir Henry
 2
Livadia Palace 348
Liverpool School of Hygiene
 and Tropical Medicine 246
Liverpool University,
 examining students in 246,
 316–17
Livingstone Dispensary,
 Edinburgh 62–4, *63*
 Livingstone, Jean *see*
 Gardner, Jean (DG's
 great-grandmother)
Local Defence Volunteers (LDV)
 44
Lochearnhead 118
Lomax-Smith, Dr J. D. 278,
 279, 280
Longmore, Dr Barrie 198, 208
Lord Mayor's Appeal for the
 Disabled, Manchester 247
Loretto School, Musselburgh
 29, 34–46
Lorna Doone 4
Los Angeles 149
Lossiemouth 19
Loury, Dr 151
Louth 91–5
 County Infirmary 90–1, *91*,
 93–5
Lowry, L. S. 236, 342
lumbar puncture 69, 94
lung cancer 81–2
lymphangitis 59

M
McArthur, Scott 313
McCance, Professor R. A. 59
McClaren Vale, Australia 283
McClure, Professor John 192,
 196, 240, 241, 273, 279–81,
 282, 317
McCormack, Dr Lawrence 146
McCormack, RJM, FRCSEd 329
McCormick, John 124
MacDonald, Dr Mary 316
McDonald, Professor Lynn 326
McDowell, Ephraim 330, *330*
McEwan, Dr Currier 206, 208

McEwan, Margaret 125
MacFarlane, Rev. David 351
McGaughey, Patrick 180
McGeough, Professor J. A. (Joe)
 314, 315
McGeown, Dr Mary Graham
 (Mollie) 192, 194
McGill University, Montreal
 137
MacGillivray, Dr D. C. 176, 179
MacGregor, Dr Agnes 130
MacGregor, John D. 157,161
Mackail, Alan 327
MacKay, J. M. K. 159
Mackay, Sister 'Tottie' 70
McKee, Philip 192
McKenzie, Max 328
Mackenzie, G. S. *40*
Mackie, Thomas Jones 66
Mackiewicz, Stefan 268
McKeown, Professor Florence
 191, *193*, 201
McKusick, Dr Victor A. 146
MacLaren, I.F. FRCSEd 323
MacLaren, Dr Kathryn 161
McLean, H. W. P. ('Squeaker')
 39, 47
MacLean, Dr Neil 161, 316, 329
McMaster University
 Medical School teaching
 programme 154
Macmillan, C. G. 148
Macmillan, Professor Duncan
 332
McNair, TJ (Tom) FRCSEd 323
Macnicol, Malcolm FRCSEd 321
McQueen, Iain Norman
 Fanshawe (RG's husband)
 186–7, 199, 200, 247, *248*,
 251
 Alastair (INFMcQ's son) 238,
 318–20, *320*, 344
 David Iain Lindsay
 (INFMcQ's son) *248*, *319*,
 320
 Anya (DILMcQs daughter)
 318, *319*
 birth 200
 family 318
 marriage 318
 Sophia (DILMcQ's
 daughter) 318, *319*

Jane Rosalind (INFMcQ's
 daughter) 200, *248*, 318,
 319, 344
 marriage 318
 Robert Andrew (INFMcQ's
 son) 250, 320, *320*, 344
McQueen, Ms M. M. FRCSEd
 315
Magdalene Chapel, Edinburgh
 62–4, *63*
magnetic resonance imaging
 338
Mahaffey, David 193, *193*
Mahler, A. H. 37–8
Mahler, Dr Robert 84
Main, Dr Judy 87
Maini, Sir Ravinder Nath (Tiny)
 175, 263
Malakoff Fort, Sevastopol 348–9
malaria 222, 224, 334
 Ross Commission 3
Malazzo, Dr Steve 276, 278
Maldyk, Professor Eugeniusz
 268
Malik, Dr 200
Manchester Royal Infirmary
 238–9
Manchester University Medical
 School 238–9
 Department of Pathology
 239–40
Mannheim 20, 21
Marack, J. R. 58
Margaret, HRH Princess 176,
 176
Marks, Dr John 114
Marks, Dr John Henry 345
Marks, Mathilda 172
Marley, Denise *see* Gardner,
 Denise (wife of CG)
Marmion, Professor Barry 159,
 280
Maroudas, Dr Alice 179, 269,
 299, 306
Marriott, Peter 198
Marshall, Bun and Lill 92
Marshall, David James 39
Marshall, Professor Tom 188–91
Masada 301–3, *302*
Mason, Dr Michael 242
Mason, James 170
Masson, Dr Alastair 328, 383

Masson, Georges 146
Masson, James 126–7, 157
maternity care in Edinburgh 62
Matthew, Dr Henry 68–9, *86*
Matthews, Dr Margaret 176,
    178
Mazuryk, Dr Roman 244
Meachim, Dr George 200
Medawar, Professor Sir Peter FRS
    181
medical practice, post-WWI 15
Medical Research Council,
    membership of Systems
    Committee 247
Medical Research Society
    199–200
Medical School new building,
    University of Edinburgh
    160, 160–1
    Department of Pathology in
    161
medical specialization 121
medicine at EMS 68
Mekie, Professor Eric FRCSEd
    329
Mekie Room 327
Melbourne 284–5, *285*
    Zoo 285
Mellor, Mark 243
Memorial Court, Clare College
    49, *50*
Menin Gate 271
meningitis 102, 249,
Menzies Campbell, John 326
    collection 330
Merchiston School 45
Meredith, Ivor 119
Mermagen, P. H. F. 37
Meteorological Centre 200
Metropole Hotel, Budapest 256
Miami 150–1
Michelangelo exhibition 109
microbiology 66–7, 114, 115
microscopes
    cartilage analysis by 212
    DG's first 56
    electron 127,
    future of 338
    laser scanning 313, 314
    interference 159
    low temperature electron
    243, *243*, 338

scanning 243
    in Manchester *239*, 240
microanalysis, electron-probe
    X-ray 178
microscopy of joints 178in
    Museum 334
    optical bench 127, *127*
    scanning electron 179, 198
    synovial microscopy 313–14
Middleton, Dr D. S. *70*
Middleton, J. F. S. (Jim) *243*
Mikimoto Pearl Island 208, *209*
Miles, Professor Sir Ashley FRS
    181
Millar, Thomas McWalter
    FRCSEd 69, 74
Miller
    Helen and Finlay 130–1, 253
    Peter (H & F's son) 130–1
Milligan, Alistair 326
Mills, Dr Michael 62, *78*, 86, *86*
'Millwood', Peebles 309, *310*
Milne
    Muriel Rose (1st wife to DG's
    father) 2, 3
    Oswald Ivan 2
Milton, R. J. 29
Minas Gerais 226–9
Minehead 18, 22–3
Minerva, MTS 346, 347
Ministry of Defence
    Microbiological Research
    Establishment (MRE) 167,
    182, 200
Mitchell, George FRCSEd 156
Mitchell, Les 327
Mitchell, Mr 311
Mitchell, Professor J.S. 116
Moberly, Mr (Swiss Ambassador
    to Iraq) 298
Moesgård Museum, Denmark
    259
Mohr, Dr Winfried 200, 244,
    247, 316
Monro, Alison 169
Monro, Dr P. A. G. 178
Mons 270–1
Montgomery, Professor George
    Lightbody 126, 134, 166,
    182, 183, 187
Montgomery of Alamein
    Science Prize 171

Montreal 154
Moody, Dr G. Howard 315
Moore, Dr R. 146
Moorfields Eye Hospital 187
More, Dr Robert 148, 152
Morgan, Dr George 10
Morgan, Dr Vaughan 281
Morgan, Lynn *see* Gardner,
    Lynn
Morgan, Robin 187
Morgan, Thomas Kirk
    ('Tommy') 37, 95
Morison, Professor John Edgar
    189
Moritz, Dr Alan 137–8, 140,
    144, *145*, 150, 163
    wife 140
Morley, Dr David 175, 177
Morley, Professor David 51
Mornard, A. J. 37
morphine 105
Morris, butler 78
Morrison, Dr J. J. 181
Morrison, F. ('Freddie') 37
Mortlake Primary School 170
mortuaries 158, 188, 195–6,
    280
Moscow 259–63, *260*, *261*
Moscow River *261*
Moule, Rev. Professor Charles
    ('Charlie') Francis Digby
    52, *52*, 200, 352
Mount Sinai Hospital 150
Mountbatten, Lord Louis 133
Moyses-Stevens, Mr and Mrs
    (HG's uncle and aunt) 170
MucKairn Castle, Taynuilt 73
Muir
    Catherine (DG's great-aunt) 1
    Jean *see* Gardner, Jean (DG's
    grandmother)
Muir, Dr Alan 162
Muir, Dr Helen FRS 175, 243,
    305
Muirden, Ken 181
Mukerjee, Dr 280
Mullaly, Dr 189
Munthe, Dr Axel 341
Murchison Scholarship of the
    Royal College of Physicians
    94
Murray

Jean (DG's cousin) *28*, 91
Madge (née Garroway) 1, *28*
Murray, Dr James Elliot *86*
Murray, R. C. *40*
Murray Bridge, Australia 283
Museum
     of Institute of Pathology,
         Belfast 188
     of Department of Pathology,
         University of Edinburgh
         162
     of Royal College of Surgeons
         of Edinburgh 321
music 16–17, 29, 39, 52–3, 73,
     93, 103–4, 141, 255, 276,
     308–9, 339, 340, 351
Musselburgh Links 34
Musson, W. A. J. 37
myalgic encephalomyelitis 171
Myers, Dr 280
Myles, A. B. 175

N
Nagasaki bomb 178
Nagle, Dr Robert (Bob) 161, 182
Nagoya 209
Nairn, Professor R. C. (Richard,
     'Richy') 180, 244, 280,
     284–5
Nanking Road, Shanghai 217
Nara 208
Nash, John 10
National Health Service (NHS)
     14, 76, 80, 241
     exhibition in Royal College
         of Surgeon of Edinburgh
         332
Nazareth *305*
Neill, Dr Desmond 194
Nelson, Professor M. Gerald
     (Gerry) 188
New Orleans 148
New York 138, *139*, 140
Newnum, Mary Cicely *see*
     Welchman, Mary Cicely
     (DG's second maternal
     grandmother)
newspapers and magazines
     26–7
Niagara Falls 141, *141*, 154
Nicholas, John J. (Jeff) and
     Barbara 140

Nicholson, Dr A. 279
Nicholson, Mr FRCS 90–1
night calls 94, 117
Noble, Captain 101, 105
nocardiosis, systemic 146
Nof Ginossar 303–5
Noosa Heads, Australia 285
North Africa 345
Northern Ireland *see* Ulster
Novartis 244 *see* Ciba Geigy
Nuffield Foundation, grant
     from 137–8
Nuffield Rheumatic Diseases
     Unit, Edinburgh *124*
Nuki, Professor George 263,
     315
nursing 7, 79, 101–2, 171

O
Oates, Dr Ken 243, *243*, 314
O'Brien, Professor Frank 191
obstetrics and gynaecology at
     EMS 67, 69
O'Connor, Dr Pat 243, 317
Odessa 349, *349*
oesophageal dilatation 224–5
Ogilvie, Dr Robertson
     Fotheringham 66, 124,
     126, 157, 159, 161
O'Hara, Dr Denis 192
Okayama 212–14
     University 211
Oldenburg 104–7
Oliver Bird Fund of Nuffield
     Foundation 124
Omar Mosque, Jerusalem 300,
     300
Orff, Carl 228
Orford, Dr Constance (Connie)
     243
Orpheus, MTS 345
Osaka 207–8
Oscroft, D. S. 37
Osler, Professor Sir William
     307, 350
osteoarthritis 293
Osteoarthritis Research Society
     269
Osteoarticular Unit, University
     of Edinburgh 307–8
osteomalacia 177
Ostergaard, Dr 316

otitis media 25
Ott, Herr Dr 203
Ouro Preto 226, 227, *228*
Overvroom Hospital 89
Owen, Dr Geronwy 101
Owen, Professor John Vallance
     194
Oxford University, examiner
     for 181, 197

P
Palmer, R. E. 29
Panayi, Dr Gabriel 175
Pantridge, Professor James
     Francis 194
Parafiniuk, Professor W. 267
Paris 269
Park, Dr James 126
Parkinson, Dr Sandy 161
Passchendaele 271
Pateman J. A. 36–7
*Pathological Basis of the
     Connective Tissue Diseases*
     317
Pathological Society of GB and
     Ireland
     Committee membership 247
     in Birmingham 116–7
     in Manchester 129
     membership 180
pathology
     Belfast 195
     Cambridge University 56–8,
         113–18
     definition vii
     EMS 66
         Lectureship 134–5
     see also Medical School new
         building, University of
         Edinburgh
     experimental 176
Pathology Department of
     Edinburgh University *see*
     under Edinburgh University
*Pathology for Surgeons in Training
     – an A to Z* 245
Pathology for the Primary FRCS
     245
Pathology of Rheumatoid Arthritis
     163
*Pathology of the Connective
     Tissue Diseases* 163, 317

Patterson, Michelle 332
Peace Palace 90
Pecs 256
Pedra, Professor Geraldo 225
Peebles 130–4, 309–12, 311, *311*
Pemberton, Nurse 11, 26
penicillin 15, 82, 106, 110
pentothal 105
perinatal care in Brazil 223
Perry, Professor Walter 162
Peters
      Derek F. 23, 28, *29*, 156
      Gladys 23
pethidine addiction 85
photography 31
Physiological Systems
      Committee of the Medical
      Research Council 247
physiology 55
Pidd, Jeremy 243
Pike , John DFC 93, 118, 200
      Florence (HG's sister) 93, 118, *166*, 308, 345–6
      Susie (HG's niece) *166*, 180, 312, 345
Pillemer, Louis 144
Pinter, Daniel 170
Piris, Dr Juan 316
Place House, Patcham 23
Playfair Anatomy Museum 321–7, *323*, 329, 330
Playfair Hall *323*, 328
platypus, duck-billed *285*
pleurisy 106
Plomley, Roy 339
Poland 267–9
poliomyelitis 94
Popper, Hans 150
Porritt, Lord 174
Portugal 253–4
Potemkin Steps, Odessa *349*, 349
Potter Dr Jacobus ('Jack') 124–5, 129, 150
      Elizabeth 150
Potts, Professor 243
Poulter, Len 175
Powells, Percy 114
Preiswerk, Dr Thomas 291, 293, 294–6, 297, 298–9
Price, Dr, EMMS 63–64

Price, Dr Frederick, physician 60
Pritchard, Professor J. J. 194
pseudarthrosis 158
pseudomyxoma peritonei 94
pulmonary embolism 116

Q
Qin Shi Huangdi, Emperor 215
Quagliata, Dr Franco 176, 178
quaich 2, *2*
Quarry Wood, W. FRCSEd 69, *70*, 83–4
Quebec 154
Queen Alexandra's Royal Army Nursing Corps (QARANC) 101
Queen's Coronation 118
Queen's University of Belfast 185
Queensland, Australia 285, 286, *287*, 288
Quorn, Australia 284

R
Race, R. R. 58
Rack, Dr John 114, 129, 192
radiation biology 160
      carcinogenesis 159
Radziwill, Mr and Mrs 170
Rae, Kenny M. 313
Rae, K.M. 232
Raick, Professor Alberto 222, 223, 223–4, 233
Ramage, Elizabeth 126–7
Rankin, Nancy 19, 33
Raso, Dr Pedro 226
Reay, Major General HAJ *84*
Red Berets 120
Red Home, Edinburgh *71*, 71–2
Red Square, Moscow 263
Refsum, Dr 269
refugees in Germany 109
Reid, Jack 193
Reith, Lord John Charles Walsham 174
religion 41–2, 52, 351
Rembrandt's *Night Watch* 89–90
renal failure 82
renin 146
research Fellowships 127–8, 137, 307

Resident House Physicians and Surgeons at RIE 76–86, *78*, *85*
respiratory medicine at EMS 68, 90
reticuloendothelial system 125
Revell, Professor Peter 247, *306*
Revere, Paul 147
Reynolds, Seymour 169
rheumatic and connective tissue disease research 128–9, 158–60
      see also Kennedy Institute of Rheumatology
Rheumatic Diseases Unit, Edinburgh 121–30, 134–5
rheumatic fever 26
rheumatoid arthritis 179, 198, 293
Rhine visit 108
rhinosporidiosis 225
Richards, Ted 279–81
Richmond, Professor John 124–5, 129, 140, 162, 180, 311
      Jenny 140, 311
Richmond, Sir Mark *243*
Richter, Dr Andreas 255, *257*
Rickard
      Grace Beatrice *see* Welchman, Grace Beatrice (DG's maternal grandmother)
      Margaret Elizabeth (née Davey) (DG's maternal great-great-grandmother) 5
Rider, W. H. *29*, 30
Rijksmuseum 89–90
Rinteln 106
Rio de Janeiro 229–31, *230*
Rizza, Dr C. R. 181
Robb, Bill 159
Robb-Smith, Dr A. H. T. 246
Roberts, Dr Stanley 194
Roberts, George and Ruth 108, 110
Robertson, Bruce 51
Robertson, Dr Kelman 68, *80*, 81, *86*, 95
Robertson, Dr R. F. 199
Robertson, Major MacGregor 105

Robertson, Mr dentist 35–6
Robinson, Geoffrey Arthur 38
Robinson, J. *40*, *46*
Robinson, Mr, carpenter 30–1
Robiony, Jules 29
Roche 293
Rockport School, Cragavad 187, 199
Rodgers, Professor Harold W. 194
Rolland, Graham 46
Romanes, Professor George 76, 134
Rosa, Dr Hitor 224
Rosemarkie 19
'Rosemount' Minehead 156
Rosenheim, Professor Max 94–5
Rosenthal Hotel, Holland 89
Ross, Dorothy 236, 250
Ross, I. A. *40*
Rossia Hotel, Moscow 260
Ross Russell, Ralph 45
  mother 61
Russell, 53
'Rote Lache' hotel *21*, 21–2
Roth, Herr 294, 295
Rothera, Miss 32
Rous, Peyton 334
Roxburgh Hotel, Edinburgh 88
Roy, Professor Arthur Douglas 194
Roy, Dr C. S. 126
Roy, Dr Linda 124
Royal Adelaide Hospital 279–81
Royal Air Force hospital, Rinteln 106
Royal Army Medical Corps (RAMC) 97, 98
Royal Ballet 110
Royal College of Pathologists
  Membership 166
  Fellowship 183
Royal College of Pathologists of Australasia 280
Royal College of Physicians of Edinburgh
  Membership 81, 90, 95
  examining students for 245
  Fellowship 166

Royal College of Physicians of London
  attempt at Murchison Scholarship 94
  Membership 183
  Fellowship 183
  Watson Smith Lecturer 199
Royal College of Surgeons of Edinburgh (RCSEd) 322
  Fellowship *328*
  examining students for 163, 245
  museum 316, 321–35, *323*, *324*
  staff meetings in 129
Royal Edinburgh Hospital for Sick Children 129–30
Royal Festival Hall 170
Royal Infirmary of Edinburgh 68, 76–86, *77*, *157*
  autopsies 157–8
  catering 79–80
  clinical care 80–5
  medicine 90
Royal Pavilion, Brighton *10*, 10
Royal Society of Medicine
  publishing author 341
  speaking to 334–5
Royal Victoria Hospital, Belfast 187–9
rubidomycin *see* daunorubicin
Russell, Bert 193
Russell, Dr Randolph 80, 81, 83, *86*
Russell, Rosalind 177
Russia 259–67, 346, 348–9
Ryan, Dr Terence 293
Ryan, Ms 293, 297

S
Saad 292, 296, 297
Saadi, A. T. 314
Sabara 226–9
sacroiliac joints 314
Salmonella enteriditis 117
Salter, Professsor Donald 312, 313, 316
Sanders, Phillippa 176
Sandison, Jocelyn 67
Sandritter, Professor 200
Sanger, Frederick 338
Santiago de Compostela 345

São Paulo 231, 233
Savage, Dr Oswald 175, 181, *181*
Sayers, Dr George 137, 144
Schiødt, Professor Torben 259
schistosomiasis 222, 225, 232
Schmaid, Dr 293
Schoenberg, Dr M. 146
Schönbrun Palace 257
Schönhals, Magda *20*, 20
  Freya, her sister 156
science writers 340
Scientific Coordinating Committee of ARC 180
Scotland, holidays in 18–19, 190–1, 245, 346
Scott, Dr J. E. 315
Scott, Dr J. T. (Tom) 175, *176*
Scottish Borders 130–4
Seahouses 165
Sellwood, Professor Ronald A. 240
Servidores do Estadu, Hopital dos 229
Sevastopol 348
Seven Dials, Brighton 13
Shaker Heights primary school 141
Shanghai 216–17
Sheehan, Professor H.L. 130
Sheffield University, applying for Chair of Pathology 166–7
Sheraton Hotel, Baghdad 292
Sherlock, Professor Sheila 224
Sherman, Professor DJC 280
Sherrington, Professor Sir Charles FRS 55
Shillington, Dr Rosemary 192
Shishinden 207
Shivas, Dr Andrew 155, 182, 183, 245
Shotton, Richard 318, *319*
  Anna 318, *319*
  Jane *see* McQueen, Jane
  Thomas 318, *319*
Signy, Dr Gordon 180
silk production 216
Silver Jubilee Express 46
Simpson, Dr Alan 323
Simpson, Professor Keith 115
Simpson, Robert (Bob) 270, 313

Simpson Memorial Maternity Pavilion 76
Sinclair, Dr Jack 124
Singapore Airport 273
Sissons, Professor H. A. 242
Skeggs, Dr Leonard 137, 146
skeleton found in RCSEd Museum 333, *333*
Skelton, Dr Floyd 148, 150
Skelton-Stroud, Dr Paul 244, 313
skiing 104, 107
Slater, Dr J. K. *86*
Sloan, Dr James 192
Sloper, Professor John 175
Smaile, Miss 73, 79
Smith, Alan 313
Smith, Marianne 245
Smith, Dr Graham 167
Smith, Dr Ian Inglis 161, 316
Smith, Dr L. S. *70*
Smith, P. J. Lancelot 37
Smyth, Michael 235
Snell, Flight Lieutenant 106
Snell, Rev. B.C.42
Sobridino District General Hospital 222
    Pathology Department 223
Sochi 348
Sokoloff, Dr Leon 244
Solomon, Neil 144
Soren, Professor Arnold 247
Souter, W. A. (Willie) FRCSEd 264, 315
Souter Strathclyde arthroplasty 315
South American Society of Rheumatology 219
South Australian Art Gallery 276
South Australian Rheumatology Association 281
South Eastern Region Hospital Board 155
Southern Railway 33
Spain 345–6
Spector, Professor Walter (Wally) 54
Speer, Albert 20
Spence, R. T. (Bob) 185
Spooner, Professor E. T. C. ('Teddy') 58, 60, 130

Springer, Miss 88, 89
St Anne's School, Edinburgh 73
St Cuthbert's Church, Edinburgh 87–8
St Louis, USA 151
St Margaret's School, Polmont 73
St Mark's University College, Adelaide 275
St Paul's School, London 169
St Peter's Cathedral, Adelaide 275
St Peter's Church, Leiden 90
St Petersburg (Leningrad) 264, 346
St Wilfred's School, Brighton 26–7
stamp collecting 17, 342, *343*
Stansfield, W. H. 29
staphylococcal endocarditis 159
State Institute of Medical and Veterinary Science, Adelaide 279
Steine 10
Stephenson, Dr D. 56
Stetson, Dr C. A. 148
Stevens, Edwin and Joan 232
Stevens, Mary 180
Stevens, Mr and Mrs and family 232
Stewart, W. I. *40*
Stockwell, Professor Robin 315
Stoddart, Dr Ian 51
Stoner, Mrs 17
    Stoner, Priscilla *see* Kennedy, Priscilla (Scilla)
'Stop Me and Buy One' 13
Stopford Building, Manchester University 238
Strachan, Dr M. J. W. 315
streptococcal infection 106
streptomycin 81, 94
Stuart, Professor Angus Erskine and Diana 134, 160, 161, 182, 183, 187, 311
Sturmabteilung (SA) 20
Sturmstaffel (SS) 21–2
Sturrock, Dr John 70
Suleiman the Great 347
Sullivan, Peter 241
sulphanilamide 15

sulphonamides 15, 82
Sumela Monastery 347, *347, 348*
Supervisor of Gold Museum, Sabara 227
Surgeon's Court, Sydney *288*
surgery at EMS 69
Suzhou 216
Svartz, Dr Nanna 180
Swann, Professor Michael Meredith, FRS 160
Swinhoe, Emily 6
Sydney *288*, 289
Symmers, Professor W. (Bill) St C. 175, 311
synovial microscopy 313–14
systemic lupus erythematosus 129, 143
Szczecin 267–8

T
Tafori, Dr 226
Tait, Barrie 181
Takarazuka Review 208
Takayasu's syndrome 232
Talbott, Dr John 219, *220, 221*, 222
Tangier 345
Tansey, Violet 328
'Tanta', Peebles 130–4
Tar Steps *4*
Tarpen, Dr 280
Taylor, Dr G. L. 58
Taylor, O. H. *40*
teaching hospitals 76, 114
television teaching 196, 240
tennis 53, 71–2, 238, 343
terracotta warriors 215, *215*
tetanus 84
Teviot Place, Edinburgh 61–2
Textbook of Medicine and Gerontology 317
theatre 227, 342
Thin, James 38, 39, 61
Third Man, The 110
Thirkhill, Henry 47
Thomas, C. D. 279
'Thomas Gardner Trust' 23
Thompson, Sir William 73
Thomson, J. Miller (HG's great uncle) 155
Thorium, cancer from 159, 334

Thwaites, Professor Sir Bryan 50, 174
thymoma 315
Tiberias 304
Tiger Moth plane 45
Tinos 346
Tinsley, Mrs 35
Tiradentes 228
Todd, Dr T.R.R. ('Tarara') 81, 95
Tokyo 203, *204*, 209, 211
Tomlinson, Dr 58
Toner, Professor Peter 201
tonsillitis, epidemic 106
toothache 25
Toronto 153
Torrens Gorge, Australia 282
Townsend, Denis 93
Trabzon 347
travel writers 340
Travers-Healy, Sean 180, 312
Trinity College, Dublin, examining students at 245
Tropical diseases 3, 222 *et seq*
tuberculosis 5, 81, 94, 103, 161, 222, 232
Tucker, Eric 187
Tulloch, Dr David 86, 158
Tunnicliffe, Dr 55
Turkey 347–8, 349–50
Turnbull, Dr and Sarah 180
Turner, Dr Hamish 161
Turner, Mrs 329
Turner Medical School building 125
Tweedle, David E. F. FRCSEd 245
Tyler Miss 214
Tzonchev, V. T. 181

U
Ulster 185–189
Umurama Hotel, Brazil 224
Uniting Glenunga Church, Adelaide 278
University of Edinburgh *see* Edinburgh University Medical School (EMS)
Unknown Soldier monument, Baghdad 295–6
uric acid levels, Iraqi vs UK 294
urinary stones 250
USA 137–53, 148–9

US Public Health Service, grants from 150

V
Vancouver 148–9
van Duren, Herr 107
varicella 102
Vasa, warship 346, *346*
Vaughan, Dame Janet FRS 181, 197
Venice 109
Venlaw Castle Hotel, Peebles 132–3, *133*
Vernon-Roberts, Professor Barrie 273, 280, 281
family 274–6
Verona 345
Veterans Administration Hospital, Cleveland 137
Vick, Sir Arthur 191
video-conferencing 146
Vieira, Dr Francisco 220
Vienna 257
vineyards 276, 283, 345, 346
virology 200
Vogt, Marthe Louise FRS 67
Volk's Electric Railway 12
von Hagens, Gunther 326
Vučković, Silva 318

W
Wade, Sir Henry 333–5, 341
Wagner, Dr Theresa 268, 269
Wailing Wall, Jerusalem 300
'Waiting Days' 78
Wakelin, J. G. *40*
Wales 171–2
Walker, Elma and Morris 278
Walker, James 329
Walker, Lieutenant 103
Walls, Professor Eldred 323, 330
Wallyford 44
Walton, Professor Kenneth 180, 267
war records 341
Warden, Paul J. 175
Warrender Park Road, Edinburgh 62
Warsaw 268, 317
Warsky, Maria 243
Wartzman, Hilda 105
Washington 148

Watson, Dr and Mrs John 278
Watson Smith Lecture 199
Watts, Mr and Mrs 112–13
daughters *113*
Waugh, James (Jimmy) 126–7, 157, 313
Webber, Robyn FRCSEd 332
Weinbren, Professor Herschell Kenneth 247
Welchman
Arthur (MG's uncle) 5–6
Emma (DG's maternal great-grandmother) (née Skeet) 5
Frank (MG's uncle) 5–6, 32
George (MG's uncle) 5
Grace Beatrice (Bici) (DG's maternal grandmother) 4, 5, 26
Herbert Guy (DG's maternal grandfather) 5, 5, 16, 18, 112
Marjorie *see* Gardner, Marjorie (DG's mother)
Mary Cicely (DG's second maternal grandmother) 5, 18
Rose 2
Thomas Guy (DG's maternal great-grandfather) 5, *5*
Wellington Park Hotel, Belfast 185
Wertzman, Luis 229
West Linton Historical Society 334
Western Reserve University Medical School 137, *143*, 143–6
Whitby, Professor Lionel 56
White, Dr M. H. Gleeson 114
Whittaker, Colonel 57
Whitteridge, Professor David FRS 166
Whyte, Dr Angus 331
Wicks, Margaret 176
Wiesbaden 258
Wijnvoord, Dr Elisabeth Christine 316
Wilhelmina Hospital 89
Wilkie, Dr Lindsay *85*
William Playfair's Anatomy Museum 321

Williams, Dr 293
Williams, Mrs 111
Williams, Professor (Sir) Alwyn
    198
Williamson, Raymond 58
Williamson, Sister 79, *80*, 88
Willmer, Dr E. N. 55, 57
Wilmot, Dr and Mrs 92
Willunga, Australia 282
Wilmington, Australia 284
Wilson, David 327, 331
Wilson, Professor Nairn H. F.
    198, 243
Wilson, Professor Clifford 159
Winchester 18
Windeyer, Sir Brian 182, 183
Windmill Restaurant, Kiev
    266–7
Winner, Professor Harold 175
Winter Palace, Leningrad 264,
    265, 346
Withington Hospital 235,
    238–9, 240–2
    DG and Chair of
        Histopathology 235
    DG's research at 242–4

Royal opening of Unit 250,
    251
staff 243–4
Wood, Joyce 313, 328, 331
Woodburn, Jenny 180
Woodruff, Professor (Sir)
    Michael FRS 157, 183, 329,
    331, 335
    Lady Woodruff 331
Woodward, David 313
woodwork 30–1
World War I 2–3, 42, 271
World War II 12, 42–6, 51–2,
    58–9
Wright, Professor Dennis H 280
Wright, Dr Selby 42
Wright, Dr M. Ingle 240
Wright, Professor Verna 315
Wu Gardens 216
Wyatt, Mrs 313
Wyke, Anne 176
Wynn-Williams, Professor Alun
    153–4, 161

X
Xian 215

Y
Yad Vashem Sanctuary,
    Jerusalem 300–1, *303*
Yalta 348, *348*, *349*
Yangrze Hotel, Shanghai 216
Yates, Dr Peter 161
Yates, Professor Peter O. 239,
    240
Young, A.H. (Harry) (DG's
    maternal great-uncle) 5
Young, Caroline (Auntie Car)
    (DG's maternal great-aunt)
    5, 248
Young, Mr and Mrs (patients of
    TG) *28*
Ypres 271
Yuan Gardens 217
Yuzen 207

Z
Zagorsk 263, *264*
Zaimis, Professor Eleanor 163
Zelazowa Wola and Chopin 268
Ziff, Dr Morris 219
Zugspitz mountain *108*
Zuki, Dr 208